Shojo Beat

Fushigi Yûgi
Genbu Kaiden

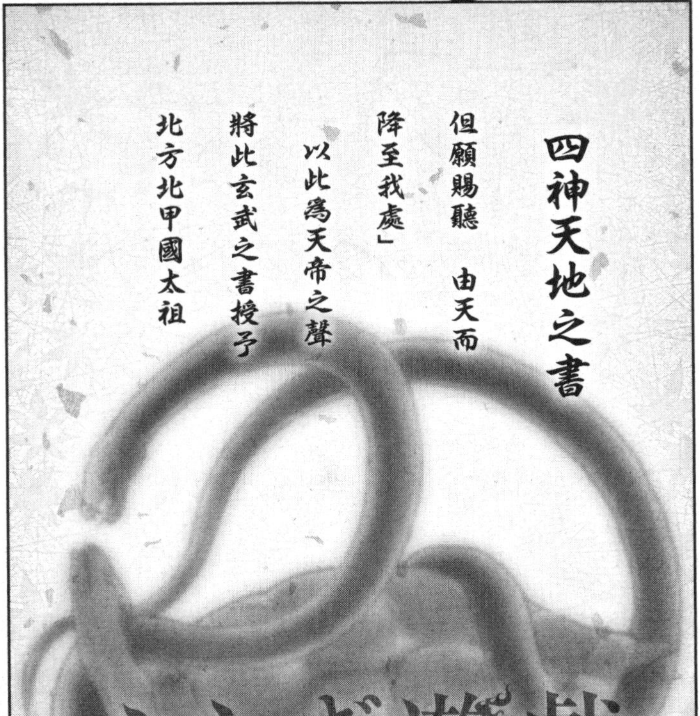
四神天地之書
但願賜聽　由天而
降至我處」
以此為天帝之聲
將此玄武之書授予
北方北甲國太祖
ふしぎ遊戯
玄武開伝
渡瀬悠宇

story and art by **YUU WATASE**

Vol. 12

CONTENTS

TRANSLATION OF "THE UNIVERSE OF THE FOUR GODS"

We summon you thus. Descend upon us from the heavens.

As the voice of the Emperor of the Heavens, this Genbu scroll is given to the progenitor of the northern country of Bêi-jîa.

Cast of Characters

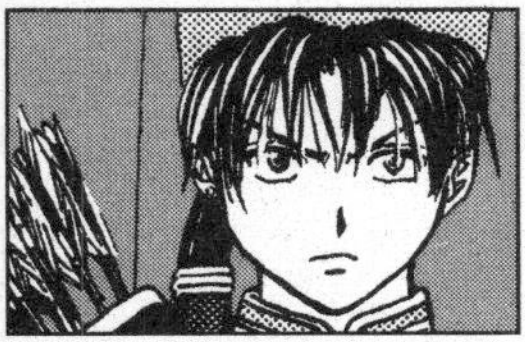

Tomite

A mischievous Celestial Warrior traveling with Takiko.

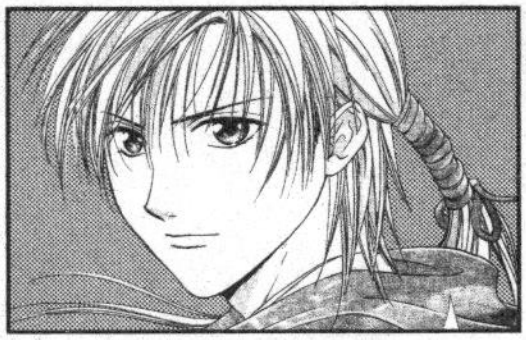

Limdo

"Uruki," a Celestial Warrior. He has the ability to take both male and female form.

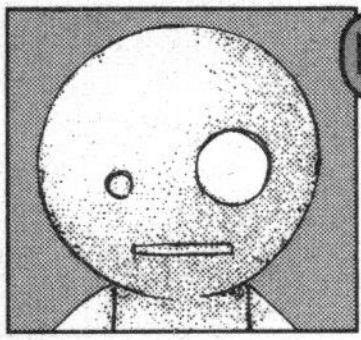

Namame

A spirit of rock made from the Star Life Stone.

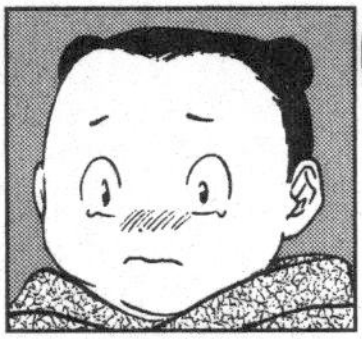

Hatsui

A Celestial Warrior, and a little timid.

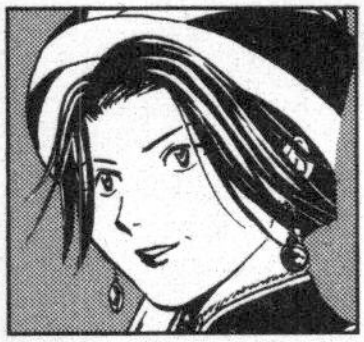

Inami

A Celestial Warrior with elastic, prehensile hair.

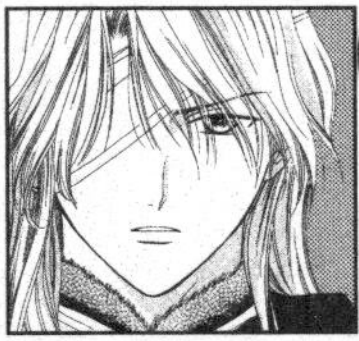

Hikitsu

A Celestial Warrior who cares deeply about his sister Ayla.

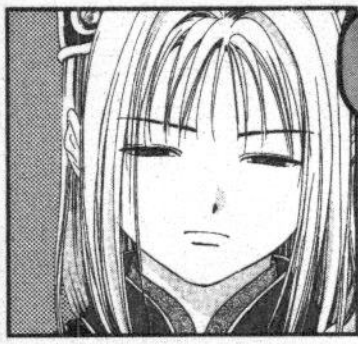

Urumiya (Teg)

A Celestial Warrior held captive in the city of Tèwulán.

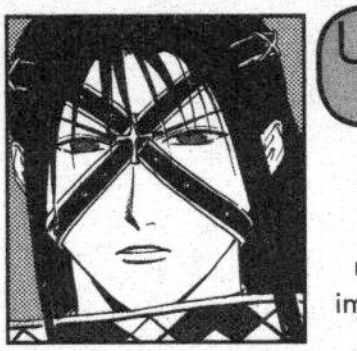

Urumiya (Hagus)

A Celestial Warrior who shares his mark with his imprisoned twin brother.

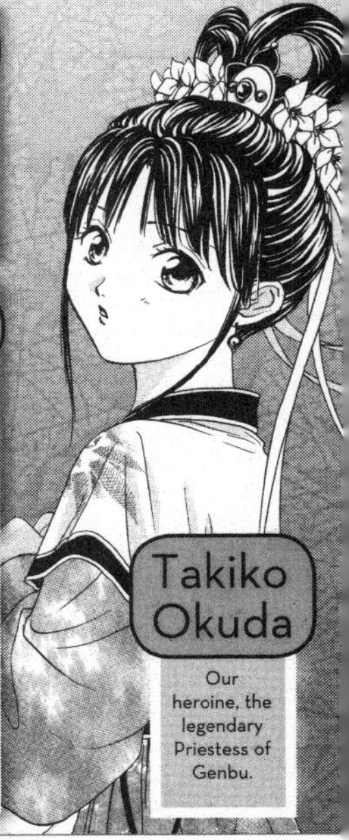

Takiko Okuda

Our heroine, the legendary Priestess of Genbu.

The Story Thus Far

The year is 1923. Takiko is drawn into the pages of *The Universe of the Four Gods*, a book her father has translated from Chinese. There, she is told that she is the legendary Priestess of Genbu, destined to save the country of Bêi-jîa. She must find the seven Celestial Warriors who will help her on her quest.

Takiko has succeeded in her quest. But when the Celestial Warriors learn that the Priestess must die to summon Genbu, they vow to protect her. Instead of sacrificing herself, Takiko marries Limdo, now the ruler of Bêi-jîa, and tries to save the country without divine intervention. Can her fate be thwarted?

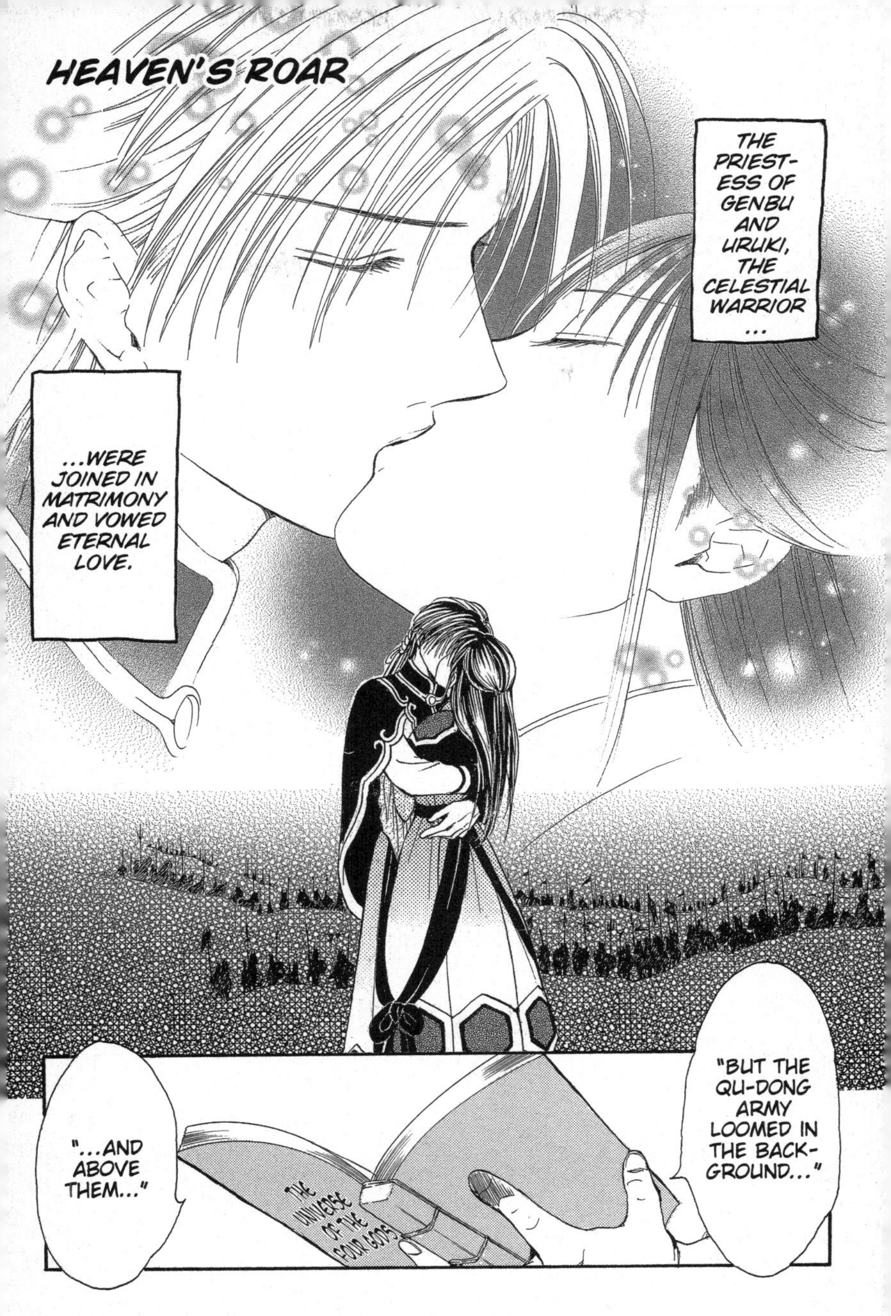
HEAVEN'S ROAR
THE PRIEST-ESS OF GENBU AND URUKI, THE CELESTIAL WARRIOR ...
...WERE JOINED IN MATRIMONY AND VOWED ETERNAL LOVE.
"BUT THE QU-DONG ARMY LOOMED IN THE BACK-GROUND..."
THE UNIVERSE OF THE FOUR GODS
"...AND ABOVE THEM..."

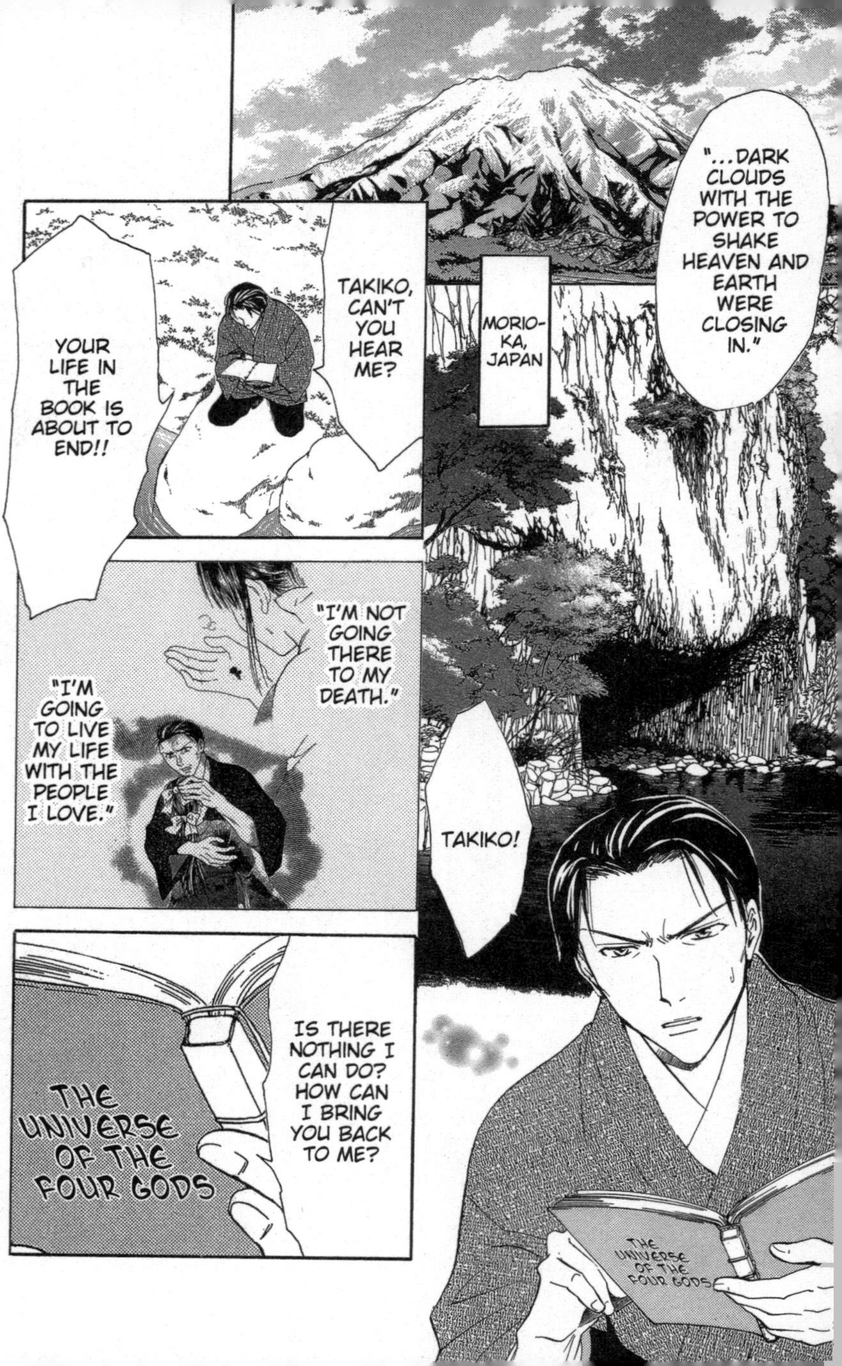
"...DARK CLOUDS WITH THE POWER TO SHAKE HEAVEN AND EARTH WERE CLOSING IN."
MORIOKA, JAPAN
TAKIKO!
THE UNIVERSE OF THE FOUR GODS
TAKIKO, CAN'T YOU HEAR ME?
YOUR LIFE IN THE BOOK IS ABOUT TO END!!
"I'M NOT GOING THERE TO MY DEATH."
"I'M GOING TO LIVE MY LIFE WITH THE PEOPLE I LOVE."
IS THERE NOTHING I CAN DO? HOW CAN I BRING YOU BACK TO ME?
THE UNIVERSE OF THE FOUR GODS

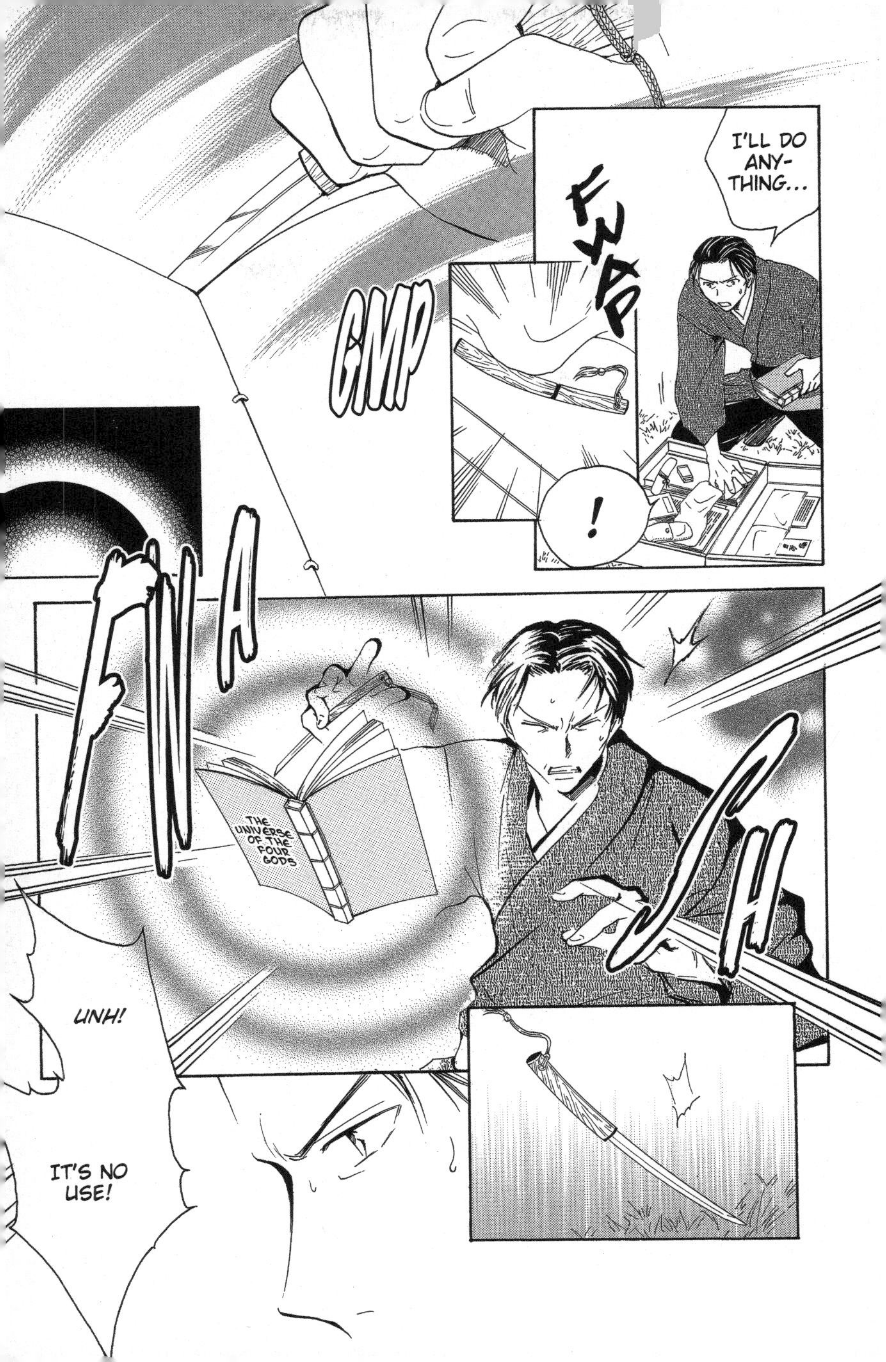
I'LL DO ANY-THING...
FWAP
GMP
!
FWA
SH
THE UNIVERSE OF THE FOUR GODS
UNH!
IT'S NO USE!

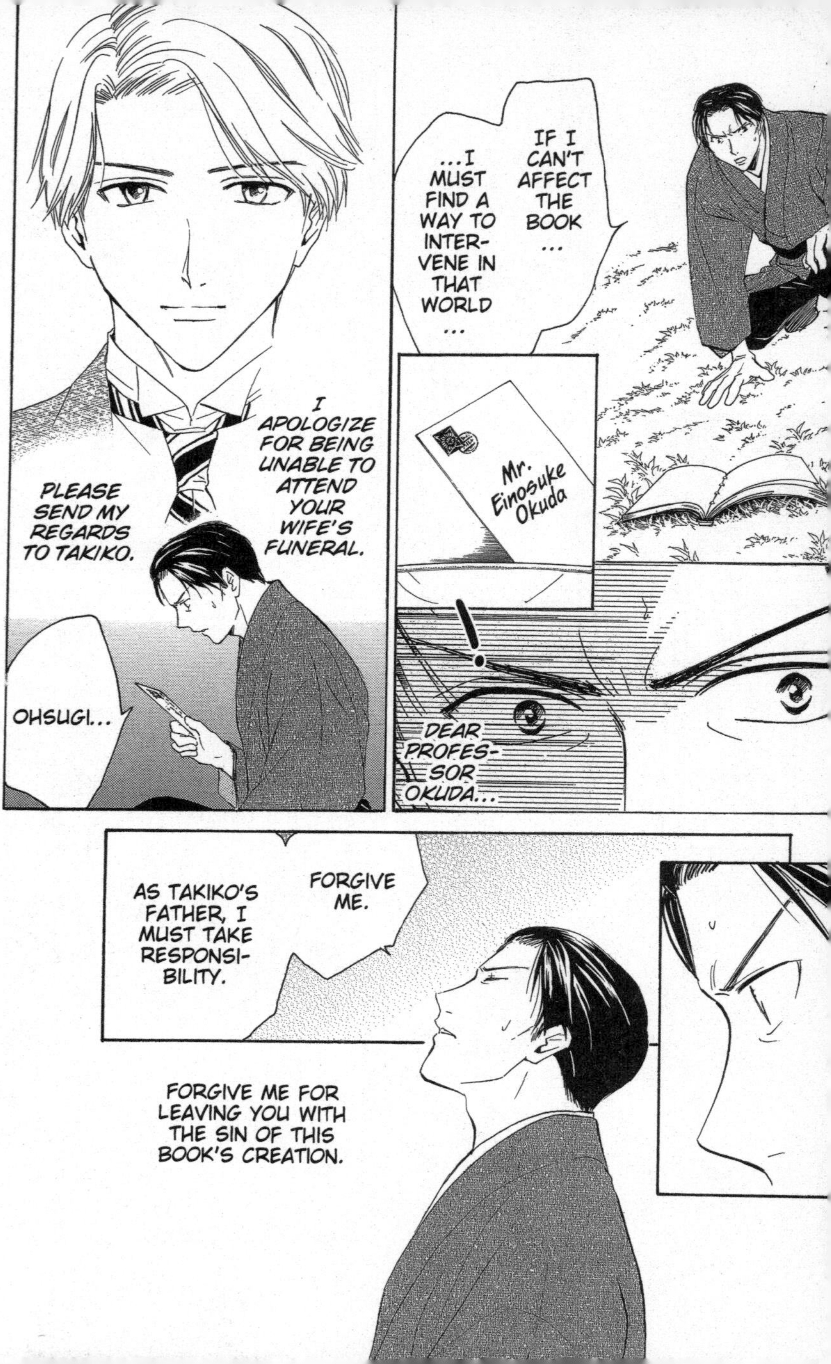
IF I CAN'T AFFECT THE BOOK...
...I MUST FIND A WAY TO INTER-VENE IN THAT WORLD...
Mr. Einosuke Okuda
!
DEAR PROFES-SOR OKUDA...
I APOLOGIZE FOR BEING UNABLE TO ATTEND YOUR WIFE'S FUNERAL.
PLEASE SEND MY REGARDS TO TAKIKO.
OHSUGI...
FORGIVE ME.
AS TAKIKO'S FATHER, I MUST TAKE RESPONSI-BILITY.
FORGIVE ME FOR LEAVING YOU WITH THE SIN OF THIS BOOK'S CREATION.

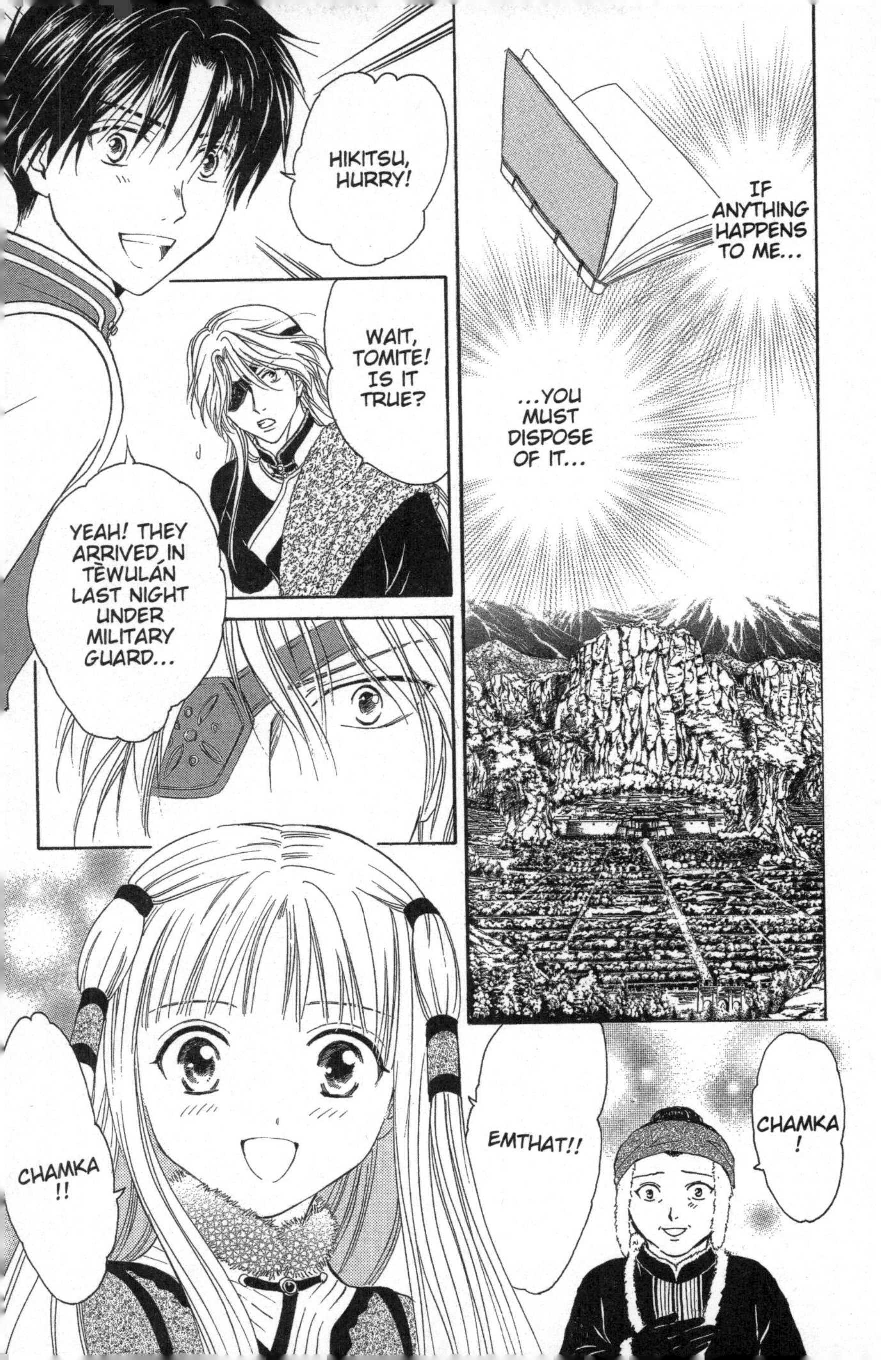
IF ANYTHING HAPPENS TO ME...
...YOU MUST DISPOSE OF IT...
HIKITSU, HURRY!
WAIT, TOMITE! IS IT TRUE?
YEAH! THEY ARRIVED IN TÈWULÁN LAST NIGHT UNDER MILITARY GUARD...
CHAMKA!
EMTHAT!!
CHAMKA!!

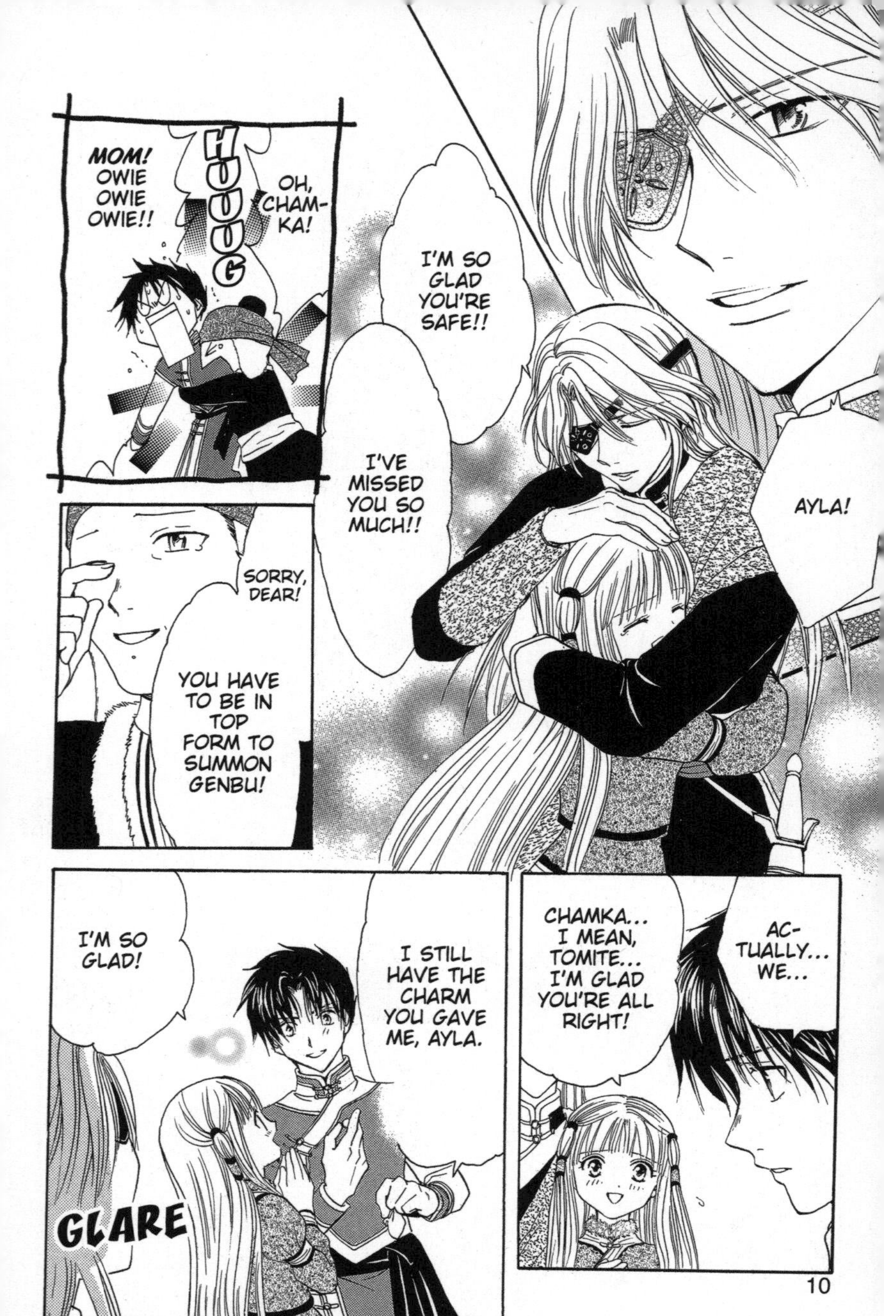
AYLA!
I'M SO GLAD YOU'RE SAFE!!
I'VE MISSED YOU SO MUCH!!
OH, CHAMKA!
HUUUG
MOM! OWIE OWIE OWIE!!
SORRY, DEAR!
YOU HAVE TO BE IN TOP FORM TO SUMMON GENBU!
AC-TUALLY... WE...
CHAMKA... I MEAN, TOMITE... I'M GLAD YOU'RE ALL RIGHT!
I STILL HAVE THE CHARM YOU GAVE ME, AYLA.
I'M SO GLAD!
GLARE

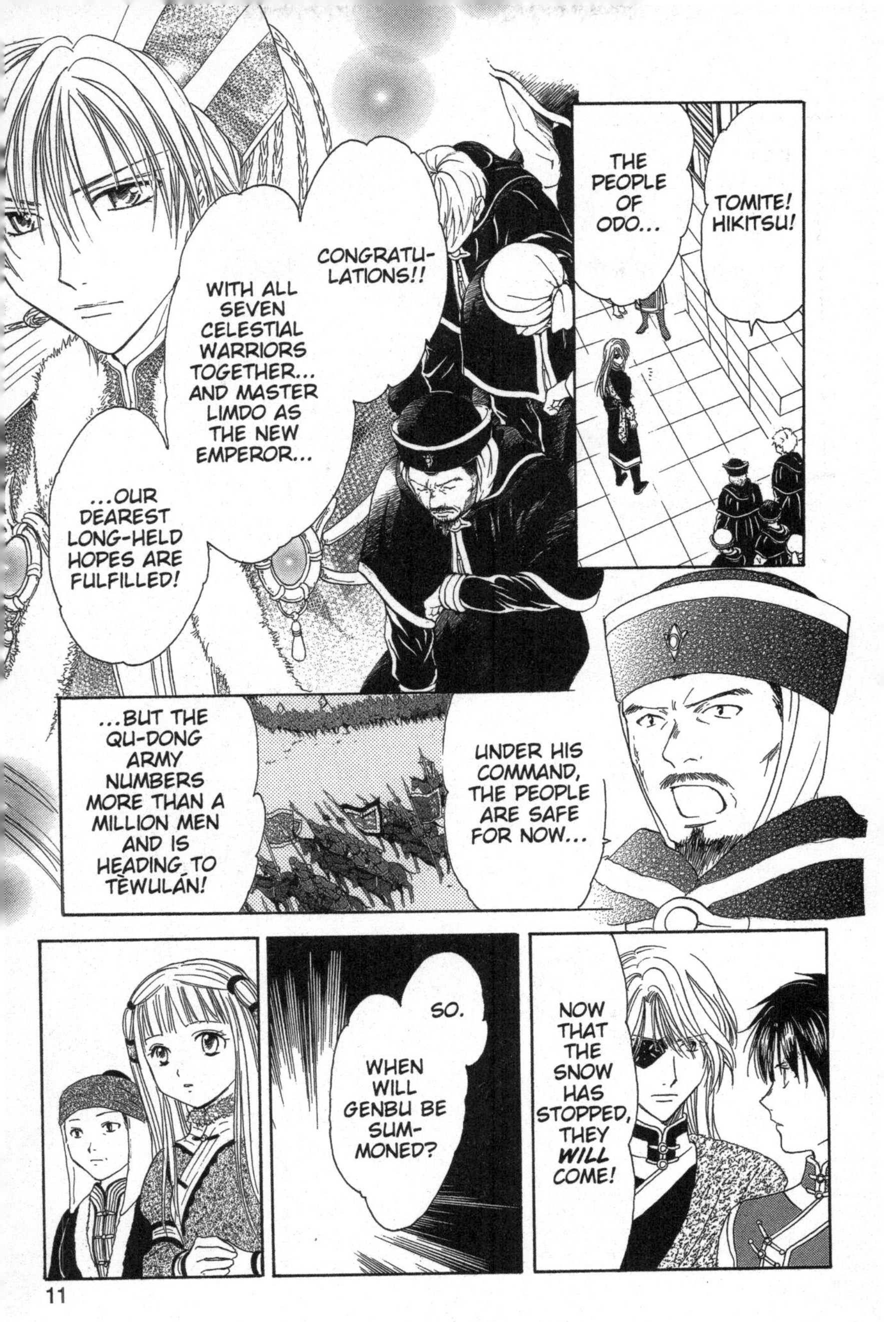
TOMITE! HIKITSU!
THE PEOPLE OF ODO...
CONGRATULATIONS!!
WITH ALL SEVEN CELESTIAL WARRIORS TOGETHER... AND MASTER LIMDO AS THE NEW EMPEROR...
...OUR DEAREST LONG-HELD HOPES ARE FULFILLED!
UNDER HIS COMMAND, THE PEOPLE ARE SAFE FOR NOW...
...BUT THE QU-DONG ARMY NUMBERS MORE THAN A MILLION MEN AND IS HEADING TO TÈWULÁN!
NOW THAT THE SNOW HAS STOPPED, THEY *WILL* COME!
SO.
WHEN WILL GENBU BE SUMMONED?

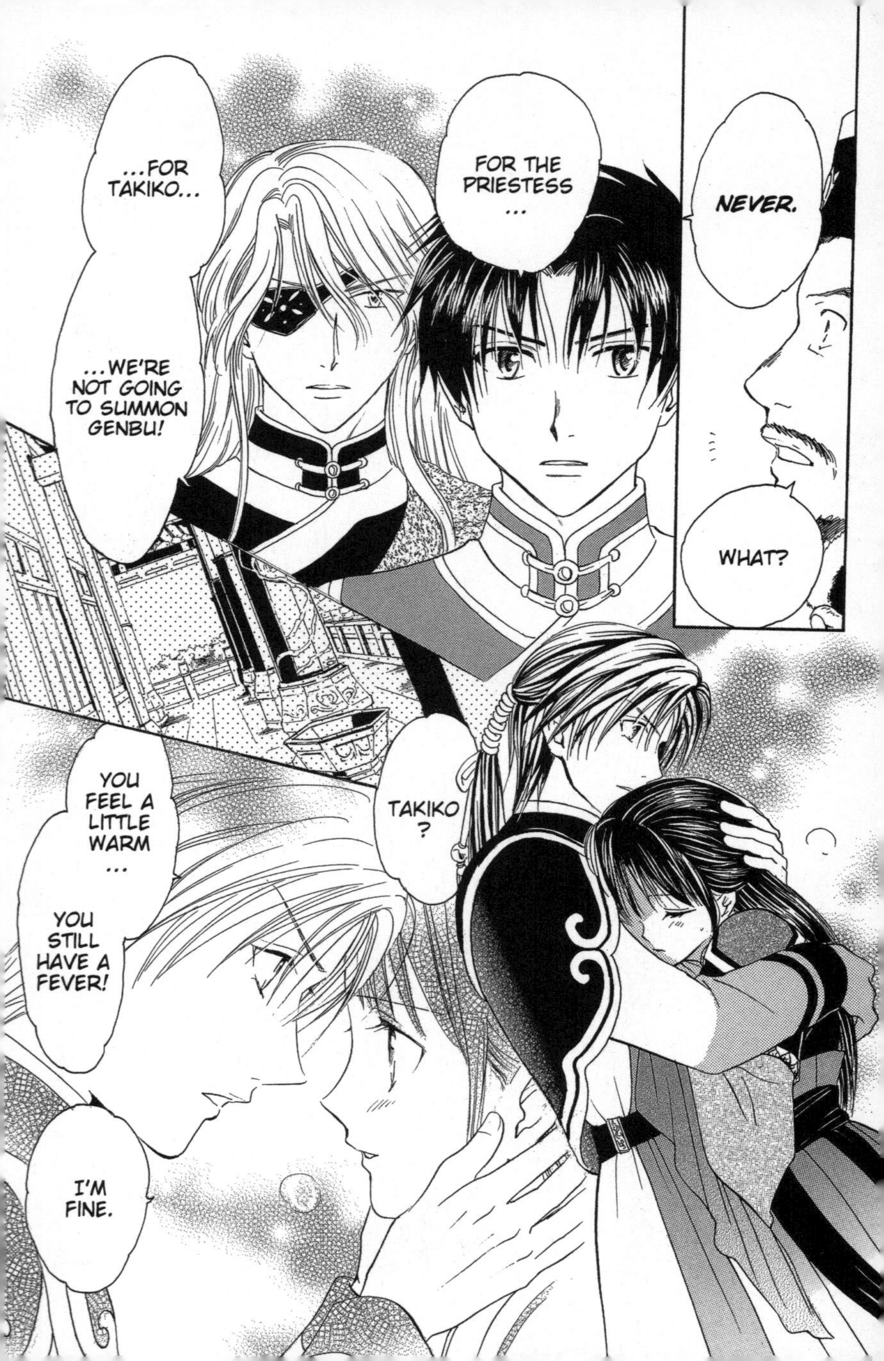
NEVER.
WHAT?
FOR THE PRIESTESS ...
...FOR TAKIKO...
...WE'RE NOT GOING TO SUMMON GENBU!
TAKIKO?
YOU FEEL A LITTLE WARM ...
YOU STILL HAVE A FEVER!
I'M FINE.

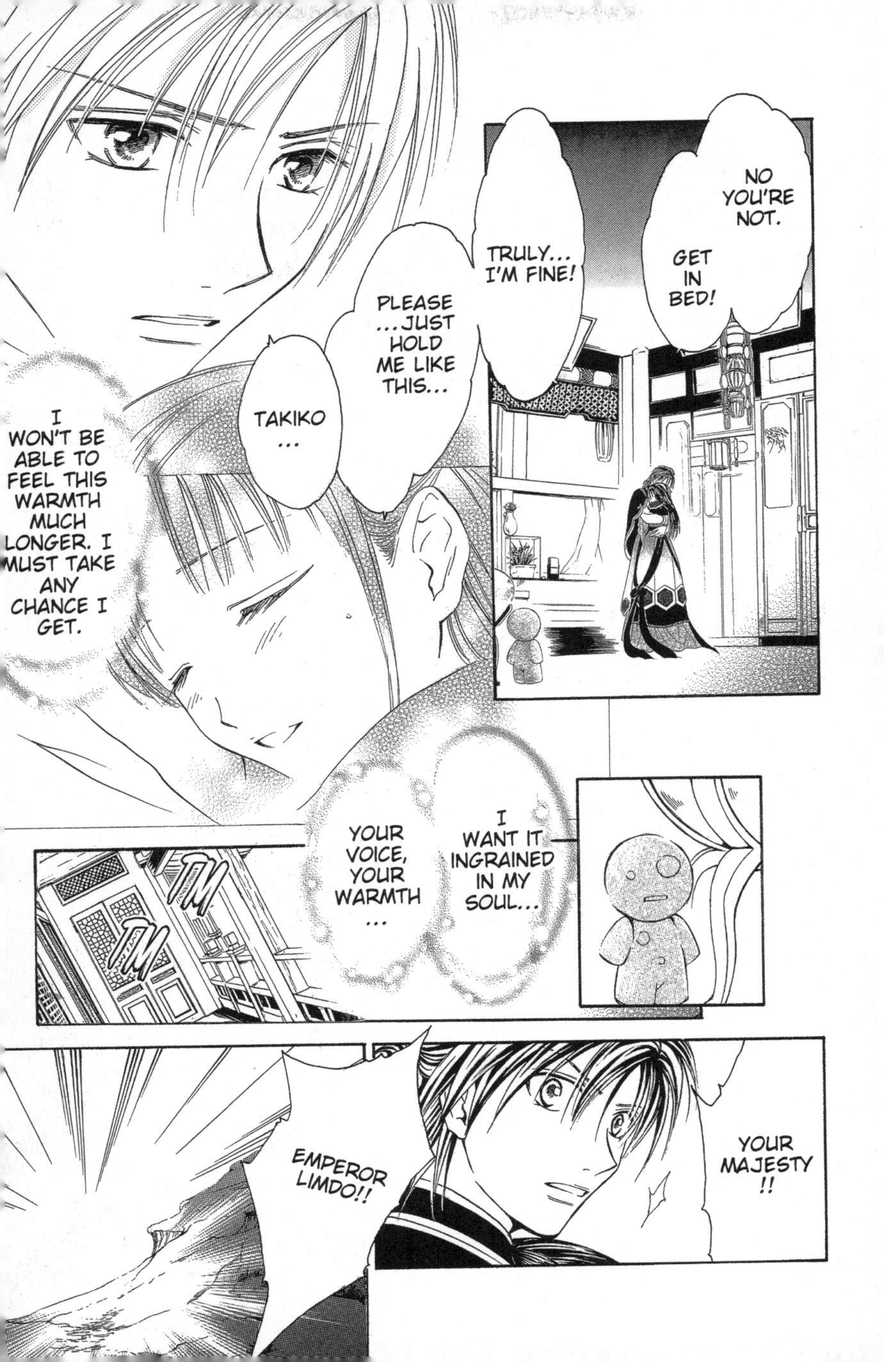
NO YOU'RE NOT.
GET IN BED!
TRULY... I'M FINE!
PLEASE ...JUST HOLD ME LIKE THIS...
TAKIKO ...
I WON'T BE ABLE TO FEEL THIS WARMTH MUCH LONGER. I MUST TAKE ANY CHANCE I GET.
I WANT IT INGRAINED IN MY SOUL...
YOUR VOICE, YOUR WARMTH ...
TM
TM
YOUR MAJESTY !!
EMPEROR LIMDO!!

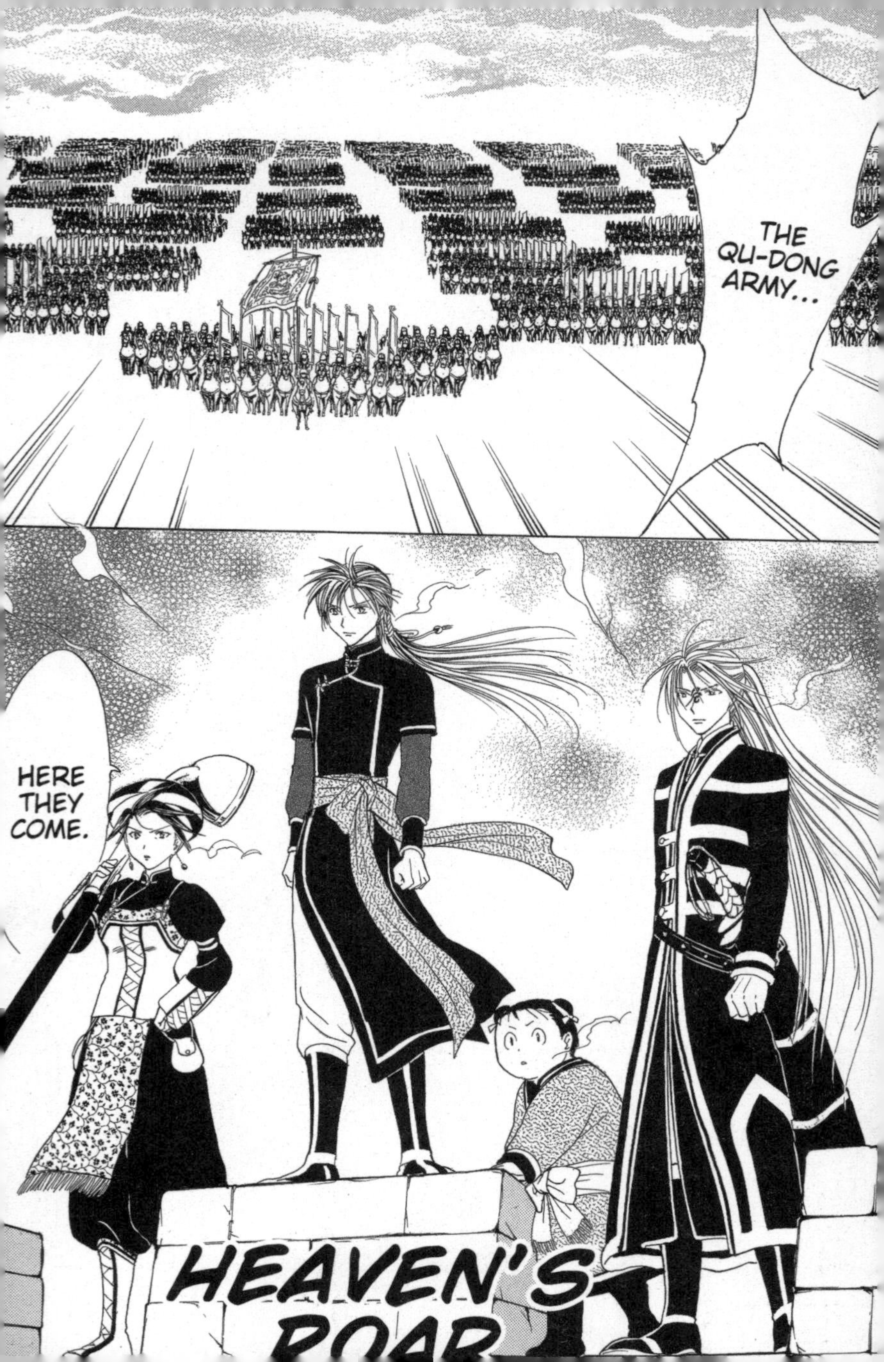
THE QU-DONG ARMY...
HERE THEY COME.
HEAVEN'S ROAR

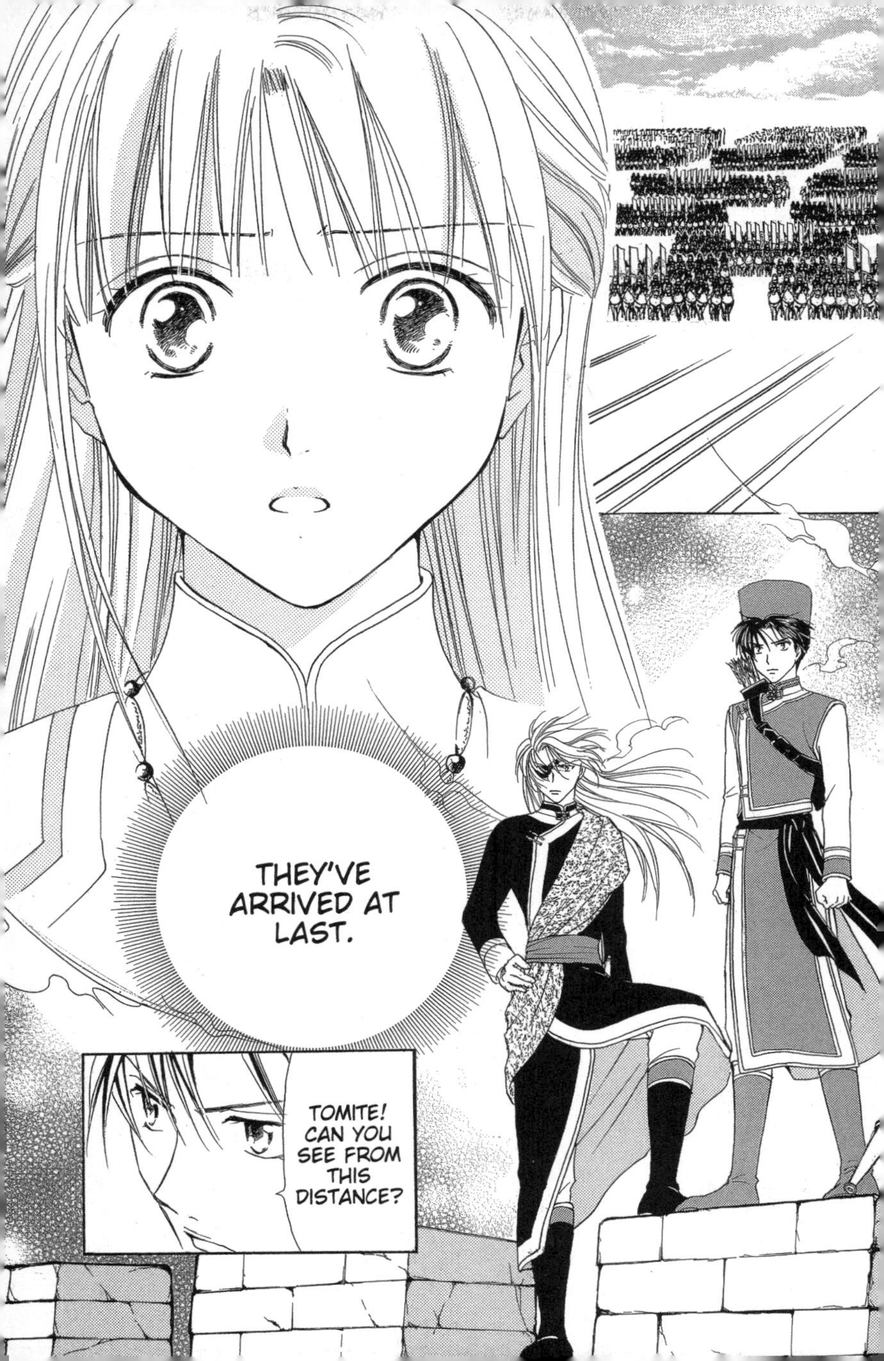
THEY'VE ARRIVED AT LAST.
TOMITE! CAN YOU SEE FROM THIS DISTANCE?

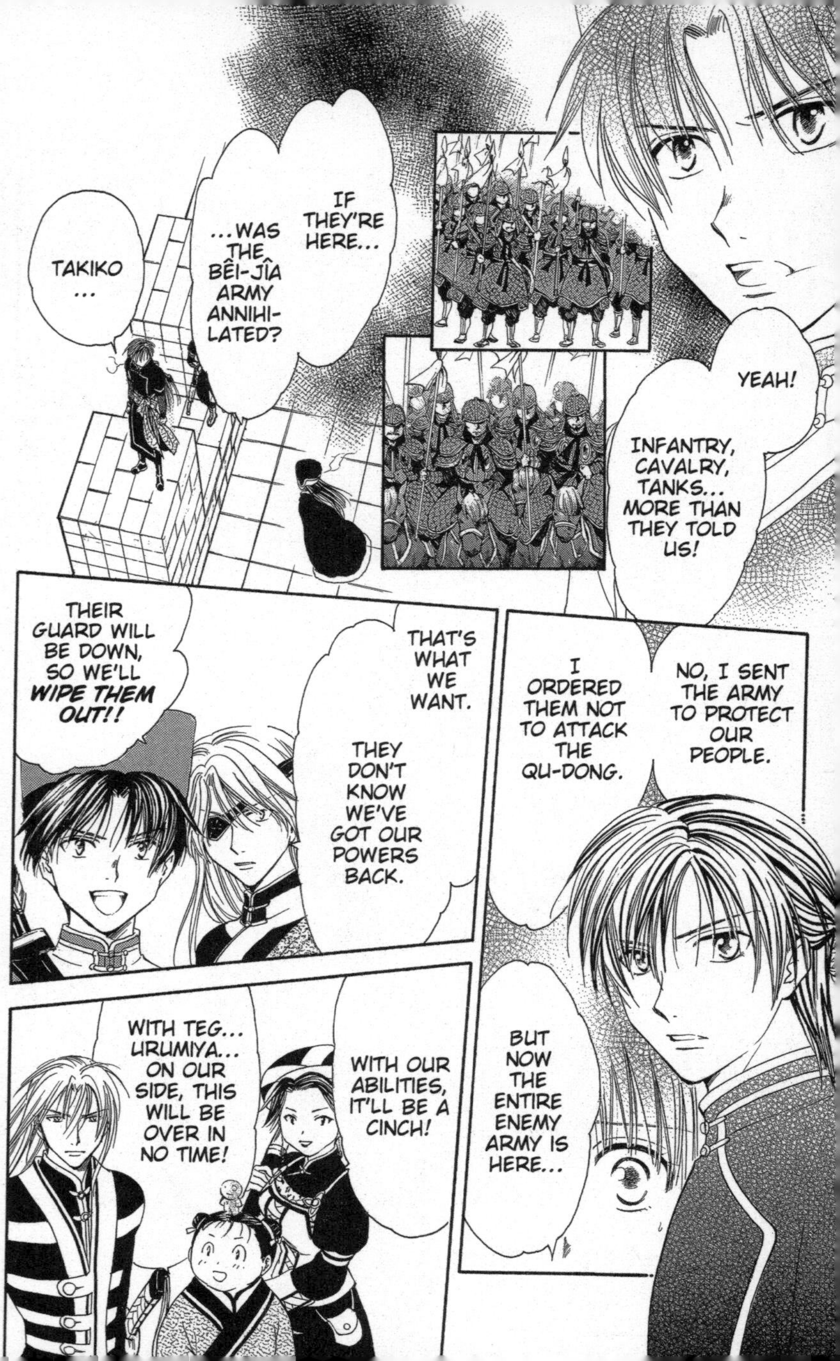
IF THEY'RE HERE...
...WAS THE BÊI-JÎA ARMY ANNIHILATED?
YEAH!
INFANTRY, CAVALRY, TANKS... MORE THAN THEY TOLD US!
TAKIKO ...
NO, I SENT THE ARMY TO PROTECT OUR PEOPLE.
I ORDERED THEM NOT TO ATTACK THE QU-DONG.
BUT NOW THE ENTIRE ENEMY ARMY IS HERE...
THAT'S WHAT WE WANT.
THEY DON'T KNOW WE'VE GOT OUR POWERS BACK.
THEIR GUARD WILL BE DOWN, SO WE'LL WIPE THEM OUT!!
WITH OUR ABILITIES, IT'LL BE A CINCH!
WITH TEG... URUMIYA... ON OUR SIDE, THIS WILL BE OVER IN NO TIME!

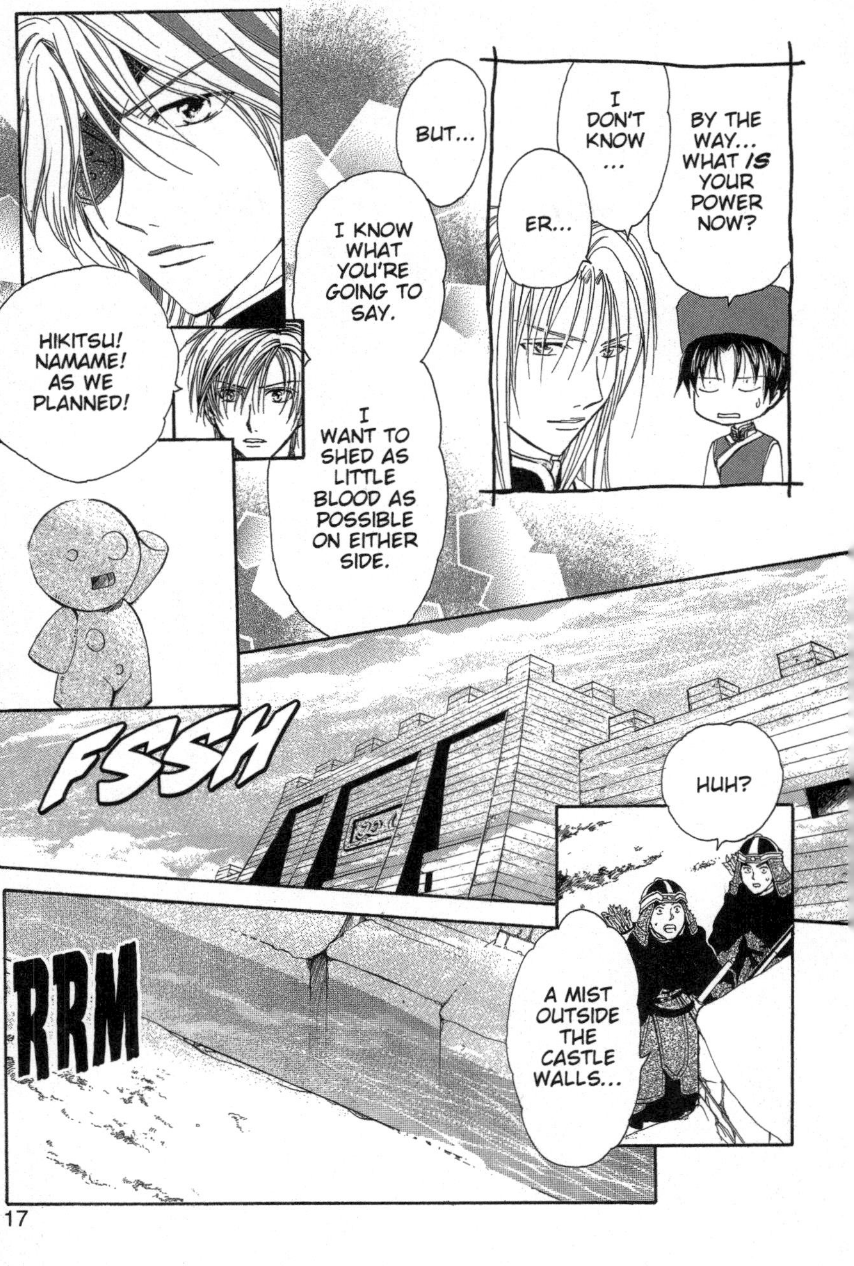
BY THE WAY... WHAT IS YOUR POWER NOW?
I DON'T KNOW ...
ER...
BUT...
I KNOW WHAT YOU'RE GOING TO SAY.
I WANT TO SHED AS LITTLE BLOOD AS POSSIBLE ON EITHER SIDE.
HIKITSU! NAMAME! AS WE PLANNED!
FSSH
HUH?
A MIST OUTSIDE THE CASTLE WALLS...
RRM

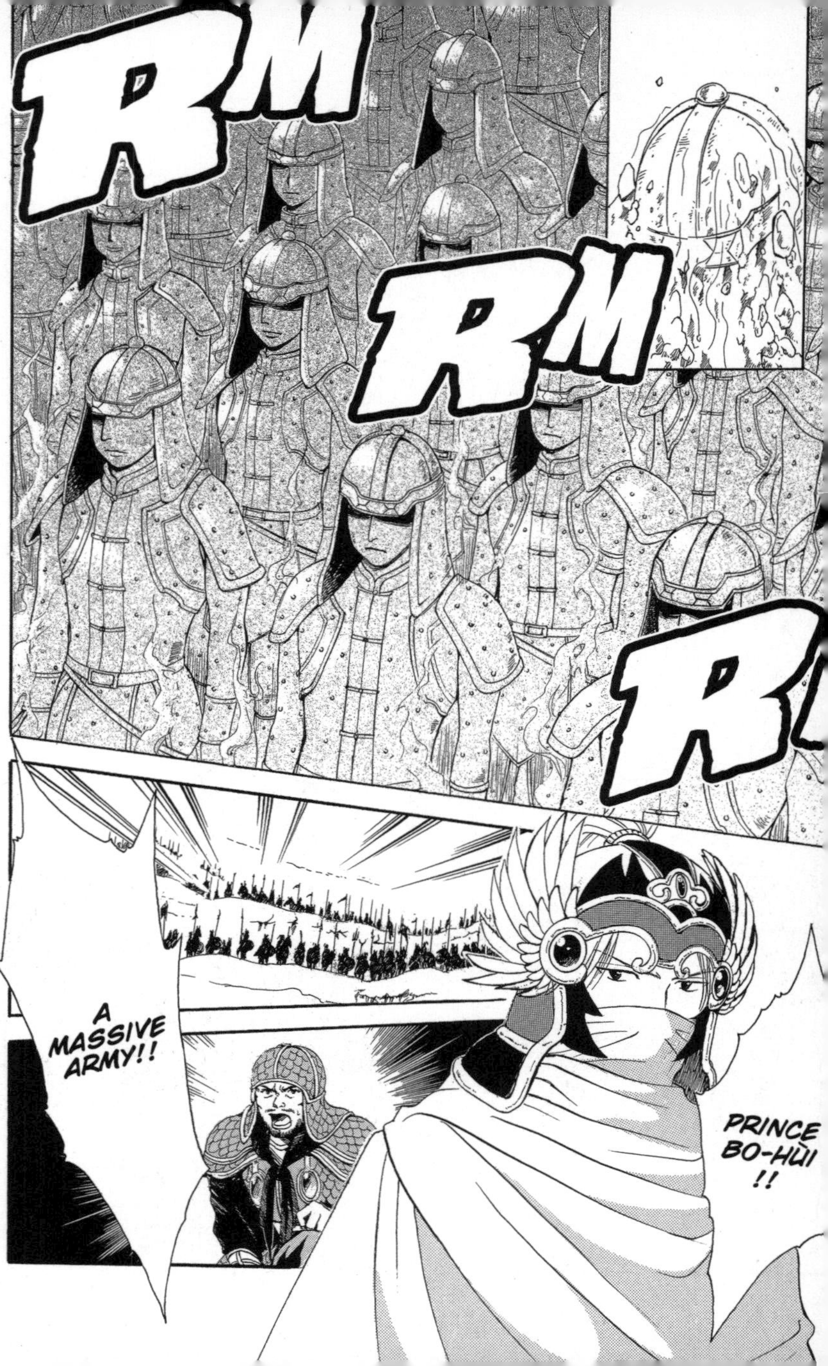
RM
RM
R
PRINCE BO-HÙI!!
A MASSIVE ARMY!!

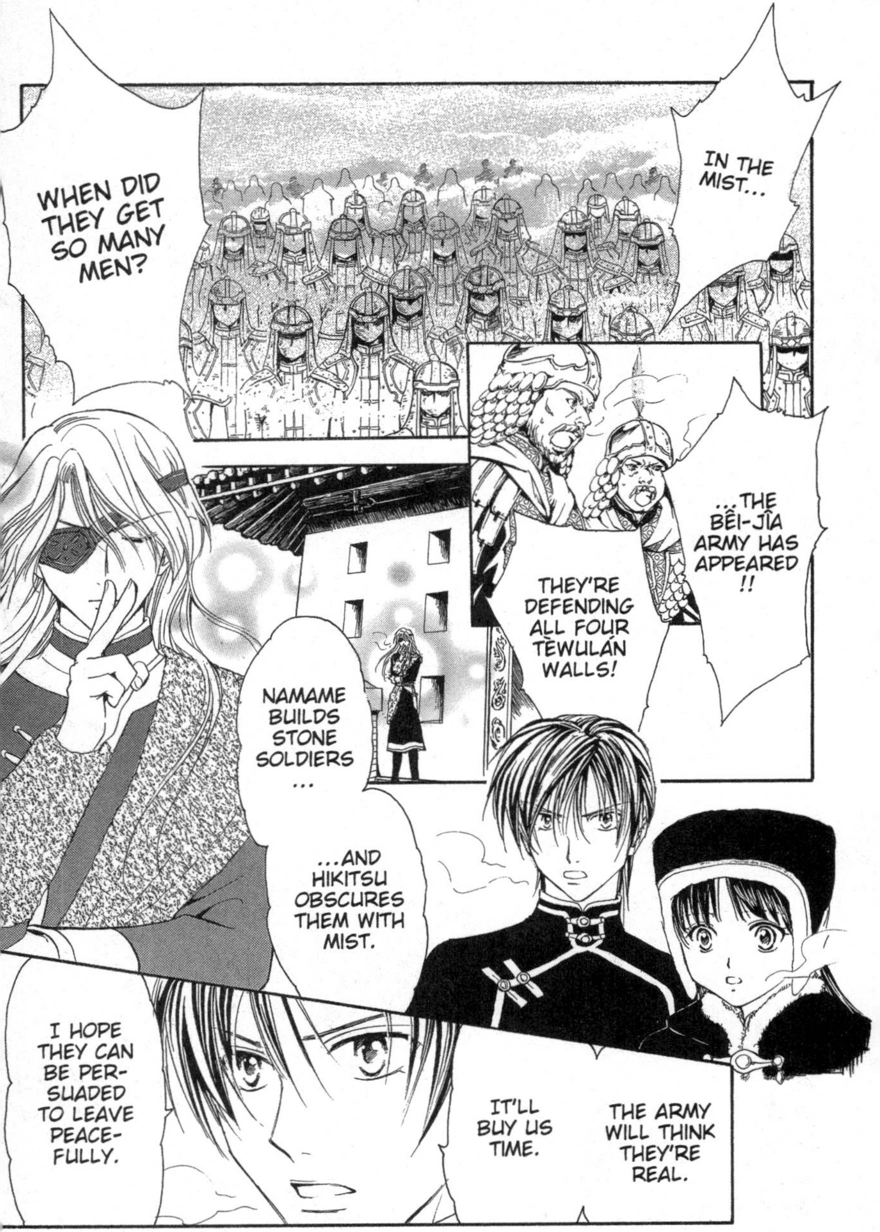
IN THE MIST...
...THE BÊI-JÎA ARMY HAS APPEARED!!
THEY'RE DEFENDING ALL FOUR TÈWULÁN WALLS!
WHEN DID THEY GET SO MANY MEN?
NAMAME BUILDS STONE SOLDIERS...
...AND HIKITSU OBSCURES THEM WITH MIST.
THE ARMY WILL THINK THEY'RE REAL.
IT'LL BUY US TIME.
I HOPE THEY CAN BE PER-SUADED TO LEAVE PEACE-FULLY.

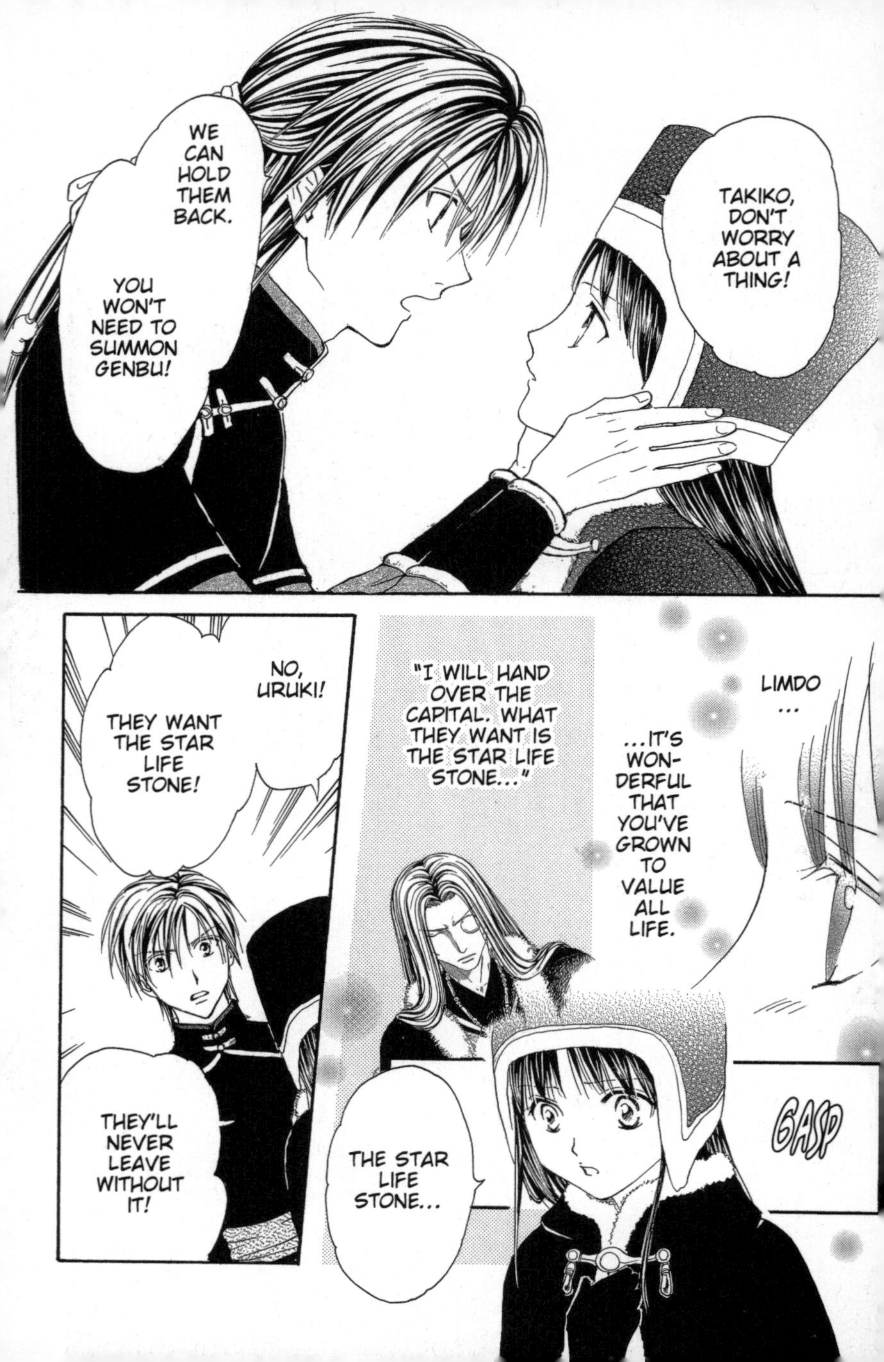
TAKIKO, DON'T WORRY ABOUT A THING!
WE CAN HOLD THEM BACK.
YOU WON'T NEED TO SUMMON GENBU!
LIMDO...
...IT'S WON-DERFUL THAT YOU'VE GROWN TO VALUE ALL LIFE.
"I WILL HAND OVER THE CAPITAL. WHAT THEY WANT IS THE STAR LIFE STONE..."
GASP
THE STAR LIFE STONE...
NO, URUKI!
THEY WANT THE STAR LIFE STONE!
THEY'LL NEVER LEAVE WITHOUT IT!

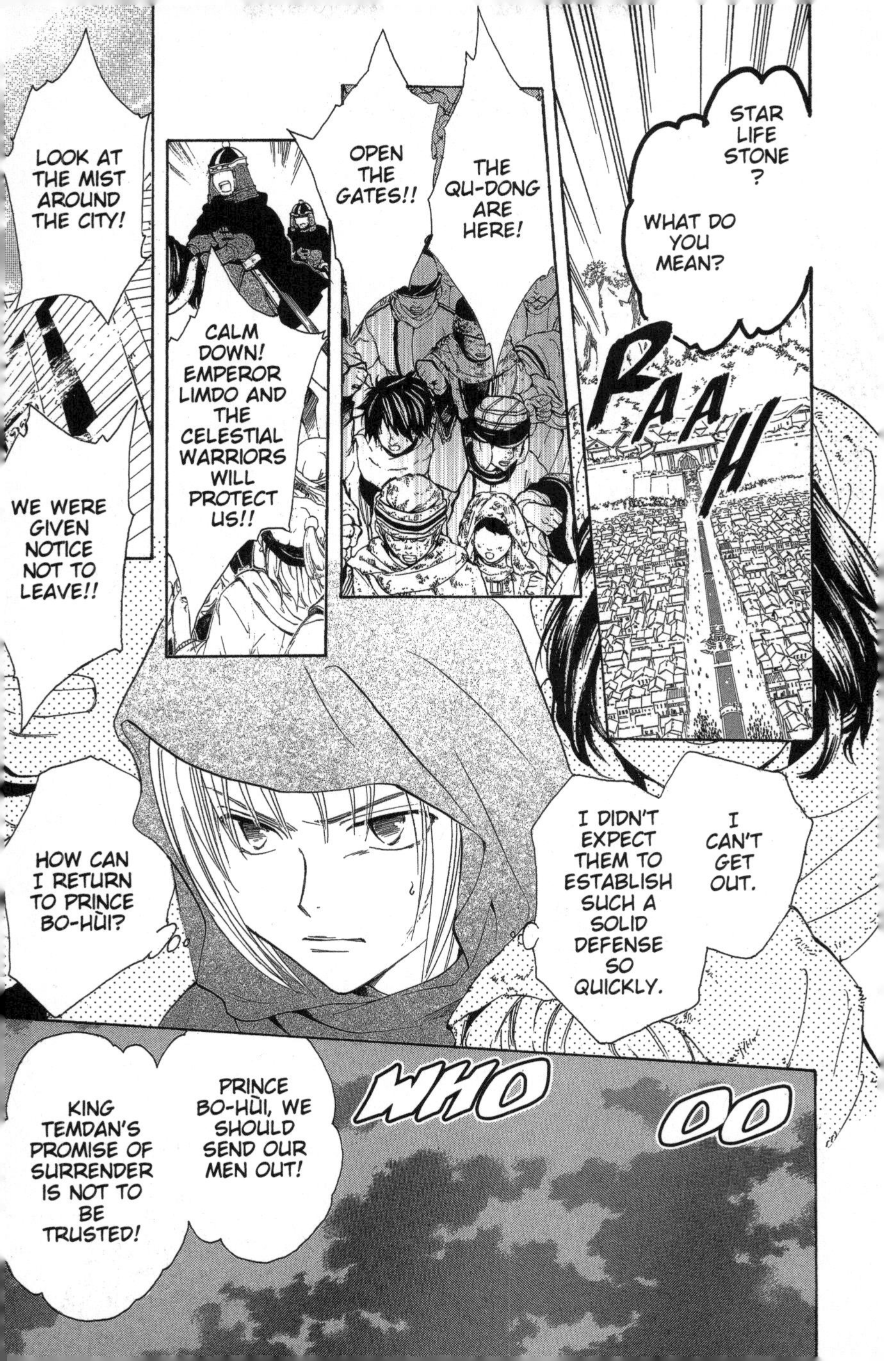
STAR LIFE STONE?
WHAT DO YOU MEAN?
PAAH
THE QU-DONG ARE HERE!
OPEN THE GATES!!
CALM DOWN! EMPEROR LIMDO AND THE CELESTIAL WARRIORS WILL PROTECT US!!
LOOK AT THE MIST AROUND THE CITY!
WE WERE GIVEN NOTICE NOT TO LEAVE!!
I CAN'T GET OUT.
I DIDN'T EXPECT THEM TO ESTABLISH SUCH A SOLID DEFENSE SO QUICKLY.
HOW CAN I RETURN TO PRINCE BO-HŬI?
WHOOO
PRINCE BO-HŬI, WE SHOULD SEND OUR MEN OUT!
KING TEMDAN'S PROMISE OF SURRENDER IS NOT TO BE TRUSTED!

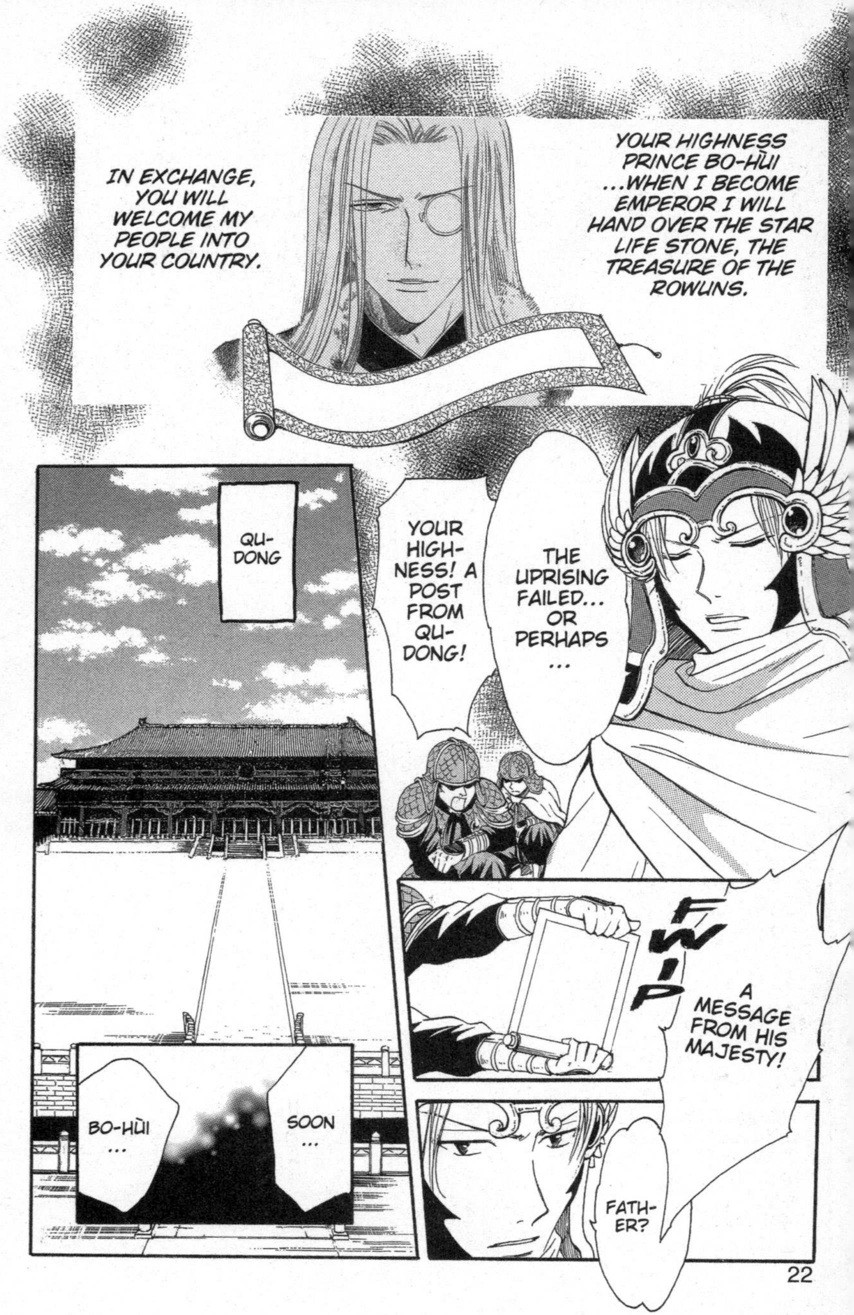
YOUR HIGHNESS PRINCE BO-HŬI ...WHEN I BECOME EMPEROR I WILL HAND OVER THE STAR LIFE STONE, THE TREASURE OF THE ROWUNS.
IN EXCHANGE, YOU WILL WELCOME MY PEOPLE INTO YOUR COUNTRY.
THE UPRISING FAILED... OR PERHAPS ...
YOUR HIGHNESS! A POST FROM QU-DONG!
FWIP
A MESSAGE FROM HIS MAJESTY!
FATHER?
QU-DONG
SOON ...
BO-HŬI ...

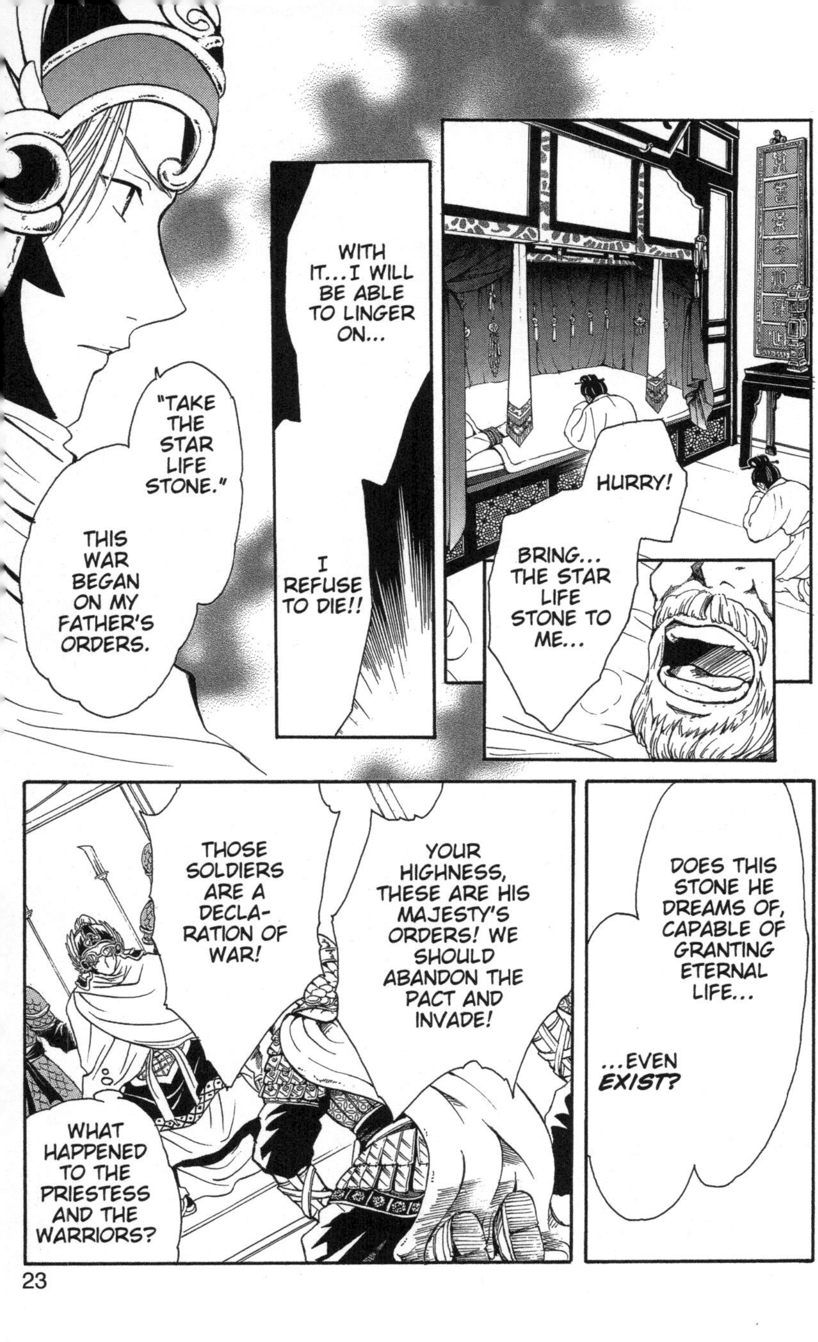
HURRY!
BRING... THE STAR LIFE STONE TO ME...
WITH IT... I WILL BE ABLE TO LINGER ON...
I REFUSE TO DIE!!
"TAKE THE STAR LIFE STONE."
THIS WAR BEGAN ON MY FATHER'S ORDERS.
DOES THIS STONE HE DREAMS OF, CAPABLE OF GRANTING ETERNAL LIFE...
...EVEN *EXIST?*
YOUR HIGHNESS, THESE ARE HIS MAJESTY'S ORDERS! WE SHOULD ABANDON THE PACT AND INVADE!
THOSE SOLDIERS ARE A DECLA-RATION OF WAR!
WHAT HAPPENED TO THE PRIESTESS AND THE WARRIORS?

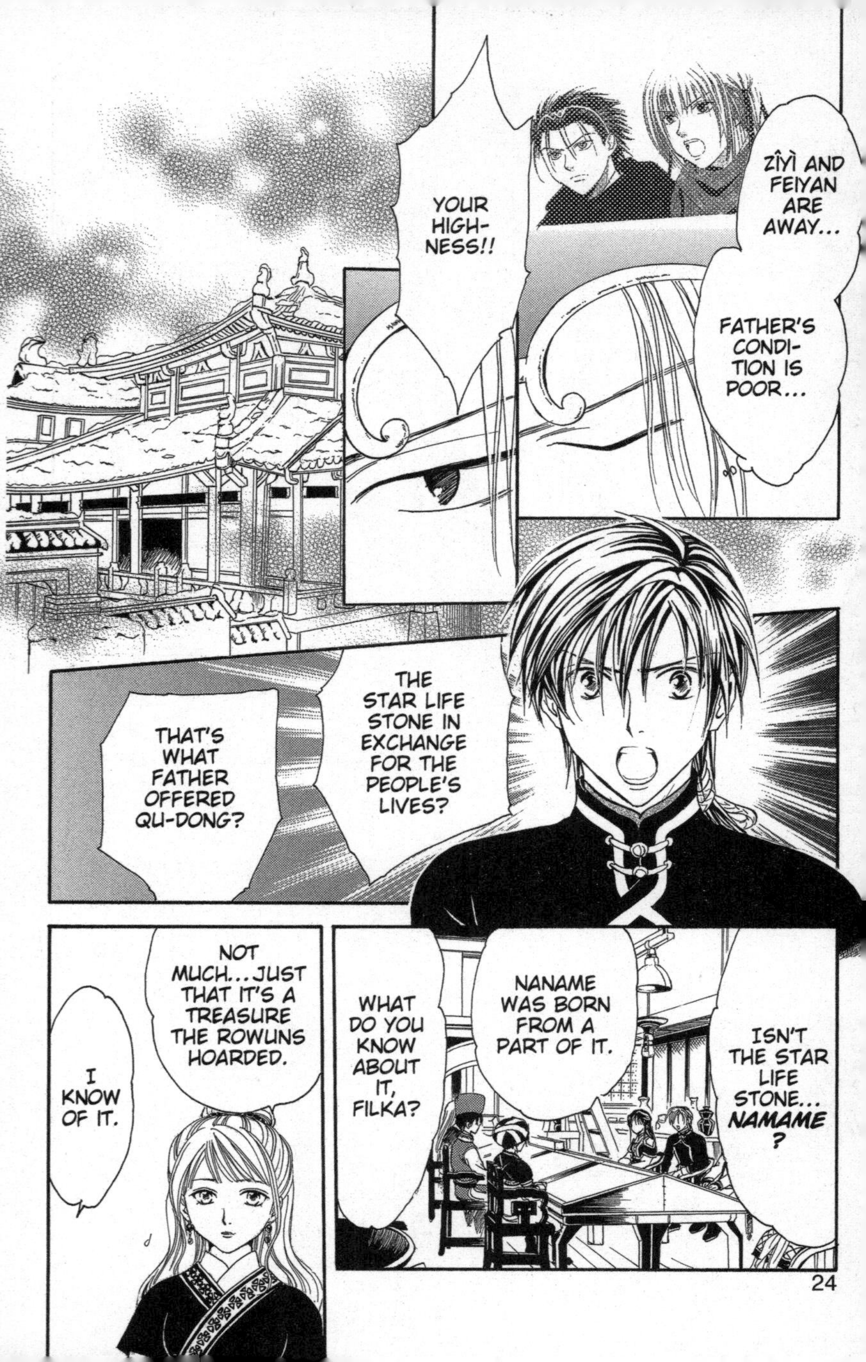
ZÎYÌ AND FEIYAN ARE AWAY...
YOUR HIGHNESS!!
FATHER'S CONDITION IS POOR...
THE STAR LIFE STONE IN EXCHANGE FOR THE PEOPLE'S LIVES?
THAT'S WHAT FATHER OFFERED QU-DONG?
ISN'T THE STAR LIFE STONE... ***NAMAME*** ?
NANAME WAS BORN FROM A PART OF IT.
WHAT DO YOU KNOW ABOUT IT, FILKA?
I KNOW OF IT.
NOT MUCH...JUST THAT IT'S A TREASURE THE ROWUNS HOARDED.

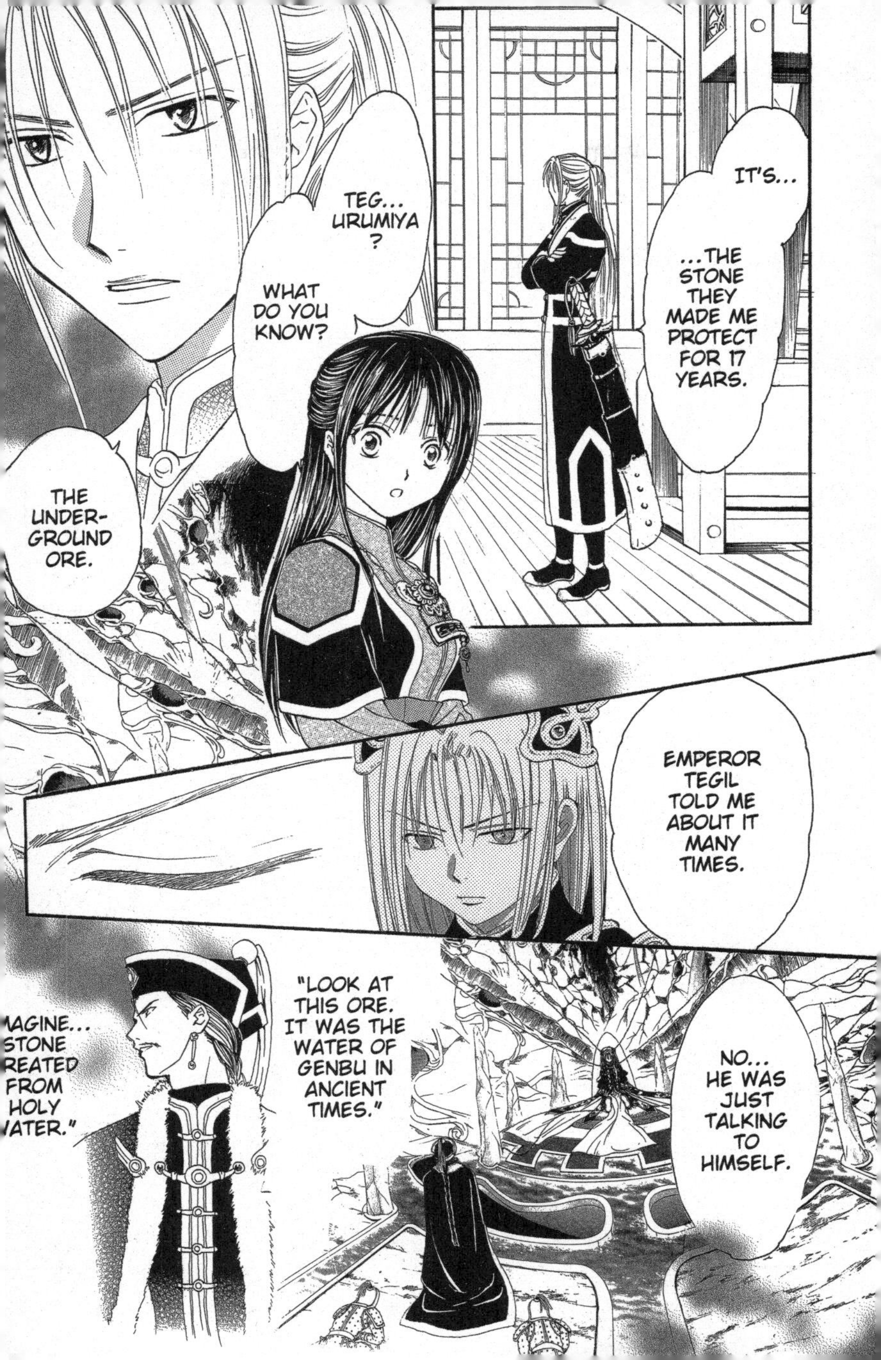
IT'S...
...THE STONE THEY MADE ME PROTECT FOR 17 YEARS.
TEG... URUMIYA?
WHAT DO YOU KNOW?
THE UNDER-GROUND ORE.
EMPEROR TEGIL TOLD ME ABOUT IT MANY TIMES.
NO... HE WAS JUST TALKING TO HIMSELF.
"LOOK AT THIS ORE. IT WAS THE WATER OF GENBU IN ANCIENT TIMES."
MAGINE... STONE REATED FROM HOLY ATER."

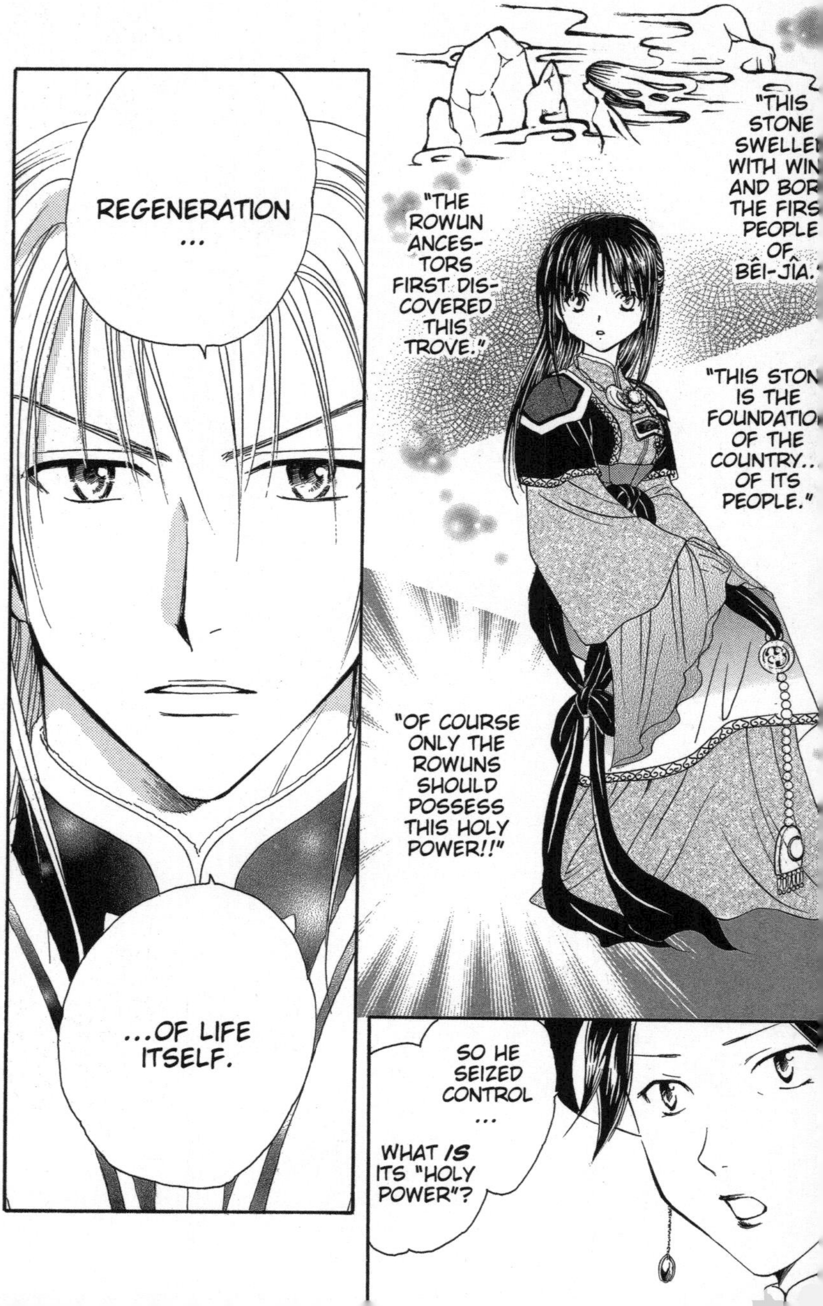
"THIS STONE SWELLE WITH WIN AND BOR THE FIRS PEOPLE OF BÊI-JÎA."
"THE ROWUN ANCES-TORS FIRST DIS-COVERED THIS TROVE."
"THIS STON IS THE FOUNDATIO OF THE COUNTRY... OF ITS PEOPLE."
"OF COURSE ONLY THE ROWUNS SHOULD POSSESS THIS HOLY POWER!!"
SO HE SEIZED CONTROL...
WHAT *IS* ITS "HOLY POWER"?
REGENERATION...
...OF LIFE ITSELF.

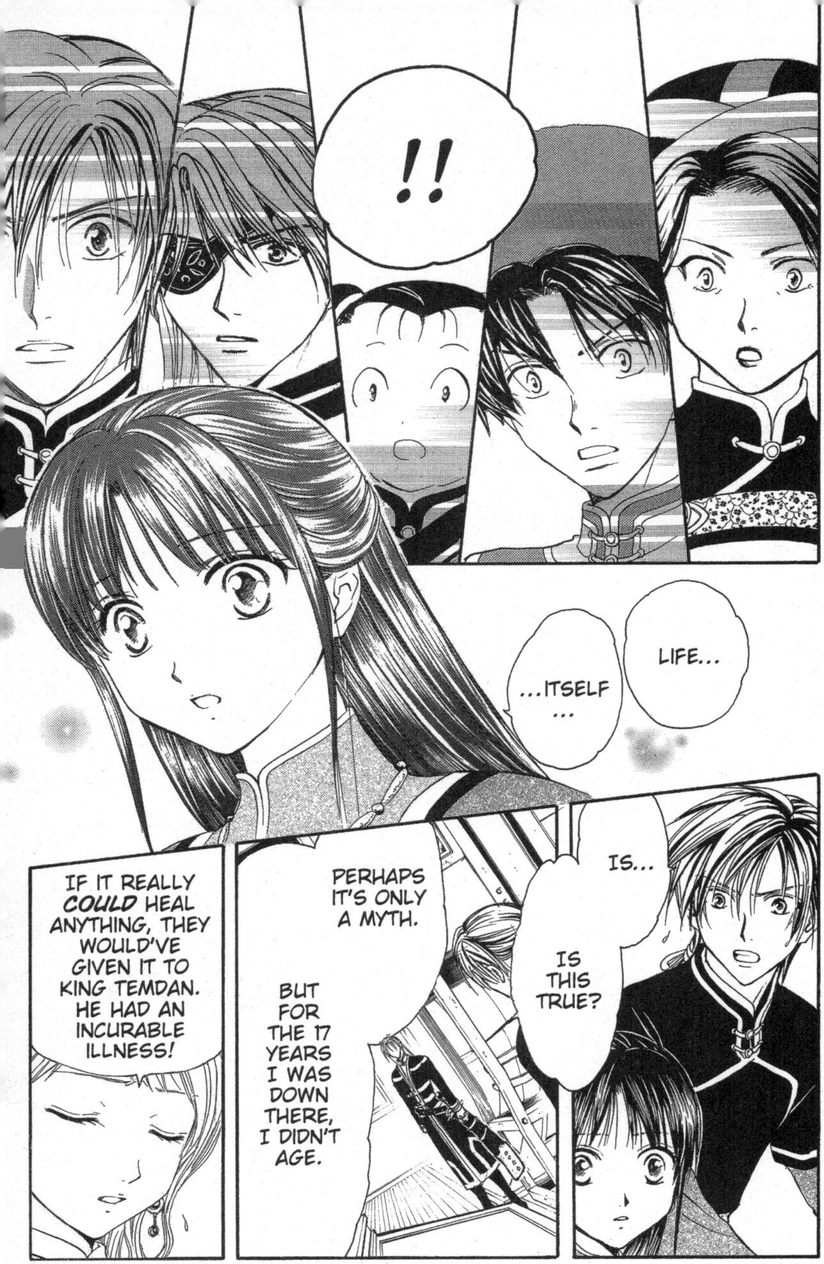
!!
LIFE...
...ITSELF ...
IS...
IS THIS TRUE?
PERHAPS IT'S ONLY A MYTH.
BUT FOR THE 17 YEARS I WAS DOWN THERE, I DIDN'T AGE.
IF IT REALLY COULD HEAL ANYTHING, THEY WOULD'VE GIVEN IT TO KING TEMDAN. HE HAD AN INCURABLE ILLNESS!

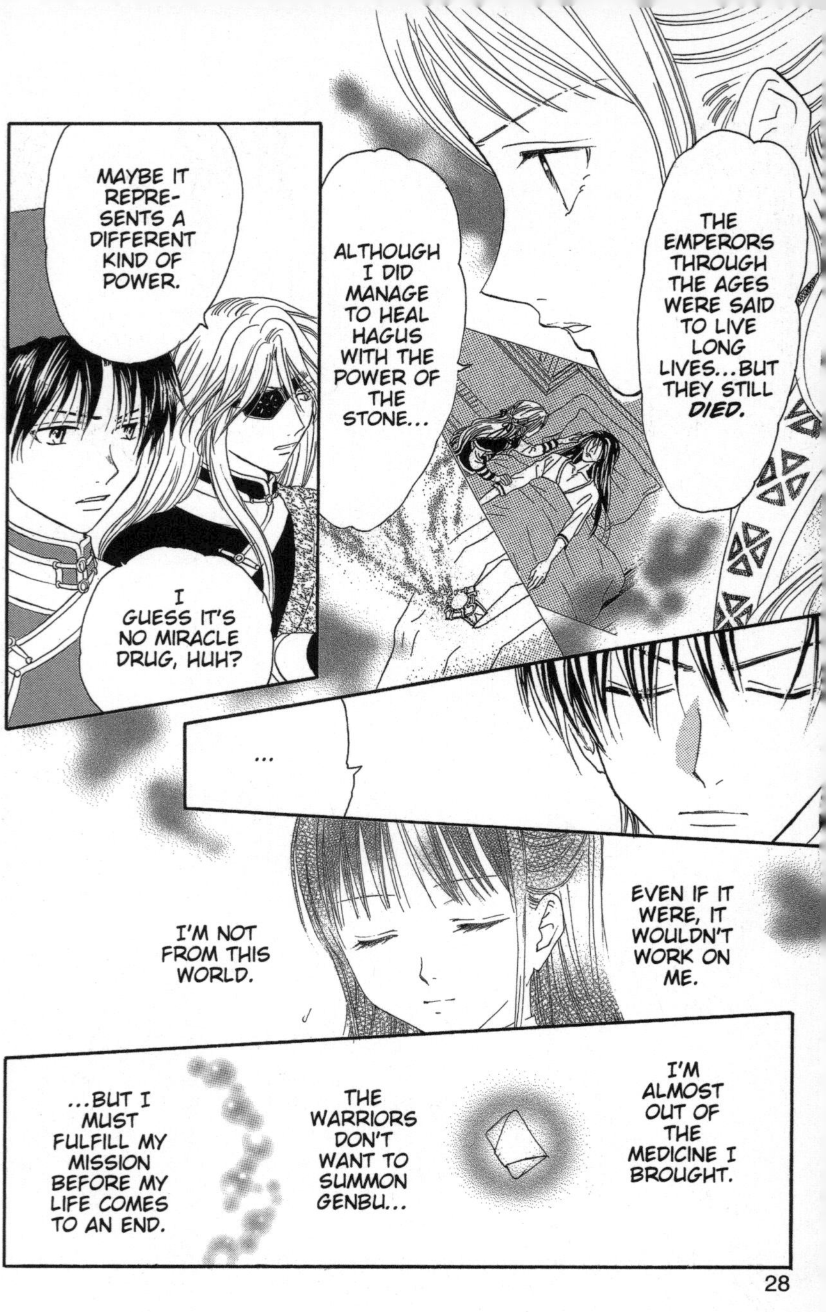
THE EMPERORS THROUGH THE AGES WERE SAID TO LIVE LONG LIVES...BUT THEY STILL ***DIED.***
ALTHOUGH I DID MANAGE TO HEAL HAGUS WITH THE POWER OF THE STONE...
MAYBE IT REPRESENTS A DIFFERENT KIND OF POWER.
I GUESS IT'S NO MIRACLE DRUG, HUH?
...
EVEN IF IT WERE, IT WOULDN'T WORK ON ME.
I'M NOT FROM THIS WORLD.
I'M ALMOST OUT OF THE MEDICINE I BROUGHT.
THE WARRIORS DON'T WANT TO SUMMON GENBU...
...BUT I MUST FULFILL MY MISSION BEFORE MY LIFE COMES TO AN END.

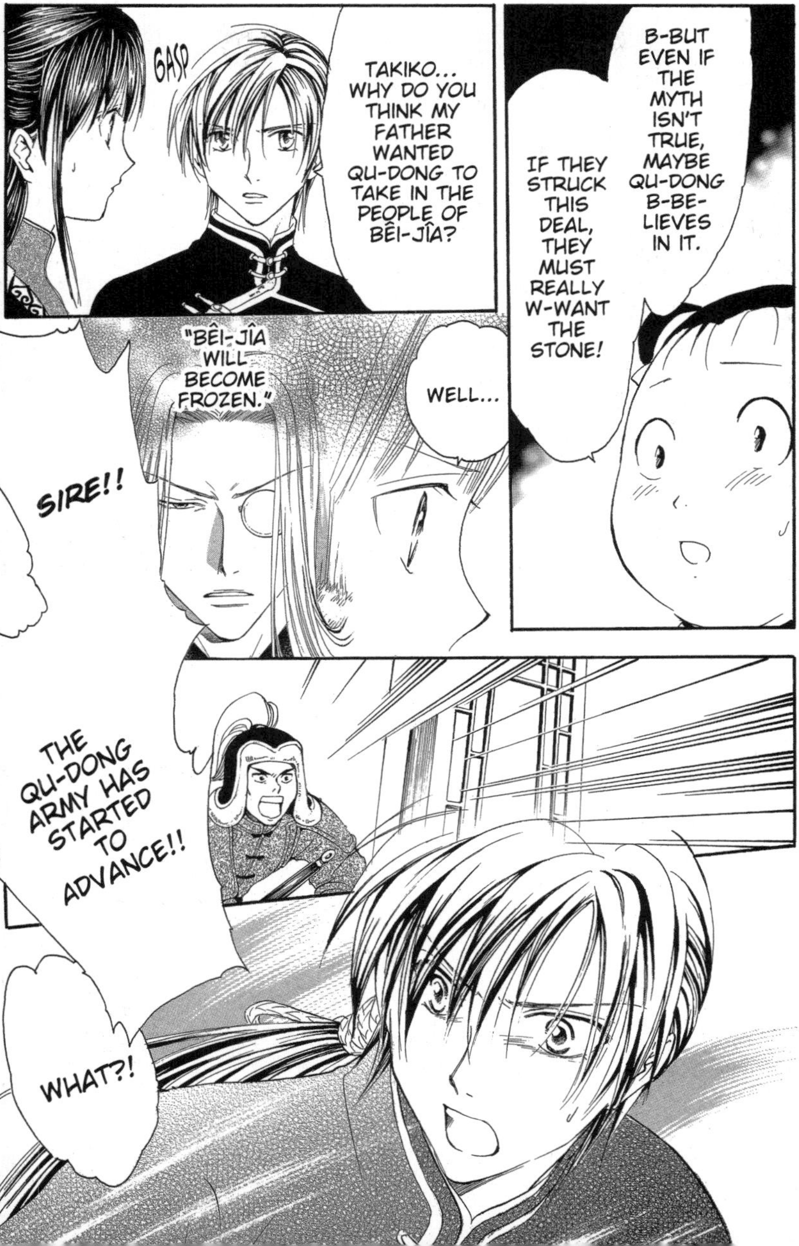
B-BUT EVEN IF THE MYTH ISN'T TRUE, MAYBE QU-DONG B-BE-LIEVES IN IT.
IF THEY STRUCK THIS DEAL, THEY MUST REALLY W-WANT THE STONE!
GASP
TAKIKO... WHY DO YOU THINK MY FATHER WANTED QU-DONG TO TAKE IN THE PEOPLE OF BÊI-JÎA?
WELL...
"BÊI-JÎA WILL BECOME FROZEN."
SIRE!!
THE QU-DONG ARMY HAS STARTED TO ADVANCE!!
WHAT?!

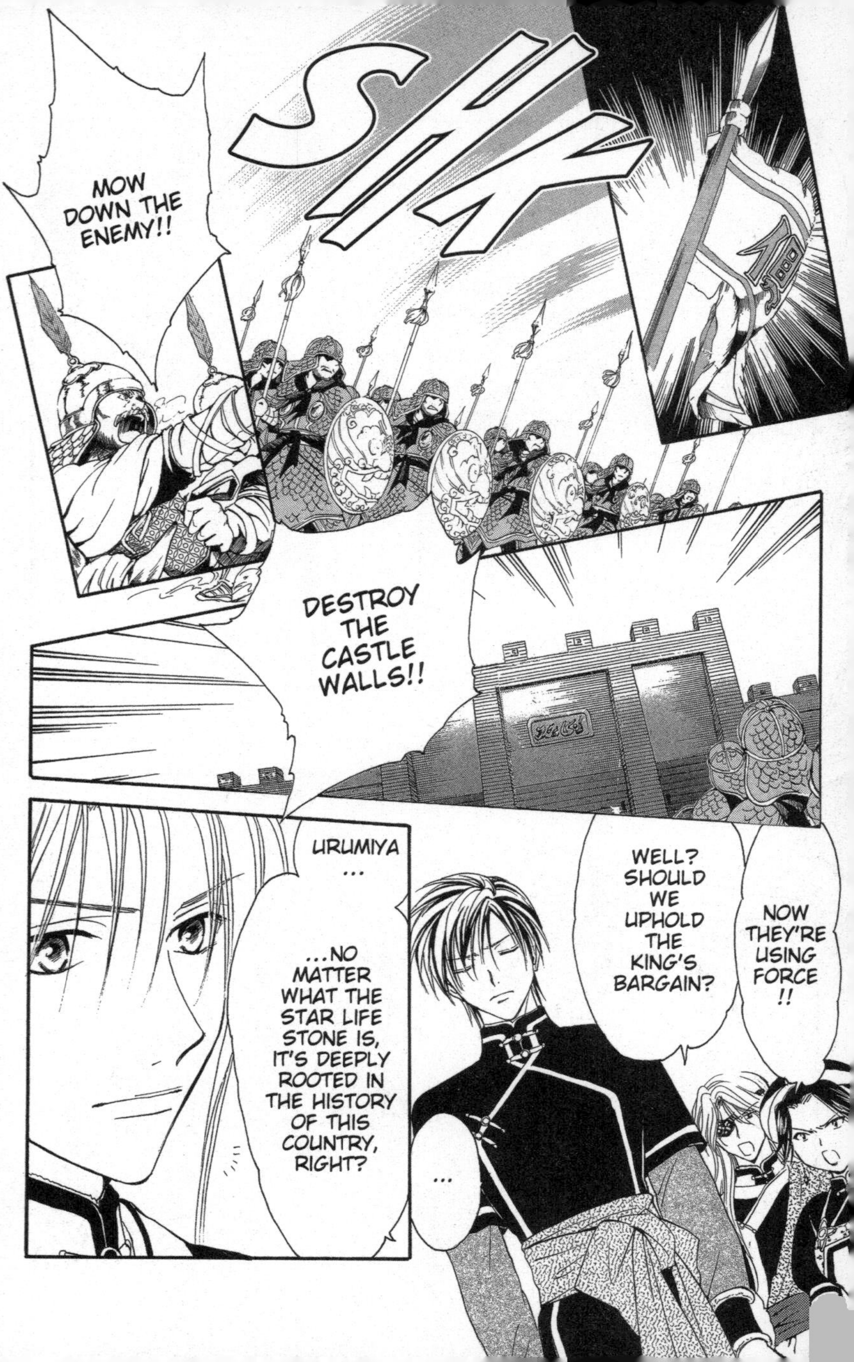
SHK
MOW DOWN THE ENEMY!!
DESTROY THE CASTLE WALLS!!
NOW THEY'RE USING FORCE!!
WELL? SHOULD WE UPHOLD THE KING'S BARGAIN?
...
URUMIYA...
...NO MATTER WHAT THE STAR LIFE STONE IS, IT'S DEEPLY ROOTED IN THE HISTORY OF THIS COUNTRY, RIGHT?

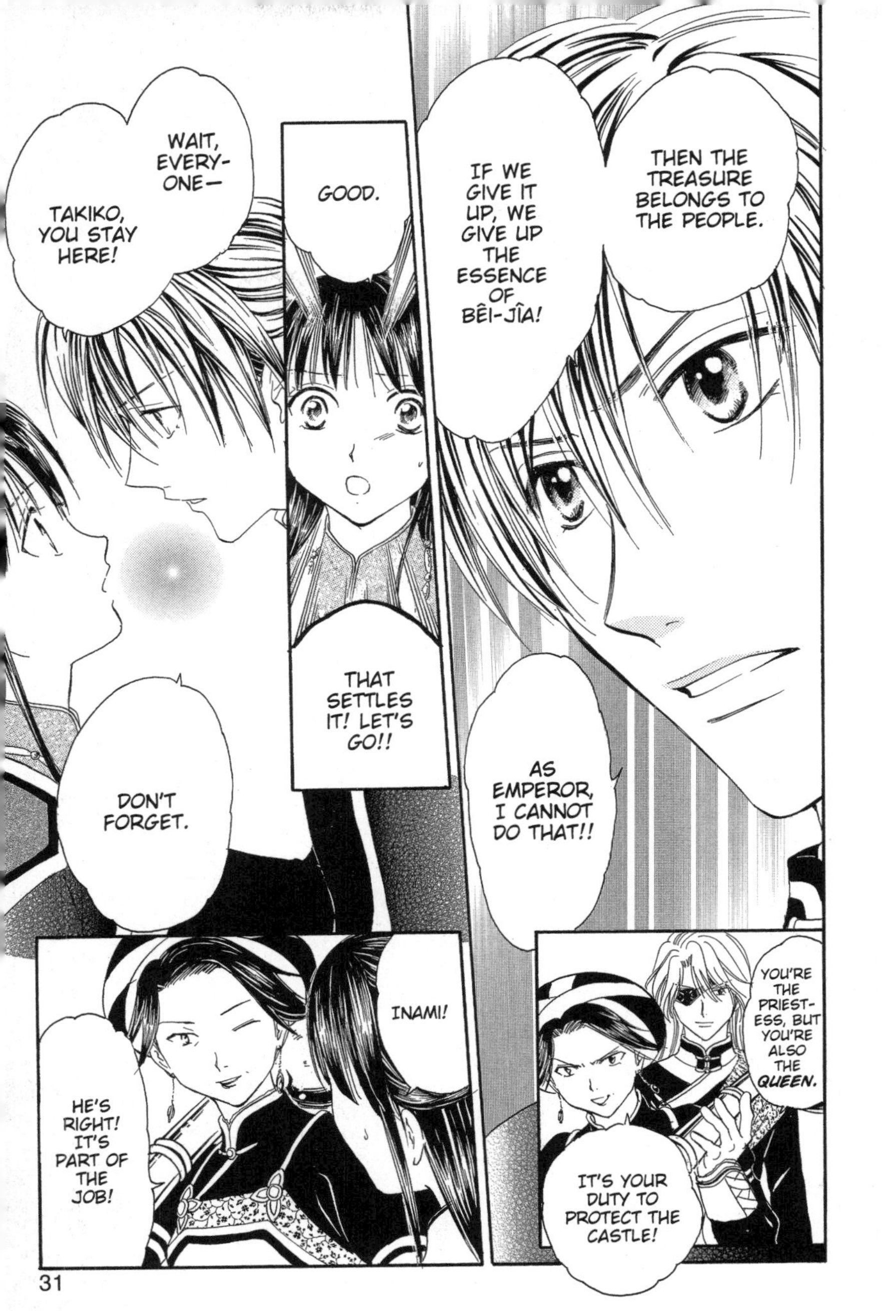
THEN THE TREASURE BELONGS TO THE PEOPLE.
IF WE GIVE IT UP, WE GIVE UP THE ESSENCE OF BÊI-JÎA!
AS EMPEROR, I CANNOT DO THAT!!
GOOD.
THAT SETTLES IT! LET'S GO!!
WAIT, EVERYONE—
TAKIKO, YOU STAY HERE!
DON'T FORGET.
YOU'RE THE PRIESTESS, BUT YOU'RE ALSO THE *QUEEN.*
IT'S YOUR DUTY TO PROTECT THE CASTLE!
INAMI!
HE'S RIGHT! IT'S PART OF THE JOB!

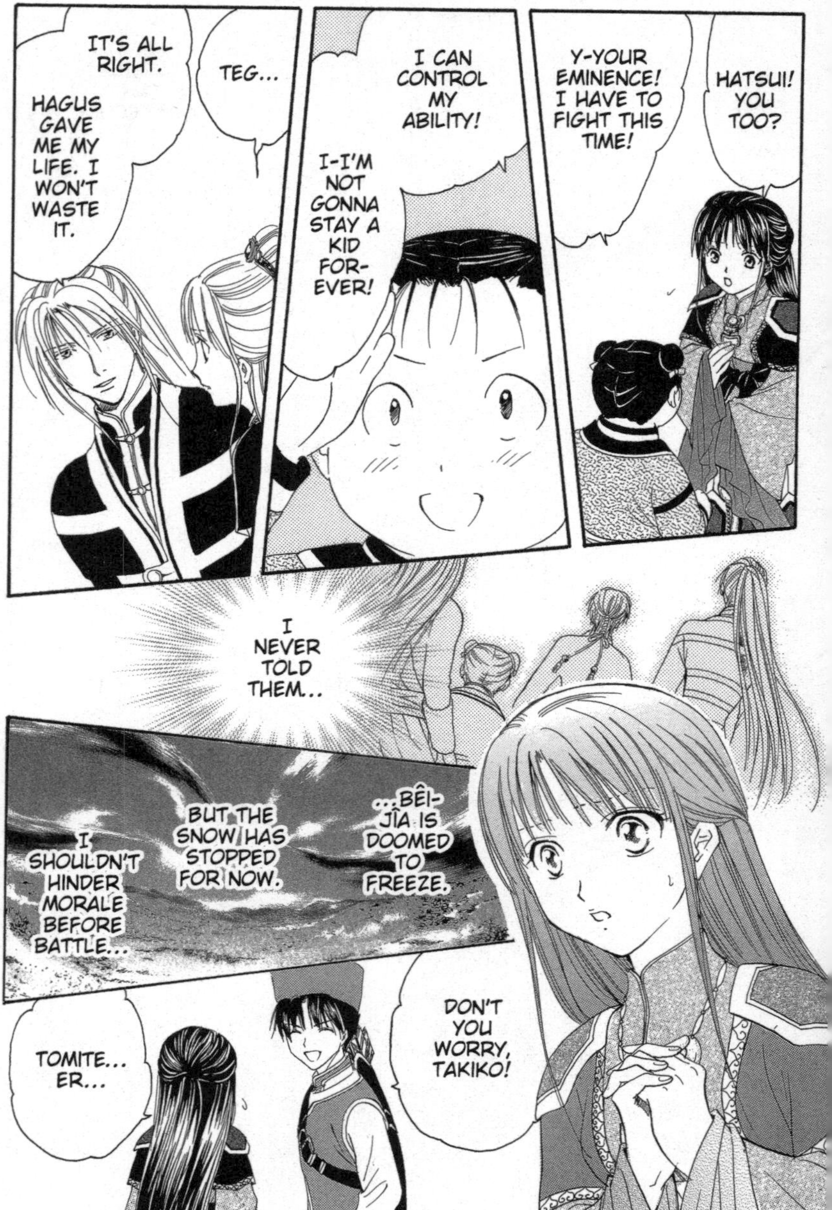

HATSUI! YOU TOO?
Y-YOUR EMINENCE! I HAVE TO FIGHT THIS TIME!
I CAN CONTROL MY ABILITY!
I-I'M NOT GONNA STAY A KID FOR-EVER!
TEG...
IT'S ALL RIGHT.
HAGUS GAVE ME MY LIFE. I WON'T WASTE IT.
I NEVER TOLD THEM...
...BÊI-JÎA IS DOOMED TO FREEZE.
BUT THE SNOW HAS STOPPED FOR NOW.
I SHOULDN'T HINDER MORALE BEFORE BATTLE...
DON'T YOU WORRY, TAKIKO!
TOMITE... ER...

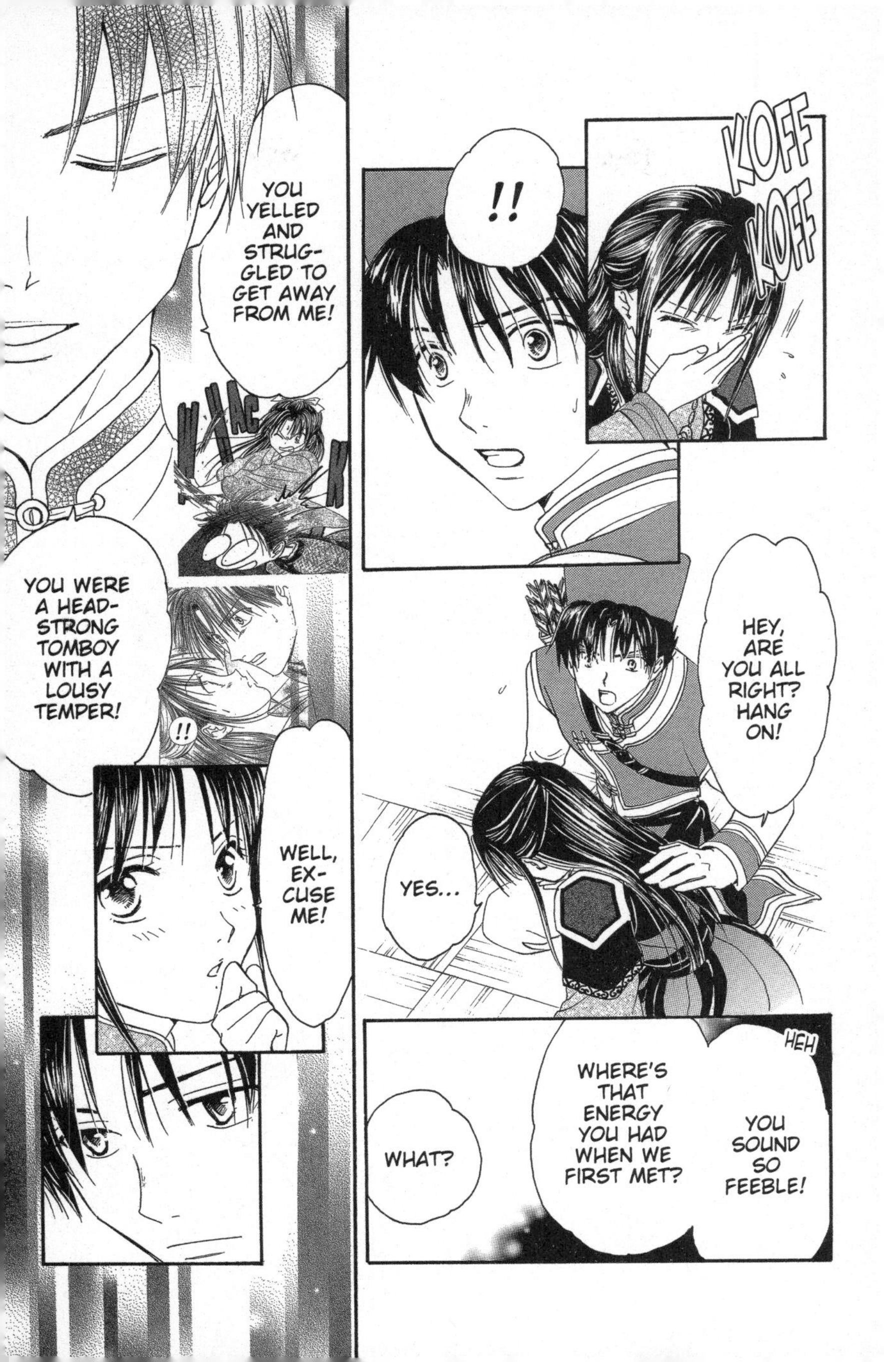
KOFF KOFF
!!
HEY, ARE YOU ALL RIGHT? HANG ON!
YES...
HEH
YOU SOUND SO FEEBLE!
WHERE'S THAT ENERGY YOU HAD WHEN WE FIRST MET?
WHAT?
YOU YELLED AND STRUGGLED TO GET AWAY FROM ME!
YOU WERE A HEADSTRONG TOMBOY WITH A LOUSY TEMPER!
!!
WELL, EXCUSE ME!

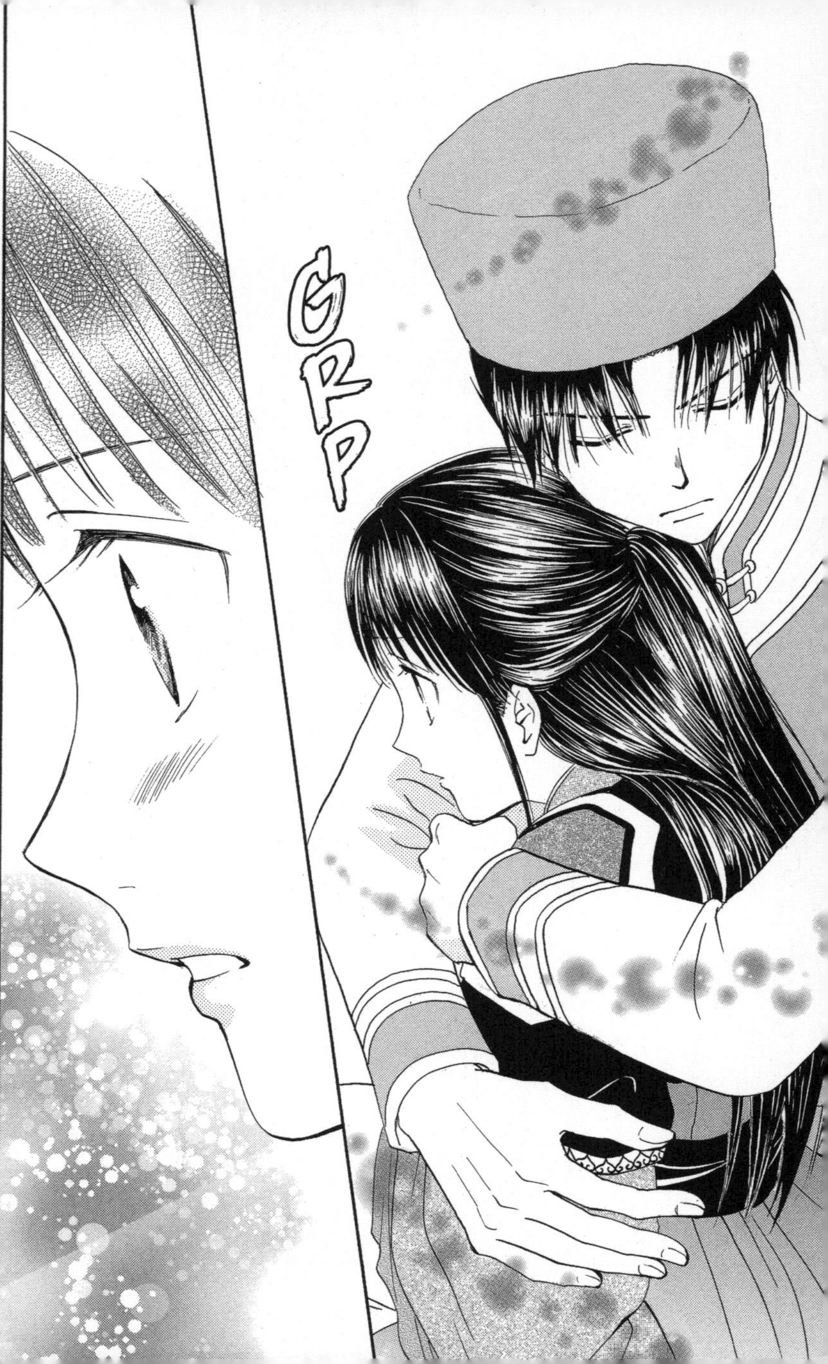
GRP

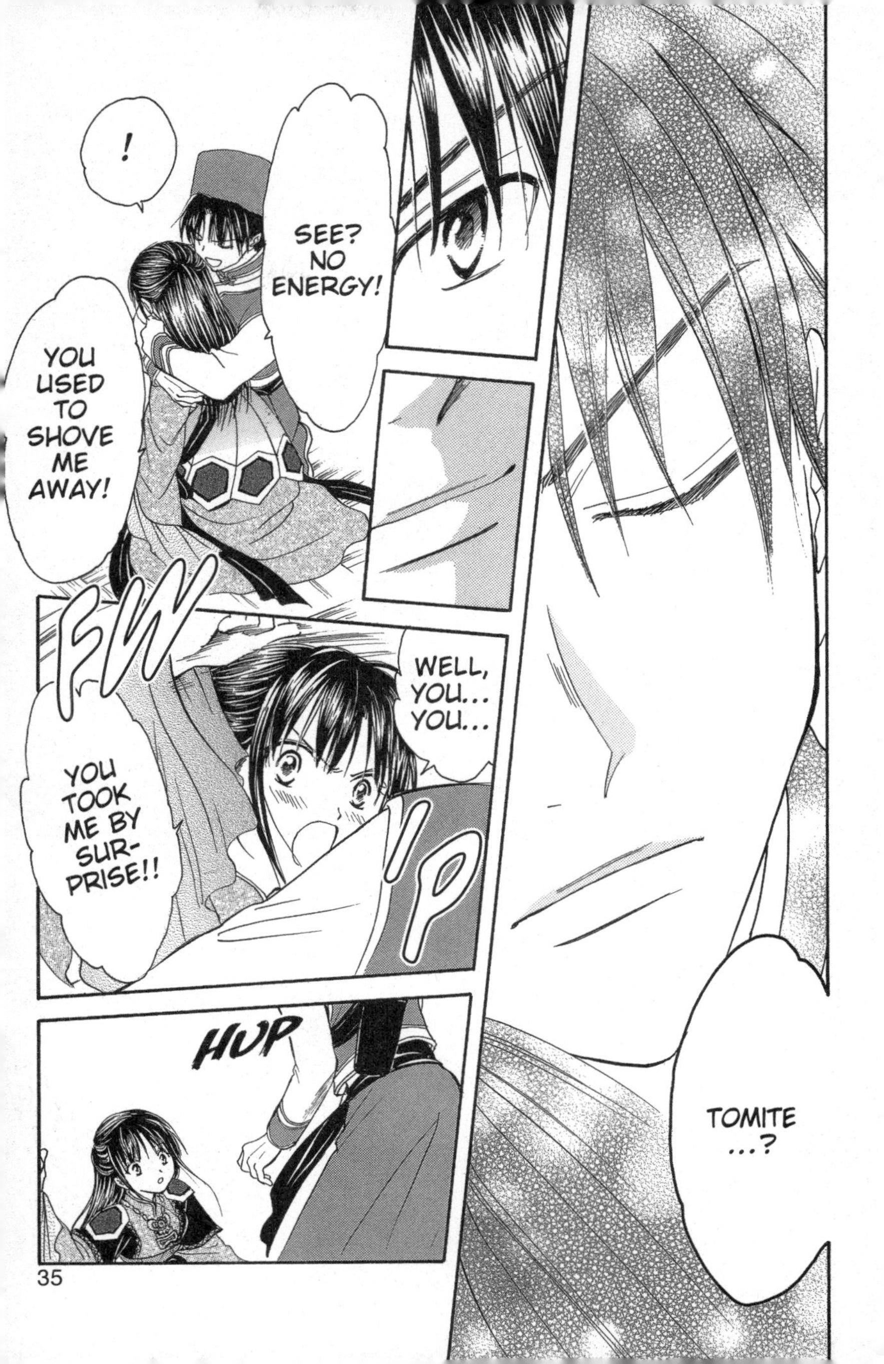
TOMITE ...?
SEE? NO ENERGY!
!
YOU USED TO SHOVE ME AWAY!
FW
WELL, YOU... YOU...
YOU TOOK ME BY SUR-PRISE!!
IP
HUP

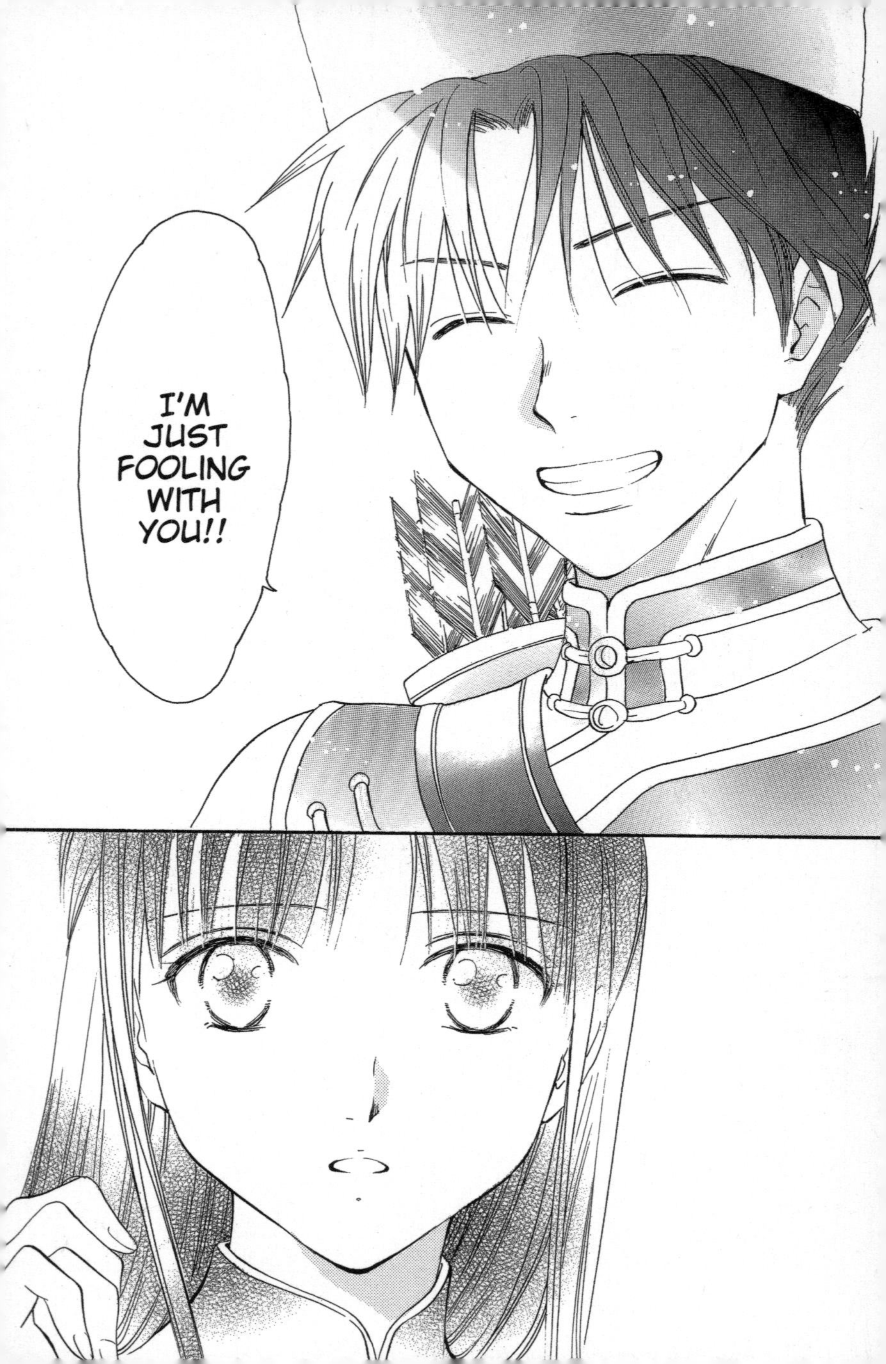
I'M JUST FOOLING WITH YOU!!

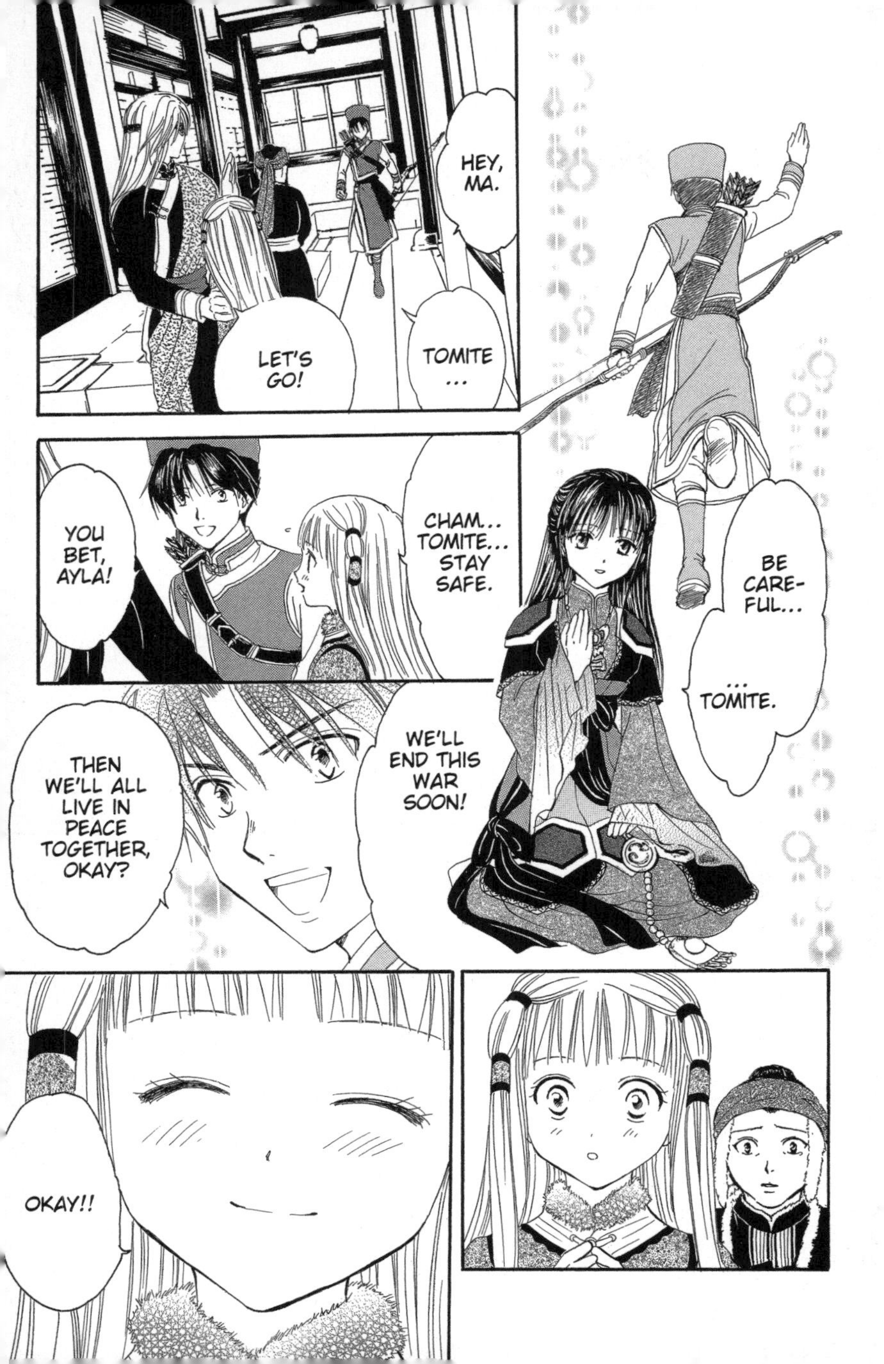
BE CAREFUL...
... TOMITE.
HEY, MA.
TOMITE ...
LET'S GO!
CHAM... TOMITE... STAY SAFE.
YOU BET, AYLA!
WE'LL END THIS WAR SOON!
THEN WE'LL ALL LIVE IN PEACE TOGETHER, OKAY?
OKAY!!

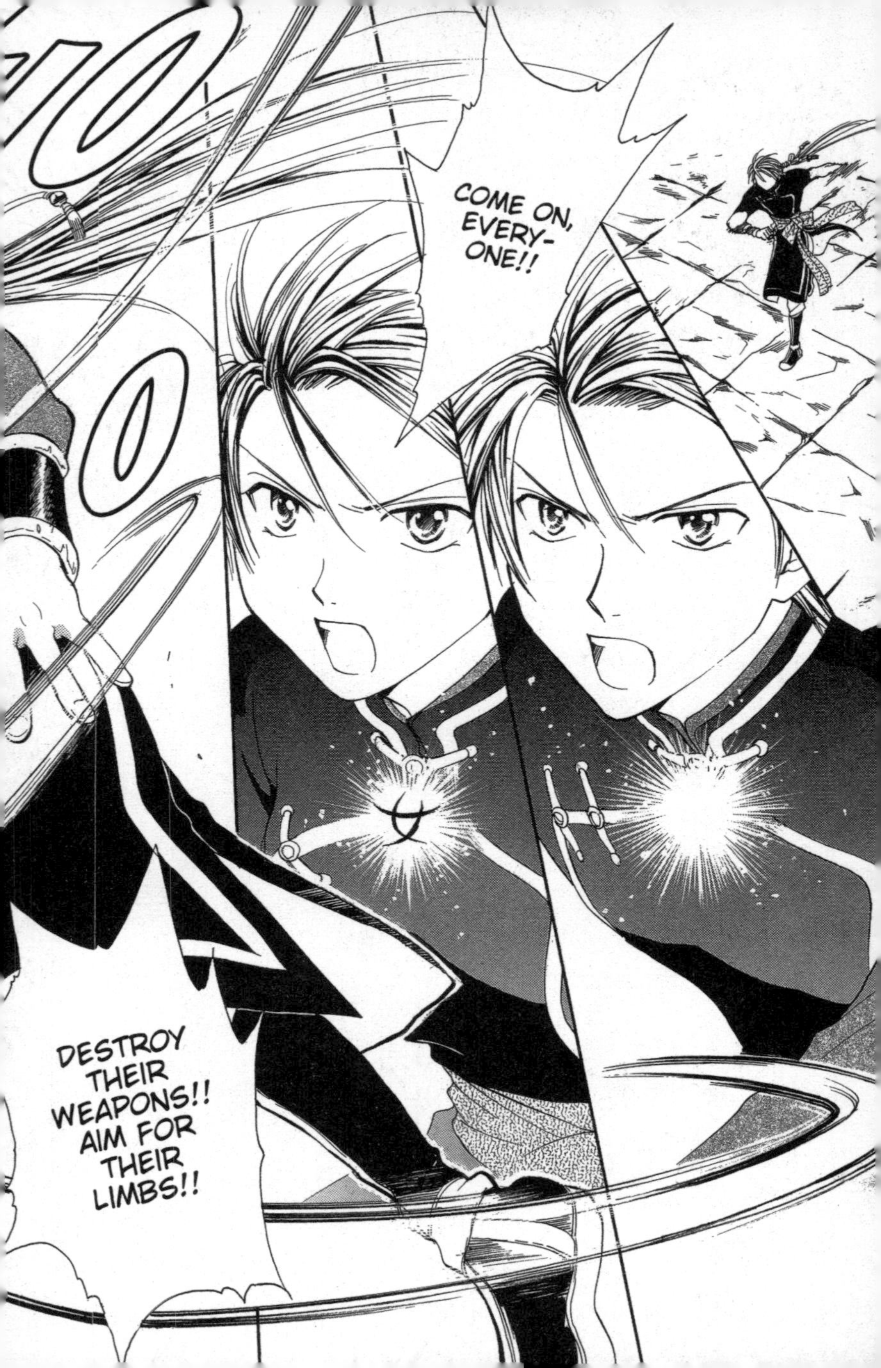
COME ON, EVERY-ONE!!
DESTROY THEIR WEAPONS!! AIM FOR THEIR LIMBS!!

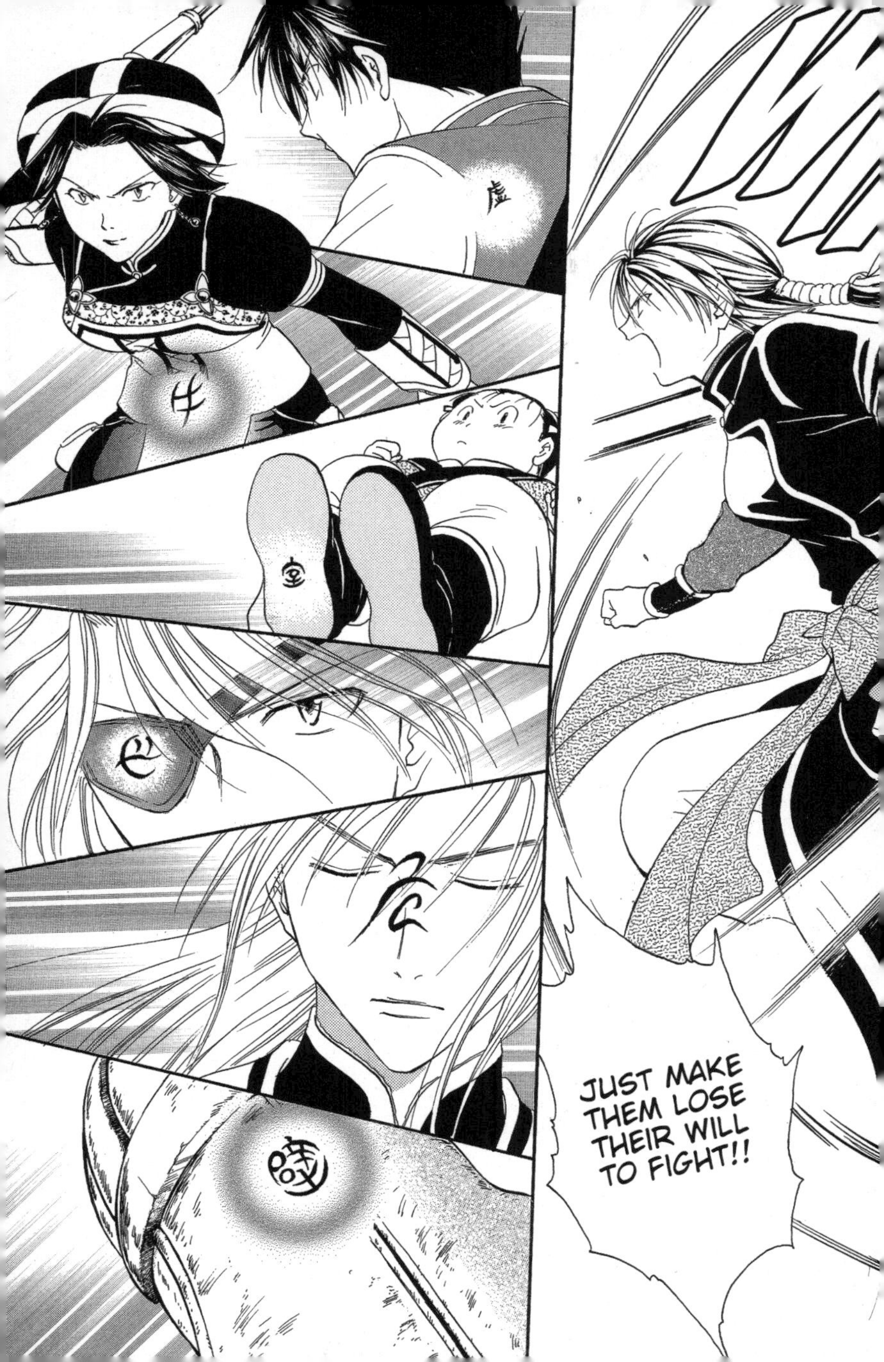
JUST MAKE THEM LOSE THEIR WILL TO FIGHT!!

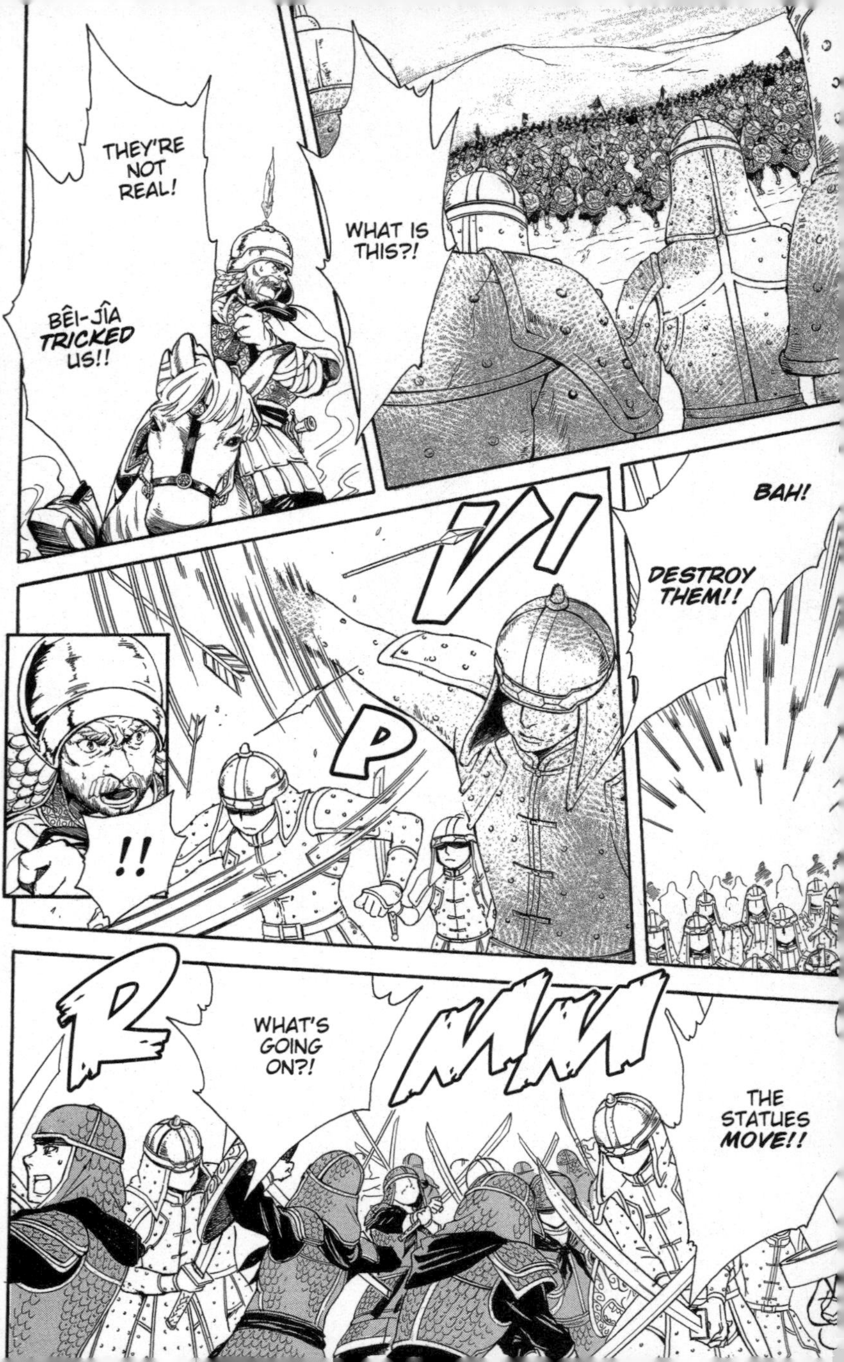
WHAT IS THIS?!
THEY'RE NOT REAL!
BÊI-JÎA *TRICKED* US!!
BAH!
DESTROY THEM!!
VIP
!!
RMM
THE STATUES *MOVE!!*
WHAT'S GOING ON?!

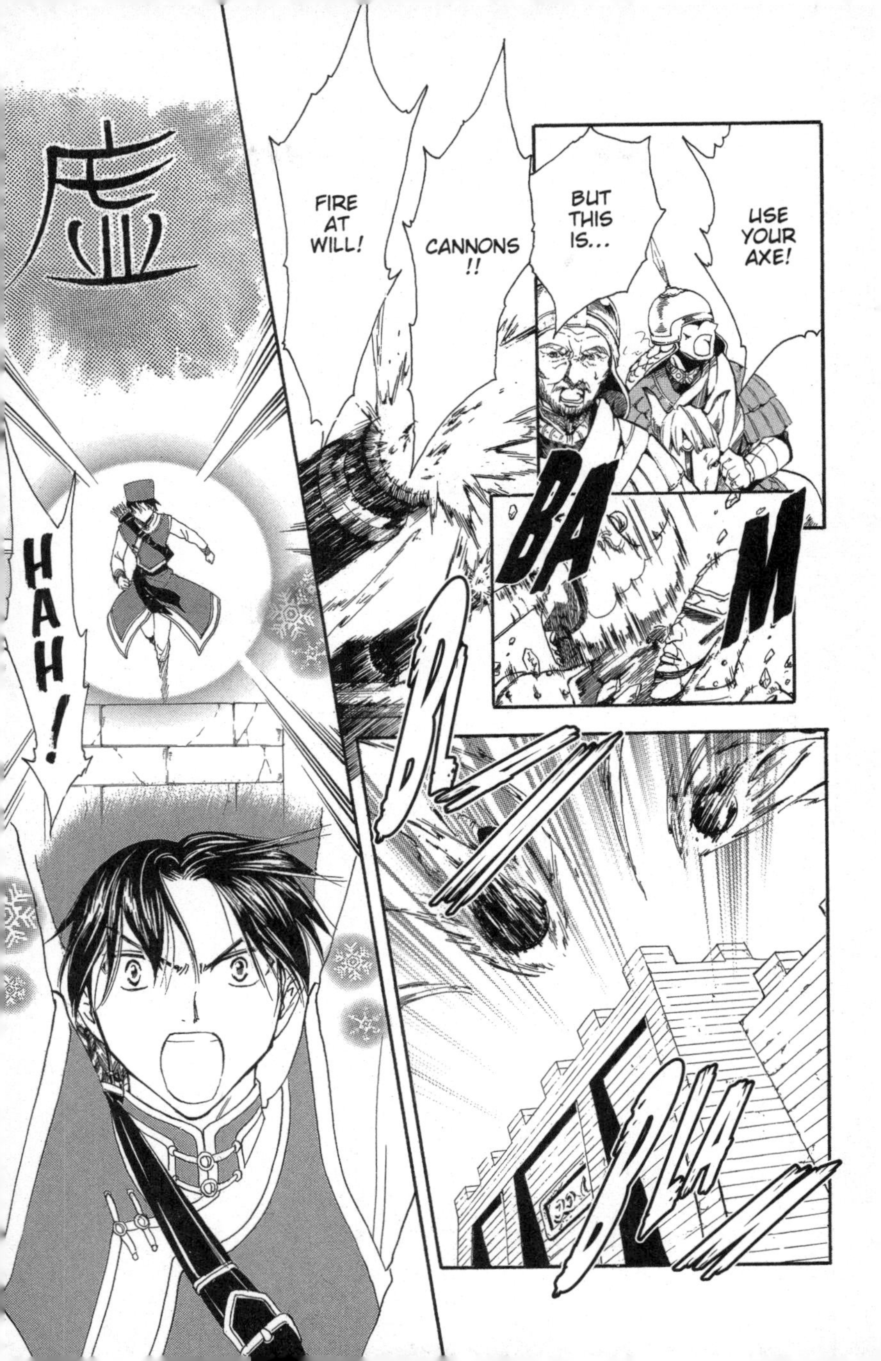
USE YOUR AXE!
BUT THIS IS...
CANNONS !!
FIRE AT WILL!
BAM
HAH!

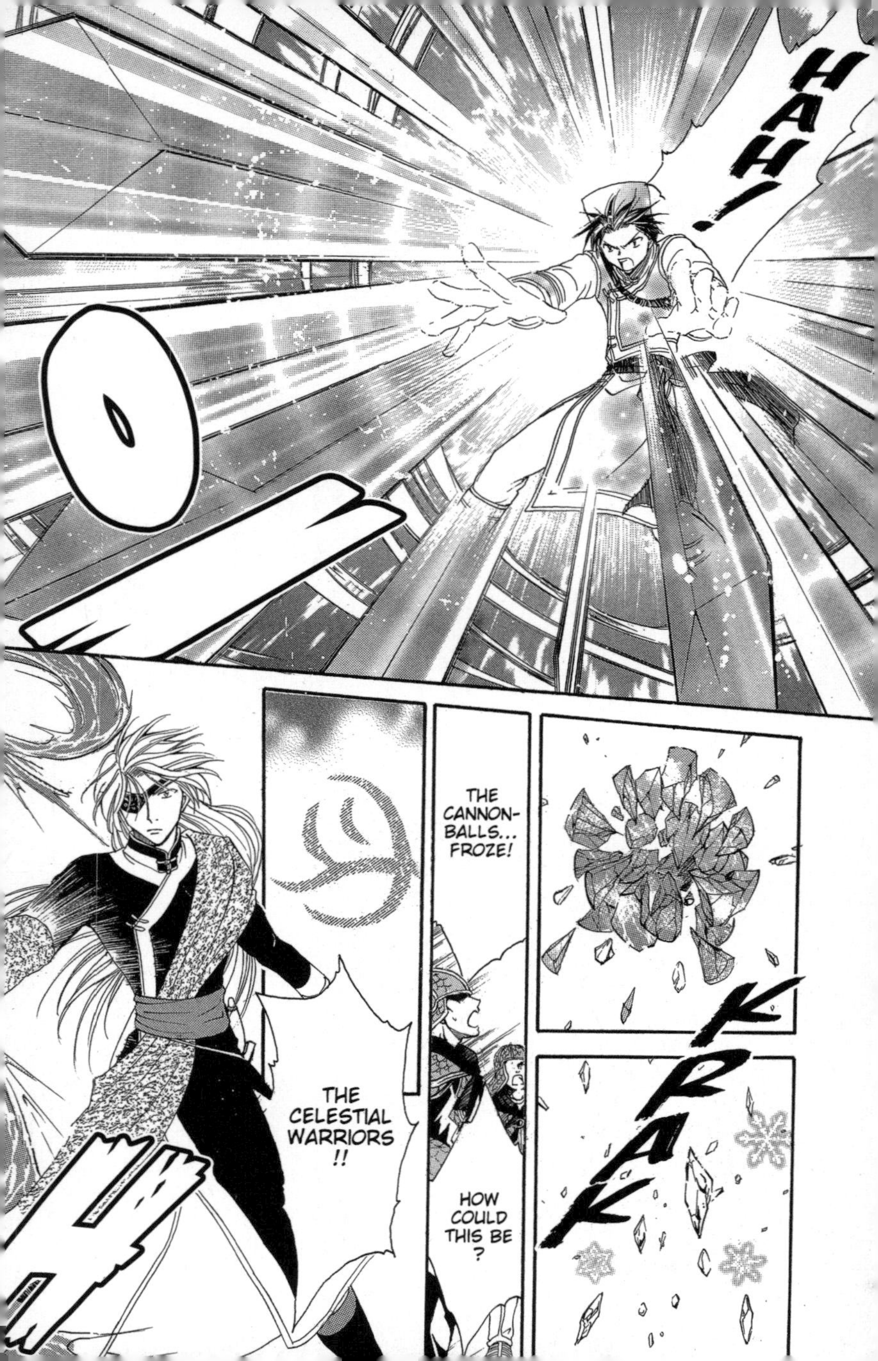
HAH!!
KRAK
THE CANNON-BALLS... FROZE!
HOW COULD THIS BE?
THE CELESTIAL WARRIORS!!

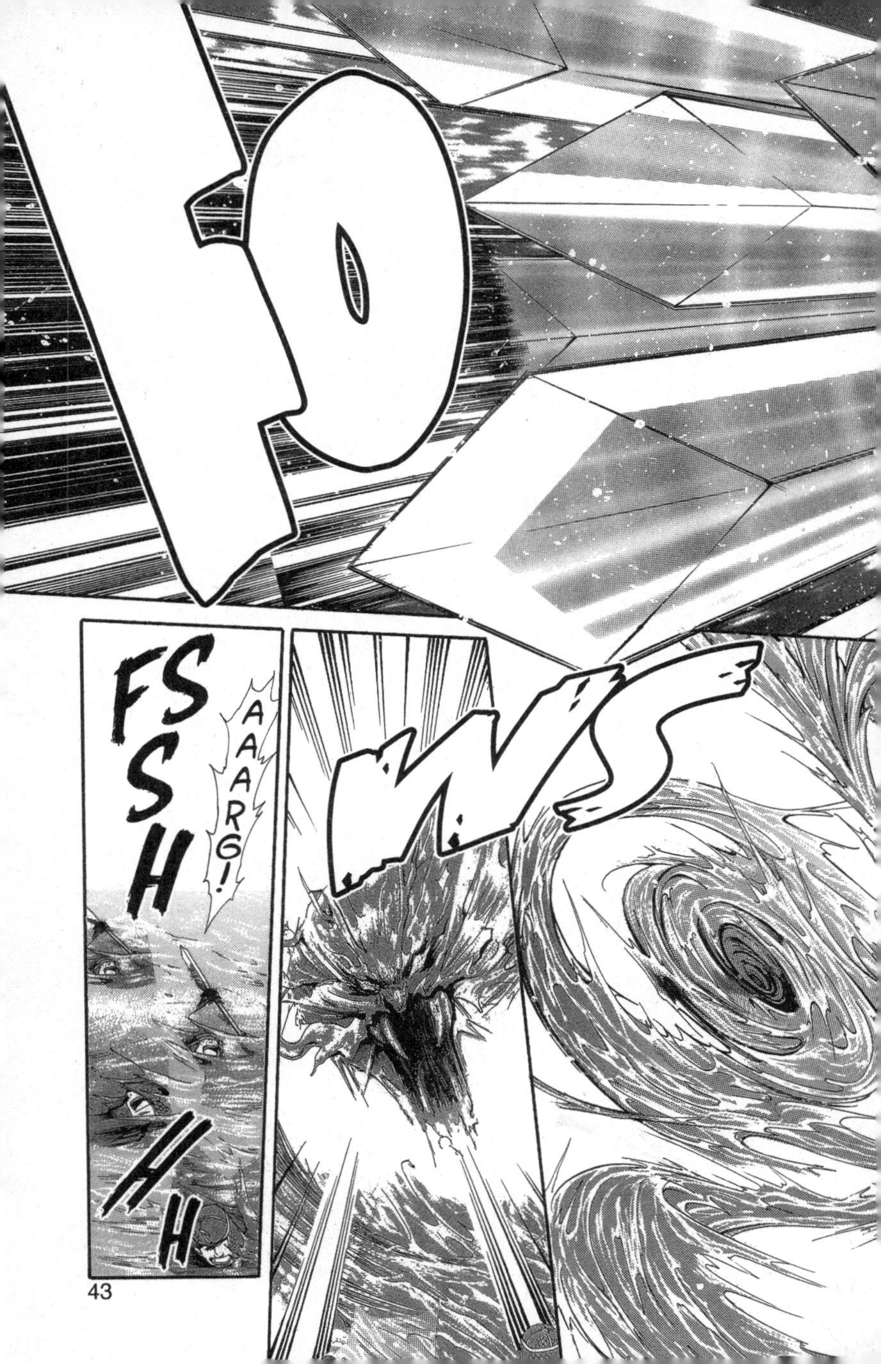
FSSH
AAAARG!
HH

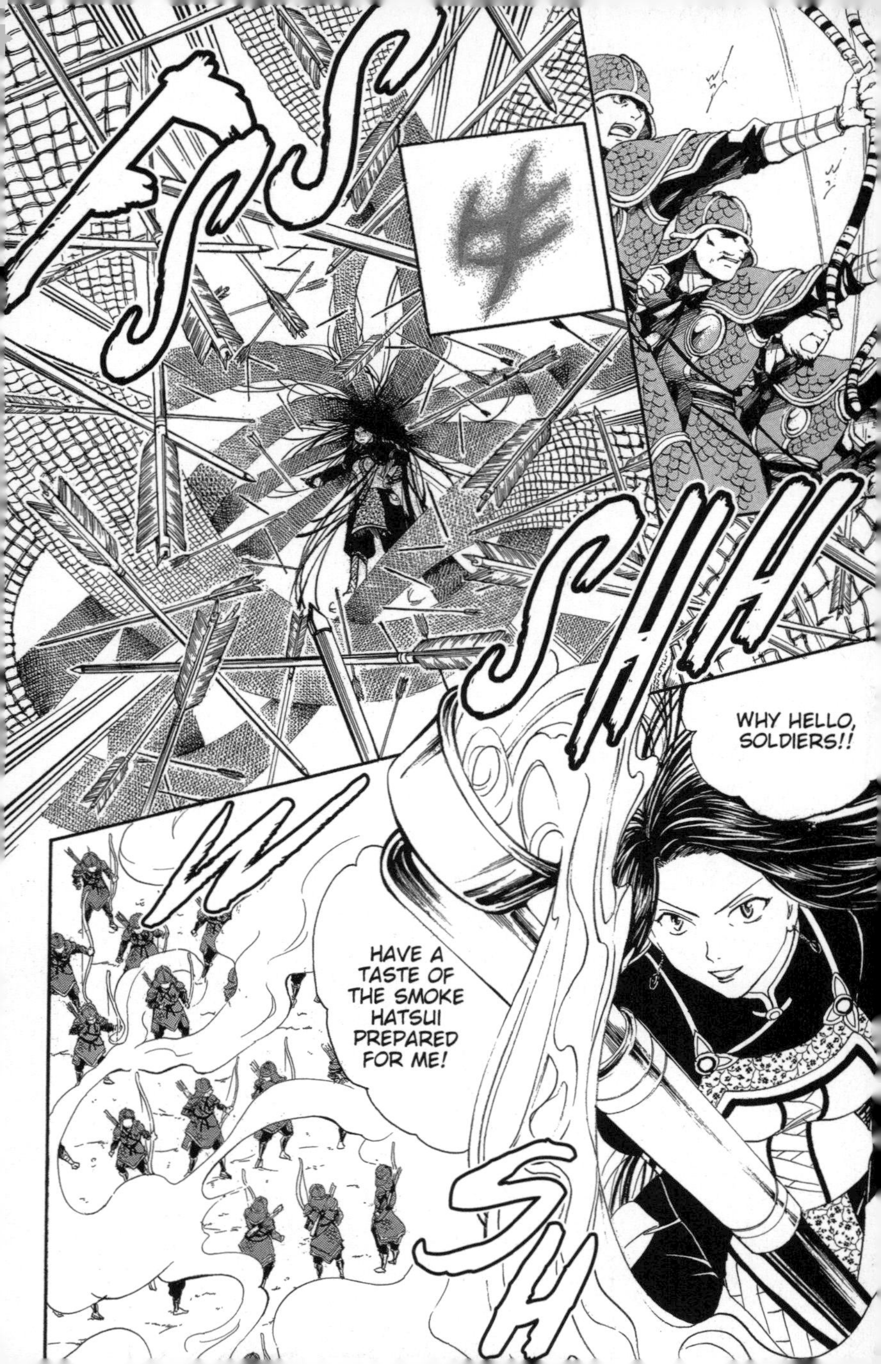
SHH
WHY HELLO, SOLDIERS!!
HAVE A TASTE OF THE SMOKE HATSUI PREPARED FOR ME!

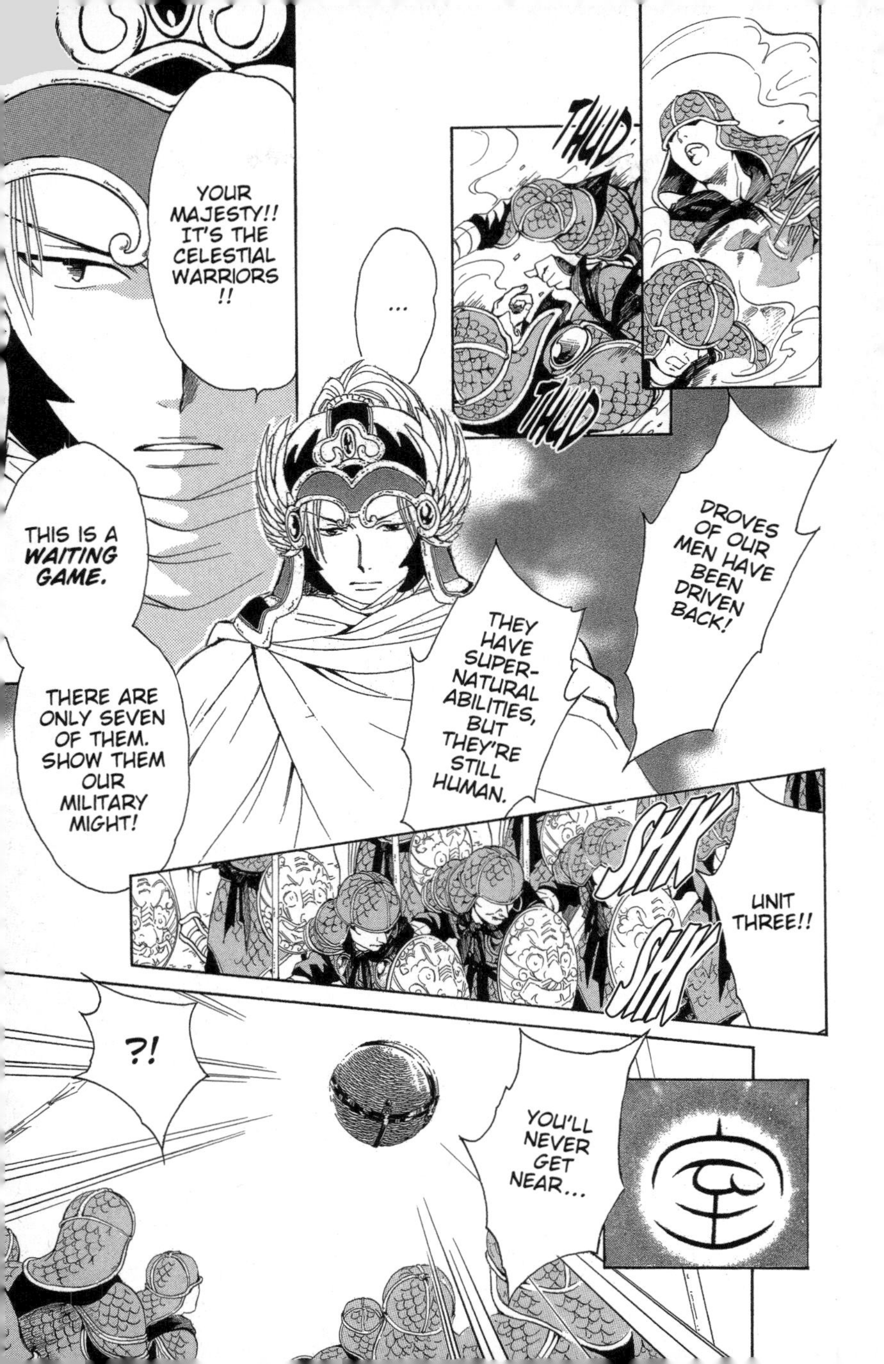
THUD
THUD
YOUR MAJESTY!! IT'S THE CELESTIAL WARRIORS!!
...
DROVES OF OUR MEN HAVE BEEN DRIVEN BACK!
THEY HAVE SUPER-NATURAL ABILITIES, BUT THEY'RE STILL HUMAN.
THIS IS A ***WAITING GAME.***
THERE ARE ONLY SEVEN OF THEM. SHOW THEM OUR MILITARY MIGHT!
UNIT THREE!!
SHK
SHK
YOU'LL NEVER GET NEAR...
?!

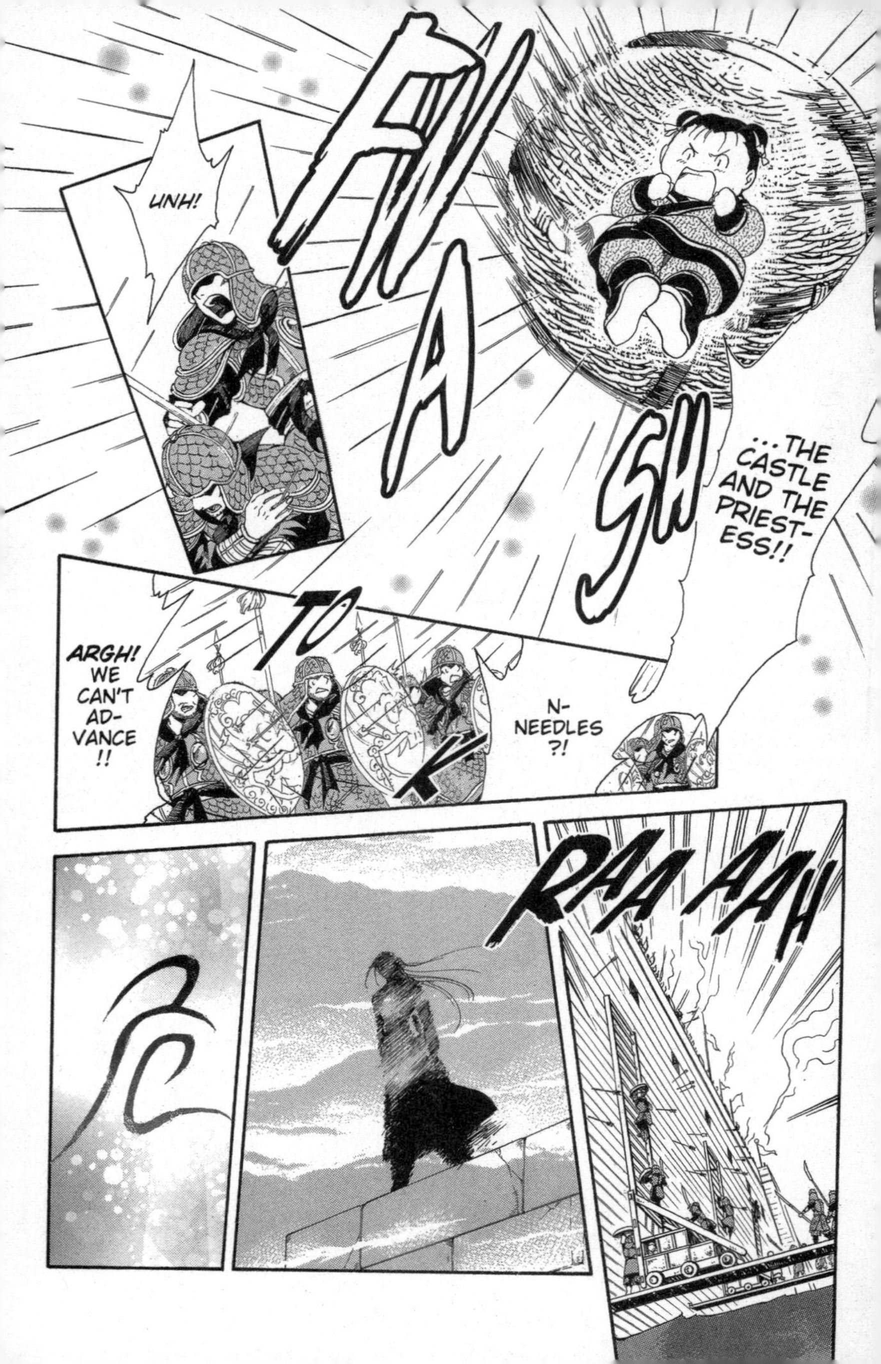
FWAASH
UNH!
...THE CASTLE AND THE PRIEST-ESS!!
TOK
N-NEEDLES ?!
ARGH! WE CAN'T AD-VANCE !!
RAAAAH

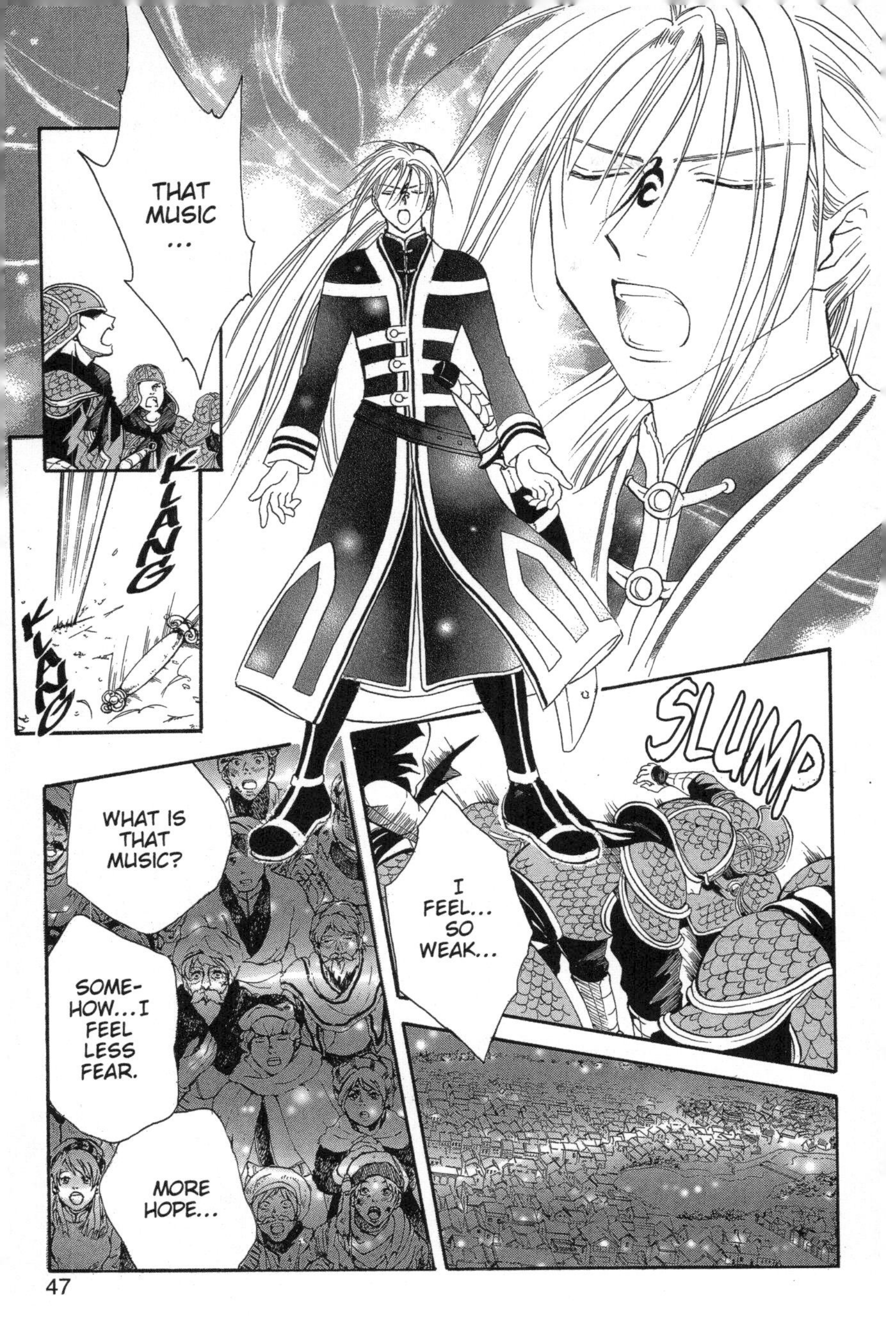
THAT MUSIC ...
KLANG
KLANG
SLUMP
I FEEL... SO WEAK...
WHAT IS THAT MUSIC?
SOME-HOW... I FEEL LESS FEAR.
MORE HOPE...

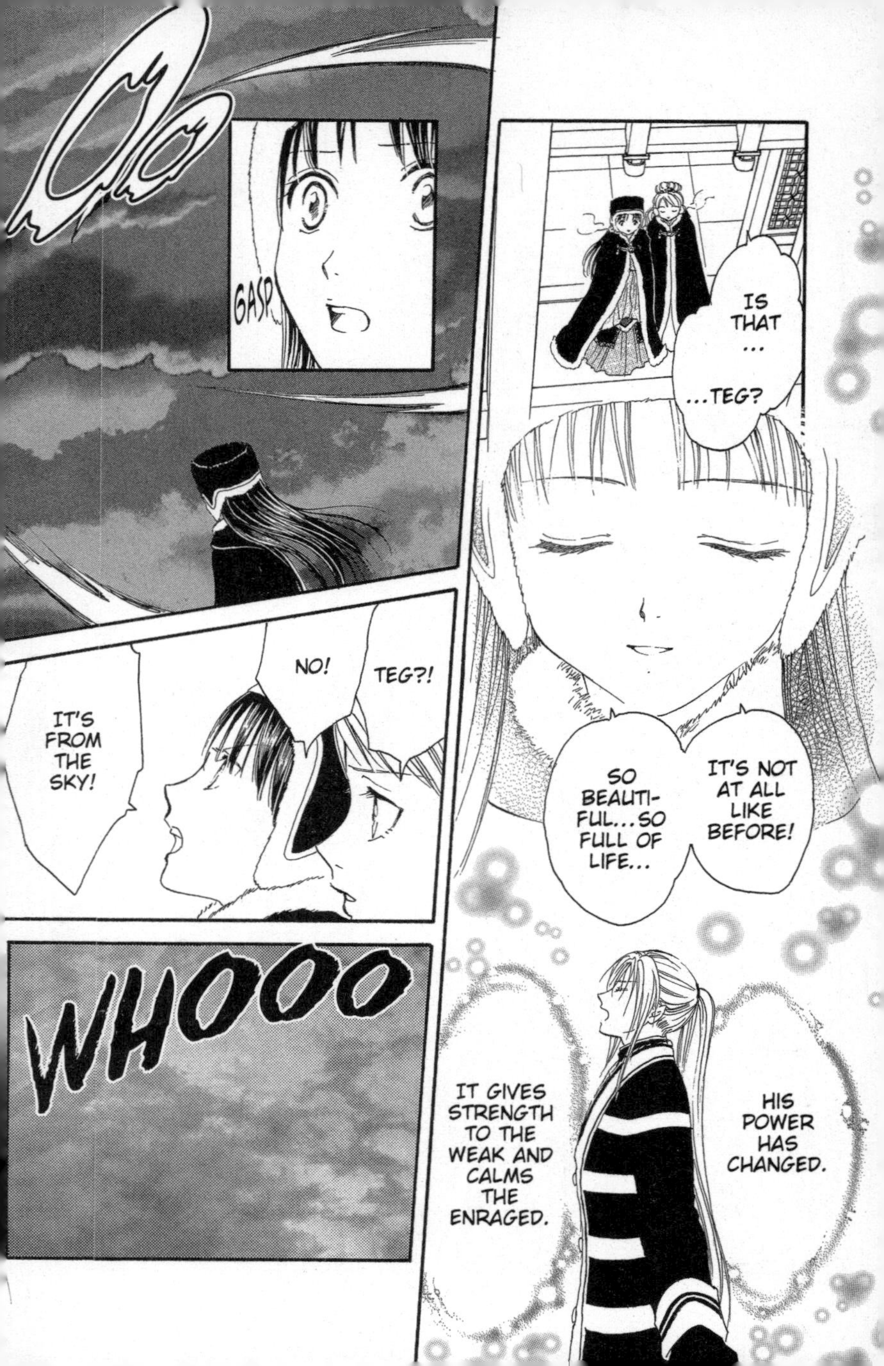
IS THAT ...
...TEG?
IT'S NOT AT ALL LIKE BEFORE!
SO BEAUTI-FUL...SO FULL OF LIFE...
HIS POWER HAS CHANGED.
IT GIVES STRENGTH TO THE WEAK AND CALMS THE ENRAGED.
GASP
TEG?!
NO!
IT'S FROM THE SKY!
WHOOO

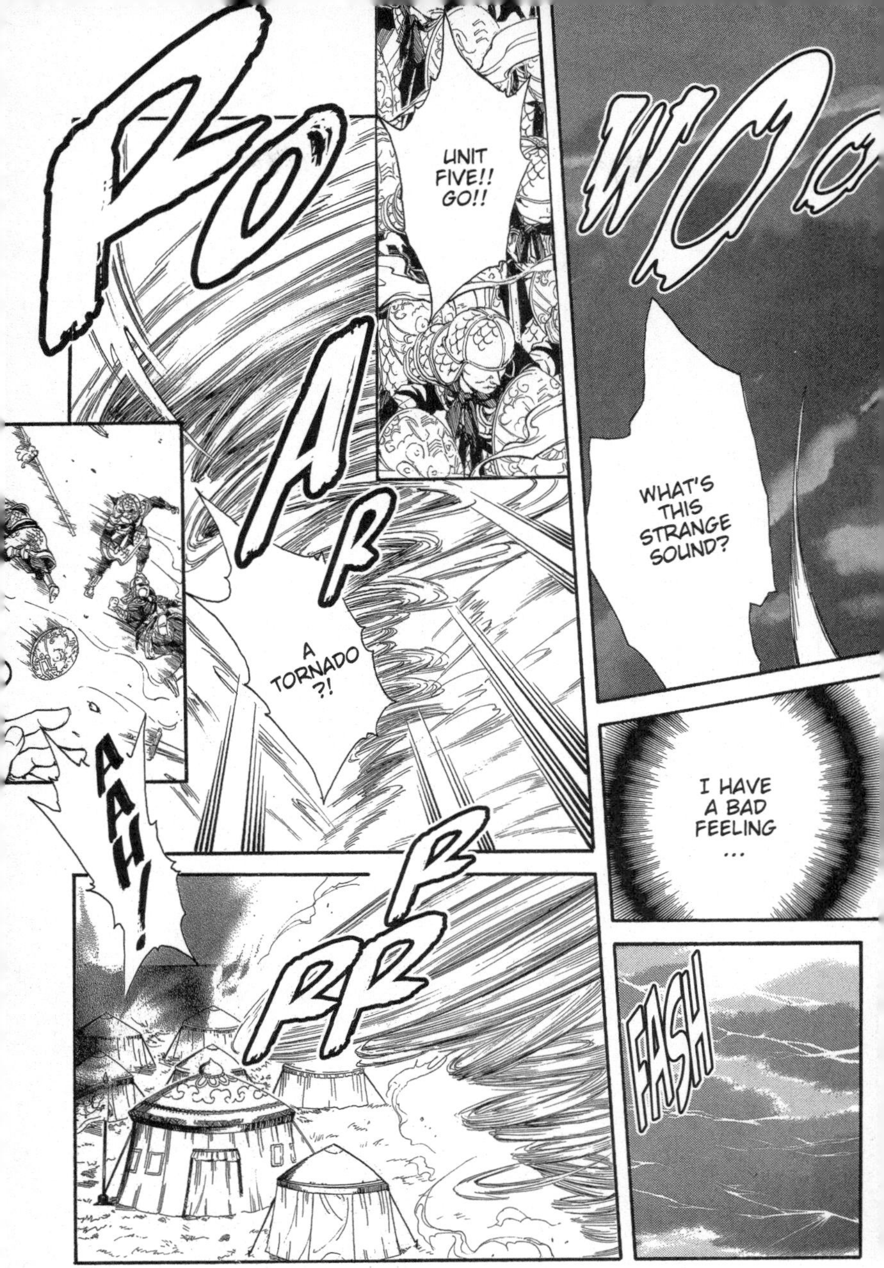
WOOO
WHAT'S THIS STRANGE SOUND?
UNIT FIVE!! GO!!
ROAR
A TORNADO?!
AAH!
I HAVE A BAD FEELING...
FASH

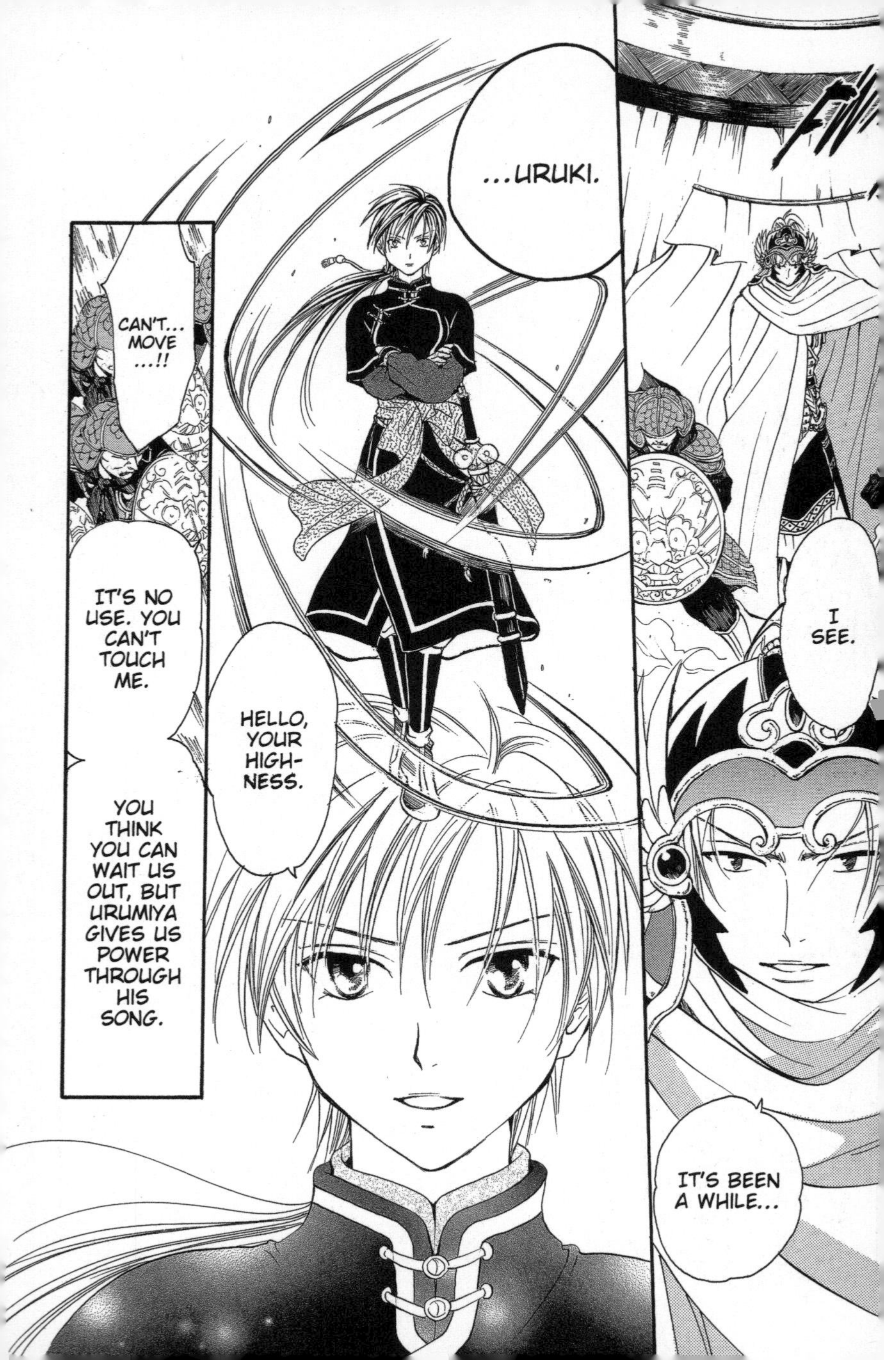
I SEE.
IT'S BEEN A WHILE...
...URUKI.
HELLO, YOUR HIGHNESS.
CAN'T... MOVE ...!!
IT'S NO USE. YOU CAN'T TOUCH ME.
YOU THINK YOU CAN WAIT US OUT, BUT URUMIYA GIVES US POWER THROUGH HIS SONG.

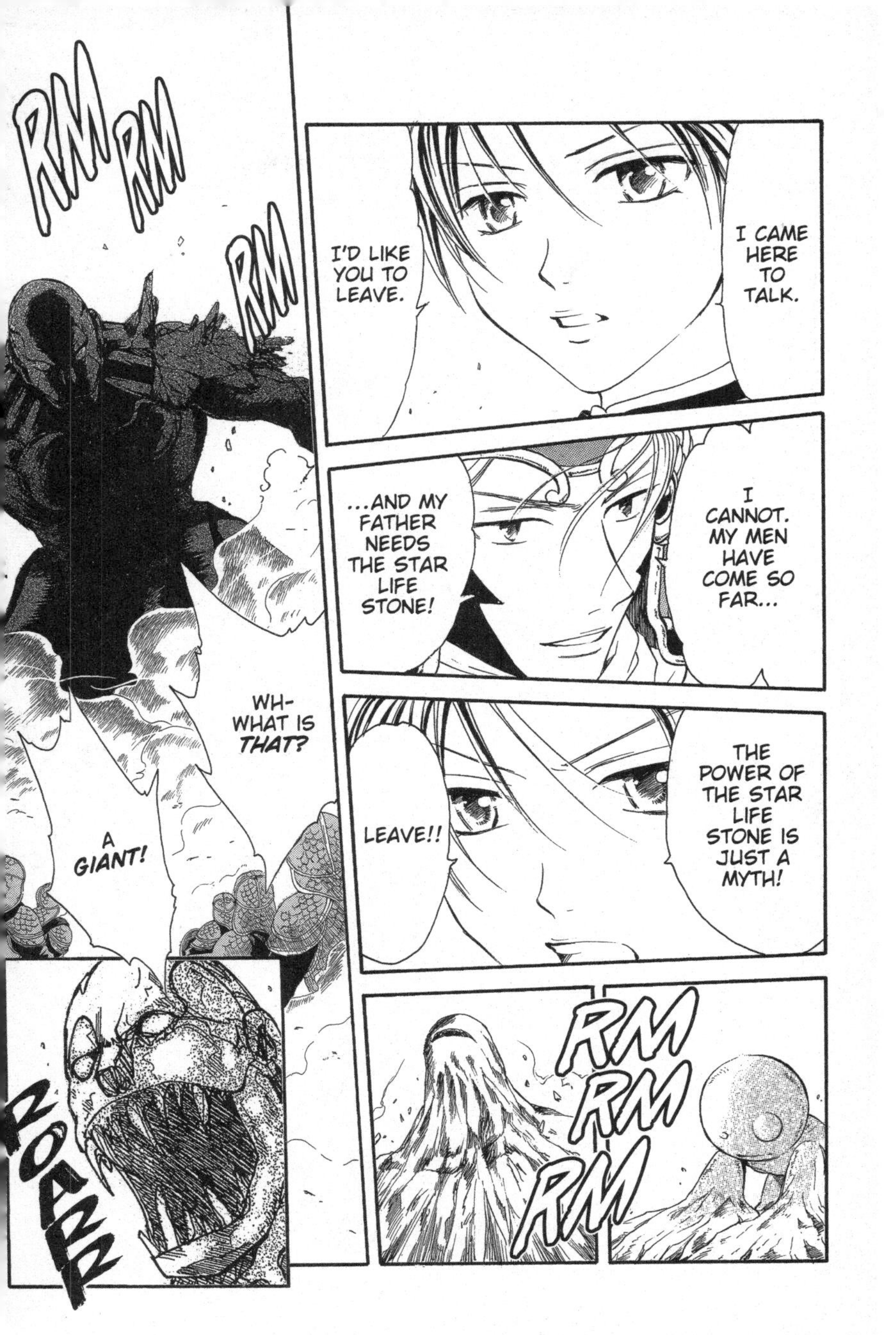
I CAME HERE TO TALK.
I'D LIKE YOU TO LEAVE.
I CANNOT. MY MEN HAVE COME SO FAR...
...AND MY FATHER NEEDS THE STAR LIFE STONE!
THE POWER OF THE STAR LIFE STONE IS JUST A MYTH!
LEAVE!!
RM RM RM
RM RM RM
WH-WHAT IS *THAT?*
A *GIANT!*
ROAR

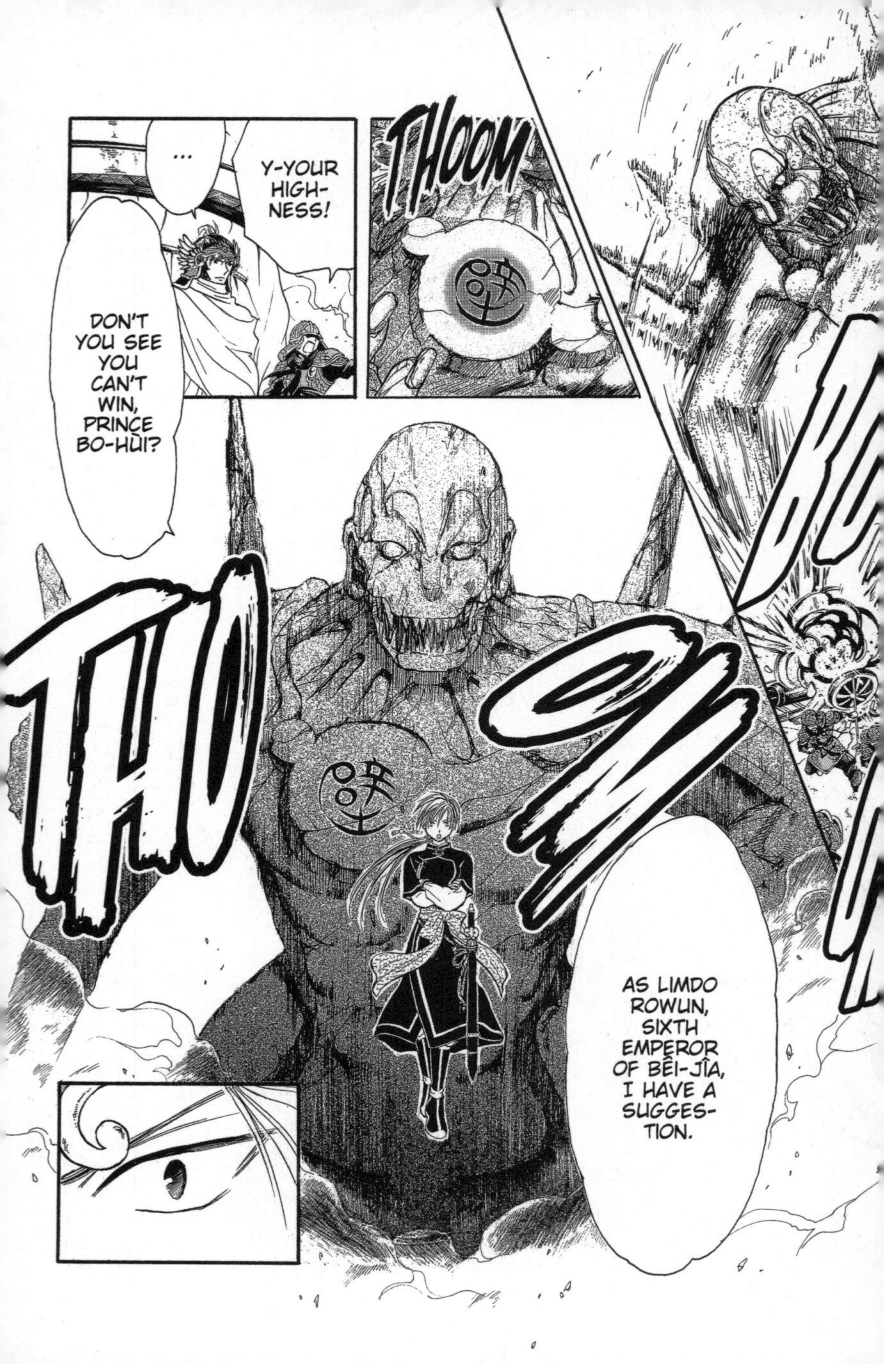
THOOM
Y-YOUR HIGHNESS!
...
DON'T YOU SEE YOU CAN'T WIN, PRINCE BO-HÜI?
AS LIMDO ROWUN, SIXTH EMPEROR OF BÊI-JÎA, I HAVE A SUGGESTION.

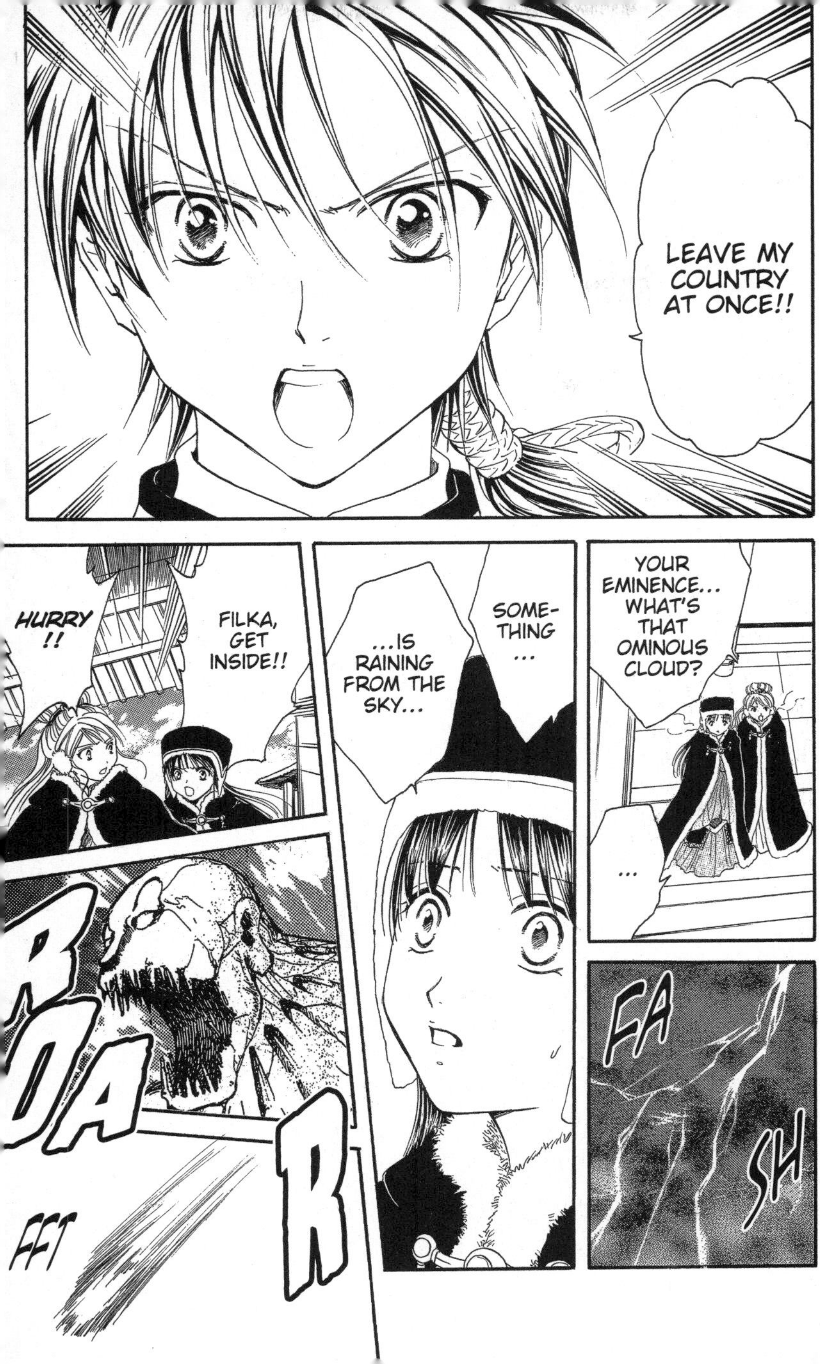
LEAVE MY COUNTRY AT ONCE!!
YOUR EMINENCE... WHAT'S THAT OMINOUS CLOUD?
...
FA SH
SOME-THING...
...IS RAINING FROM THE SKY...
FILKA, GET INSIDE!!
HURRY!!
RDAR
FFT

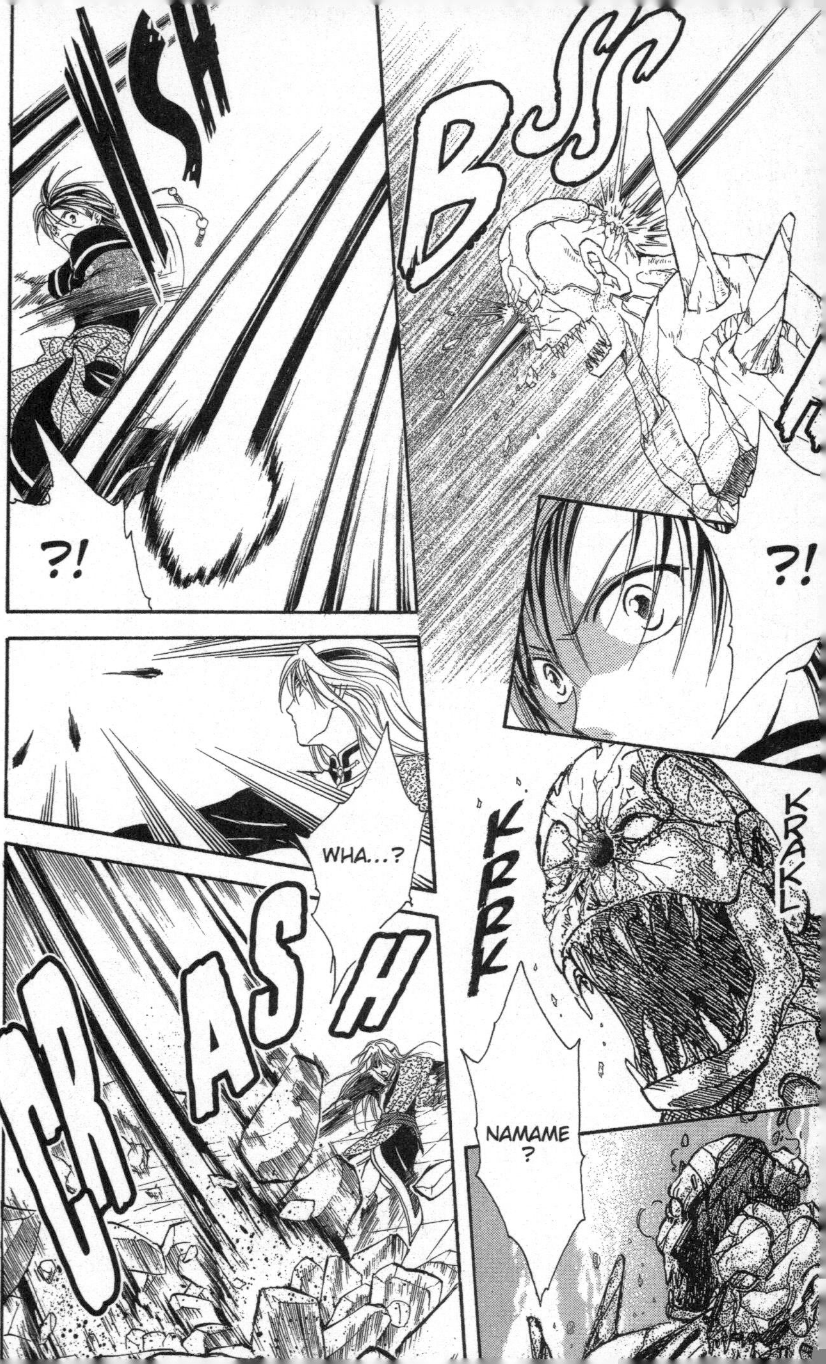

BSSS
?!
?!
WHA...?
KRAKL
KRRRK
NAMAME ?
CRASH

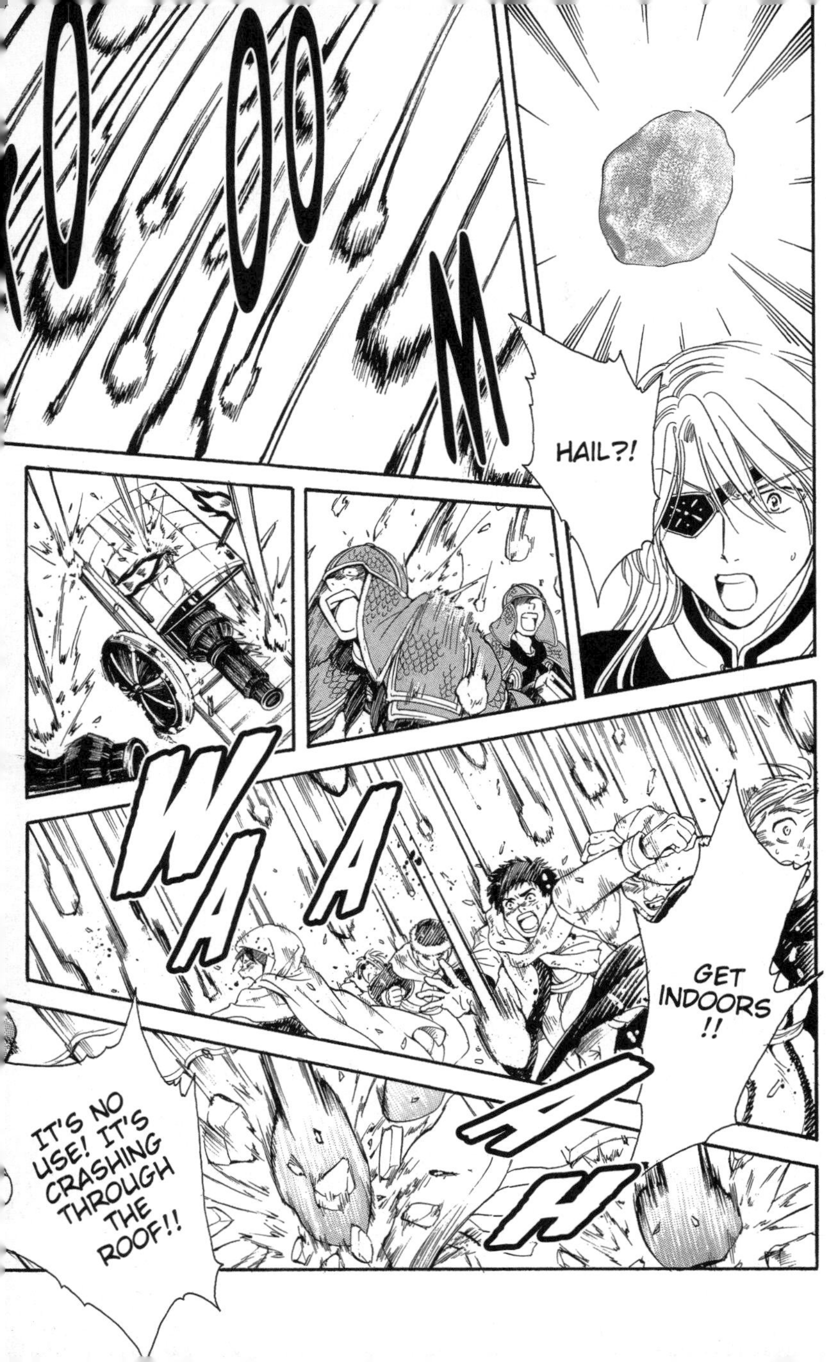
OOOM
HAIL?!
WAAAAH
GET INDOORS!!
IT'S NO USE! IT'S CRASHING THROUGH THE ROOF!!

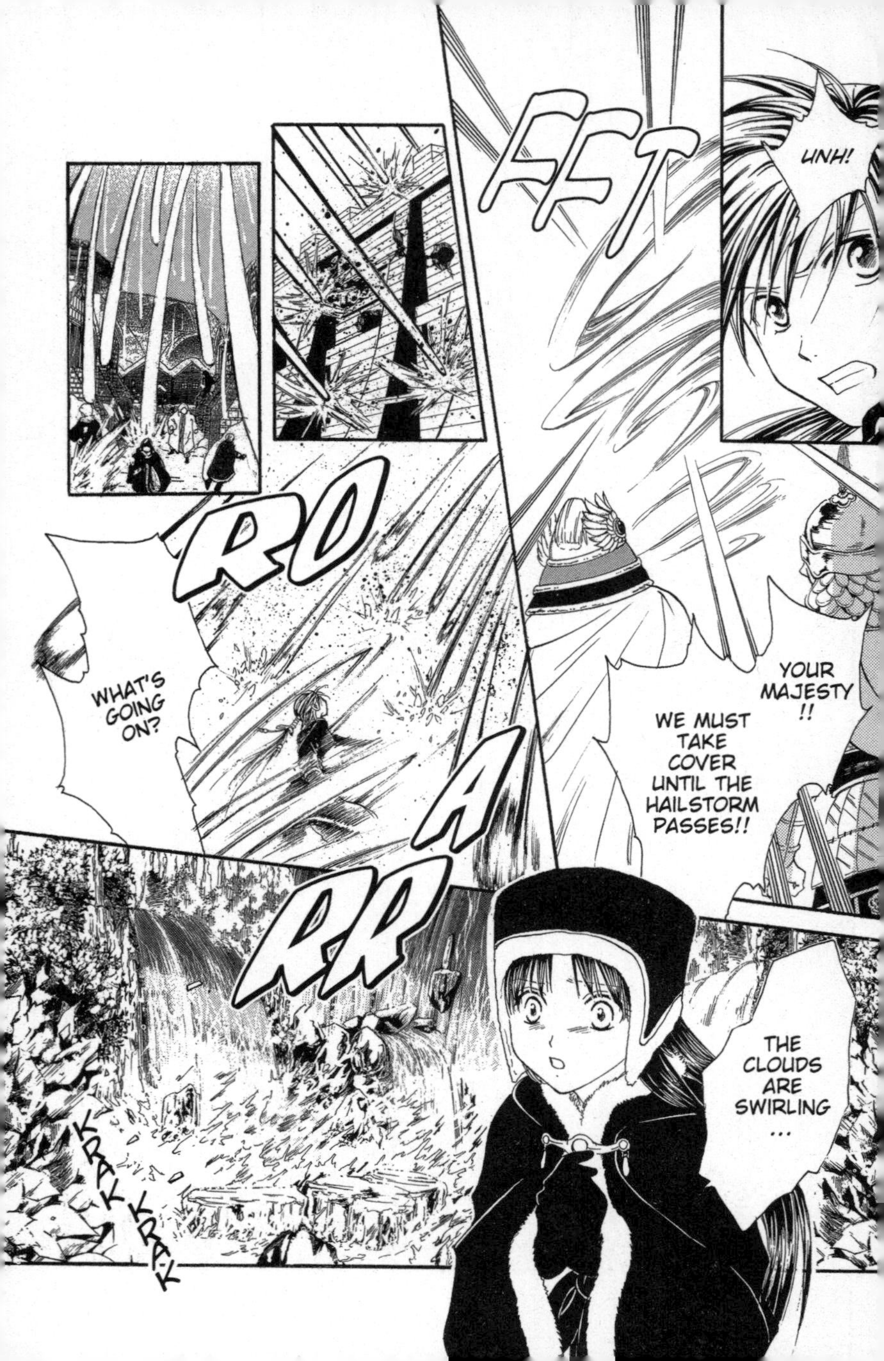
UNH!
FFT
YOUR MAJESTY!!
WE MUST TAKE COVER UNTIL THE HAILSTORM PASSES!!
ROARR
WHAT'S GOING ON?
THE CLOUDS ARE SWIRLING ...
KRAK KRAK

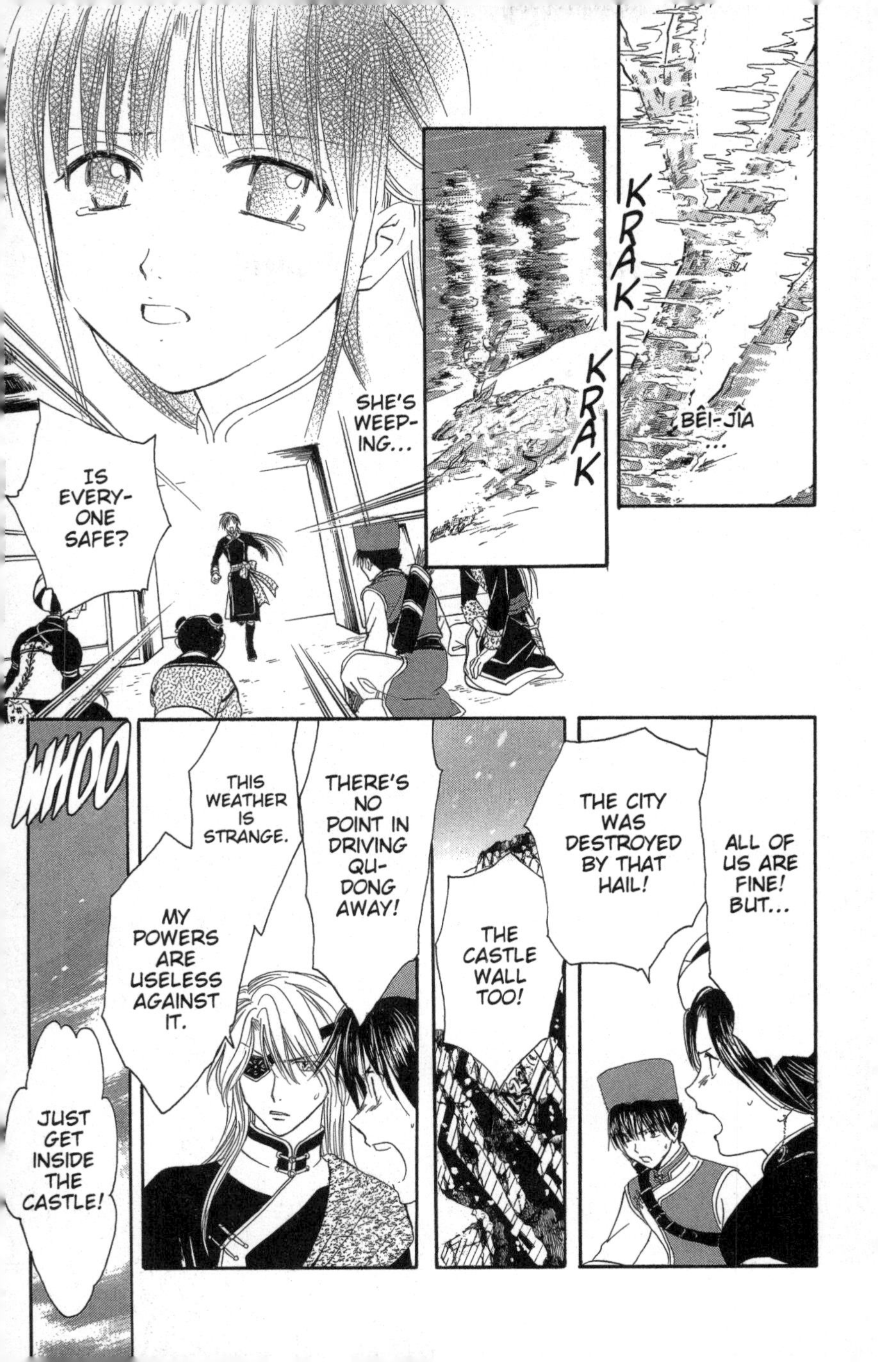
BÊI-JÎA ...
KRAK
KRAK
SHE'S WEEPING...
IS EVERYONE SAFE?
ALL OF US ARE FINE! BUT...
THE CITY WAS DESTROYED BY THAT HAIL!
THE CASTLE WALL TOO!
THERE'S NO POINT IN DRIVING QU-DONG AWAY!
THIS WEATHER IS STRANGE.
MY POWERS ARE USELESS AGAINST IT.
WHOO
JUST GET INSIDE THE CASTLE!

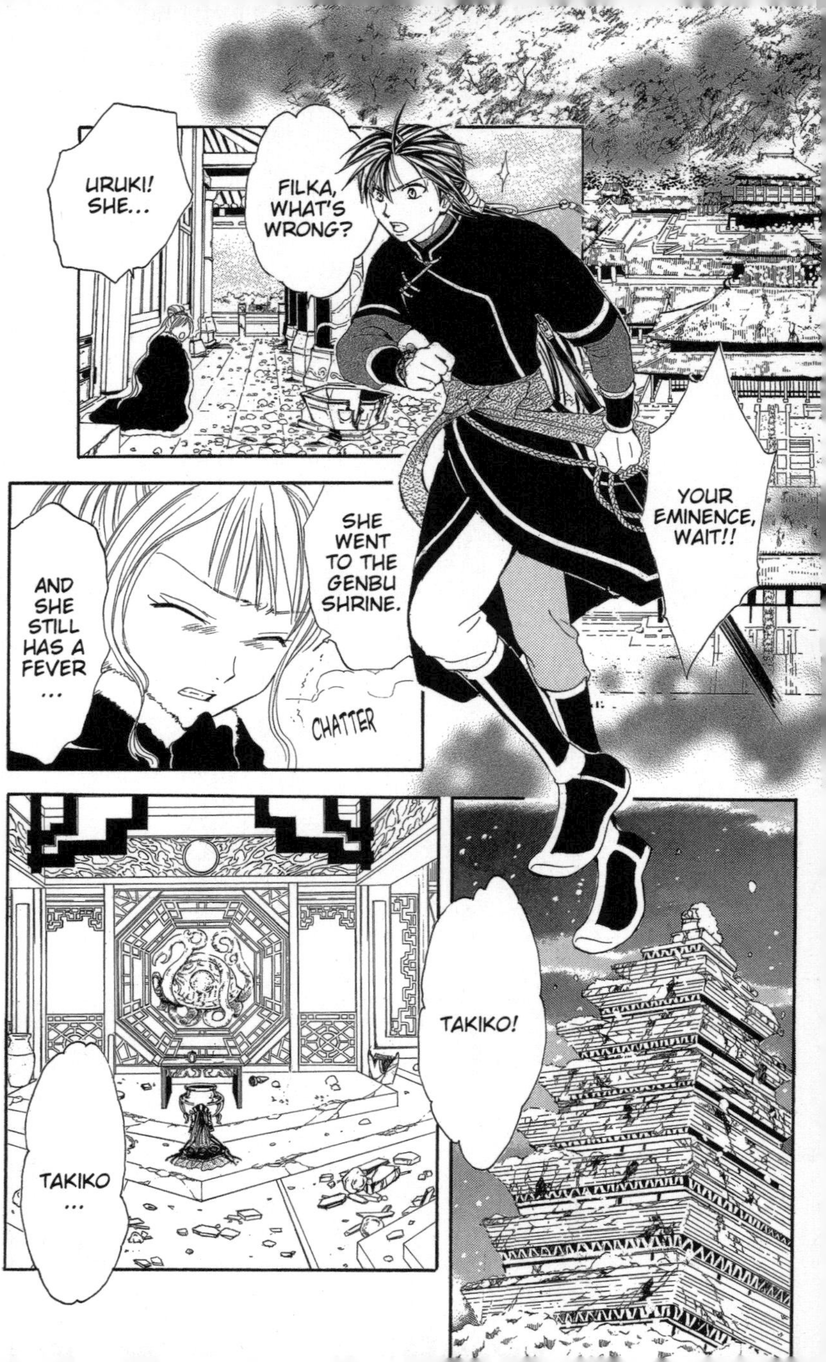
YOUR EMINENCE, WAIT!!
FILKA, WHAT'S WRONG?
URUKI! SHE...
SHE WENT TO THE GENBU SHRINE.
AND SHE STILL HAS A FEVER ...
CHATTER
TAKIKO!
TAKIKO ...

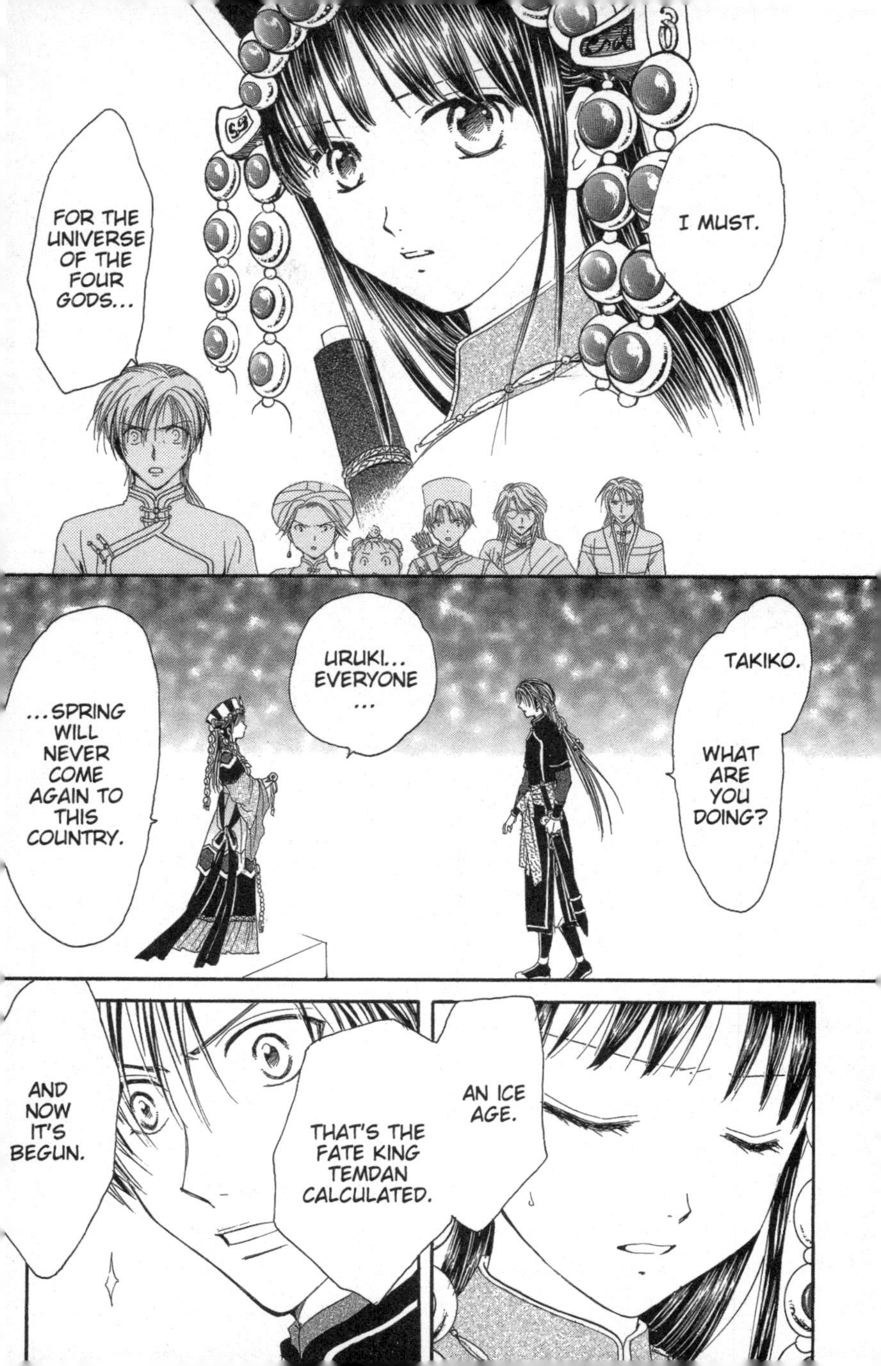
I MUST.
FOR THE UNIVERSE OF THE FOUR GODS...
TAKIKO.
WHAT ARE YOU DOING?
URUKI... EVERYONE ...
...SPRING WILL NEVER COME AGAIN TO THIS COUNTRY.
AN ICE AGE.
THAT'S THE FATE KING TEMDAN CALCULATED.
AND NOW IT'S BEGUN.

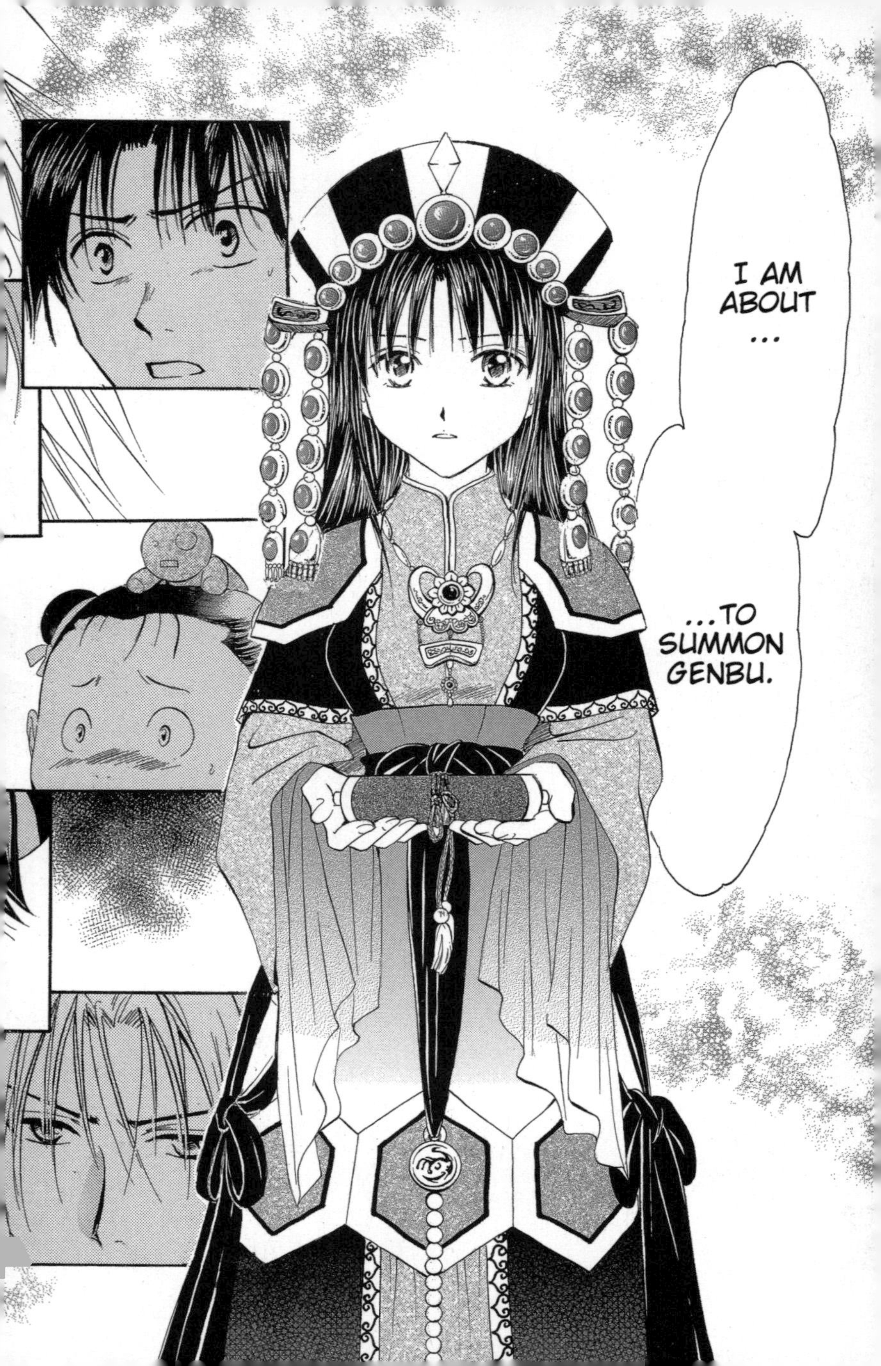
I AM ABOUT ...
...TO SUMMON GENBU.

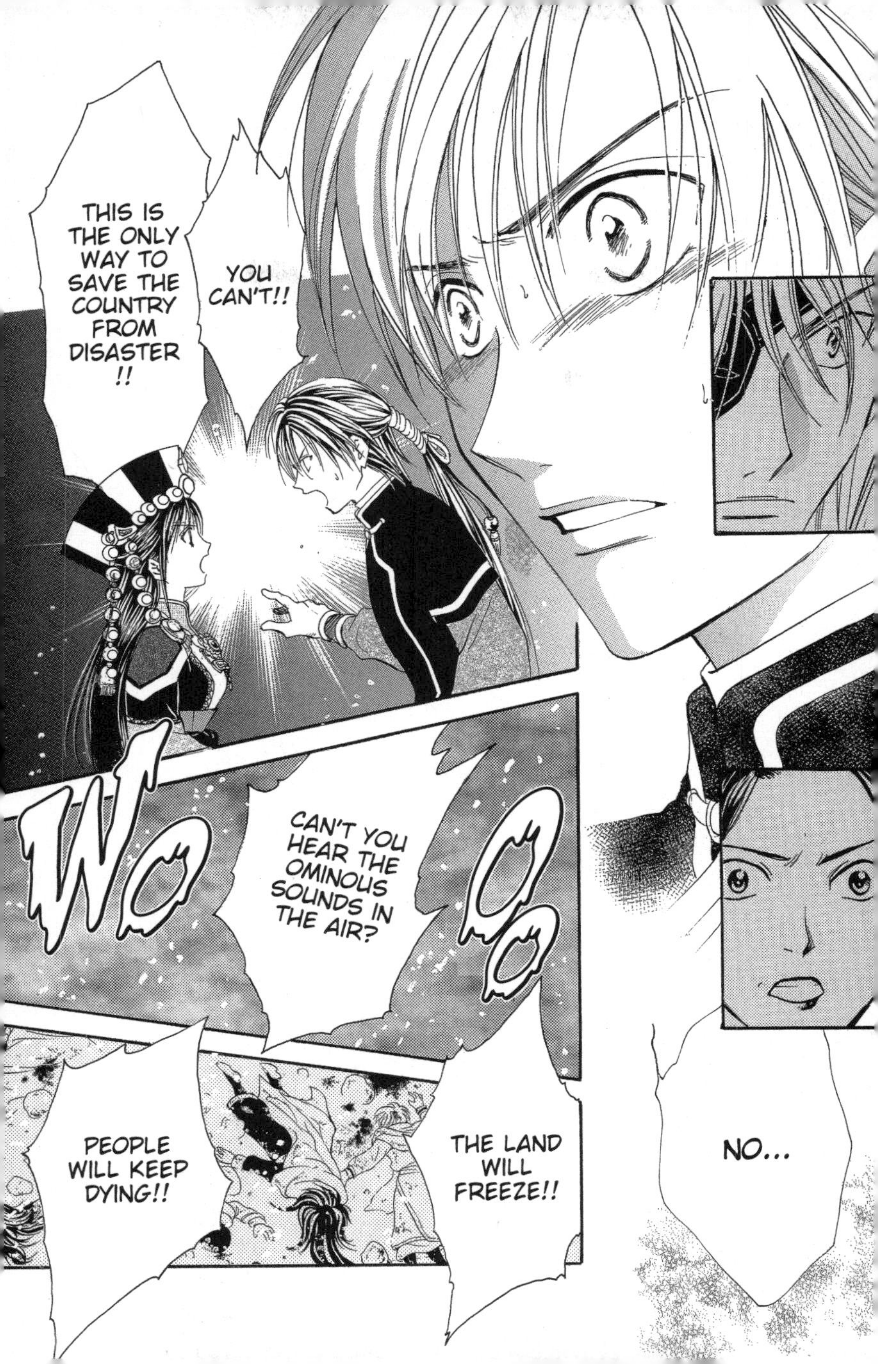
YOU CAN'T!!
THIS IS THE ONLY WAY TO SAVE THE COUNTRY FROM DISASTER!!
WOOO
CAN'T YOU HEAR THE OMINOUS SOUNDS IN THE AIR?
THE LAND WILL FREEZE!!
PEOPLE WILL KEEP DYING!!
NO...

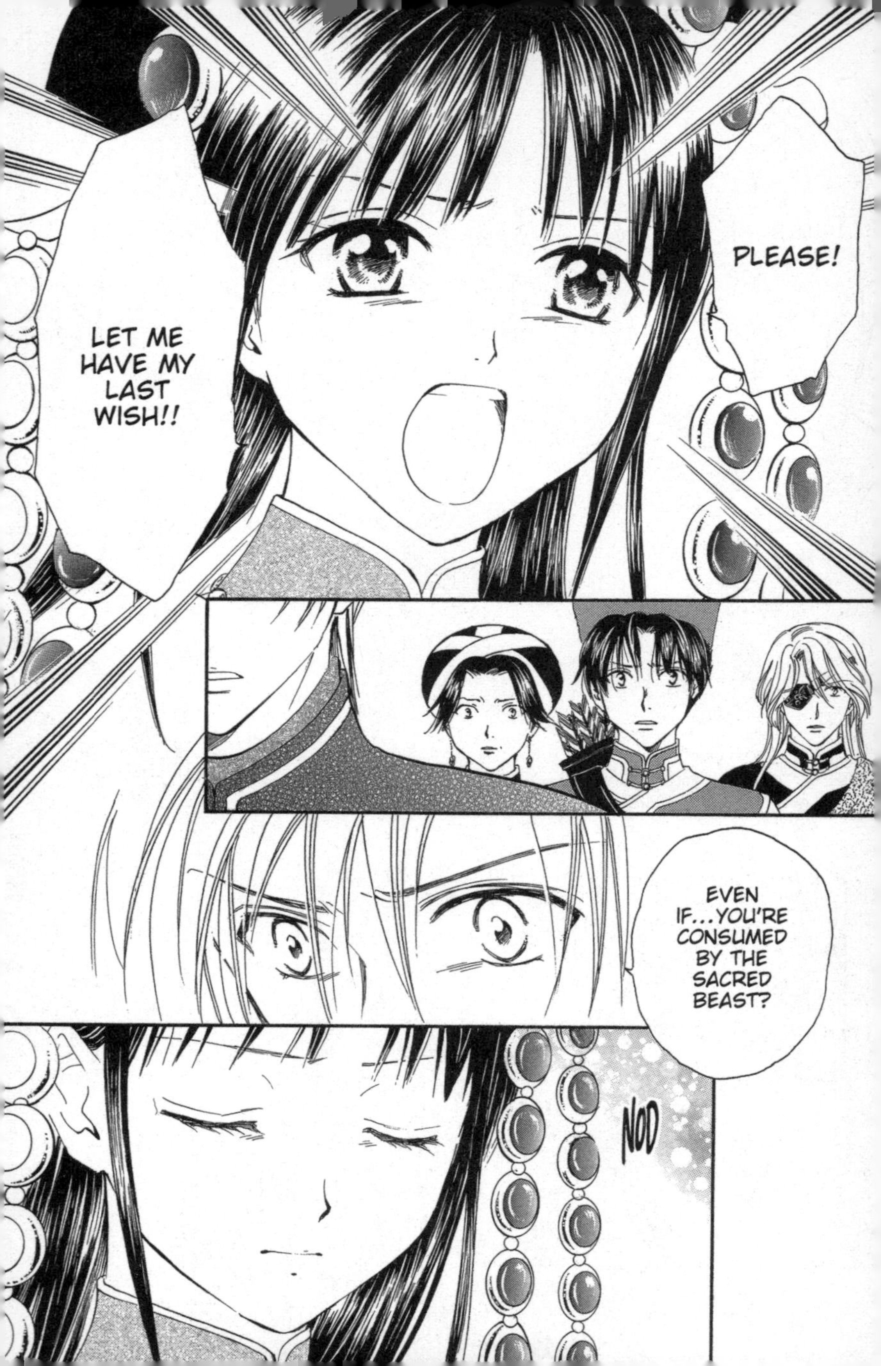
PLEASE!
LET ME HAVE MY LAST WISH!!
EVEN IF...YOU'RE CONSUMED BY THE SACRED BEAST?
NOD

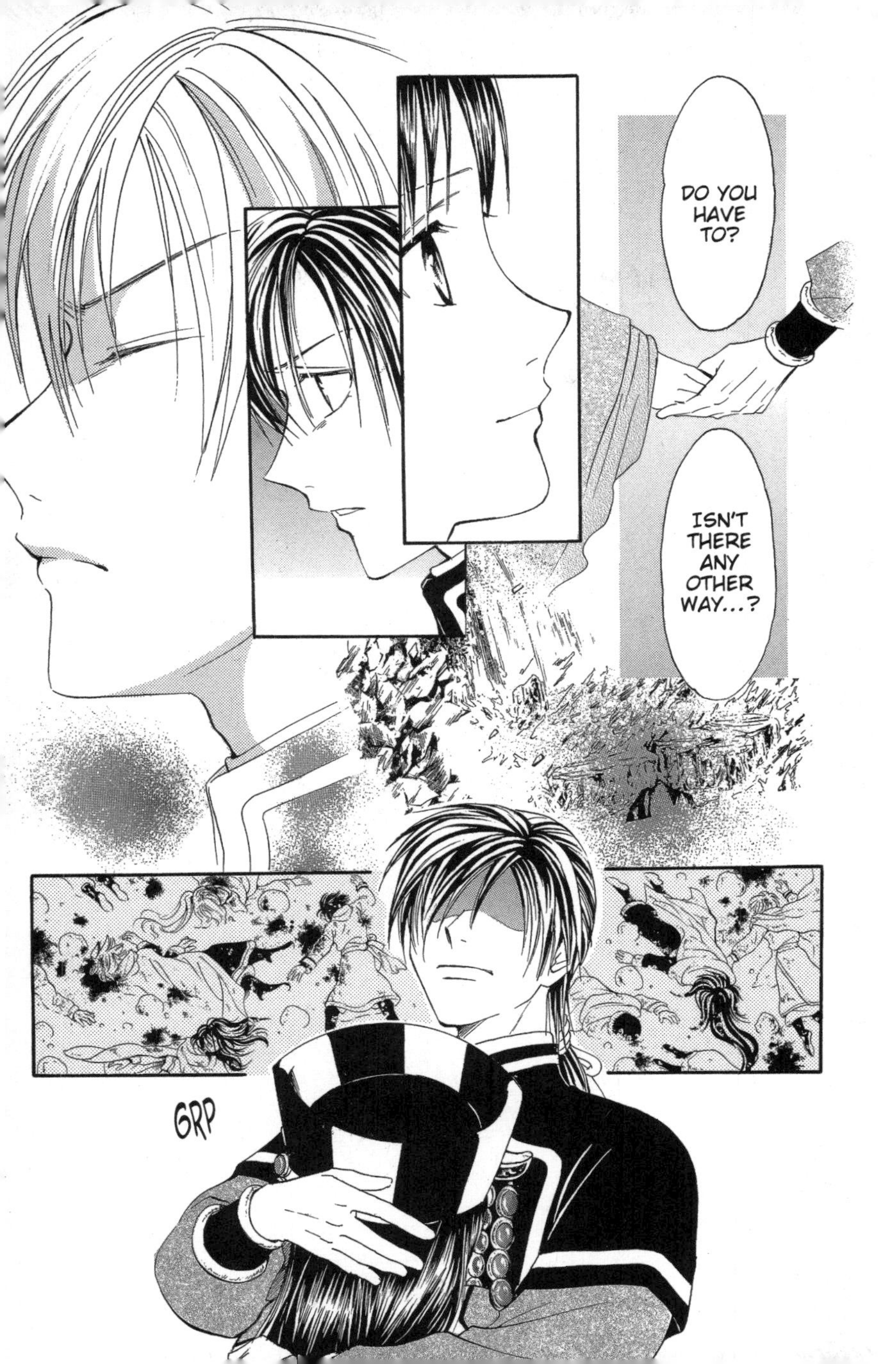
DO YOU HAVE TO?
ISN'T THERE ANY OTHER WAY...?
GRP

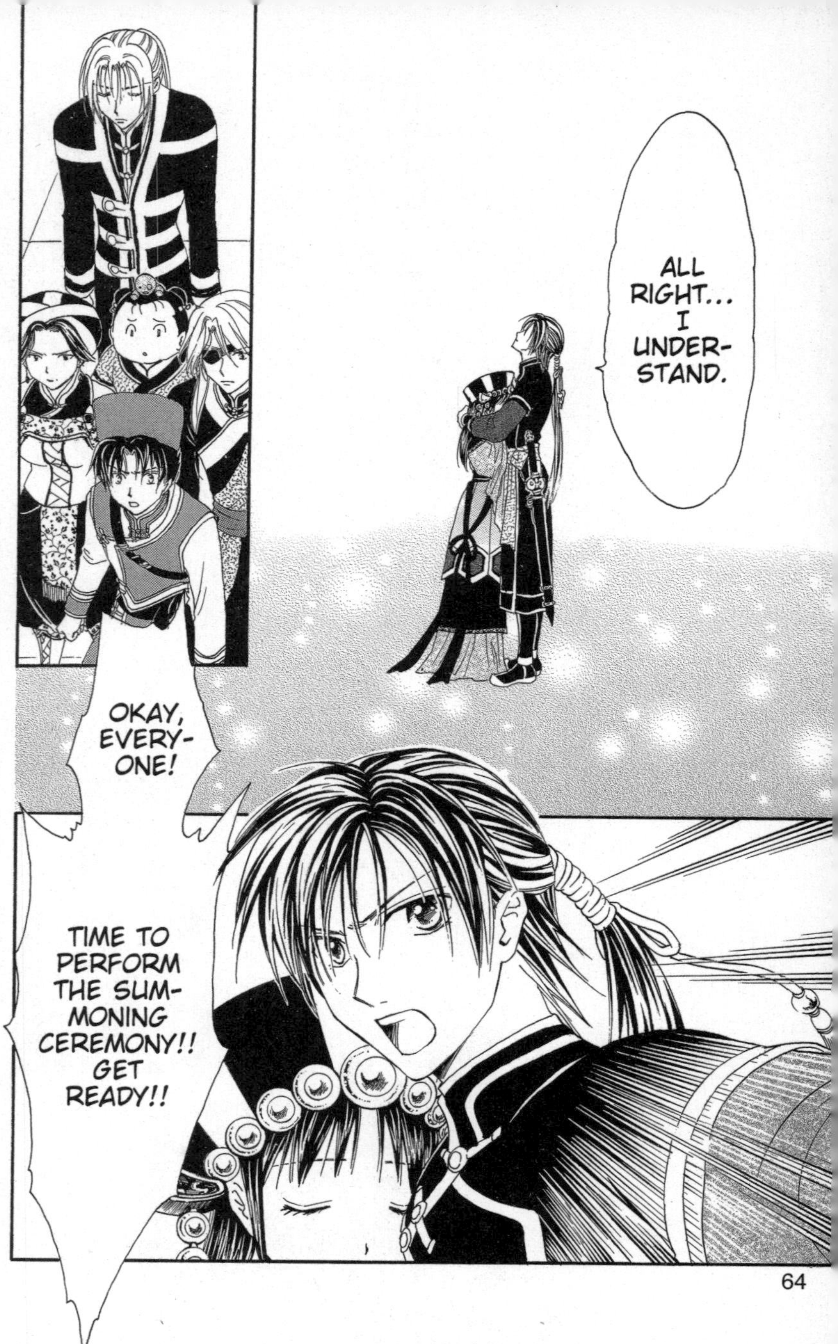
ALL RIGHT... I UNDER-STAND.
OKAY, EVERY-ONE!
TIME TO PERFORM THE SUM-MONING CEREMONY!! GET READY!!

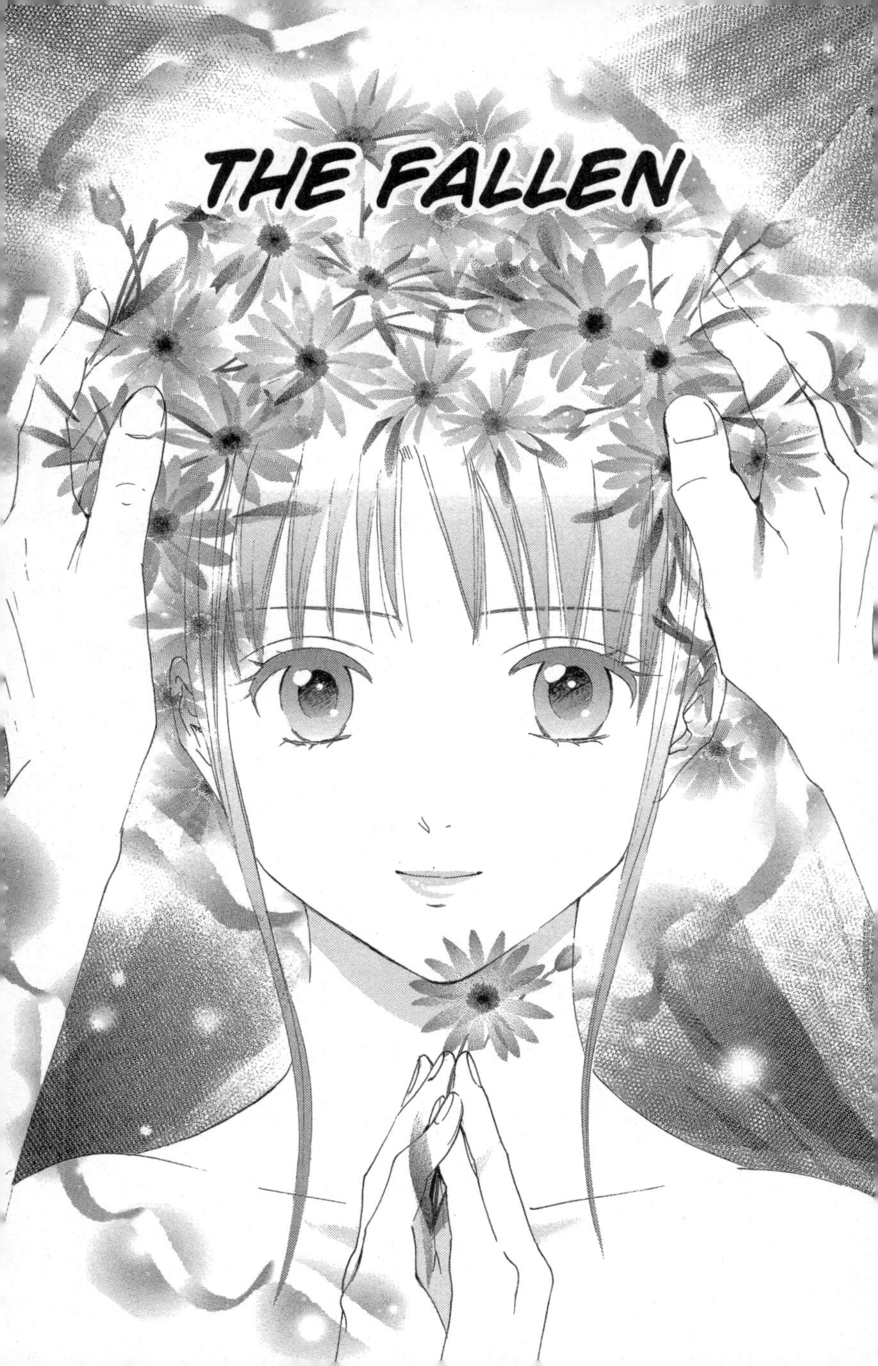
THE FALLEN

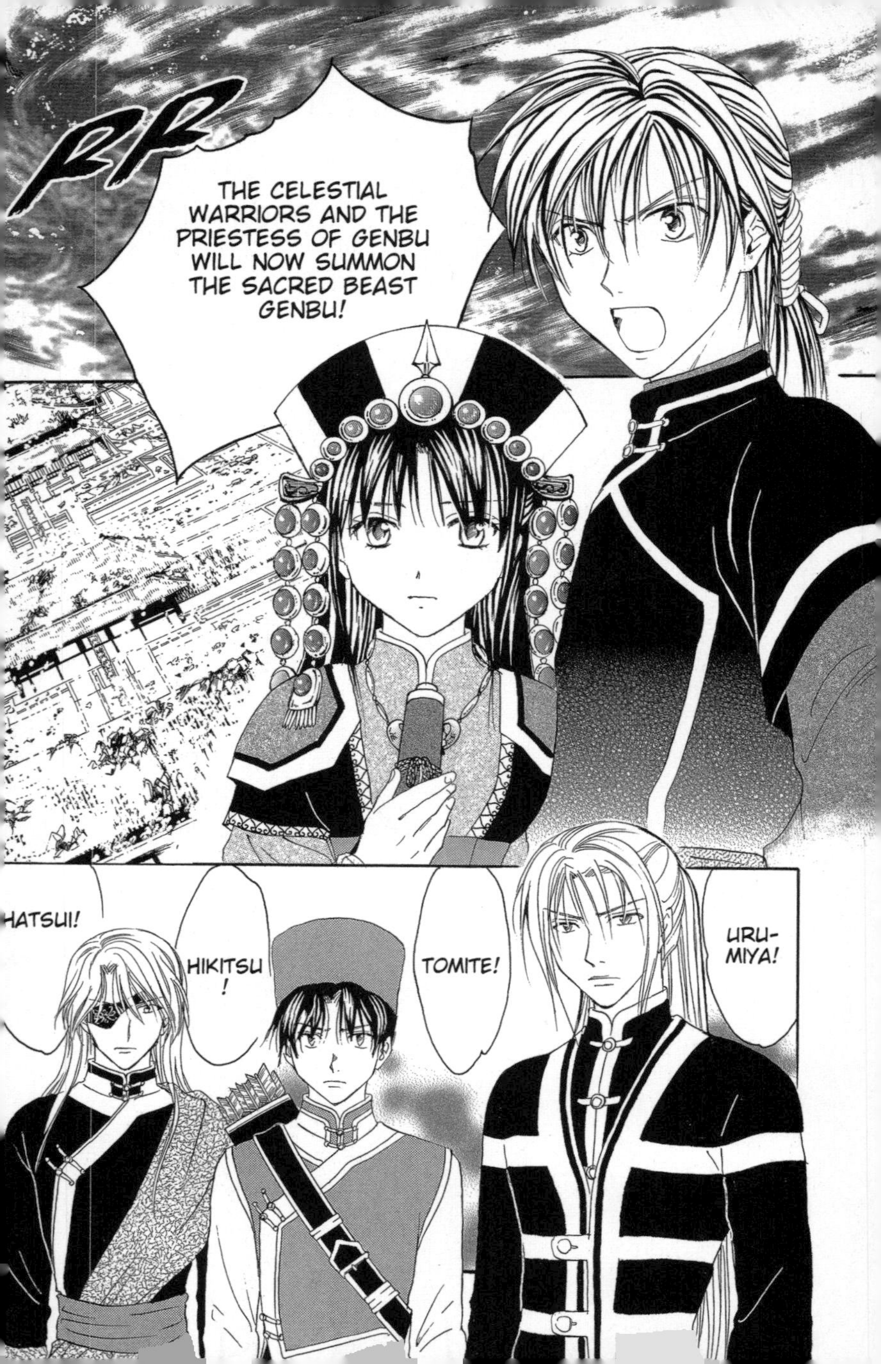
RR
THE CELESTIAL WARRIORS AND THE PRIESTESS OF GENBU WILL NOW SUMMON THE SACRED BEAST GENBU!
URU-MIYA!
TOMITE!
HIKITSU!
HATSUI!

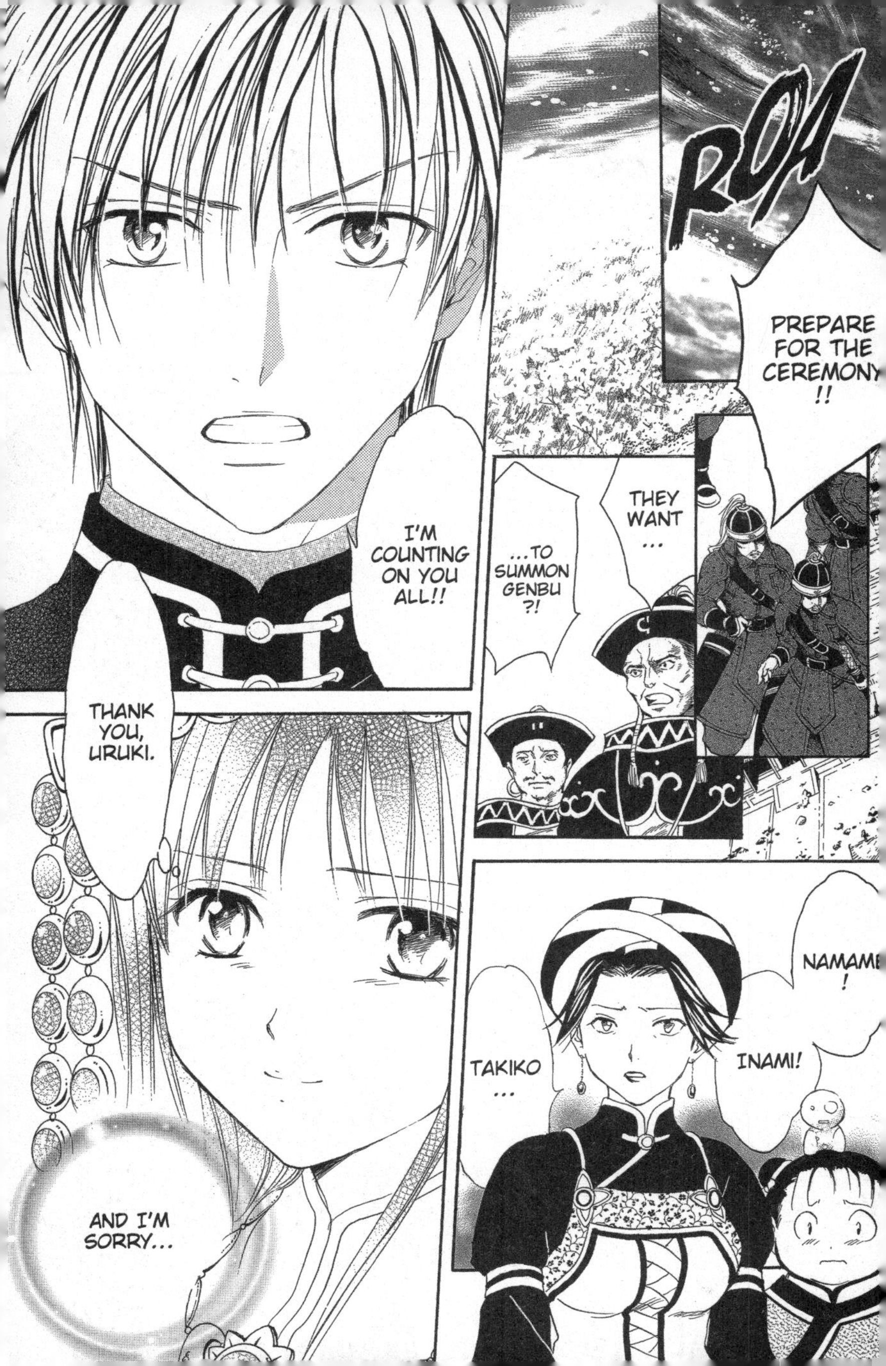
ROA
PREPARE FOR THE CEREMONY!!
THEY WANT...
...TO SUMMON GENBU?!
I'M COUNTING ON YOU ALL!!
NAMAME!
INAMI!
TAKIKO...
THANK YOU, URUKI.
AND I'M SORRY...

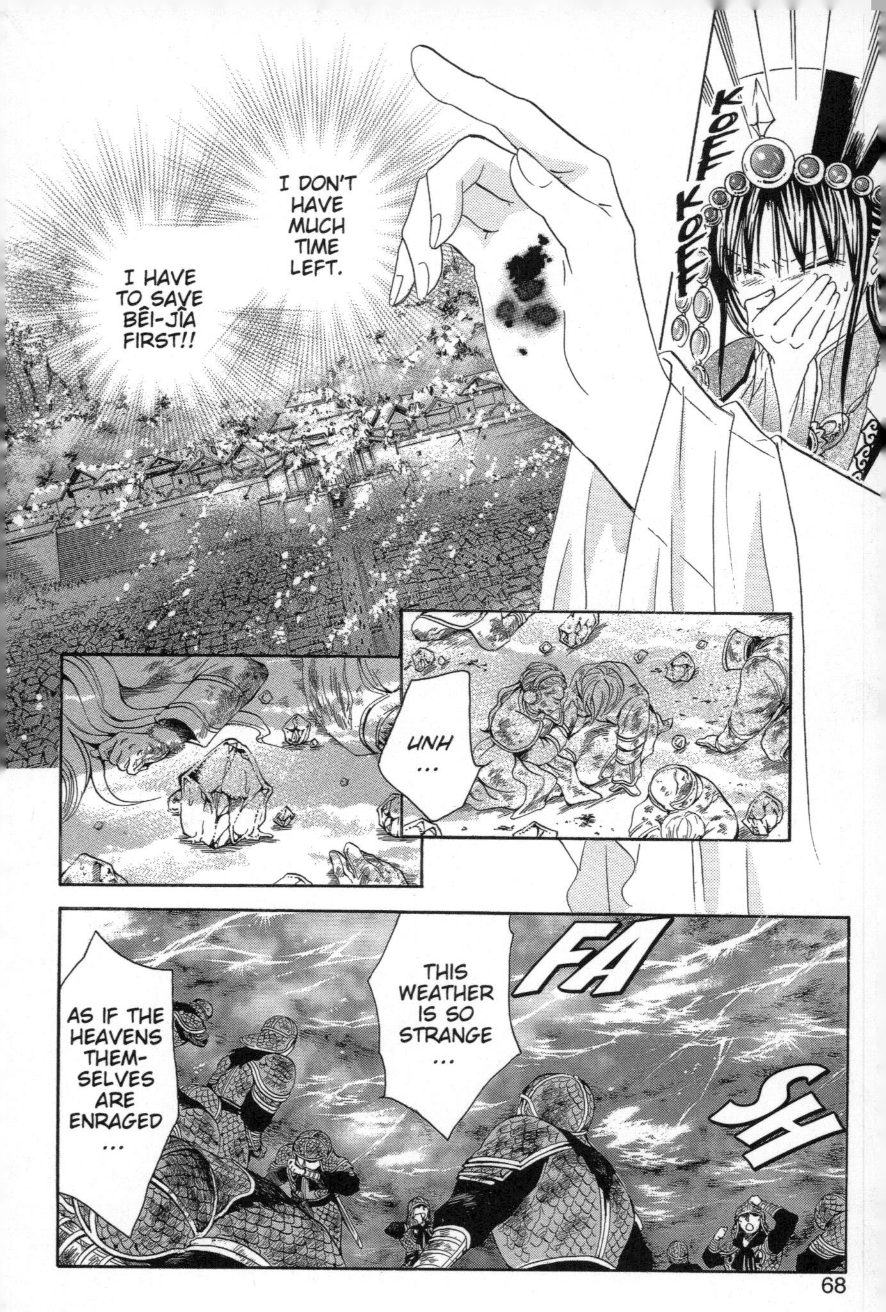
KOFF KOFF KOFF
I DON'T HAVE MUCH TIME LEFT.
I HAVE TO SAVE BÊI-JÎA FIRST!!
UNH ...
SH
FA
THIS WEATHER IS SO STRANGE ...
AS IF THE HEAVENS THEM-SELVES ARE ENRAGED ...

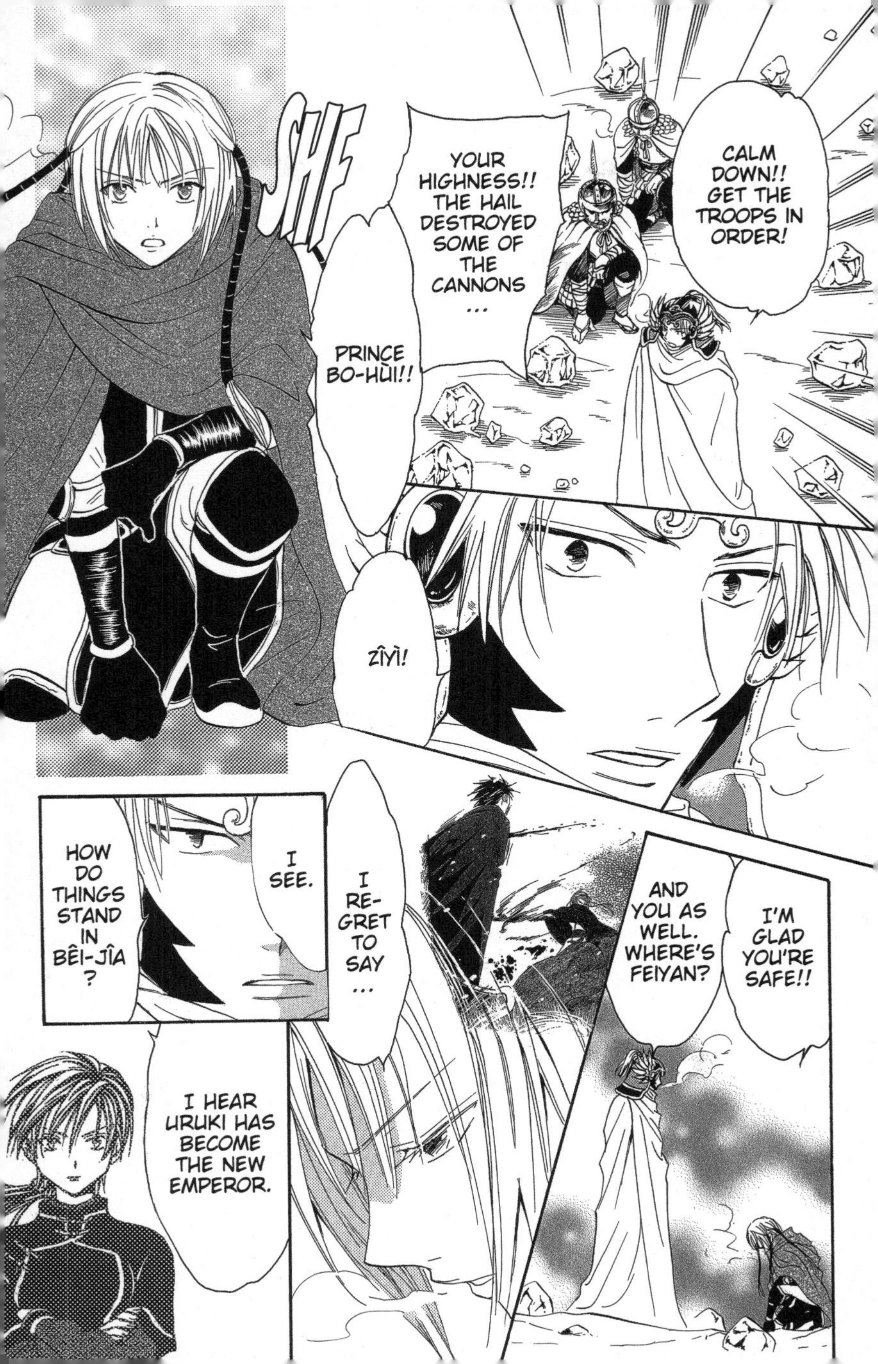
CALM DOWN!! GET THE TROOPS IN ORDER!
YOUR HIGHNESS!! THE HAIL DESTROYED SOME OF THE CANNONS ...
PRINCE BO-HŪI!!
SHE
ZÎYÌ!
I'M GLAD YOU'RE SAFE!!
AND YOU AS WELL. WHERE'S FEIYAN?
I RE-GRET TO SAY ...
I SEE.
HOW DO THINGS STAND IN BÊI-JÎA?
I HEAR URUKI HAS BECOME THE NEW EMPEROR.

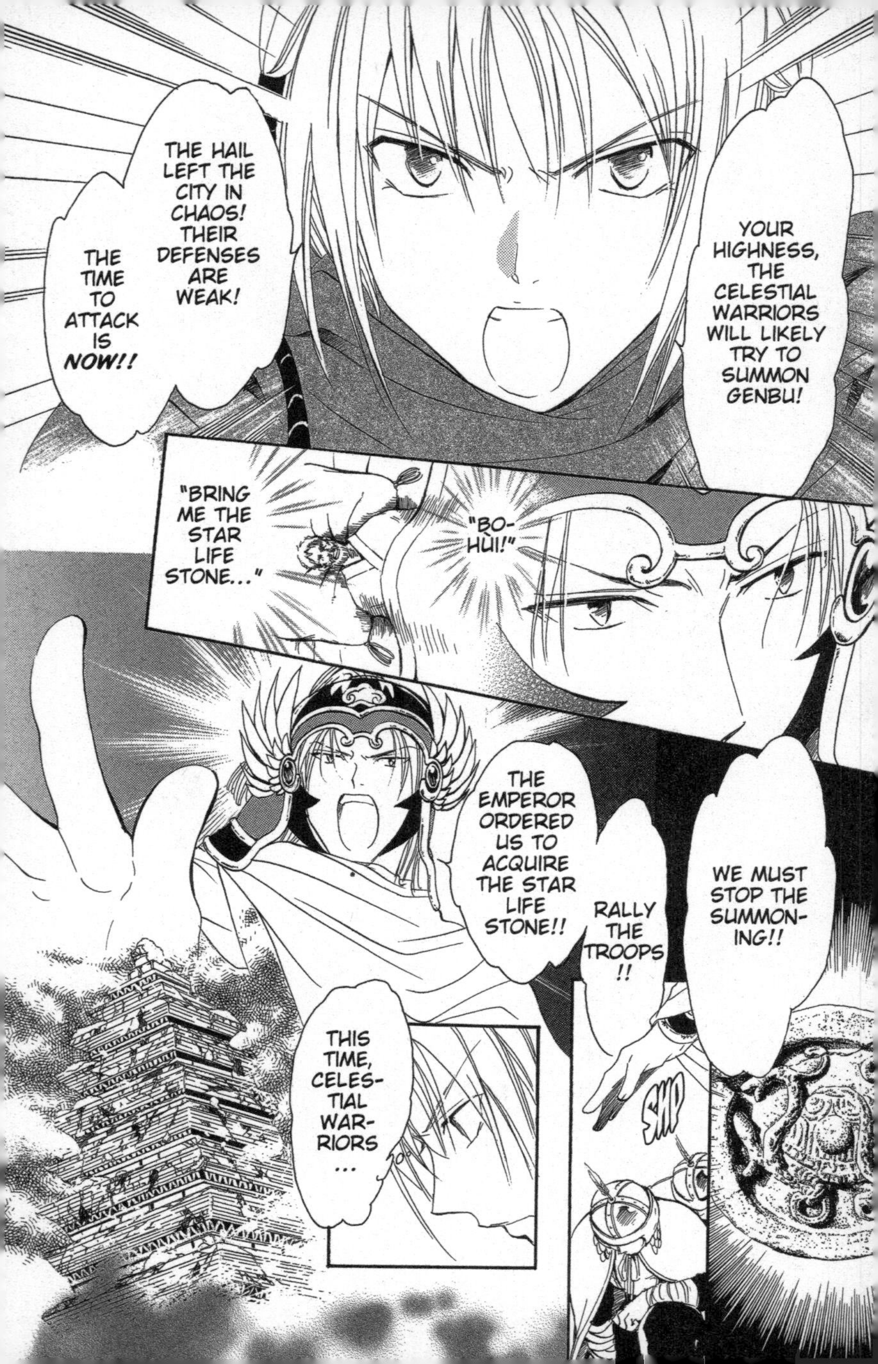
YOUR HIGHNESS, THE CELESTIAL WARRIORS WILL LIKELY TRY TO SUMMON GENBU!
THE HAIL LEFT THE CITY IN CHAOS! THEIR DEFENSES ARE WEAK!
THE TIME TO ATTACK IS *NOW!!*
"BO-HÜI!"
"BRING ME THE STAR LIFE STONE..."
WE MUST STOP THE SUMMON-ING!!
RALLY THE TROOPS!!
THE EMPEROR ORDERED US TO ACQUIRE THE STAR LIFE STONE!!
SHP
THIS TIME, CELES-TIAL WAR-RIORS...

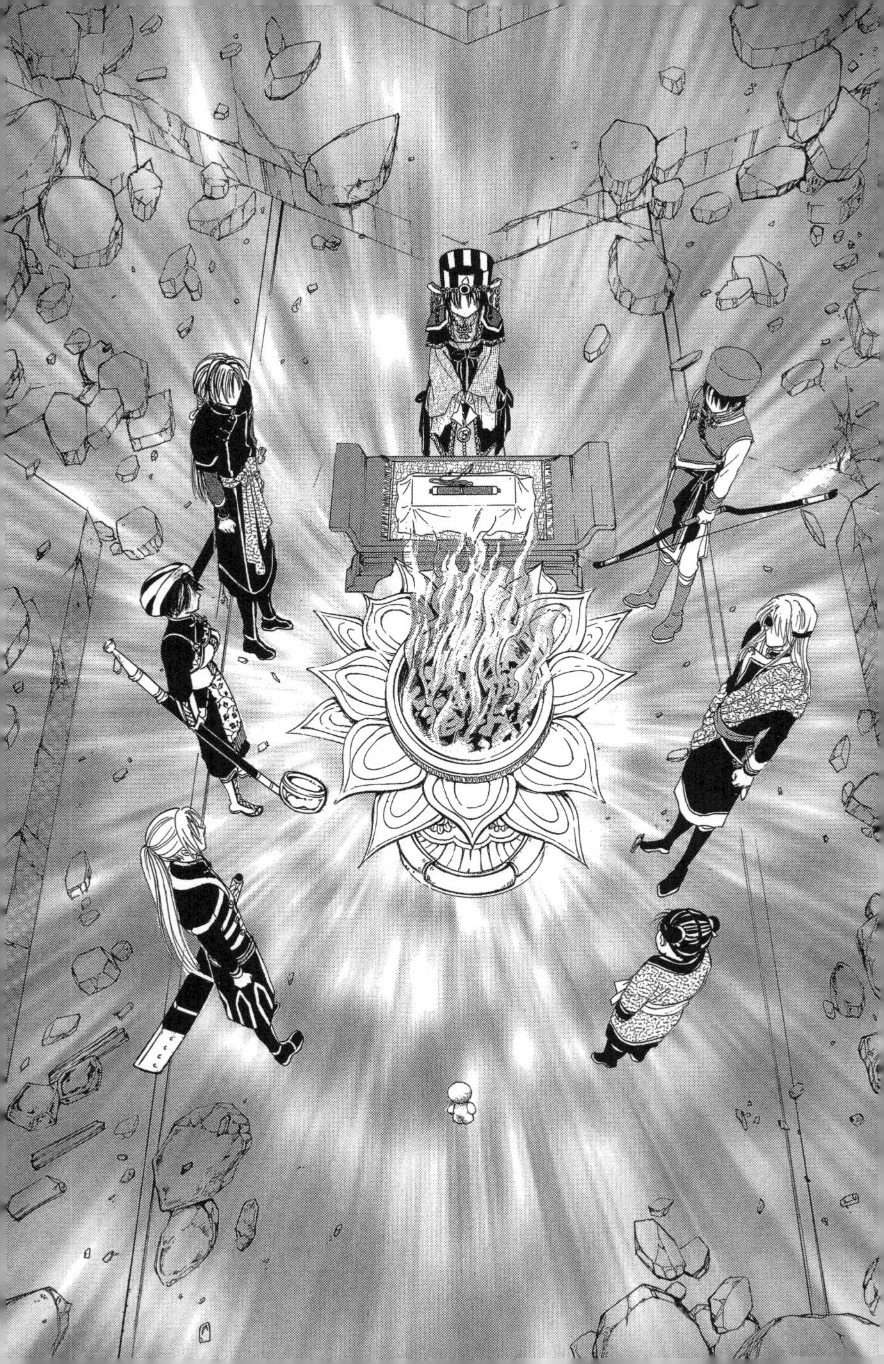

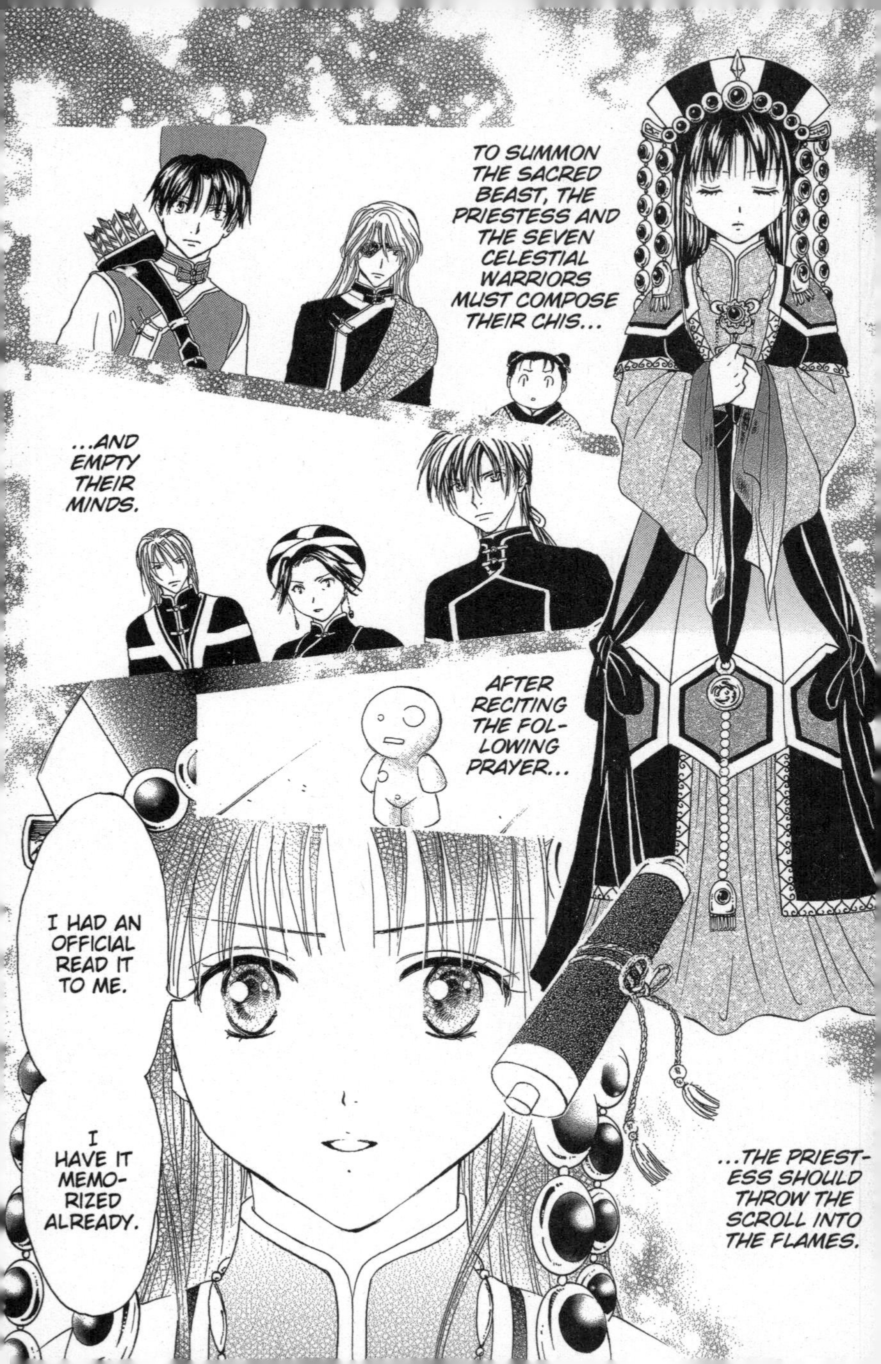
TO SUMMON THE SACRED BEAST, THE PRIESTESS AND THE SEVEN CELESTIAL WARRIORS MUST COMPOSE THEIR CHIS...
...AND EMPTY THEIR MINDS.
AFTER RECITING THE FOL-LOWING PRAYER...
...THE PRIEST-ESS SHOULD THROW THE SCROLL INTO THE FLAMES.
I HAD AN OFFICIAL READ IT TO ME.
I HAVE IT MEMO-RIZED ALREADY.

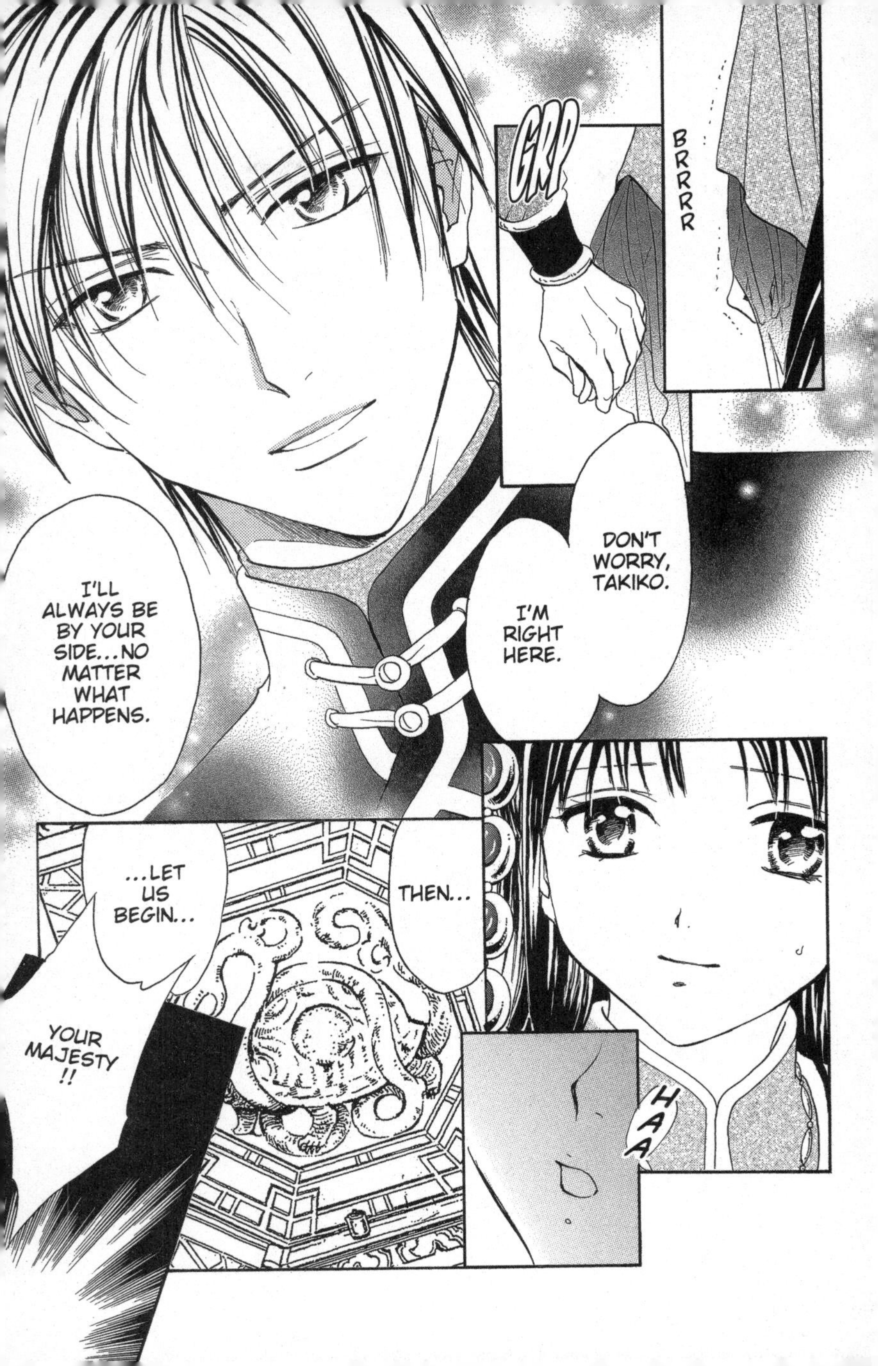
BRRRR
GRP
DON'T WORRY, TAKIKO.
I'M RIGHT HERE.
I'LL ALWAYS BE BY YOUR SIDE...NO MATTER WHAT HAPPENS.
THEN...
...LET US BEGIN...
YOUR MAJESTY !!
HAA

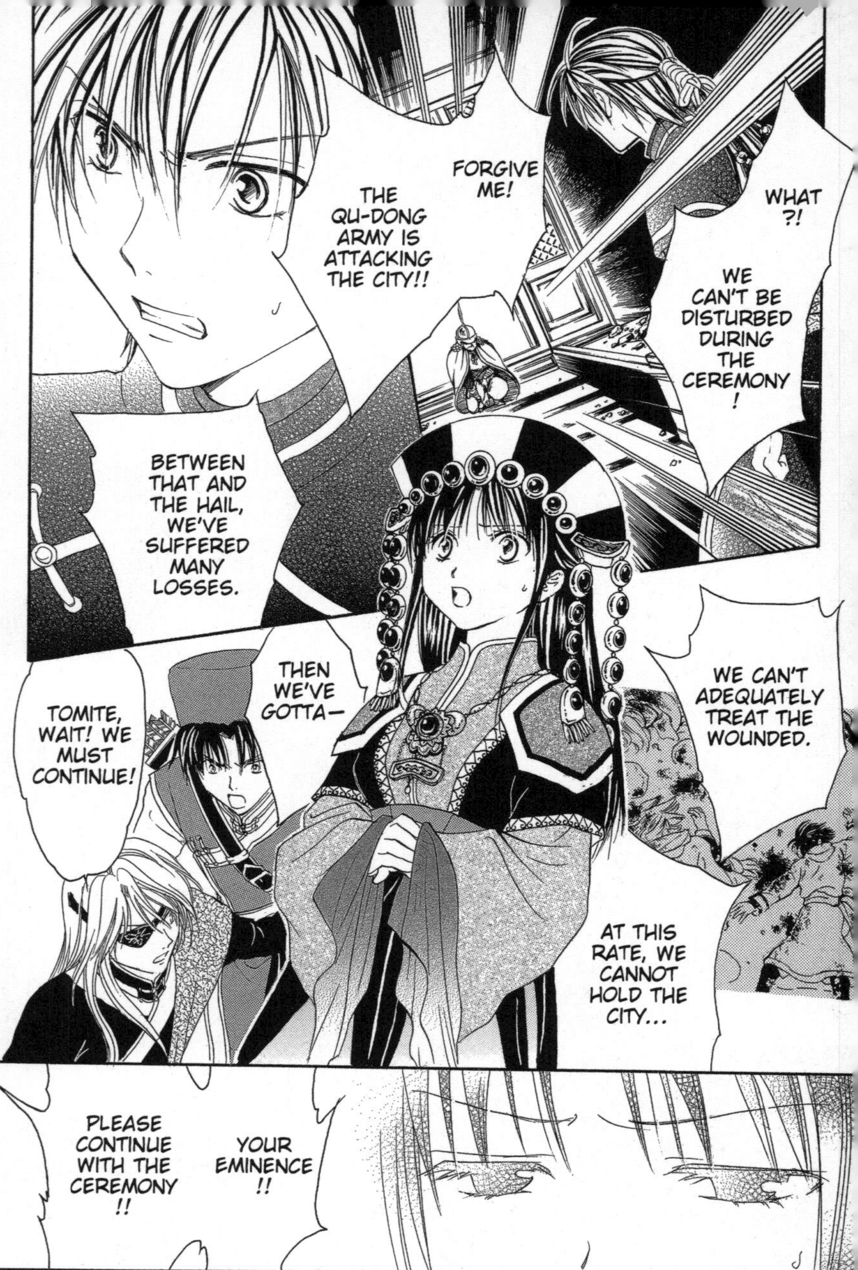
WHAT?!
WE CAN'T BE DISTURBED DURING THE CEREMONY!
FORGIVE ME!
THE QU-DONG ARMY IS ATTACKING THE CITY!!
BETWEEN THAT AND THE HAIL, WE'VE SUFFERED MANY LOSSES.
WE CAN'T ADEQUATELY TREAT THE WOUNDED.
AT THIS RATE, WE CANNOT HOLD THE CITY...
THEN WE'VE GOTTA—
TOMITE, WAIT! WE MUST CONTINUE!
YOUR EMINENCE!!
PLEASE CONTINUE WITH THE CEREMONY!!

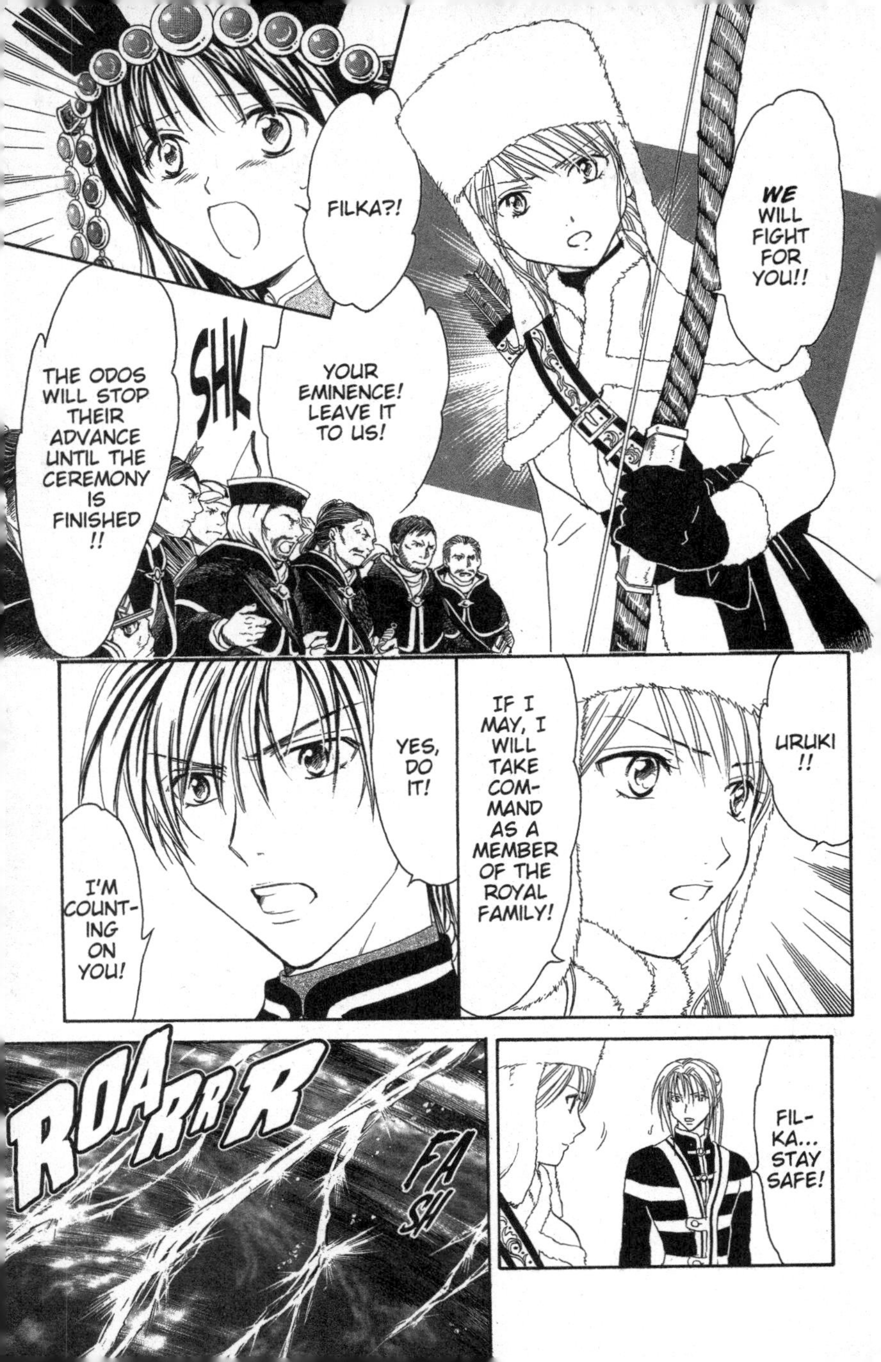
WE WILL FIGHT FOR YOU!!
FILKA?!
YOUR EMINENCE! LEAVE IT TO US!
SHK
THE ODOS WILL STOP THEIR ADVANCE UNTIL THE CEREMONY IS FINISHED!!
URUKI!!
IF I MAY, I WILL TAKE COM-MAND AS A MEMBER OF THE ROYAL FAMILY!
YES, DO IT!
I'M COUNT-ING ON YOU!
FIL-KA... STAY SAFE!
ROARRR
FASH

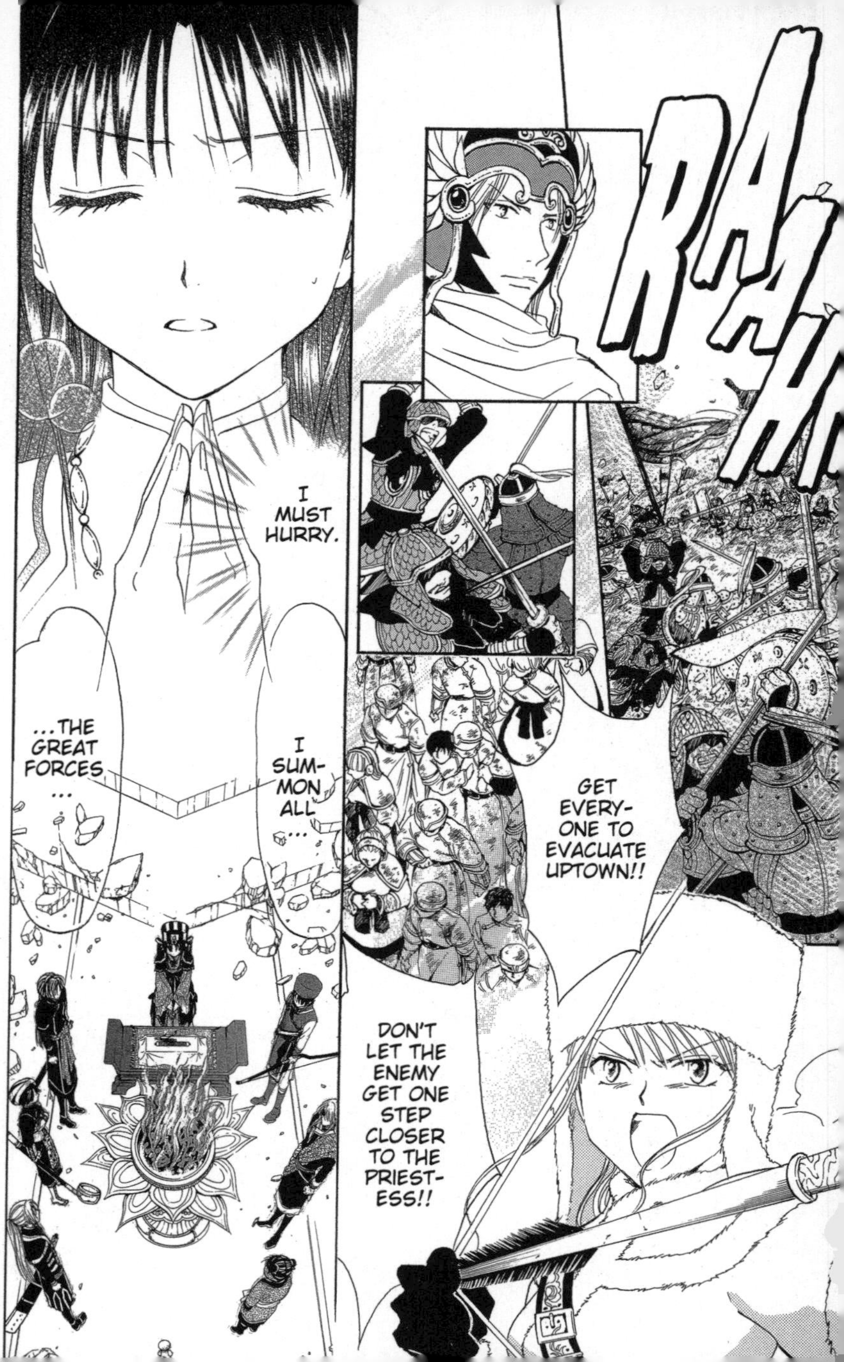

RAAH
GET EVERY-ONE TO EVACUATE UPTOWN!!
DON'T LET THE ENEMY GET ONE STEP CLOSER TO THE PRIEST-ESS!!
I MUST HURRY.
I SUM-MON ALL...
...THE GREAT FORCES...

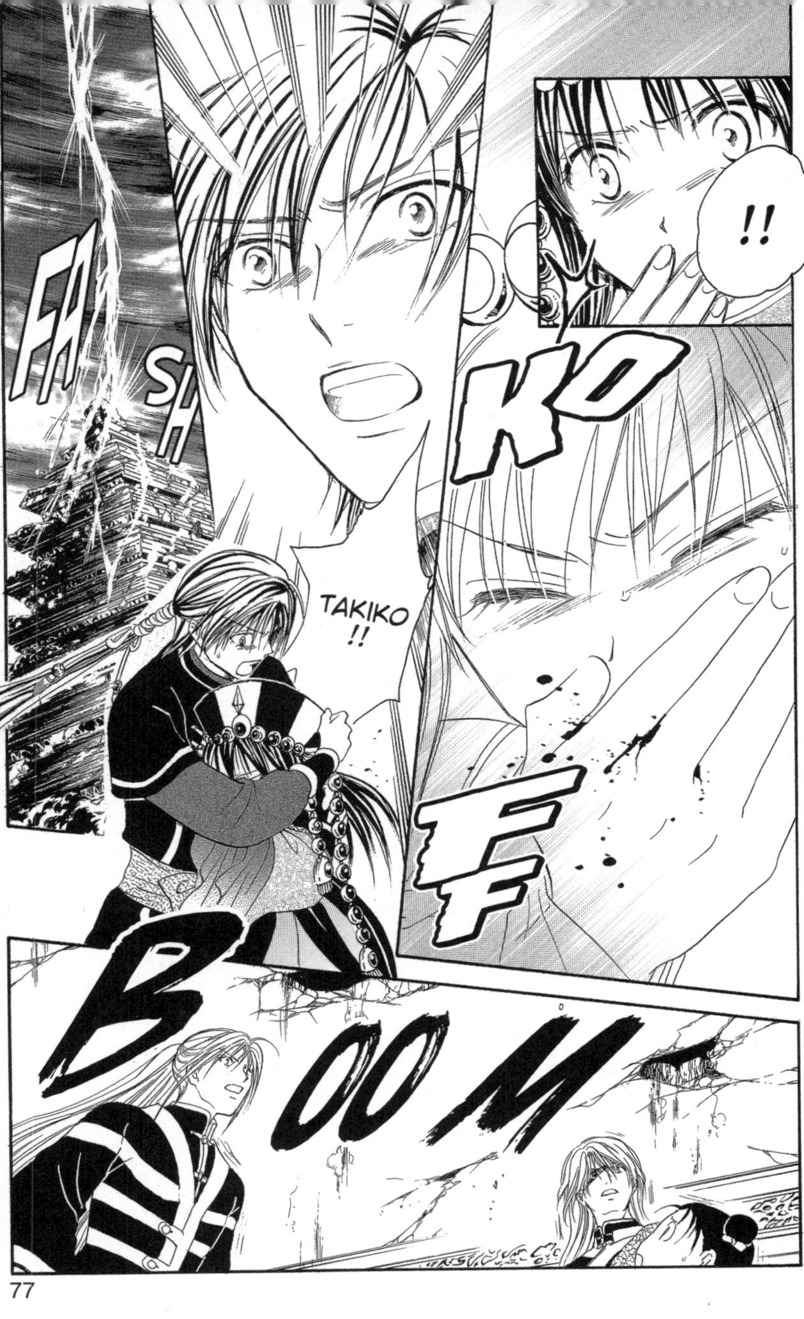
!!
KOFF
TAKIKO !!
FASH
BOOM

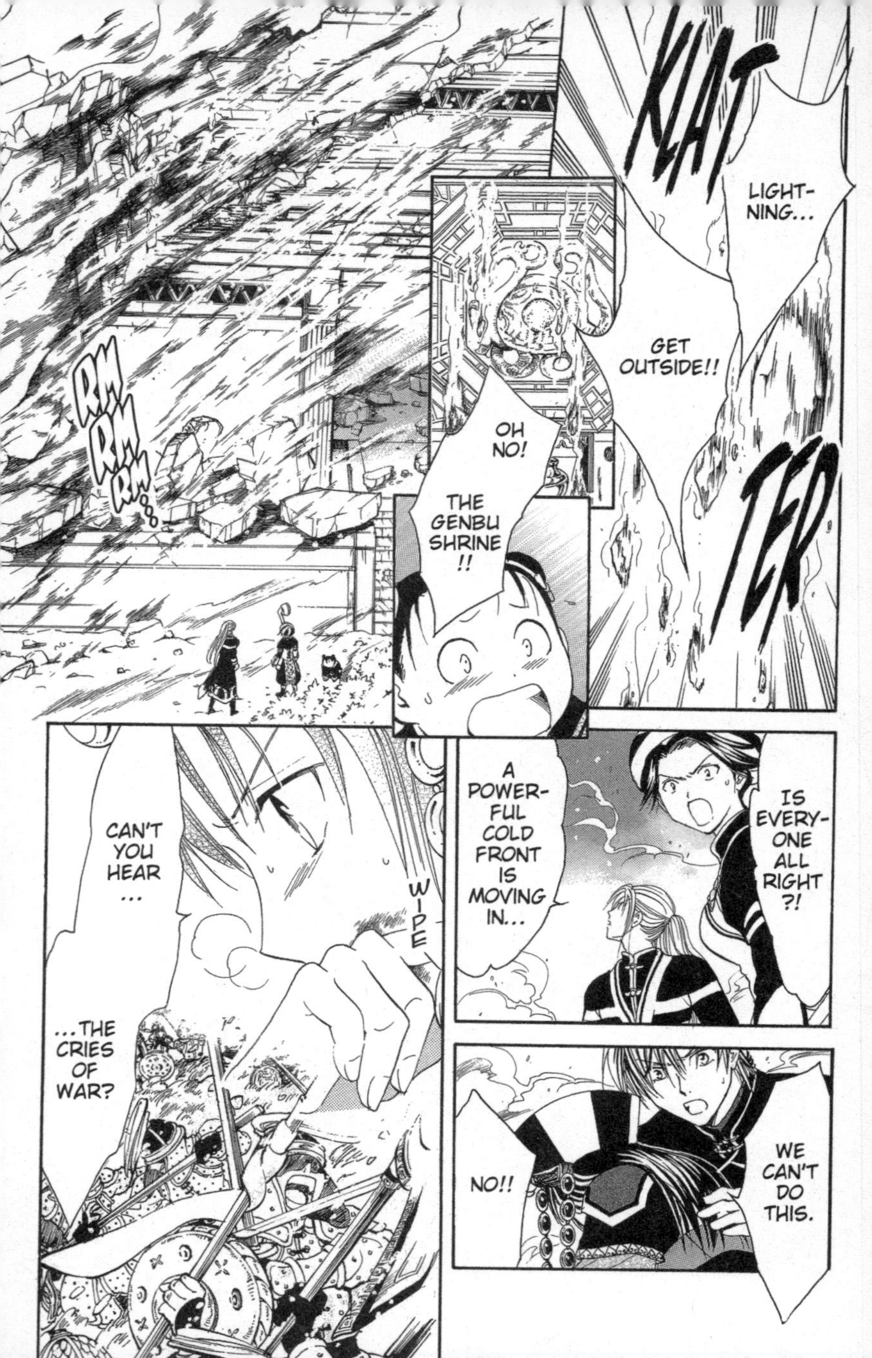
KLATTER
LIGHTNING...
GET OUTSIDE!!
OH NO!
THE GENBU SHRINE!!
RMRMRM
IS EVERYONE ALL RIGHT?!
A POWERFUL COLD FRONT IS MOVING IN...
WE CAN'T DO THIS.
NO!!
WIPE
CAN'T YOU HEAR...
...THE CRIES OF WAR?

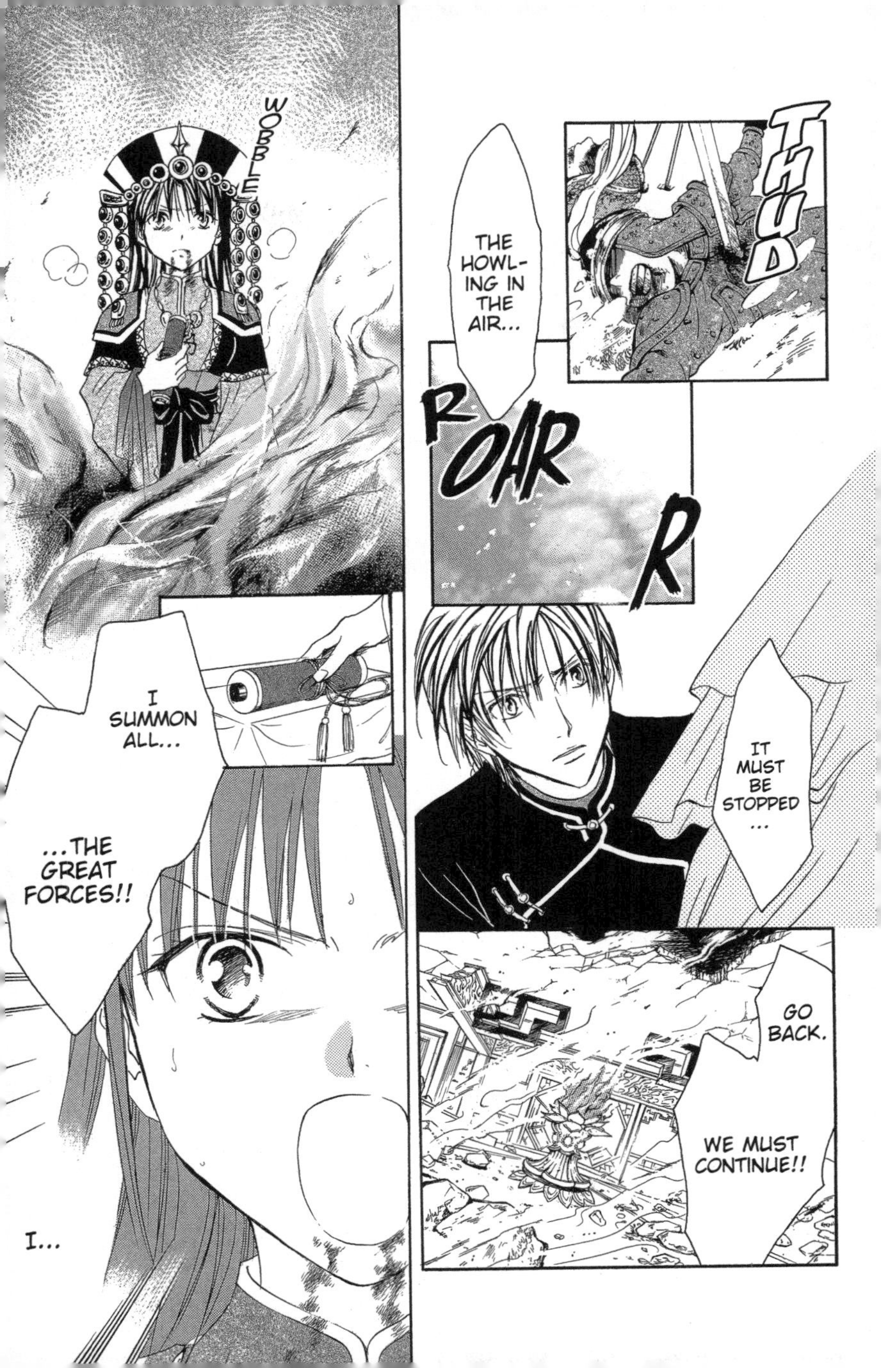
THUD
THE HOWLING IN THE AIR...
ROARR
IT MUST BE STOPPED...
GO BACK.
WE MUST CONTINUE!!
WOBBLE
I SUMMON ALL...
...THE GREAT FORCES!!
I...

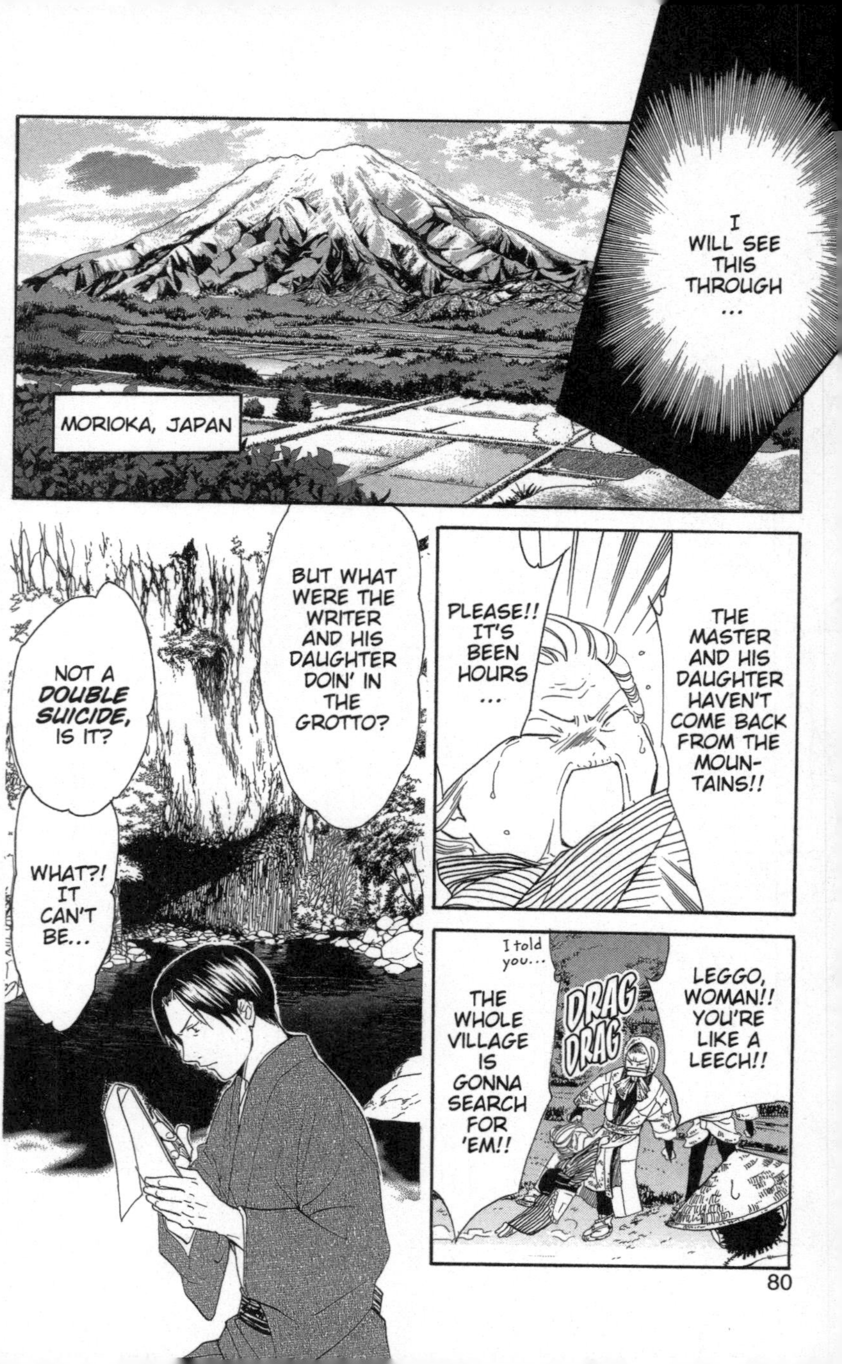
I WILL SEE THIS THROUGH...
MORIOKA, JAPAN
THE MASTER AND HIS DAUGHTER HAVEN'T COME BACK FROM THE MOUN-TAINS!!
PLEASE!! IT'S BEEN HOURS...
LEGGO, WOMAN!! YOU'RE LIKE A LEECH!!
DRAG DRAG
I told you...
THE WHOLE VILLAGE IS GONNA SEARCH FOR 'EM!!
BUT WHAT WERE THE WRITER AND HIS DAUGHTER DOIN' IN THE GROTTO?
NOT A *DOUBLE SUICIDE*, IS IT?
WHAT?! IT CAN'T BE...

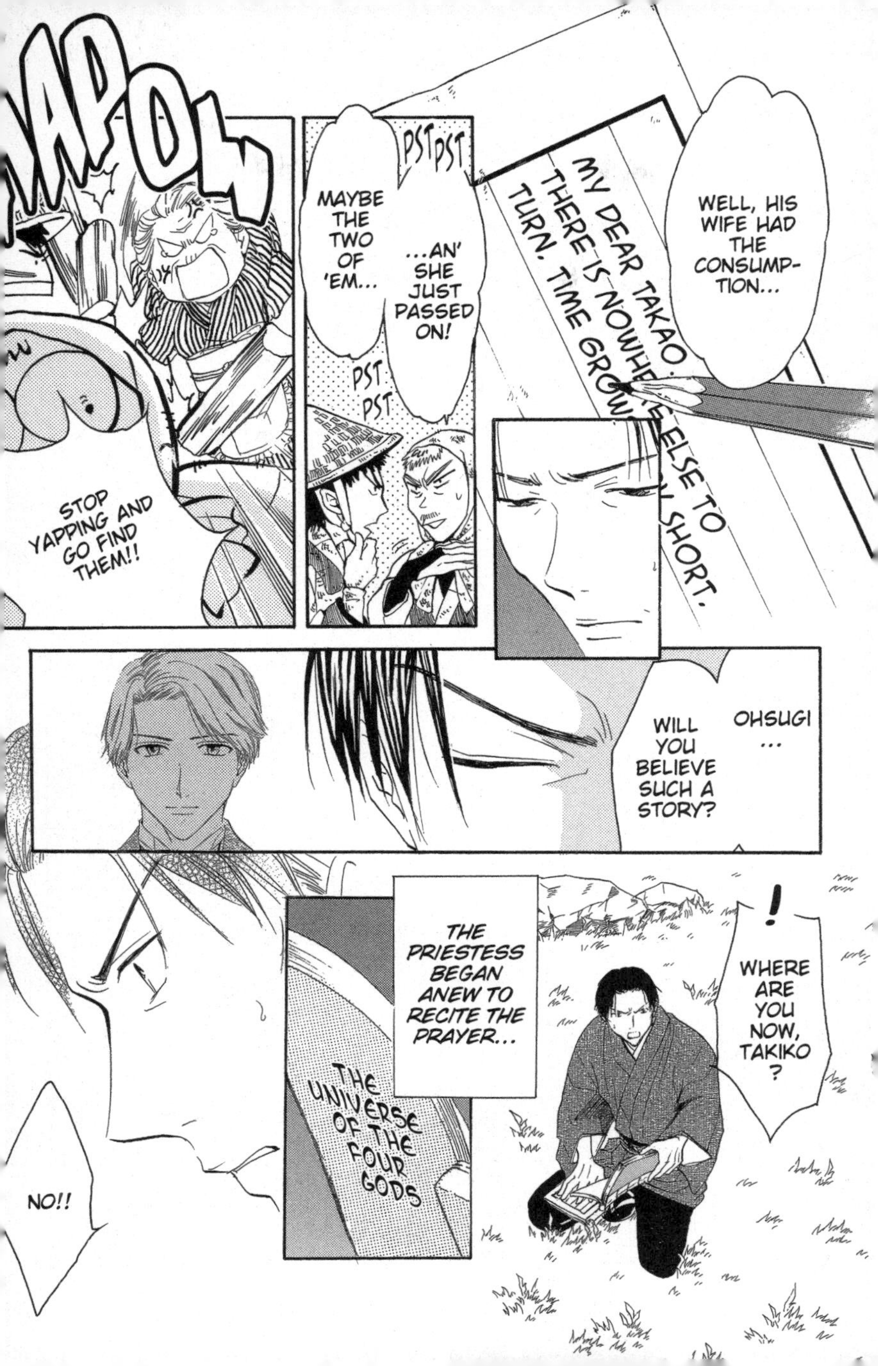
WELL, HIS WIFE HAD THE CONSUMPTION...
MY DEAR TAKAO.
THERE IS NOWHE ELSE TO
TURN. TIME GROW SHORT.
PST PST
...AN' SHE JUST PASSED ON!
MAYBE THE TWO OF 'EM...
PST PST
WAPOW
STOP YAPPING AND GO FIND THEM!!
OHSUGI...
WILL YOU BELIEVE SUCH A STORY?
!
WHERE ARE YOU NOW, TAKIKO?
THE PRIESTESS BEGAN ANEW TO RECITE THE PRAYER...
THE UNIVERSE OF THE FOUR GODS
NO!!

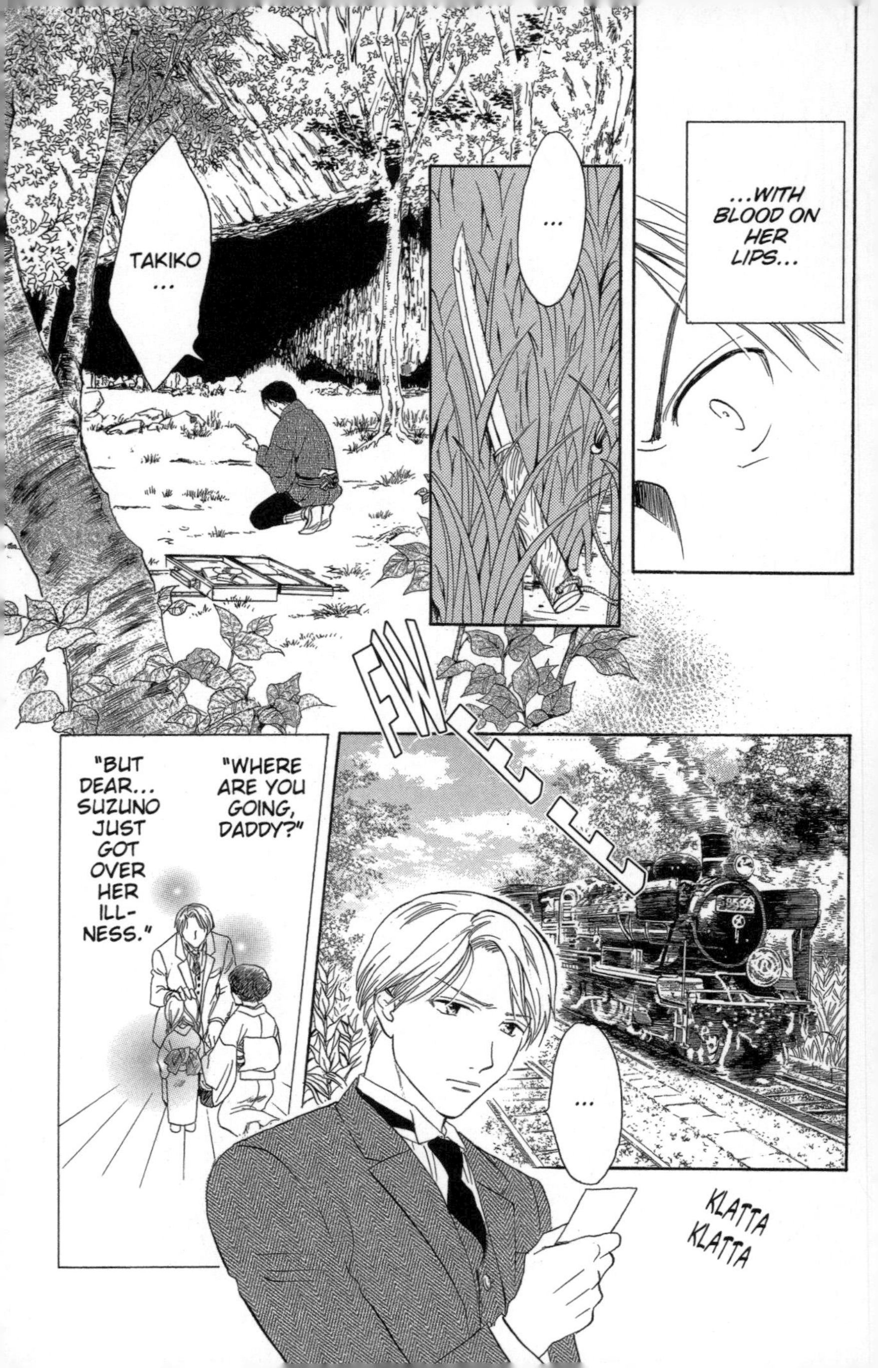

...WITH BLOOD ON HER LIPS...
...
TAKIKO ...
FWEEEE
...
KLATTA KLATTA
"WHERE ARE YOU GOING, DADDY?"
"BUT DEAR... SUZUNO JUST GOT OVER HER ILL-NESS."

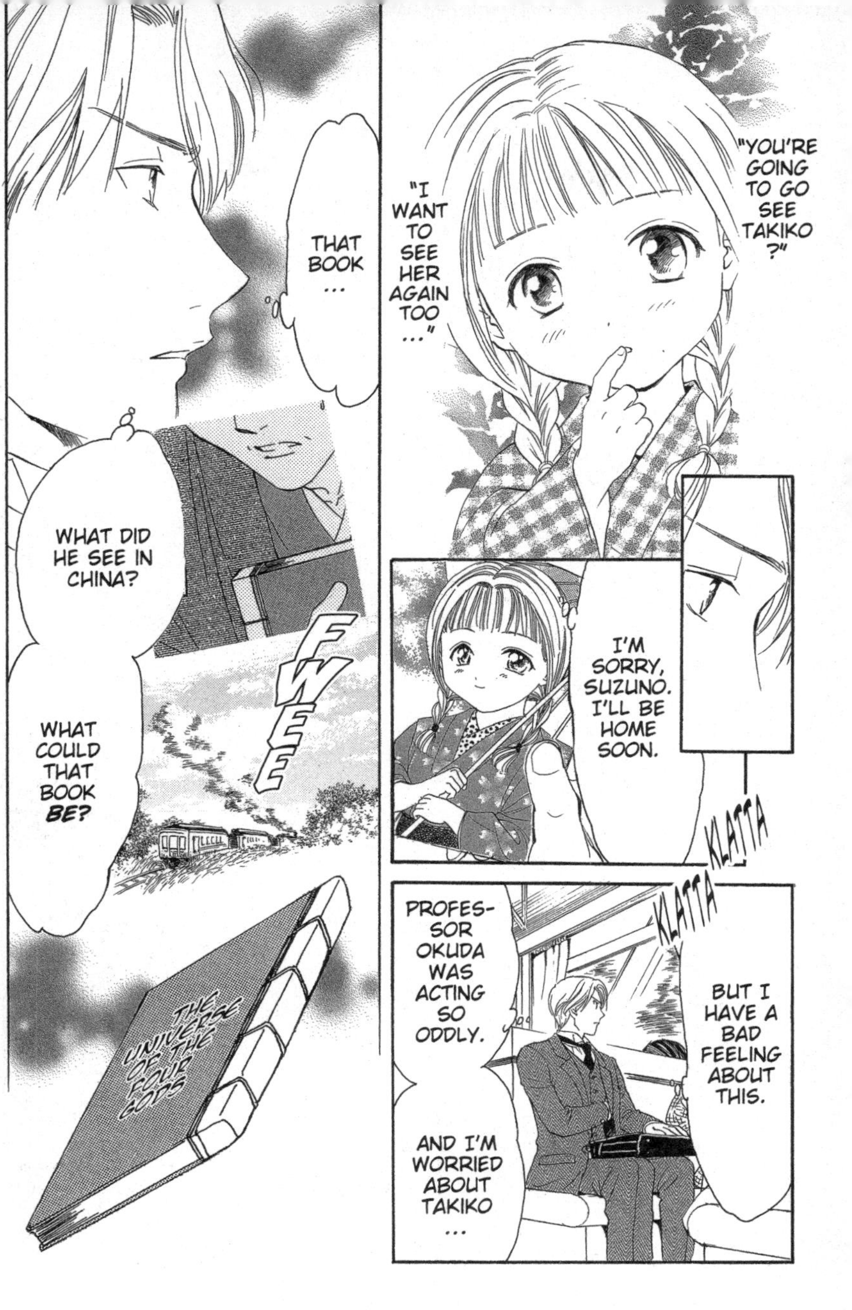
"YOU'RE GOING TO GO SEE TAKIKO?"
"I WANT TO SEE HER AGAIN TOO..."
I'M SORRY, SUZUNO. I'LL BE HOME SOON.
KLATTA
KLATTA
BUT I HAVE A BAD FEELING ABOUT THIS.
PROFES-SOR OKUDA WAS ACTING SO ODDLY.
AND I'M WORRIED ABOUT TAKIKO...
THAT BOOK...
WHAT DID HE SEE IN CHINA?
FWEEE
WHAT COULD THAT BOOK *BE?*
THE UNIVERSE OF THE FOUR GODS

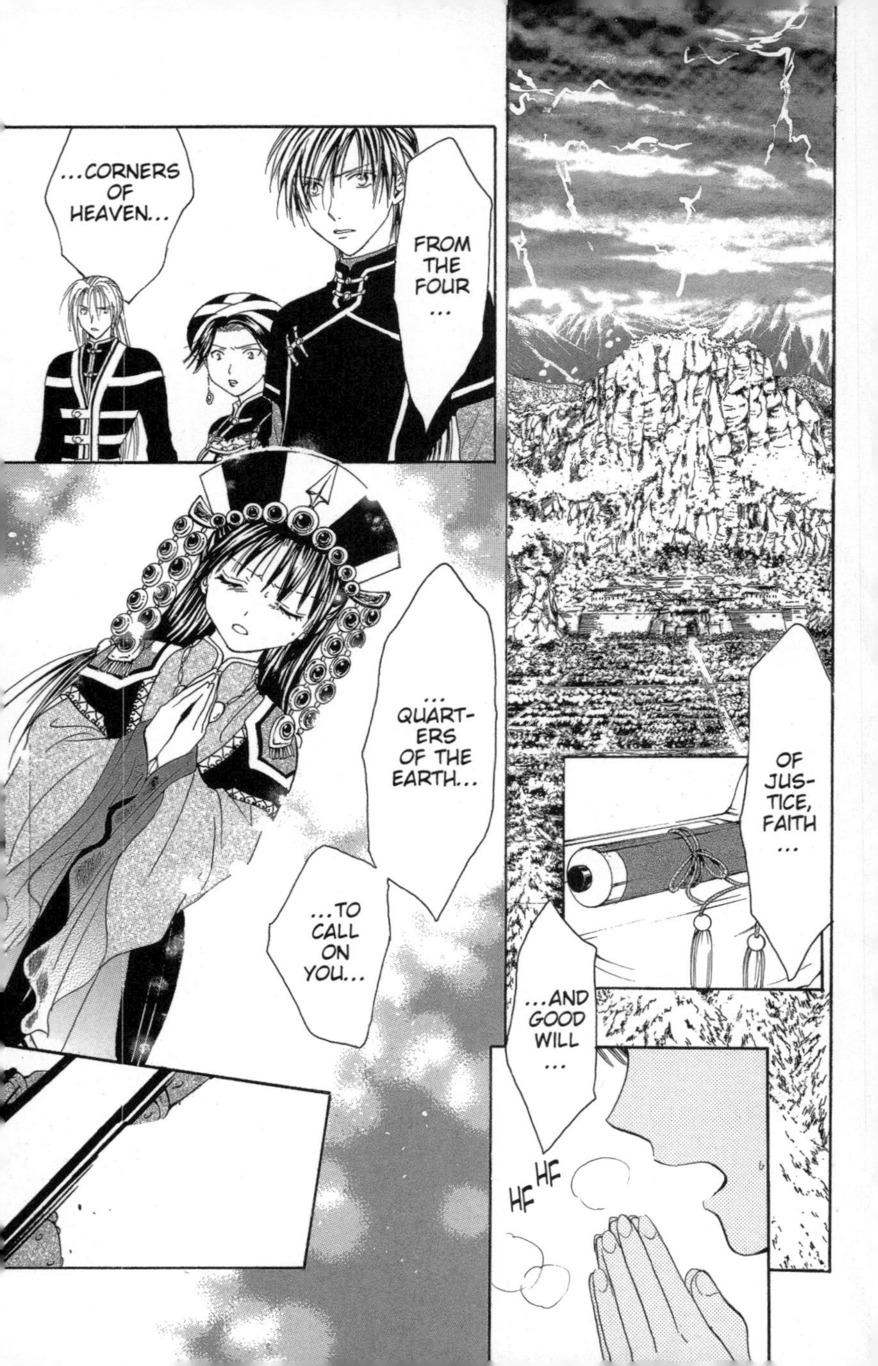
FROM THE FOUR ...
...CORNERS OF HEAVEN...
... QUARTERS OF THE EARTH...
...TO CALL ON YOU...
OF JUS-TICE, FAITH ...
...AND GOOD WILL ...
HF HF

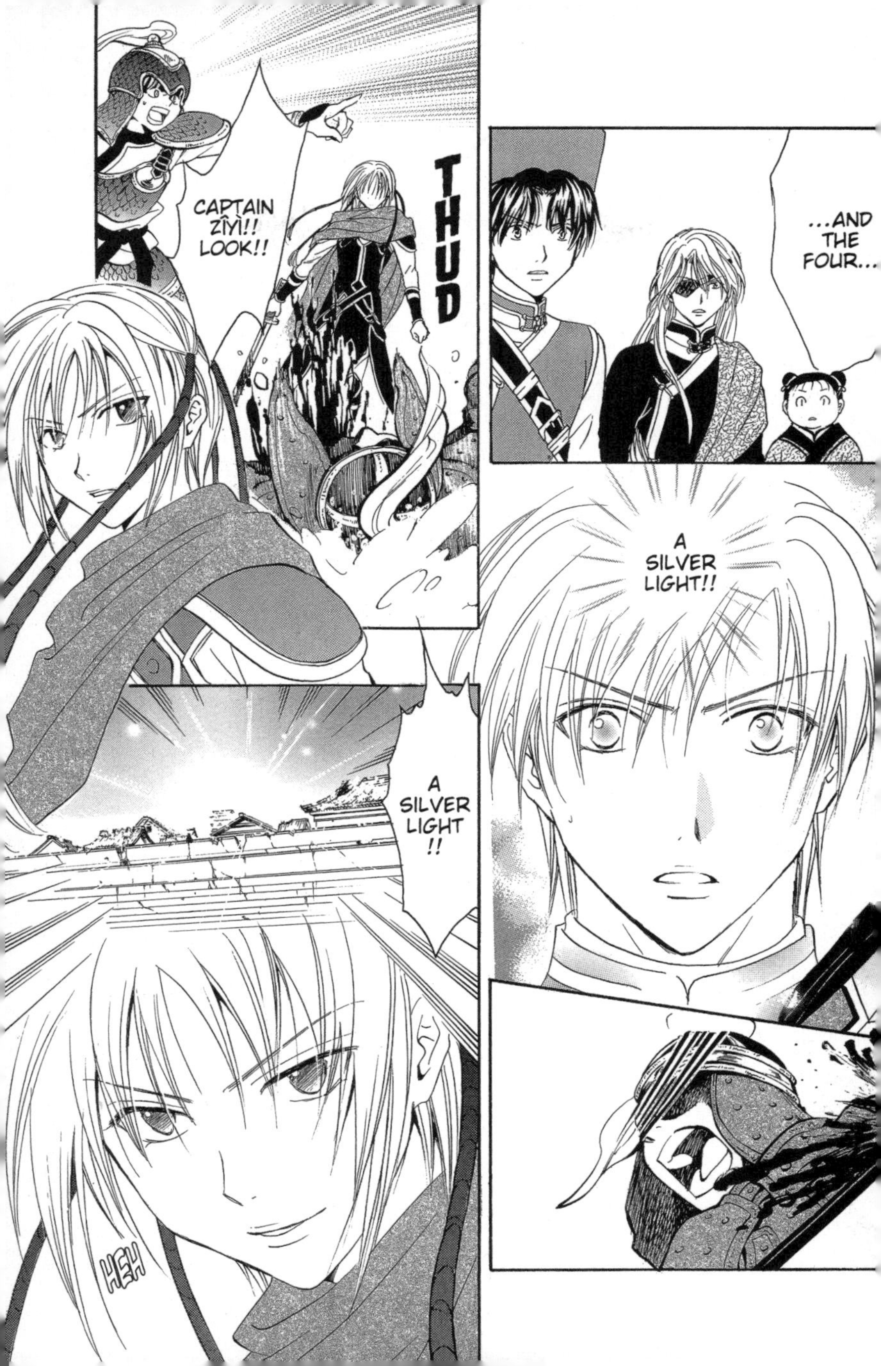
...AND THE FOUR...
CAPTAIN ZÎYÌ!! LOOK!!
THUD
A SILVER LIGHT!!
A SILVER LIGHT !!
HEH

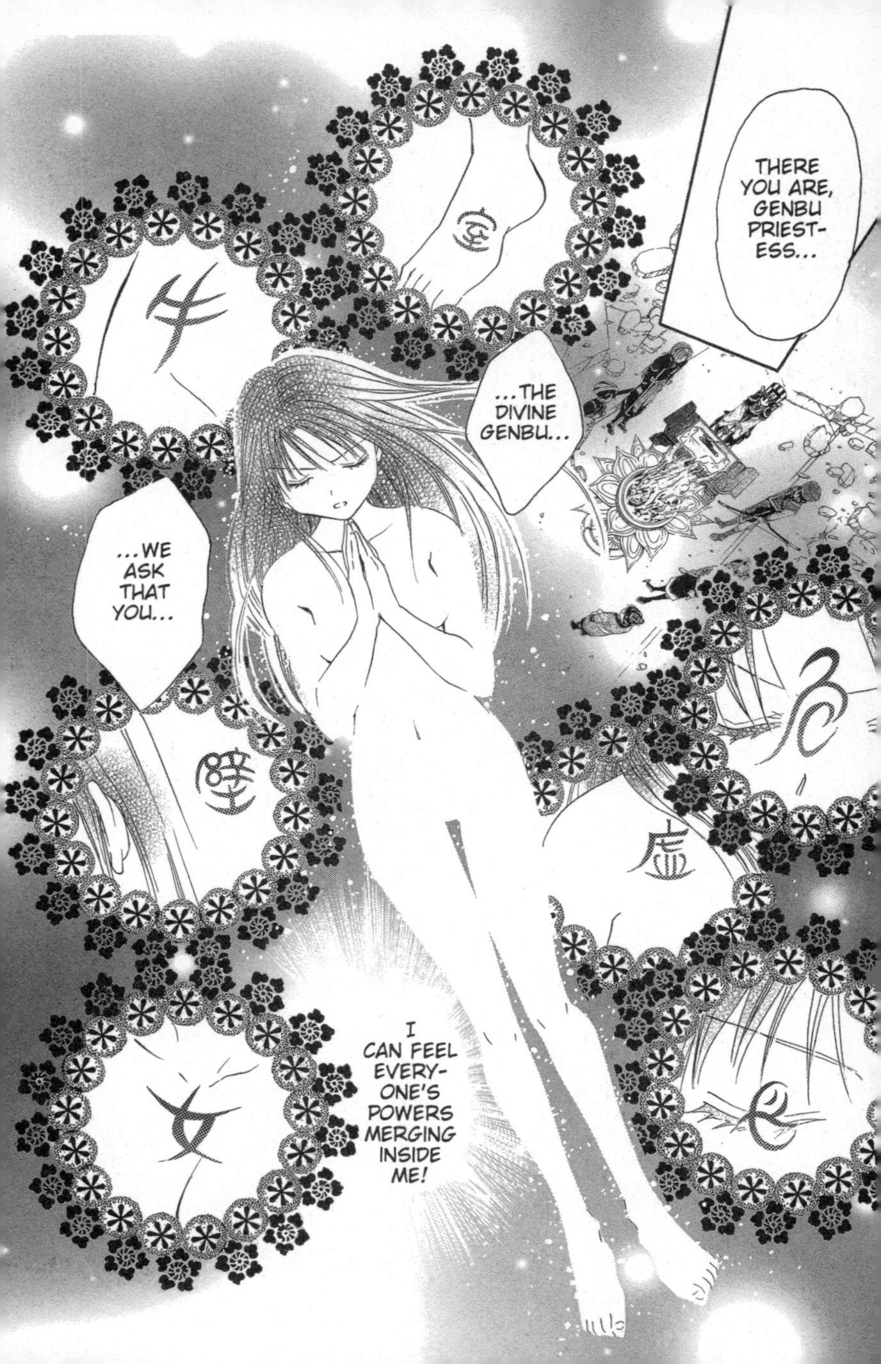
THERE YOU ARE, GENBU PRIEST-ESS...
...THE DIVINE GENBU...
...WE ASK THAT YOU...
I CAN FEEL EVERY-ONE'S POWERS MERGING INSIDE ME!

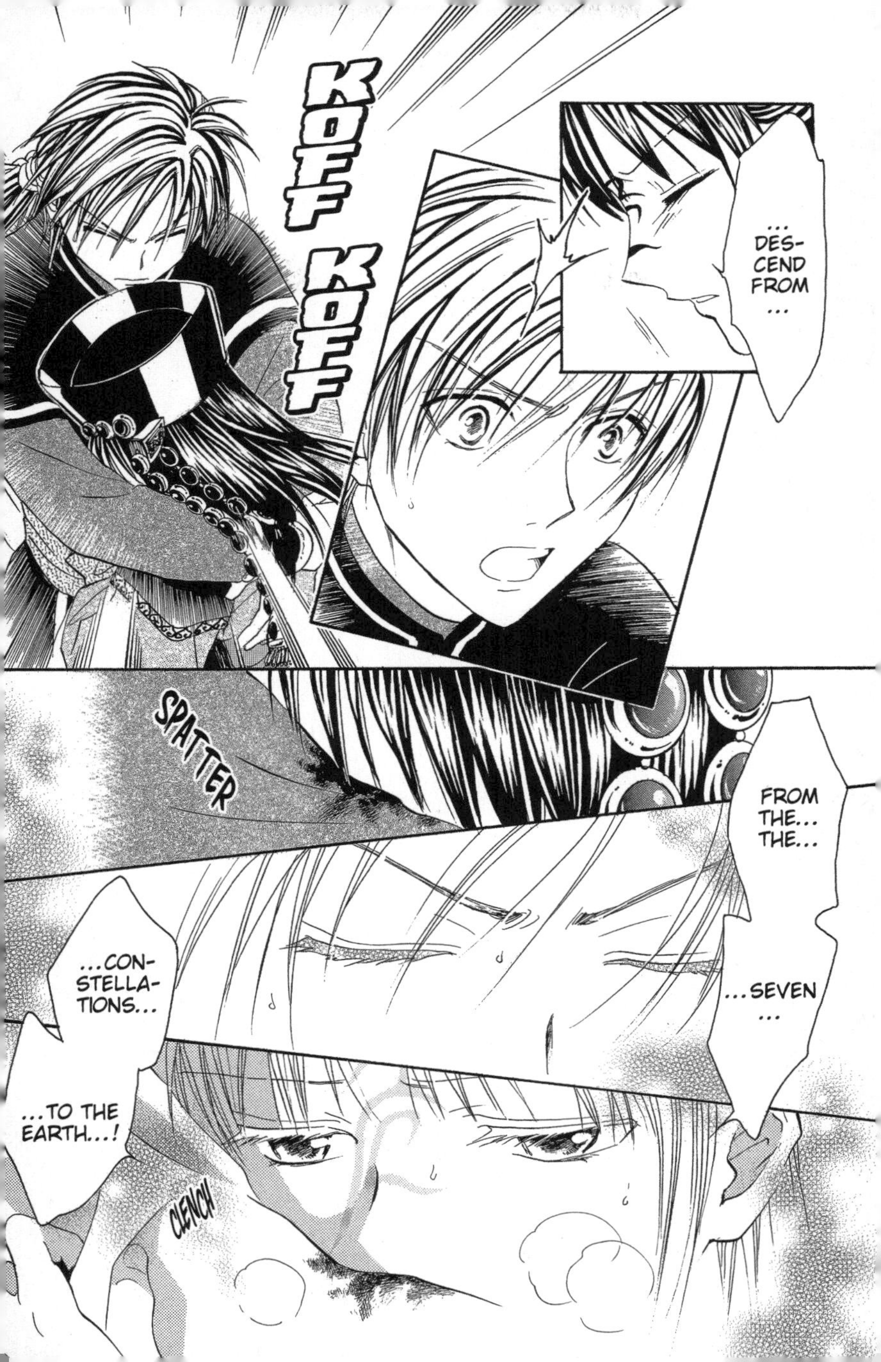
...DES-CEND FROM...
KOFF KOFF
FROM THE... THE...
SPATTER
...SEVEN...
...CON-STELLA-TIONS...
...TO THE EARTH...!
CLENCH

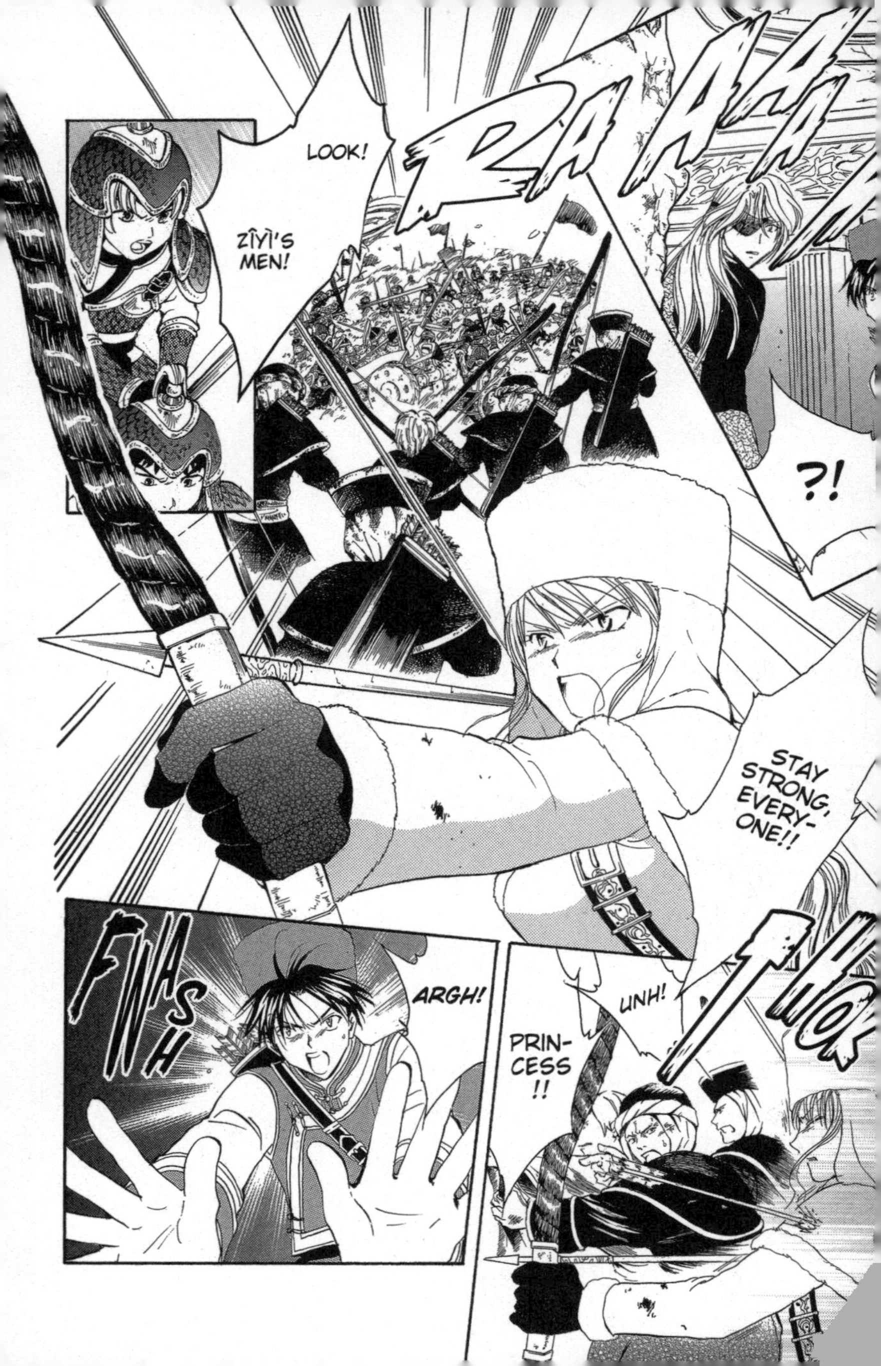
RAAA
?!
LOOK!
ZÎYÌ'S MEN!
STAY STRONG, EVERY-ONE!!
THOK
UNH!
PRIN-CESS!!
ARGH!
FWASH

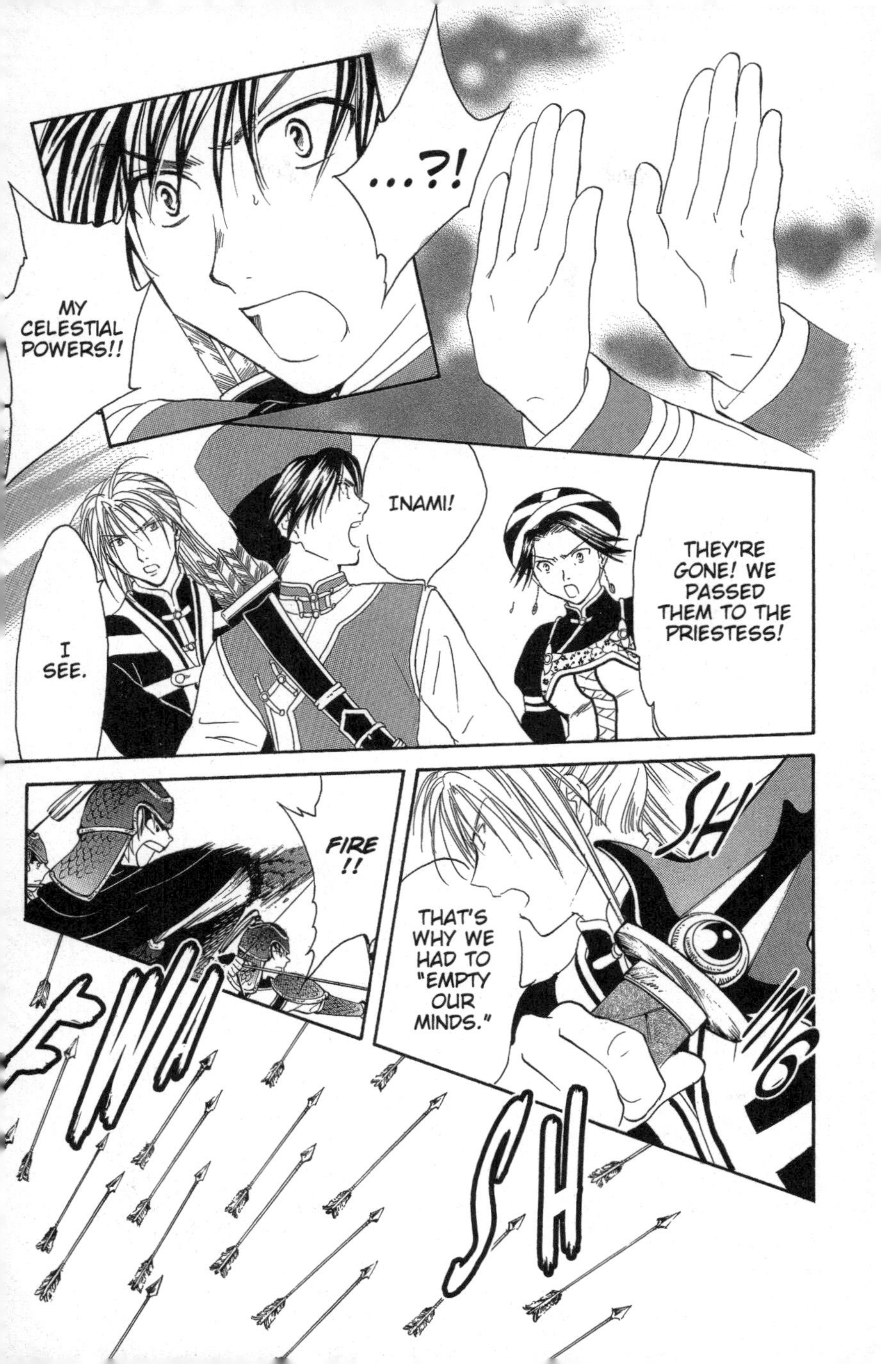
...?!
MY CELESTIAL POWERS!!
THEY'RE GONE! WE PASSED THEM TO THE PRIESTESS!
INAMI!
I SEE.
THAT'S WHY WE HAD TO "EMPTY OUR MINDS."
FIRE!!

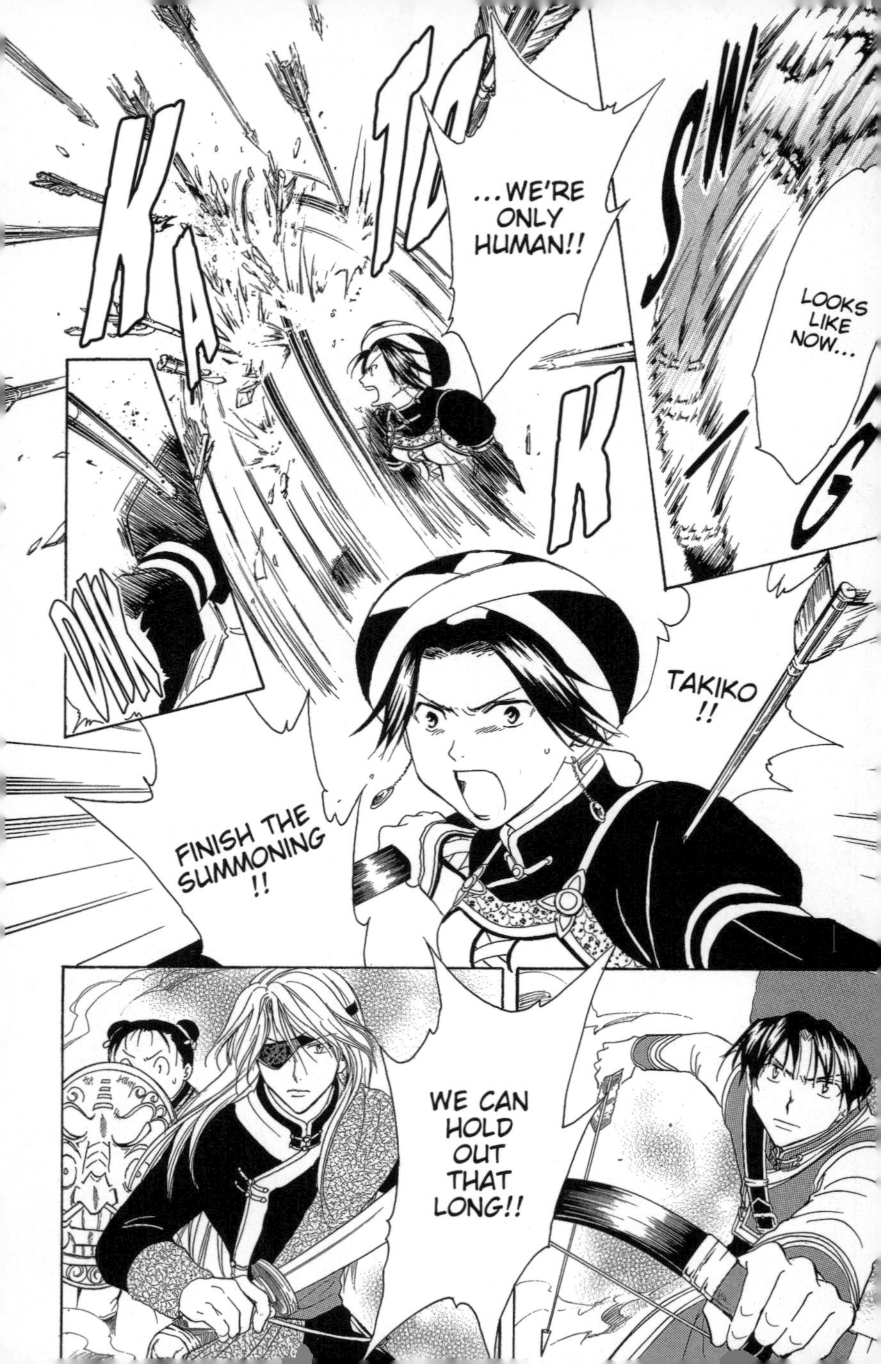
SWING
LOOKS LIKE NOW...
...WE'RE ONLY HUMAN!!
TAKIKO!!
FINISH THE SUMMONING!!
WE CAN HOLD OUT THAT LONG!!

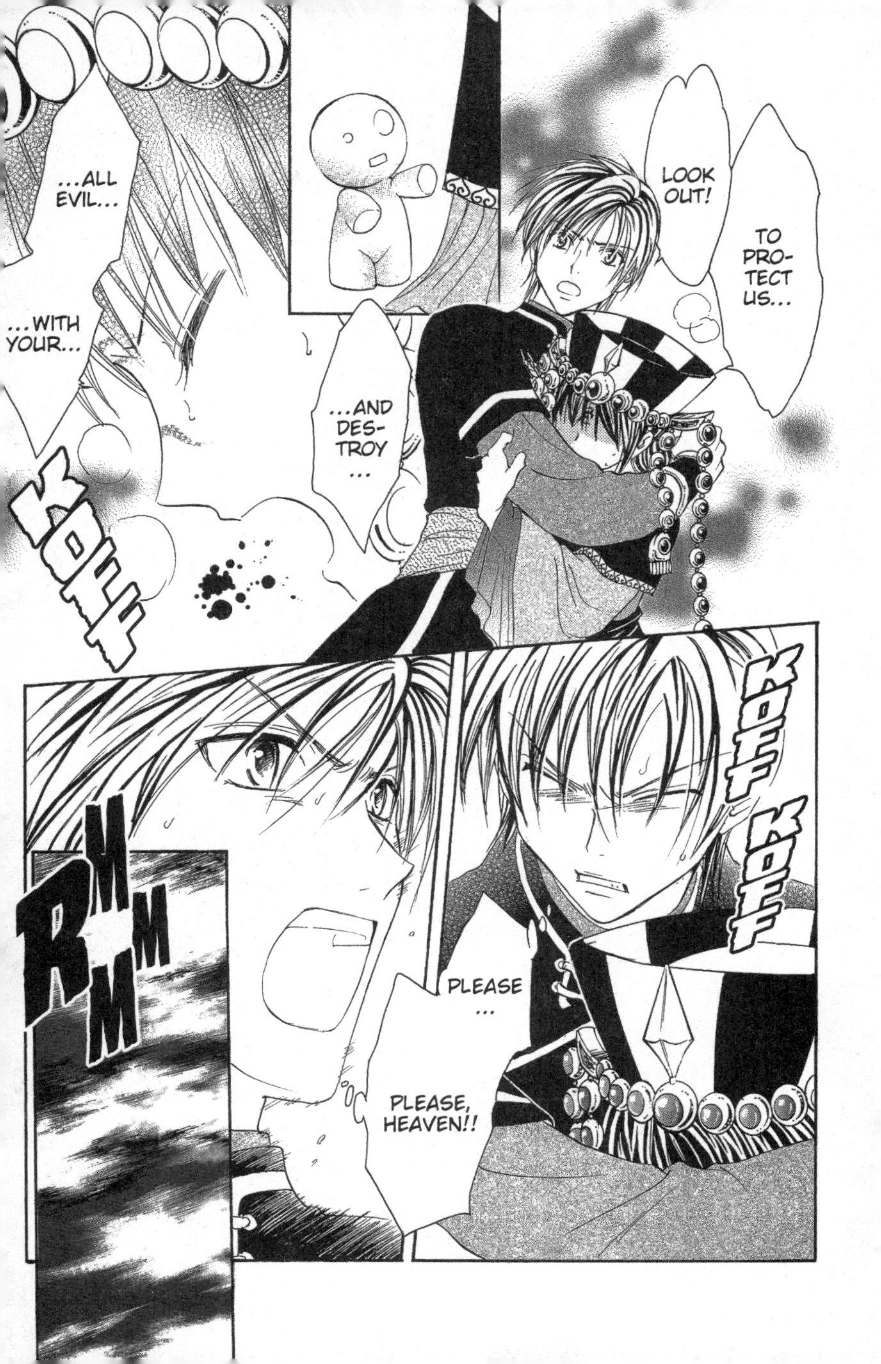
LOOK OUT!
TO PROTECT US...
...AND DESTROY...
...ALL EVIL...
...WITH YOUR...
KOFF
KOFF KOFF KOFF
PLEASE...
PLEASE, HEAVEN!!
RMMMM

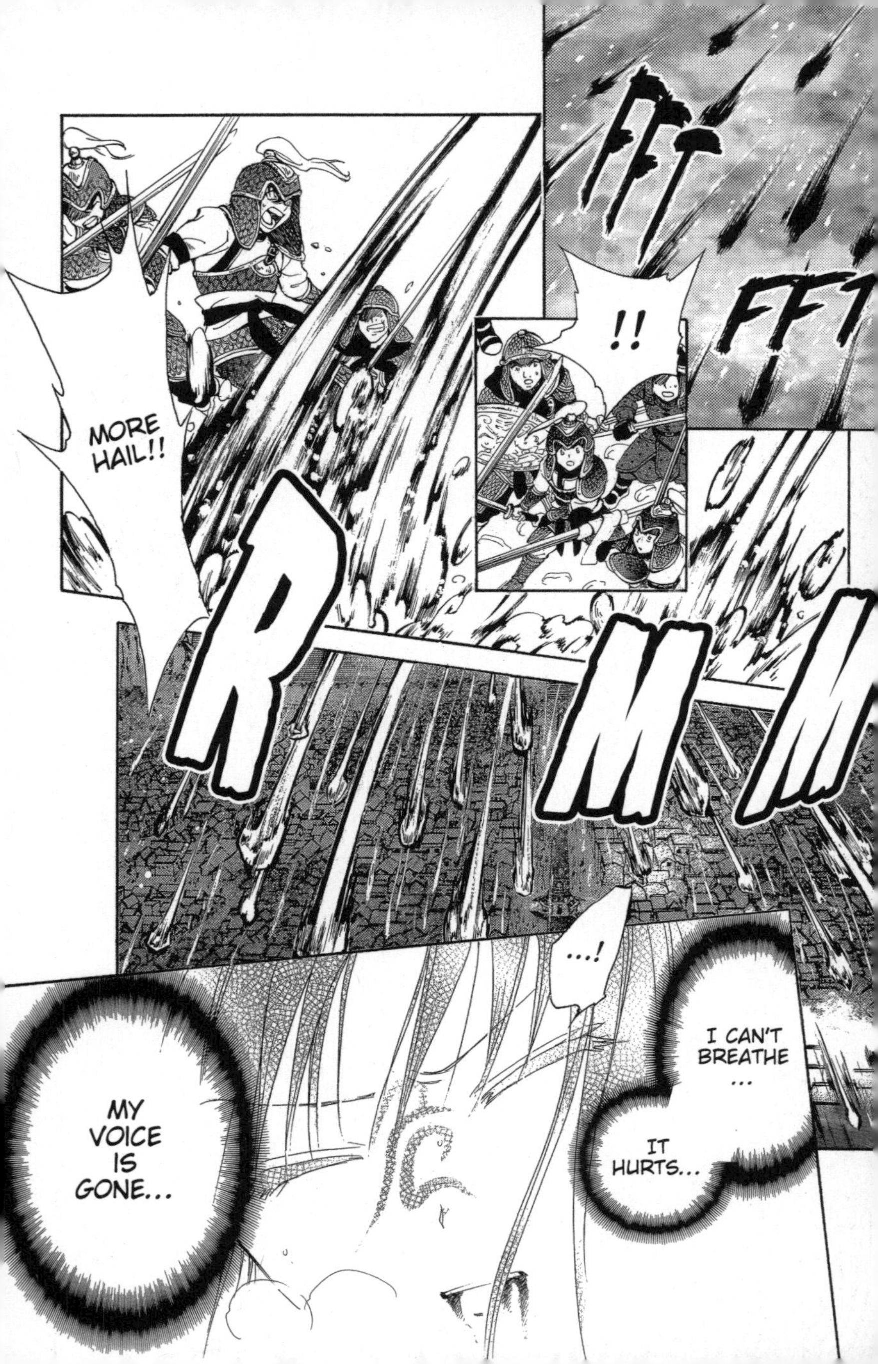
FFT
FFT
!!
MORE HAIL!!
RMM
...!
I CAN'T BREATHE ...
IT HURTS...
MY VOICE IS GONE...

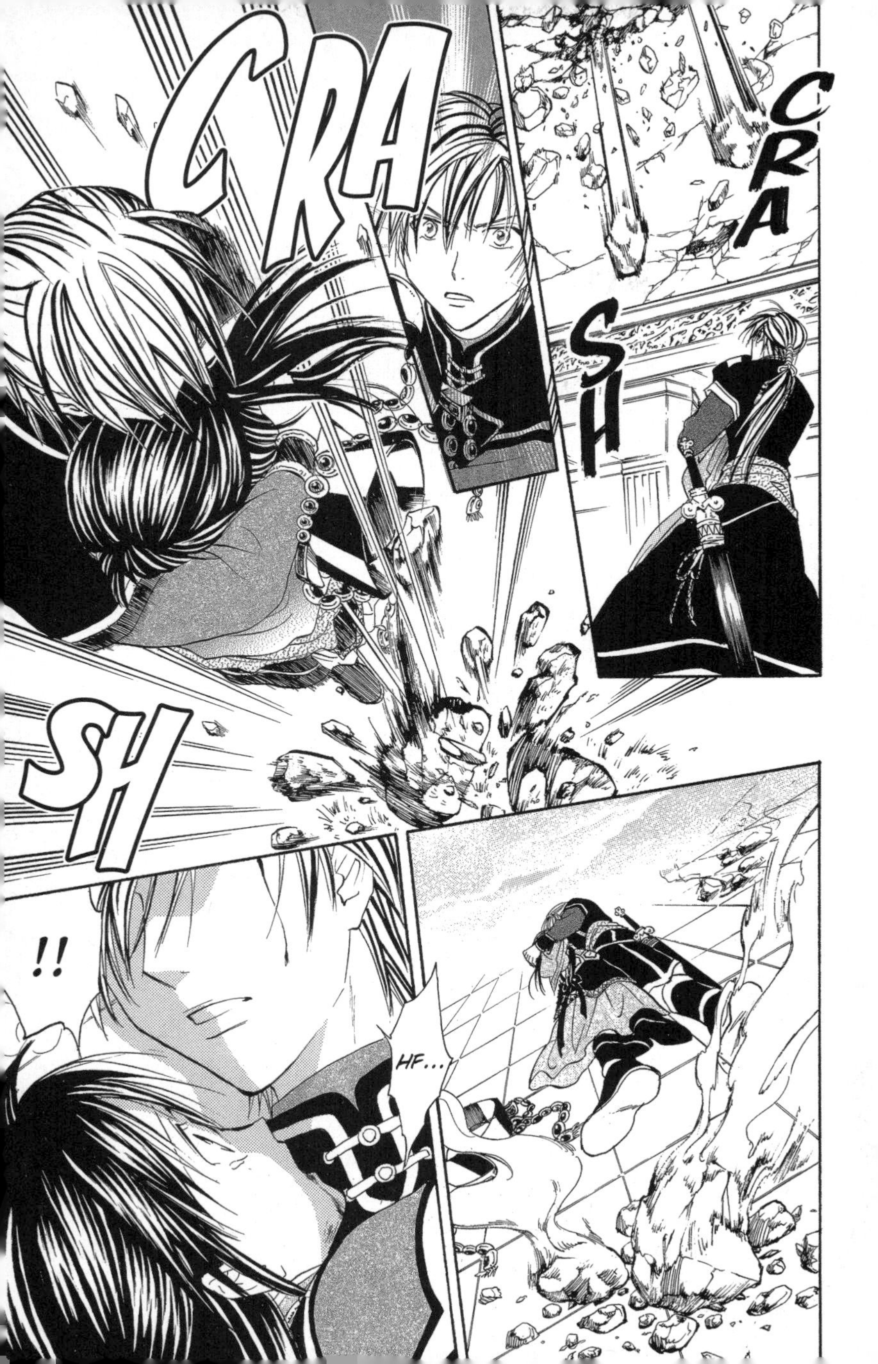
CRA
CRA
SH
SH
!!
HF...

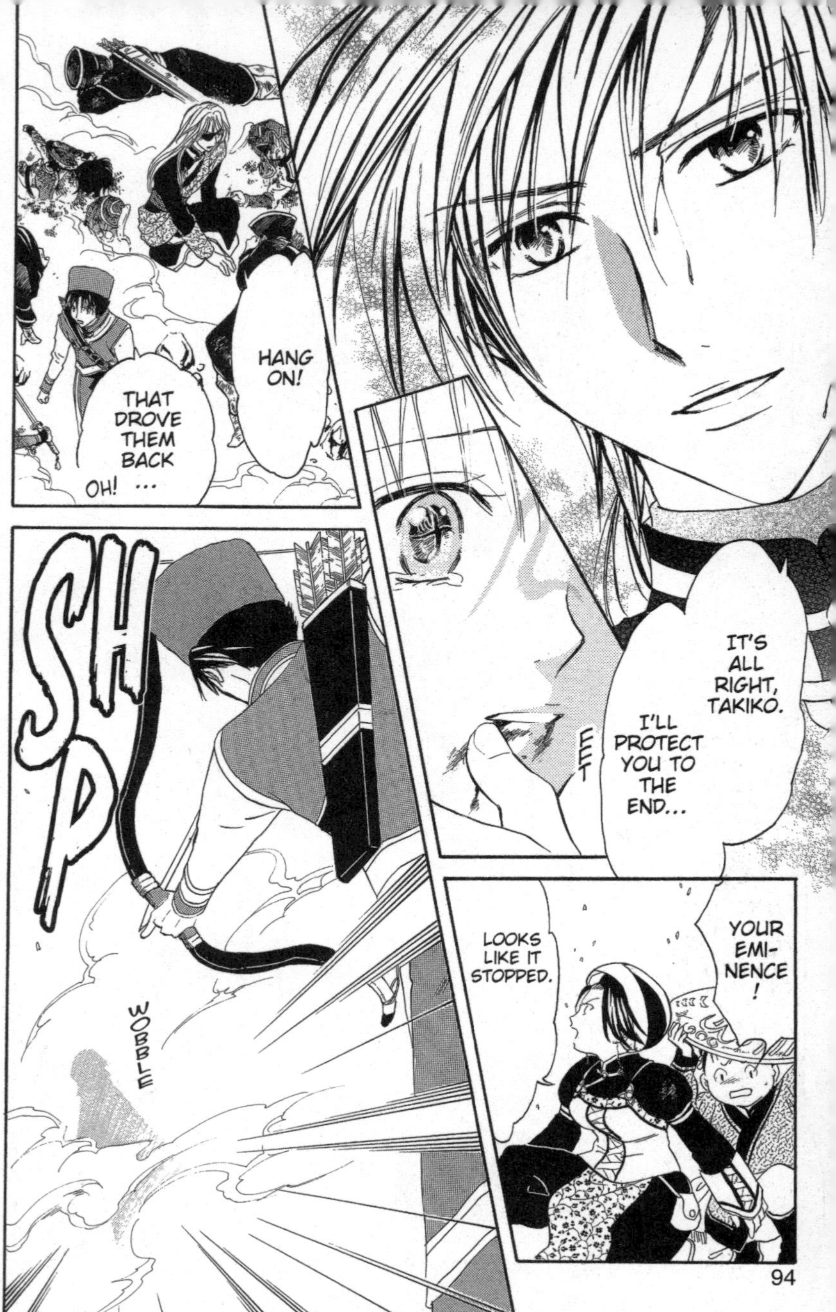
IT'S ALL RIGHT, TAKIKO.
I'LL PROTECT YOU TO THE END...
HANG ON!
THAT DROVE THEM BACK ...
OH!
EET
YOUR EMI-NENCE!
LOOKS LIKE IT STOPPED.
SHP
WOBBLE

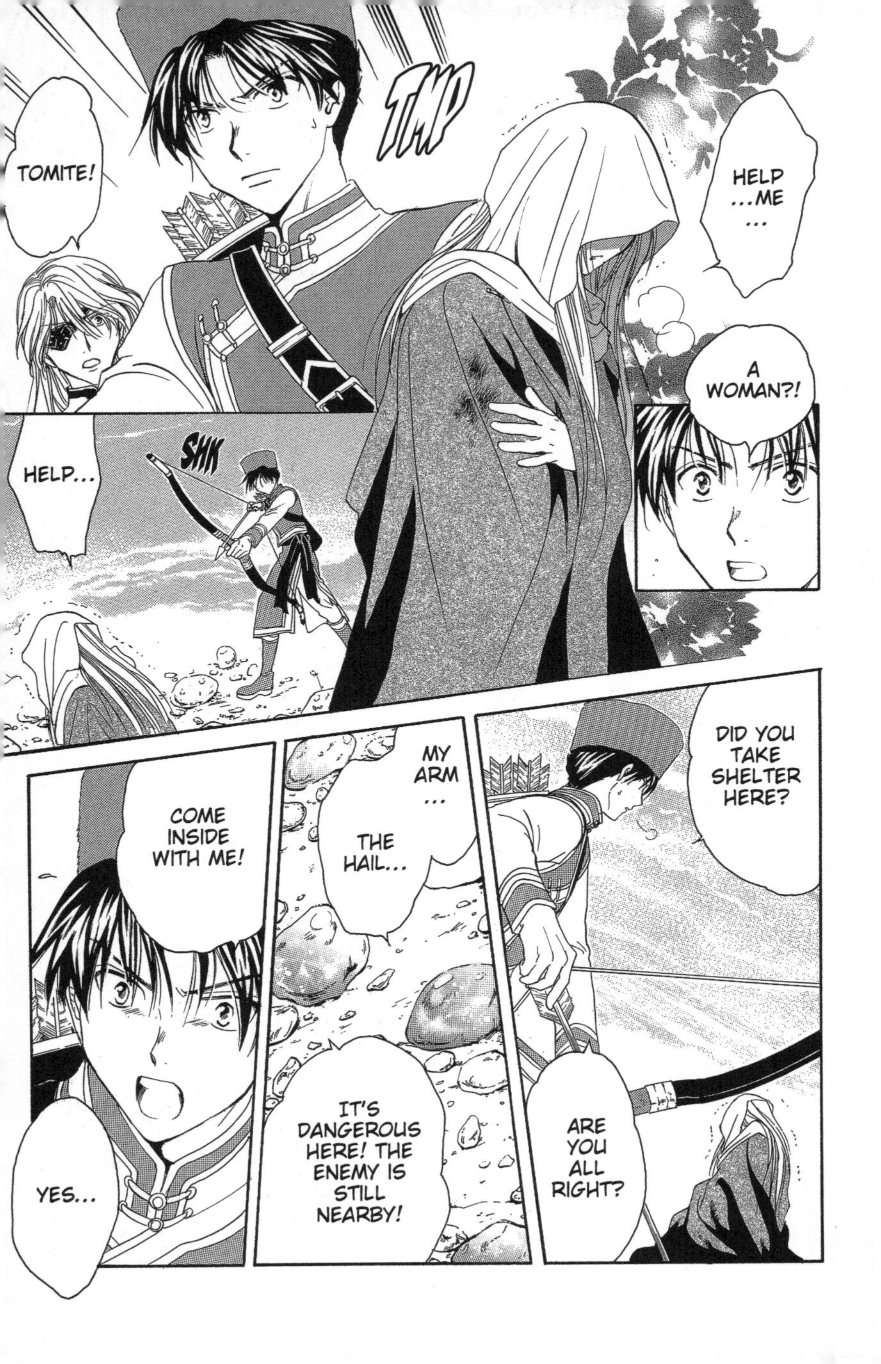
HELP ...ME ...
TMP
TOMITE!
A WOMAN?!
SHK
HELP...
DID YOU TAKE SHELTER HERE?
ARE YOU ALL RIGHT?
MY ARM ...
THE HAIL...
IT'S DANGEROUS HERE! THE ENEMY IS STILL NEARBY!
COME INSIDE WITH ME!
YES...

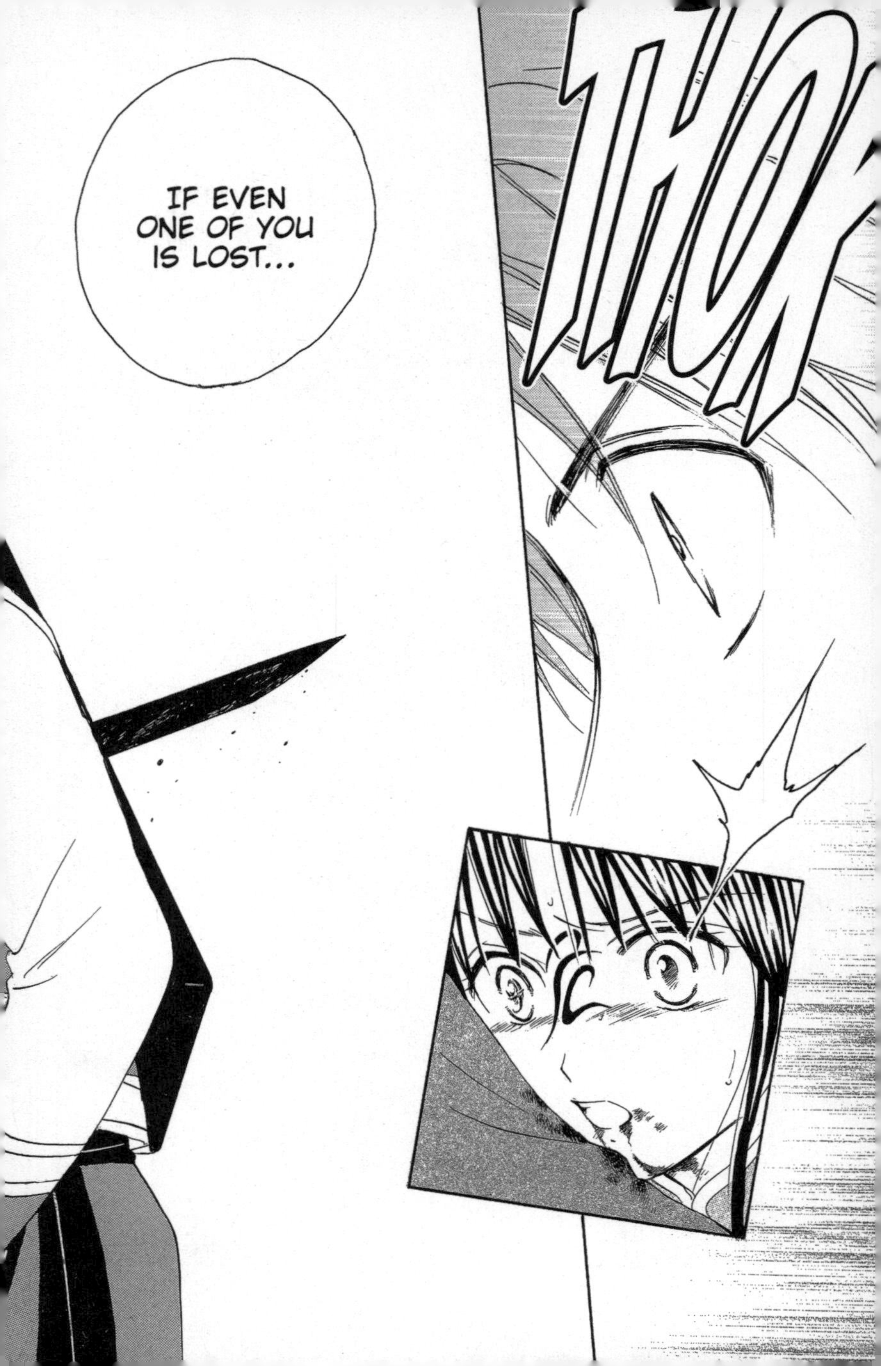
IF EVEN ONE OF YOU IS LOST...

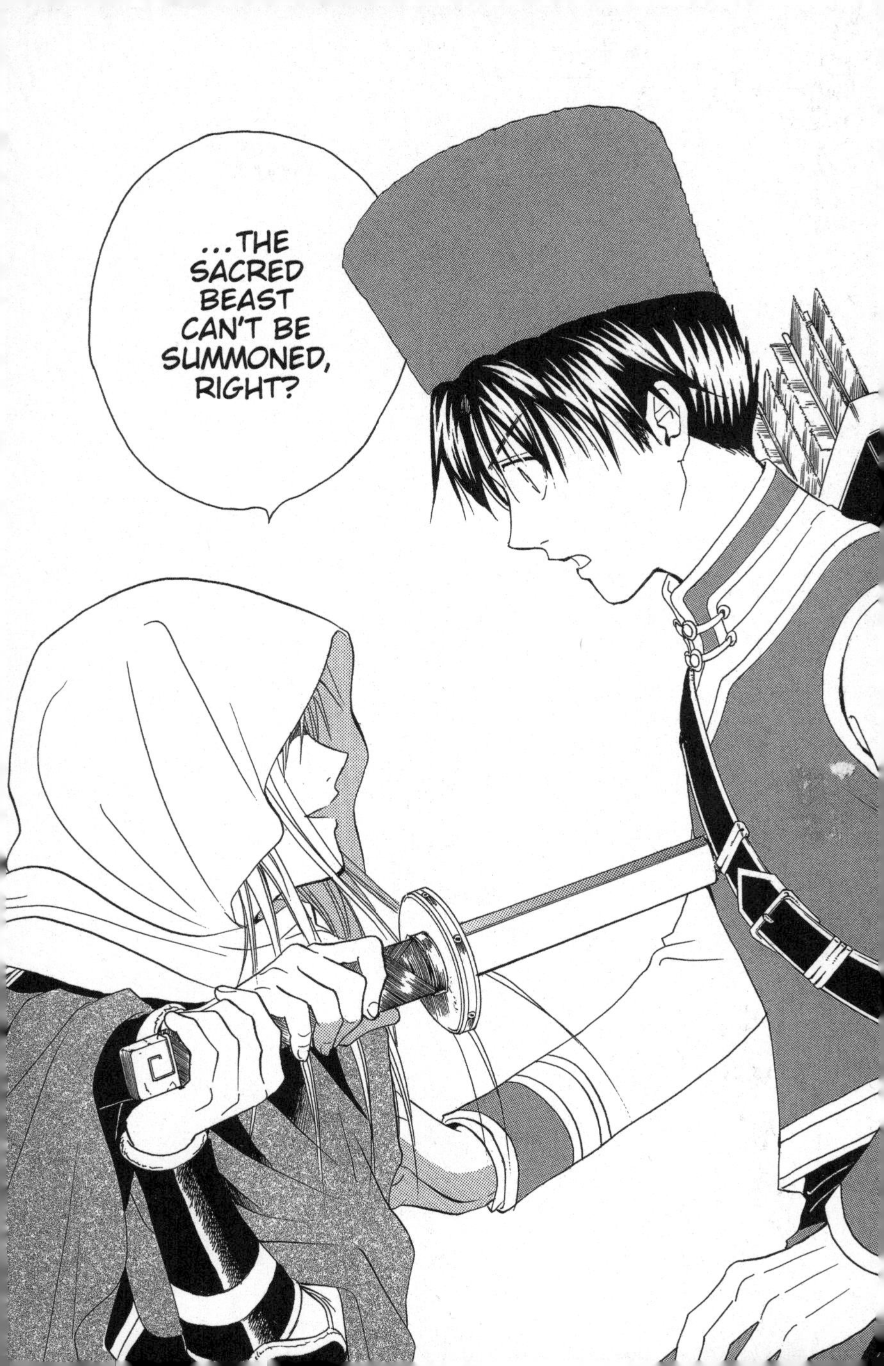
...THE SACRED BEAST CAN'T BE SUMMONED, RIGHT?

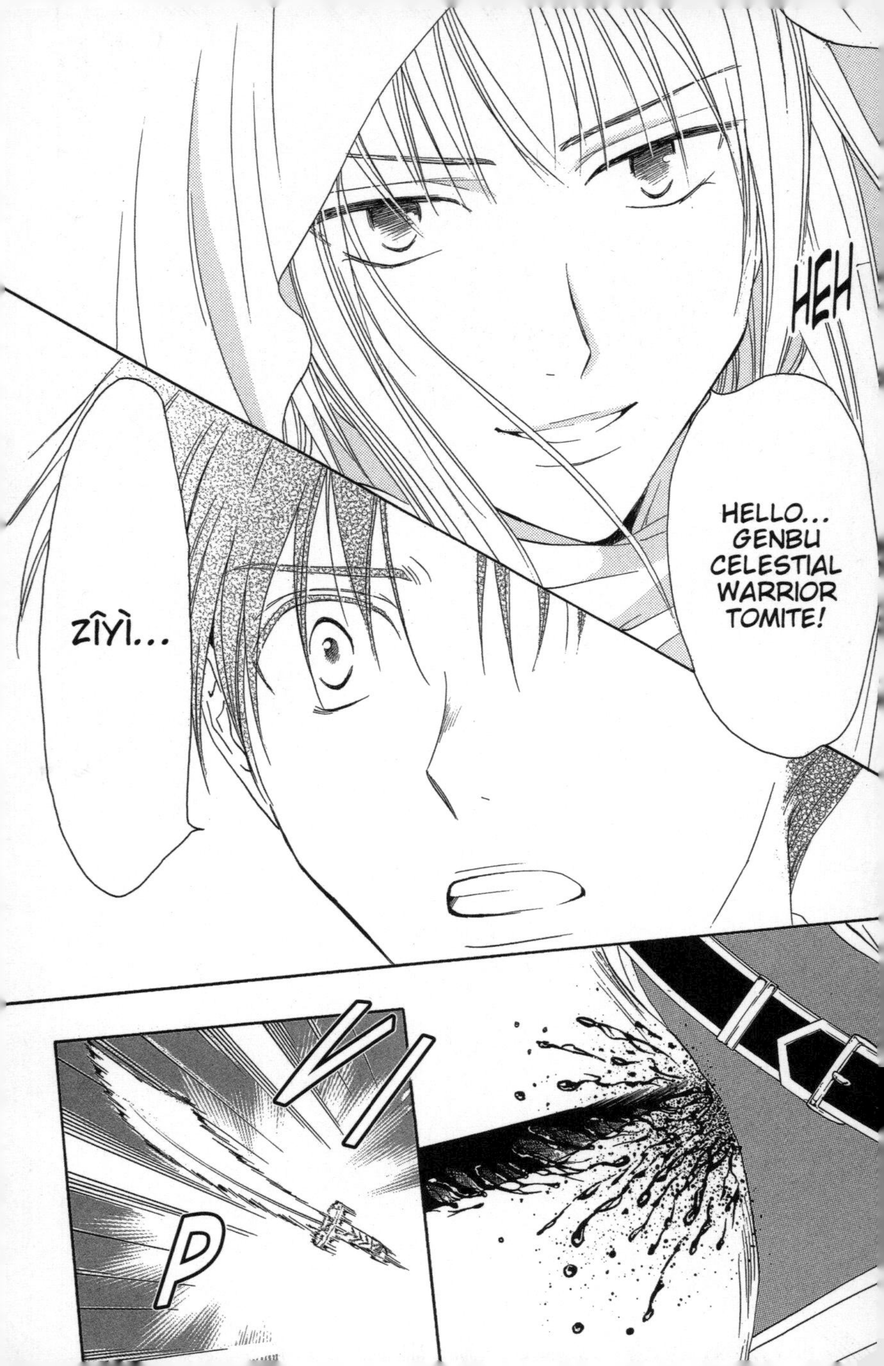
HEH
HELLO... GENBU CELESTIAL WARRIOR TOMITE!
ZÎYÌ...

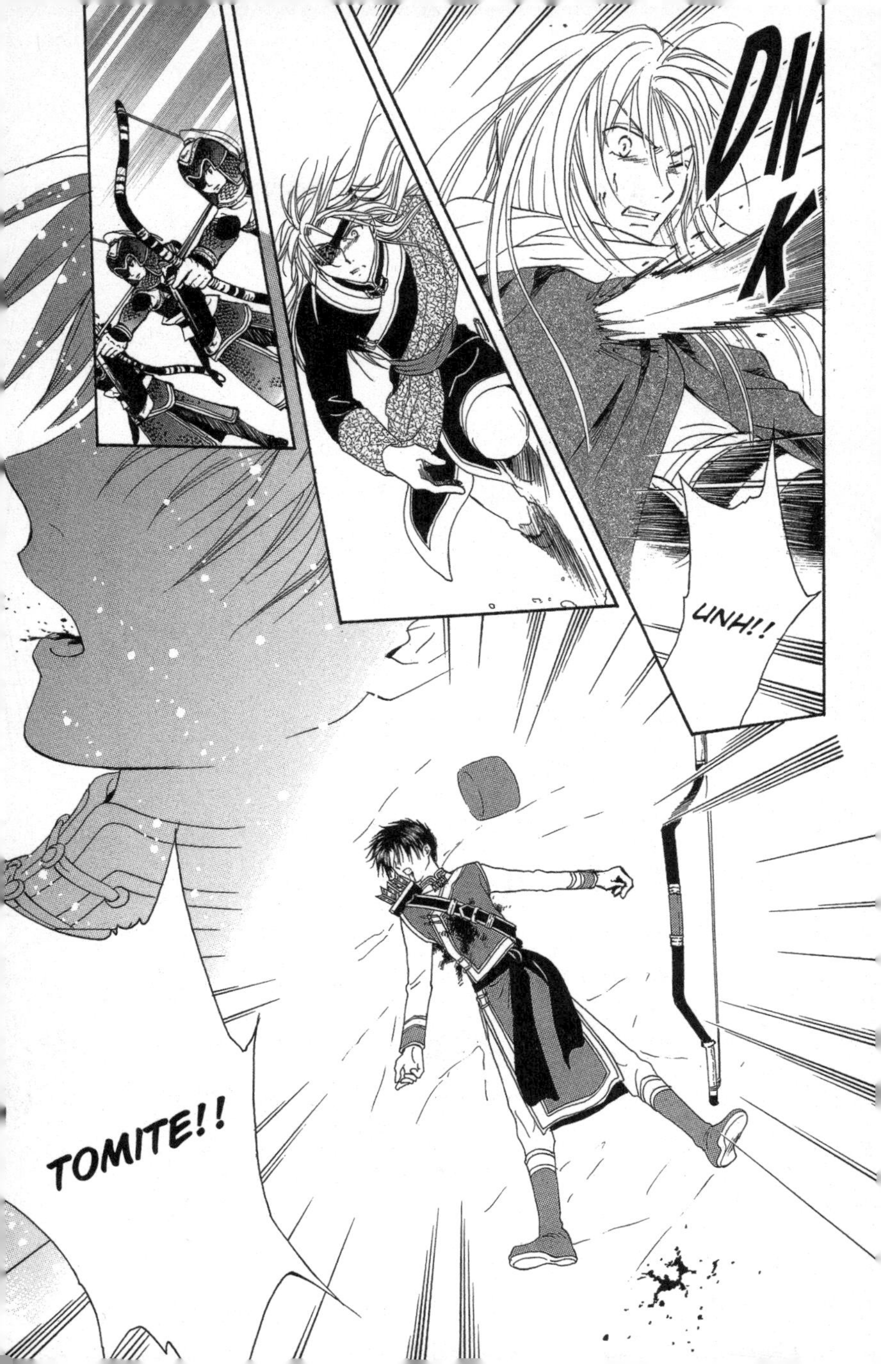
DNK
UNH!!
TOMITE!!

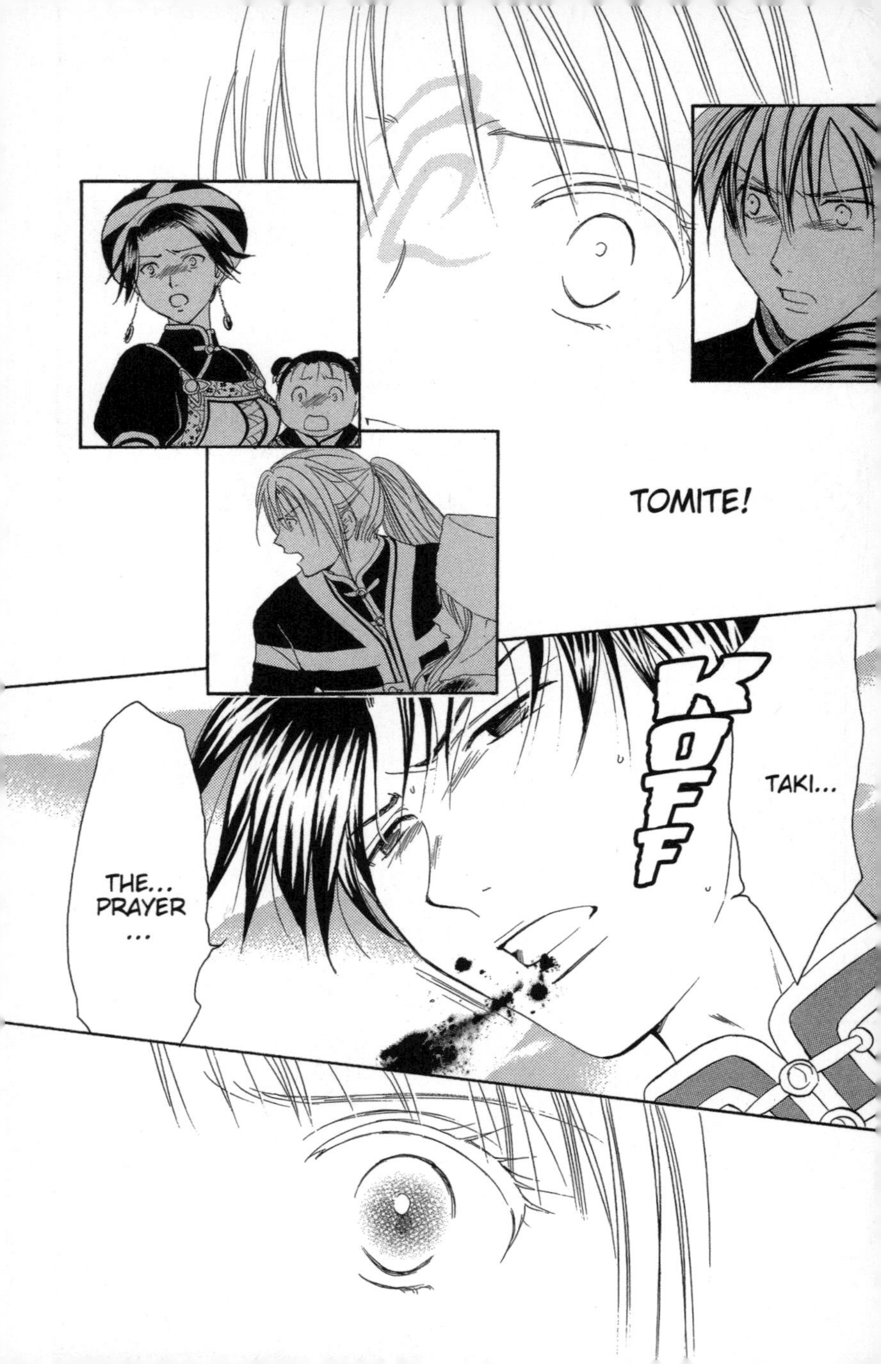
TOMITE!
KOFF
TAKI...
THE... PRAYER ...

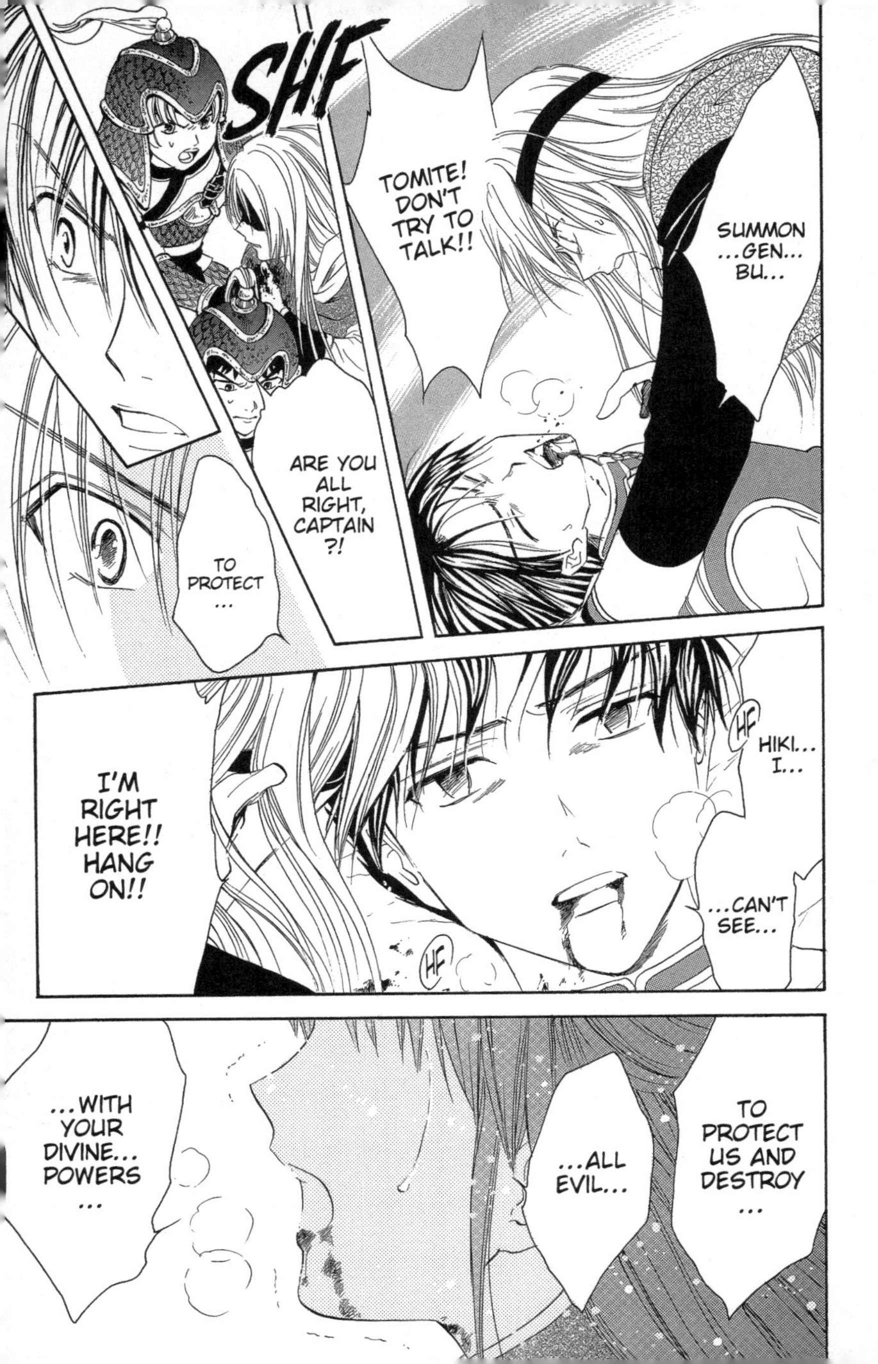
SUMMON ...GEN... BU...
TOMITE! DON'T TRY TO TALK!!
SHF
ARE YOU ALL RIGHT, CAPTAIN?!
TO PROTECT ...
HF
HIKI... I...
...CAN'T SEE...
HF
I'M RIGHT HERE!! HANG ON!!
TO PROTECT US AND DESTROY ...
...ALL EVIL...
...WITH YOUR DIVINE... POWERS ...

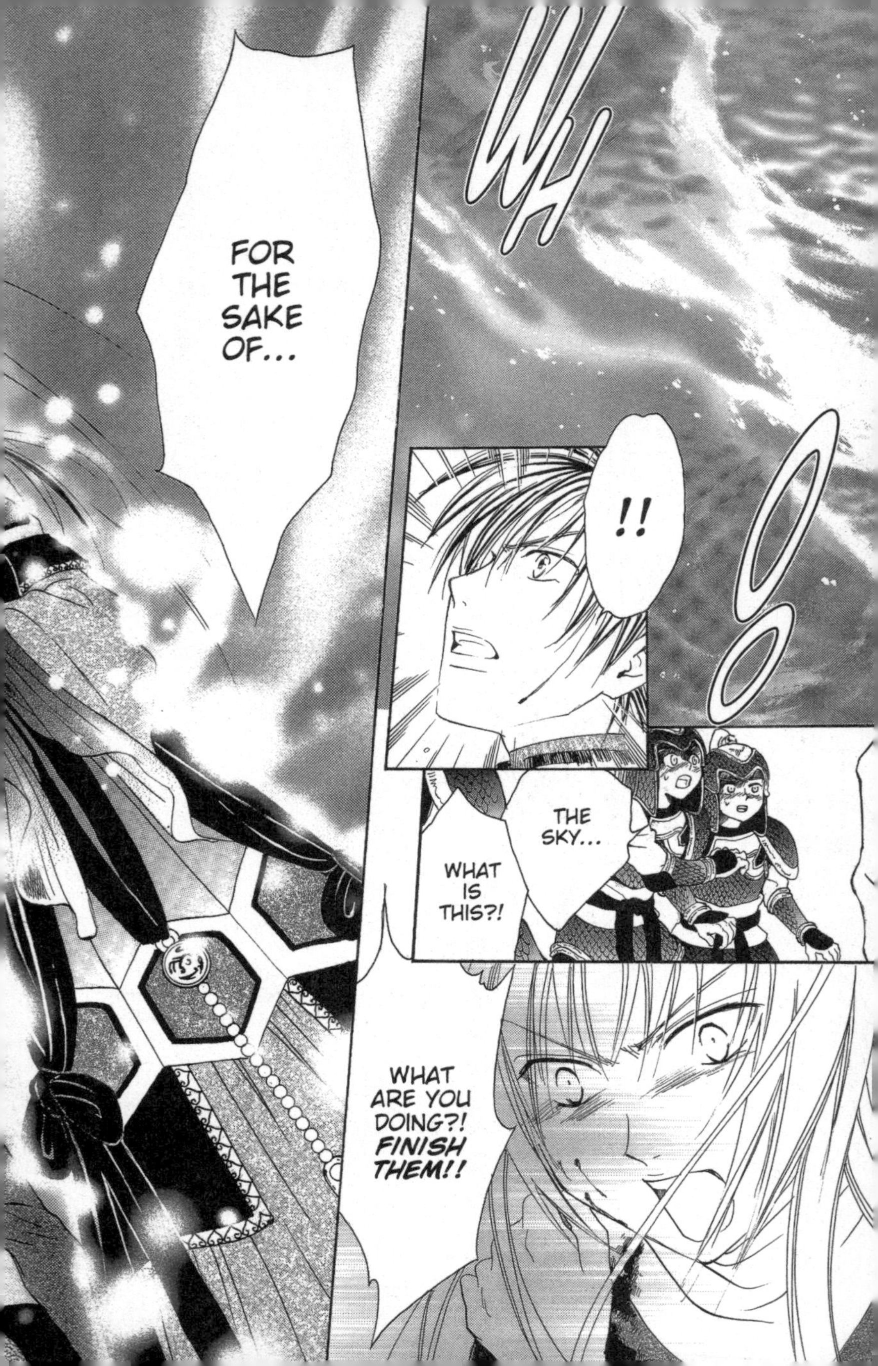
!!
THE SKY...
WHAT IS THIS?!
WHAT ARE YOU DOING?! ***FINISH THEM!!***
FOR THE SAKE OF...

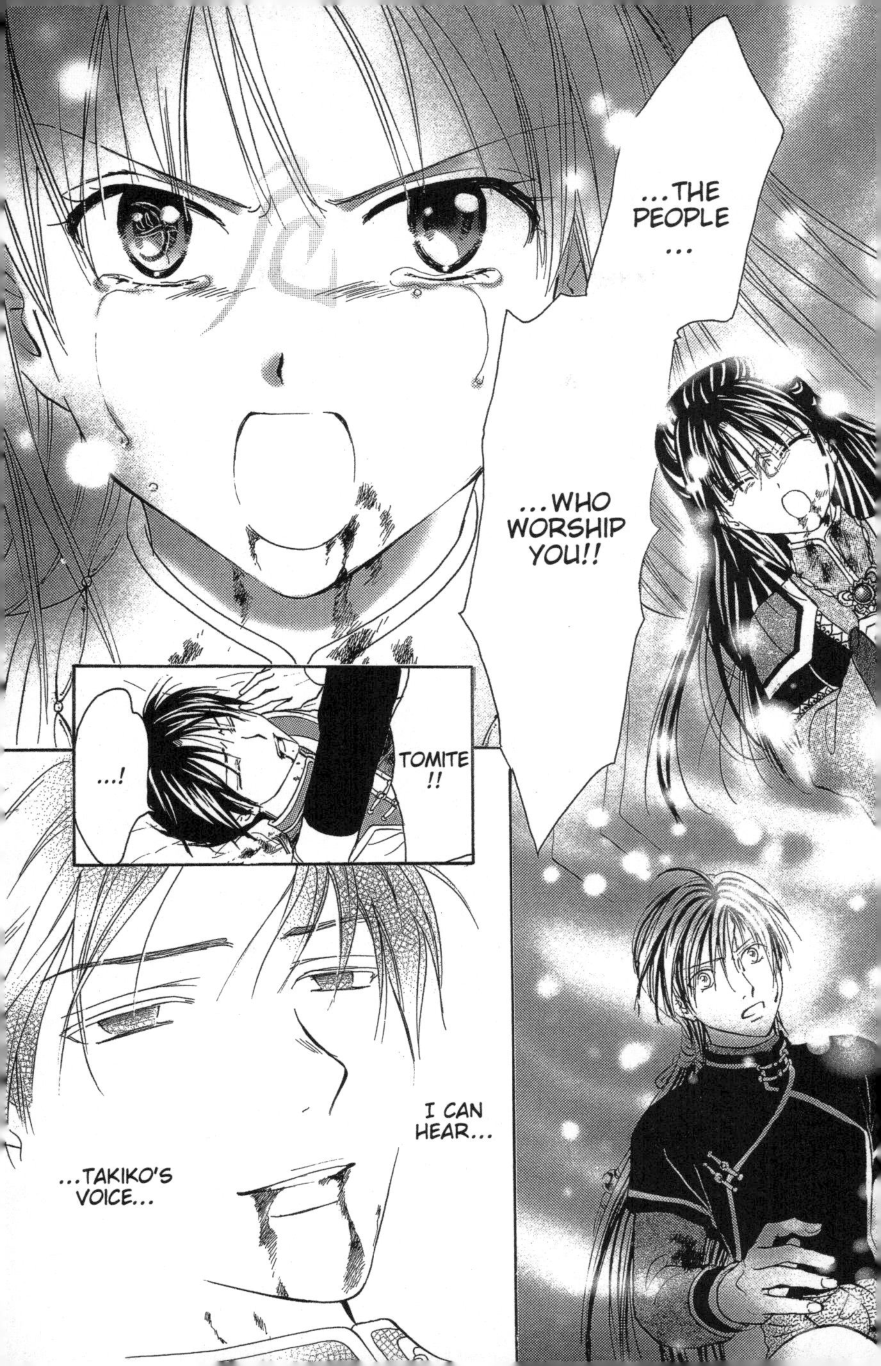
...THE PEOPLE ...
...WHO WORSHIP YOU!!
TOMITE !!
...!
I CAN HEAR...
...TAKIKO'S VOICE...

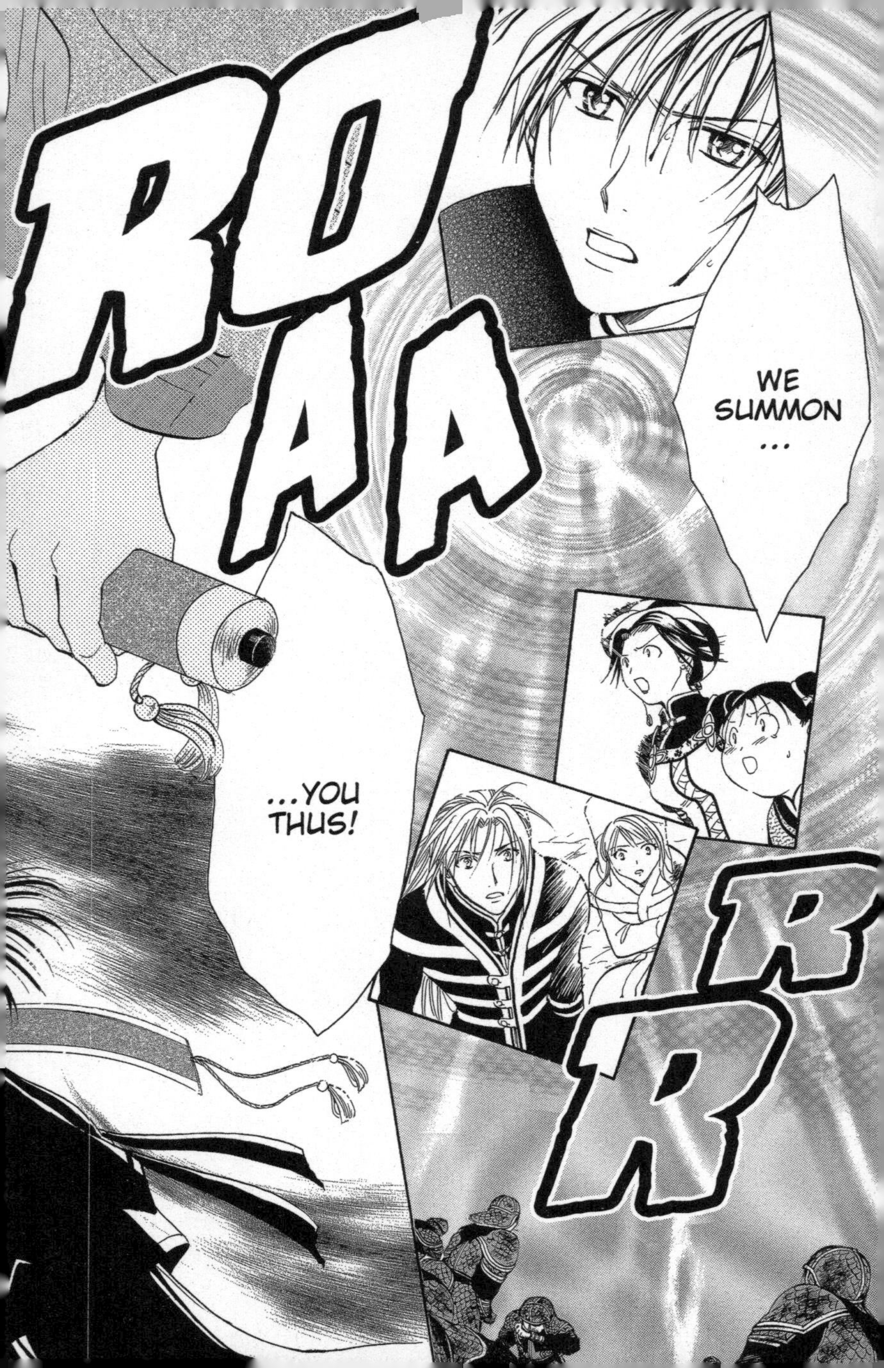
WE SUMMON ...
...YOU THUS!
ROAARR

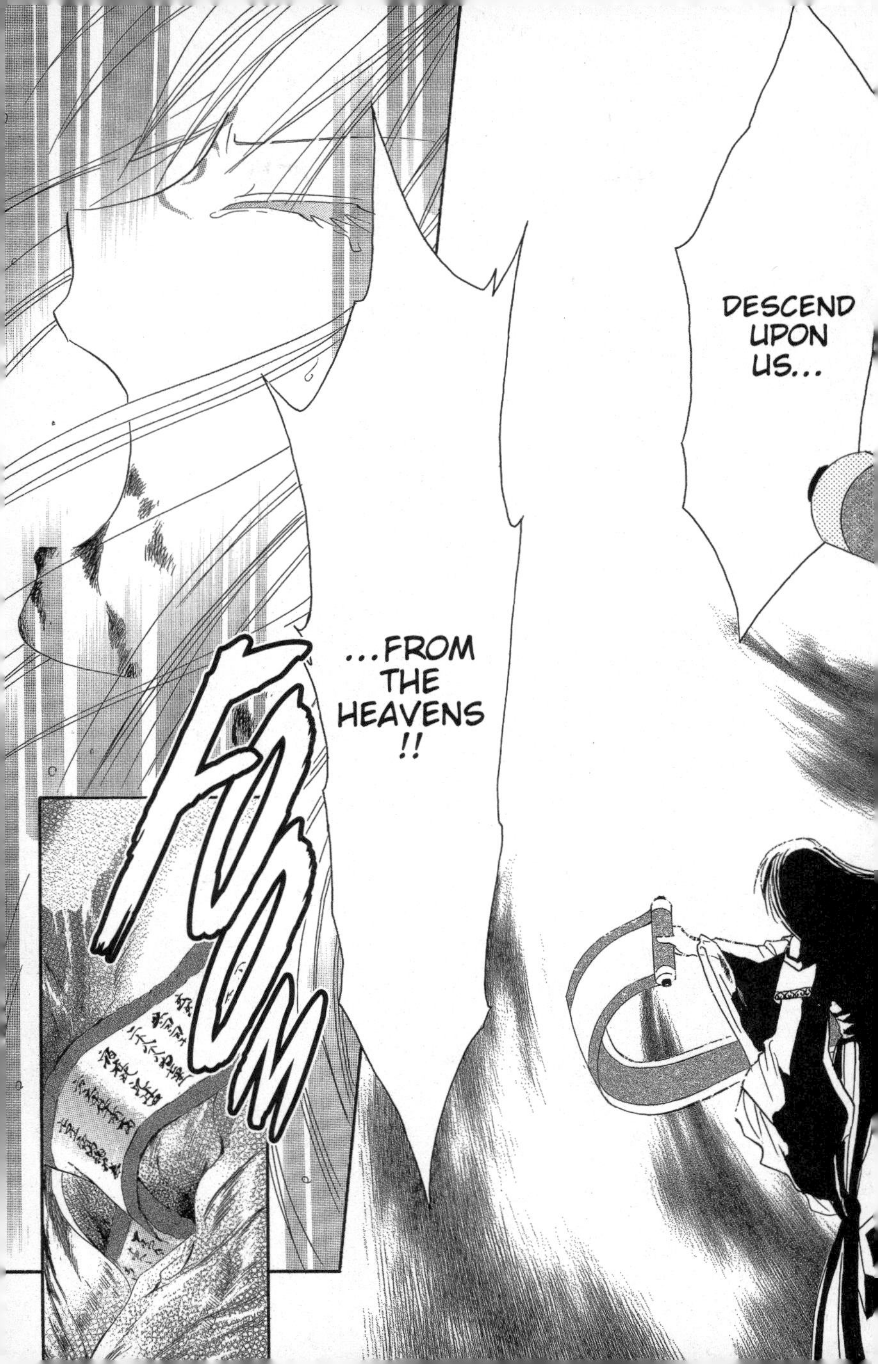
DESCEND UPON US...
...FROM THE HEAVENS !!

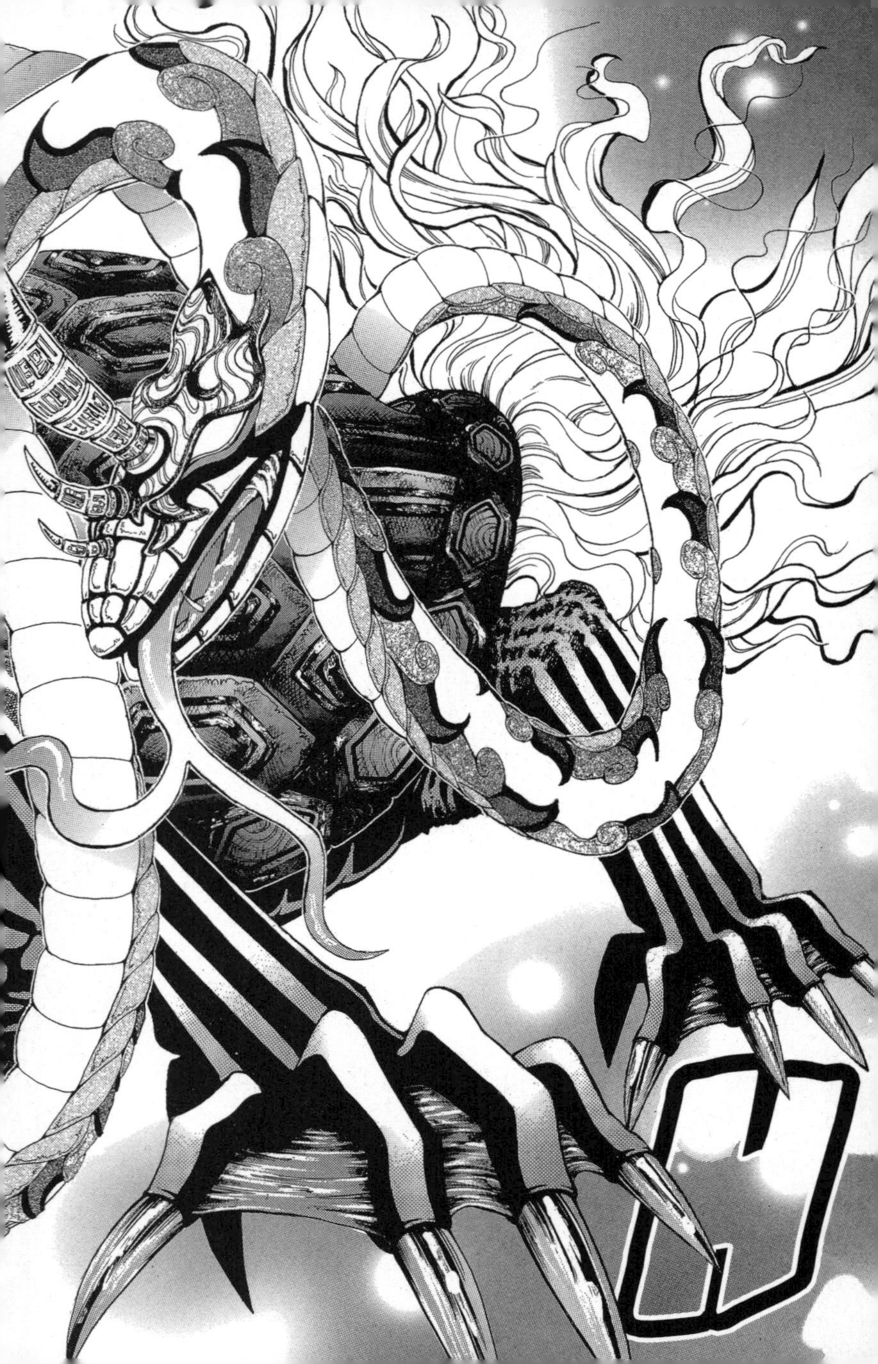

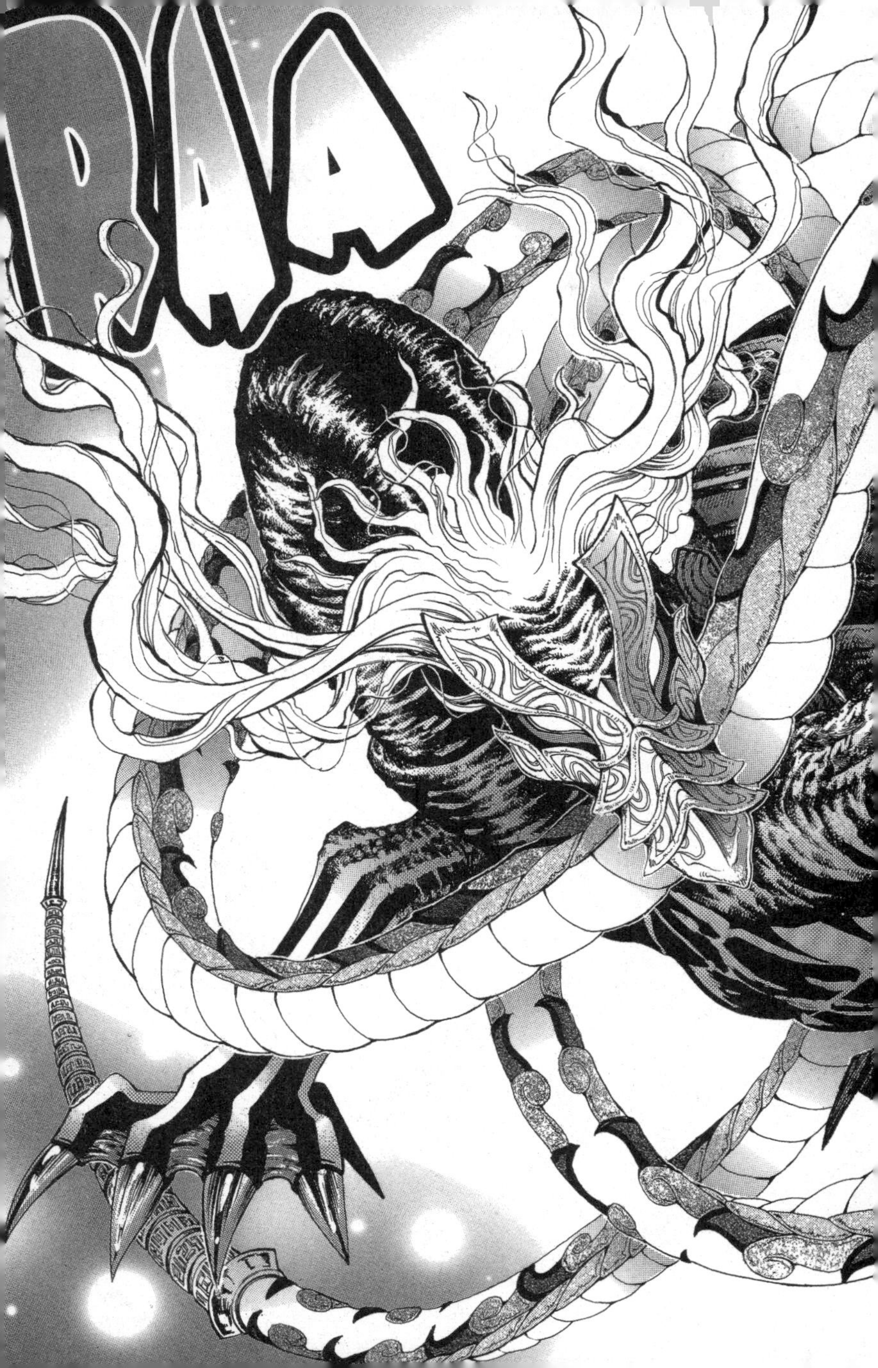
DAA

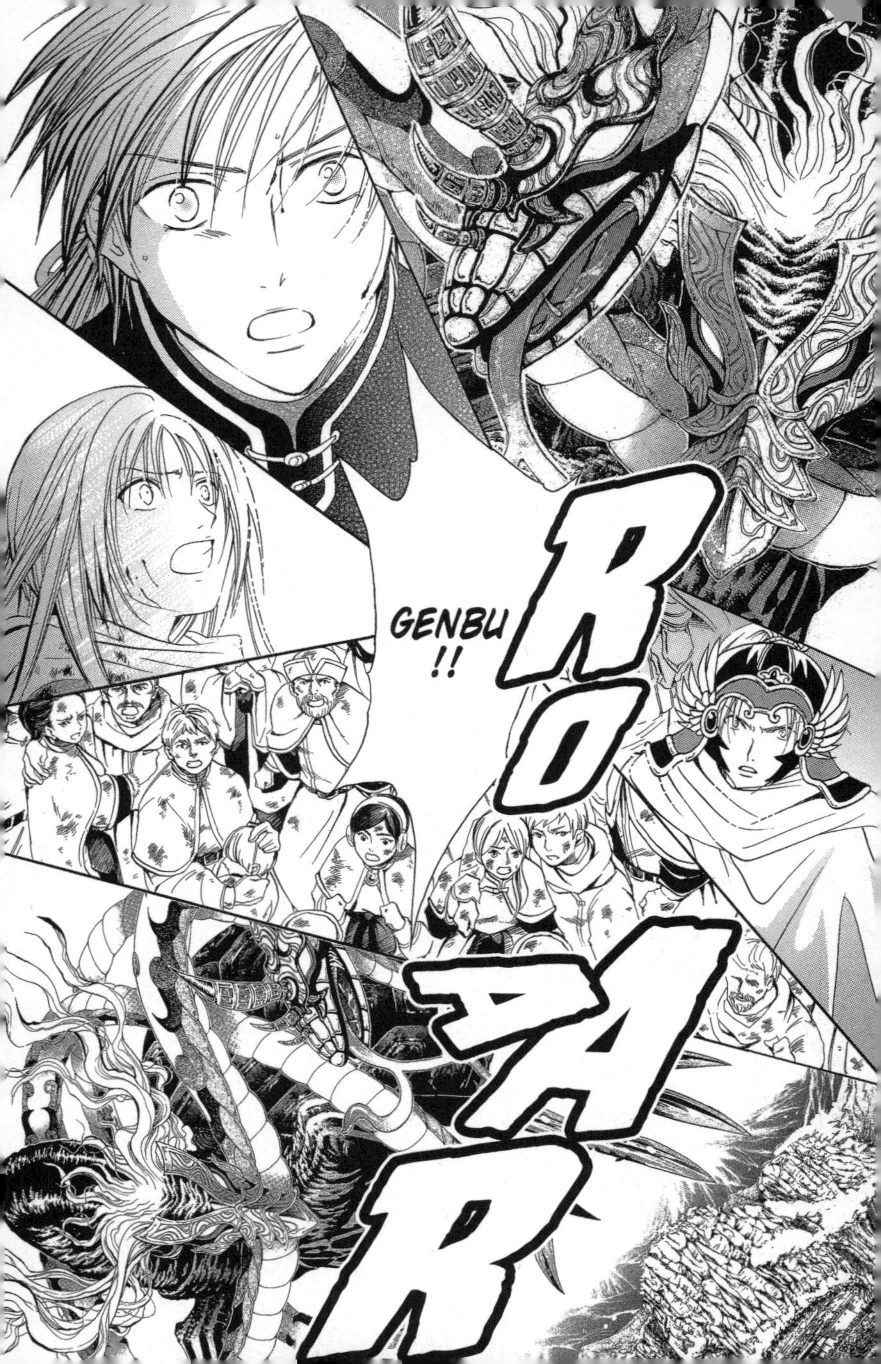
GENBU!!
ROAAR

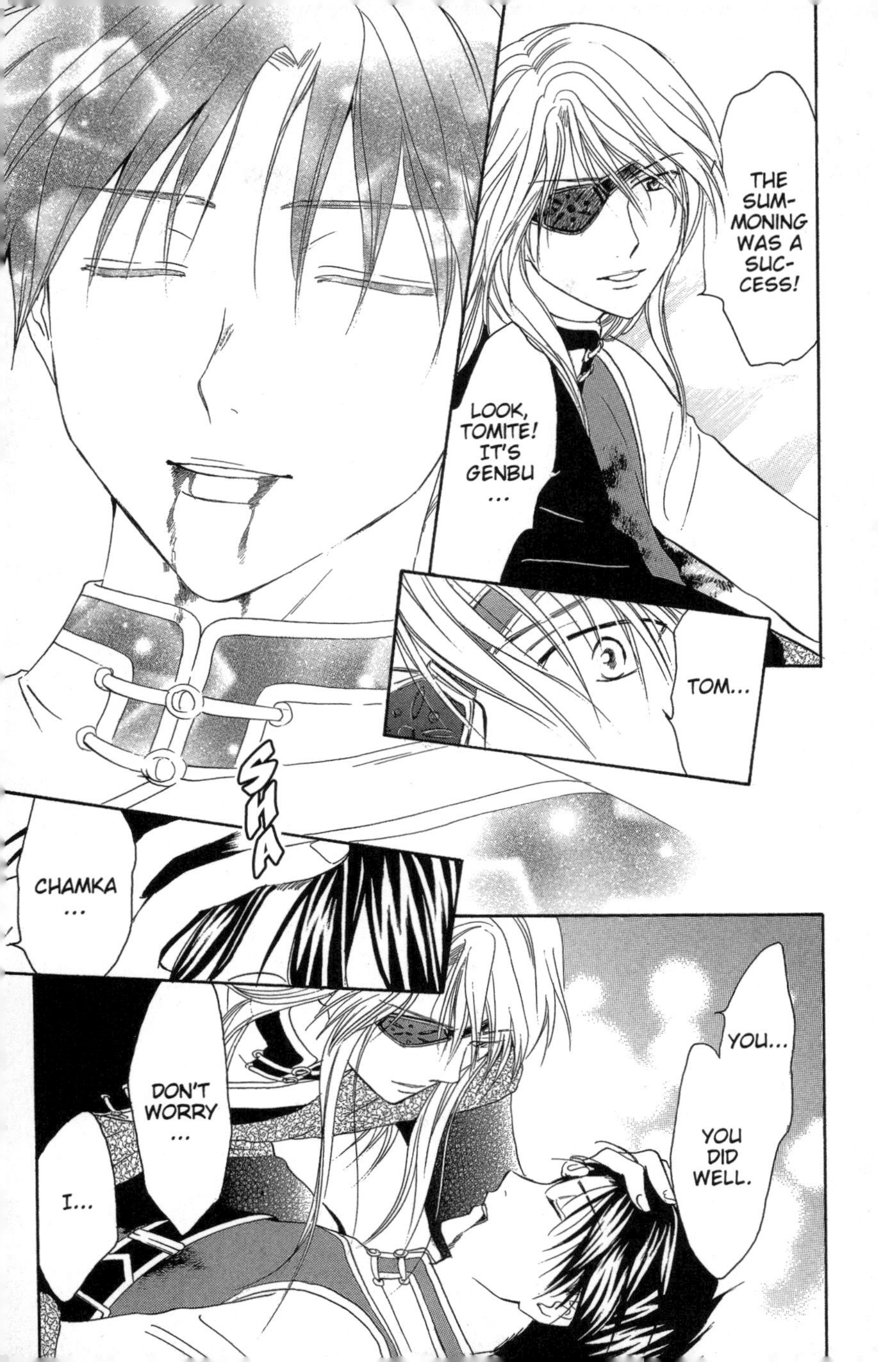
THE SUM-MONING WAS A SUC-CESS!
LOOK, TOMITE! IT'S GENBU ...
TOM...
SHA
CHAMKA ...
YOU...
YOU DID WELL.
DON'T WORRY ...
I...

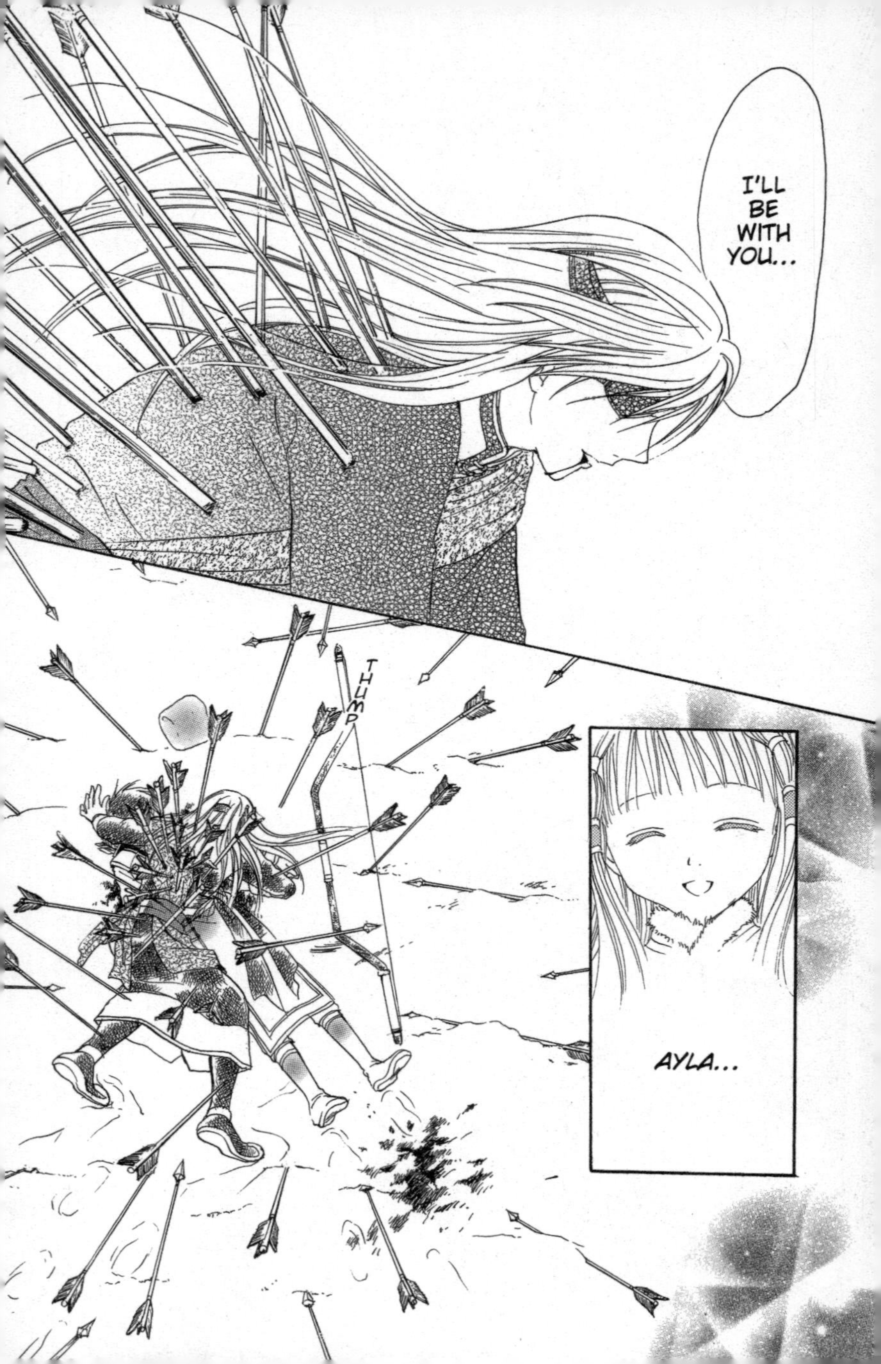
I'LL BE WITH YOU...
THUMP
AYLA...

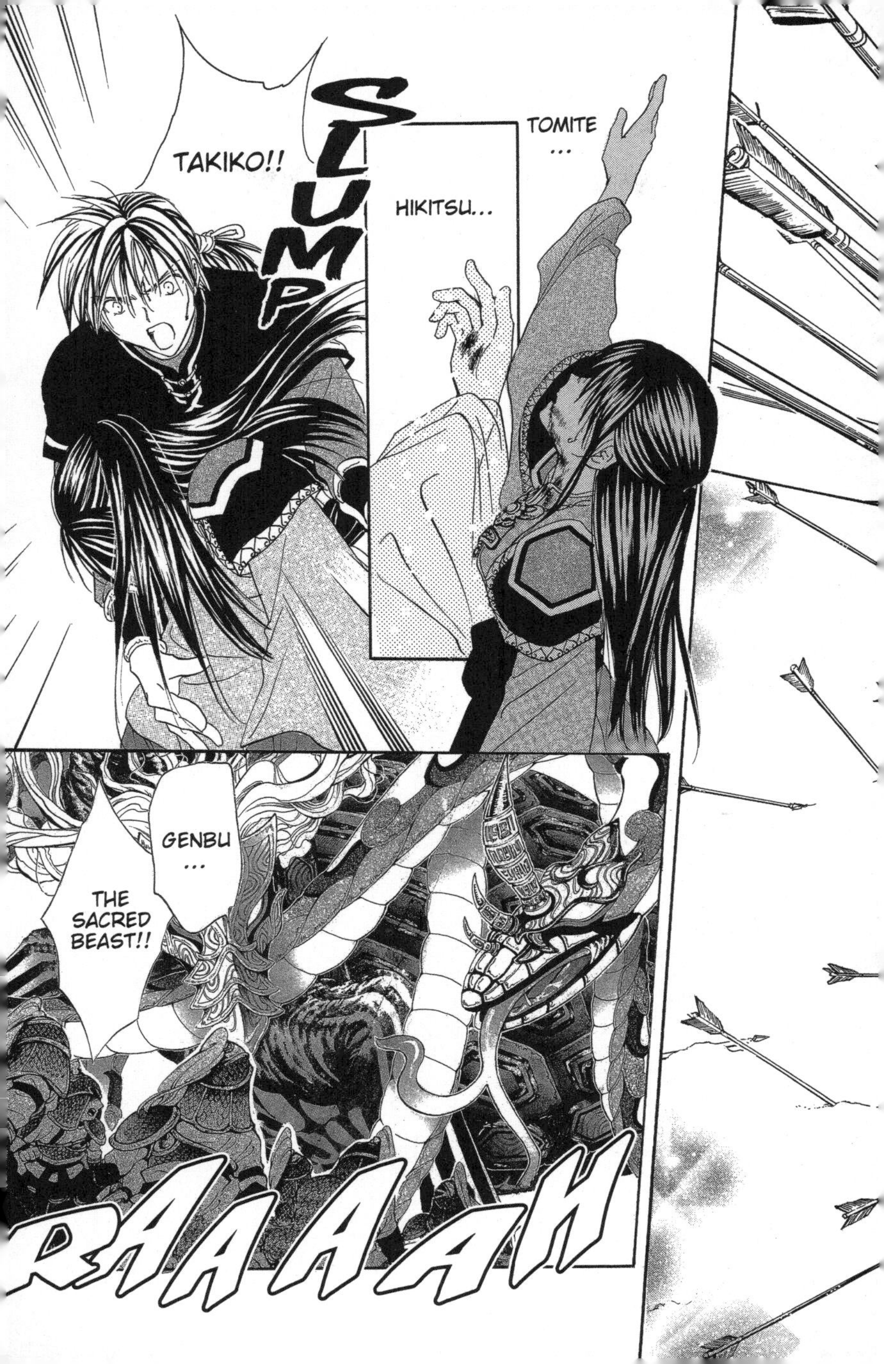
TOMITE ...
HIKITSU...
TAKIKO!!
SLUMP
GENBU ...
THE SACRED BEAST!!
RAAAAH

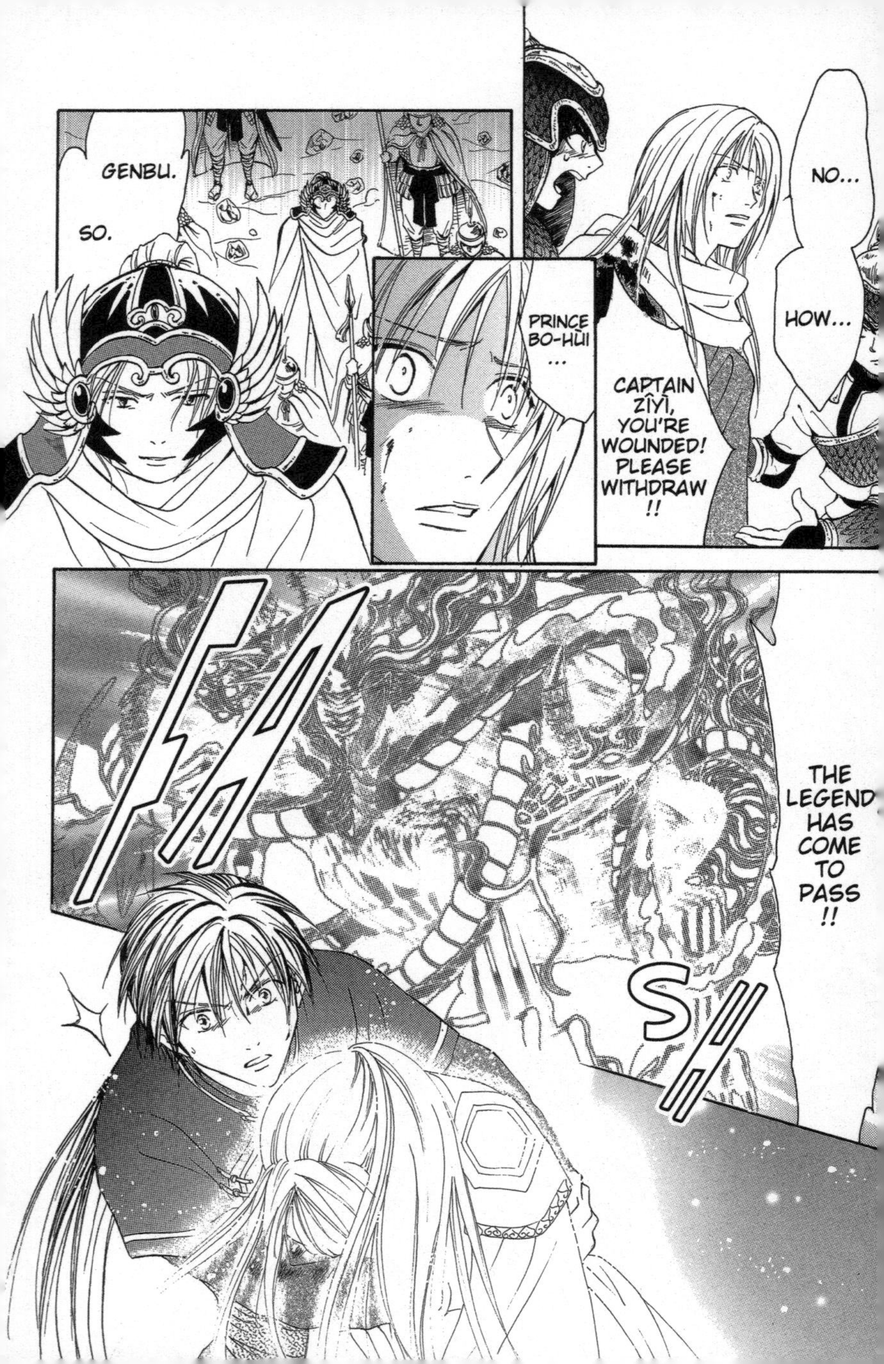
NO...
HOW...
CAPTAIN ZÎYÌ, YOU'RE WOUNDED! PLEASE WITHDRAW!!
PRINCE BO-HÙI...
GENBU.
SO.
THE LEGEND HAS COME TO PASS!!
S

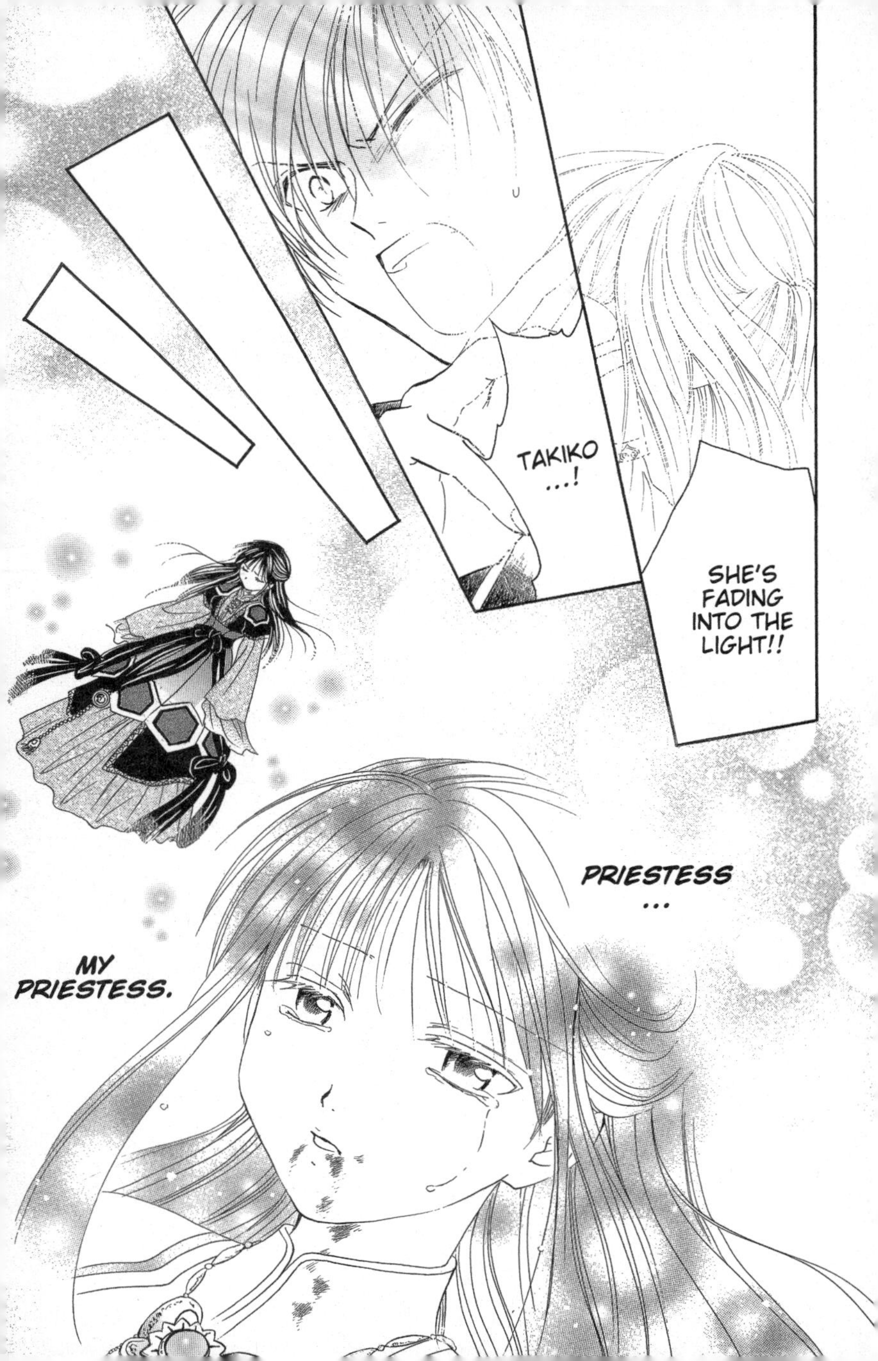
SHE'S FADING INTO THE LIGHT!!
TAKIKO ...!
PRIESTESS ...
MY PRIESTESS.

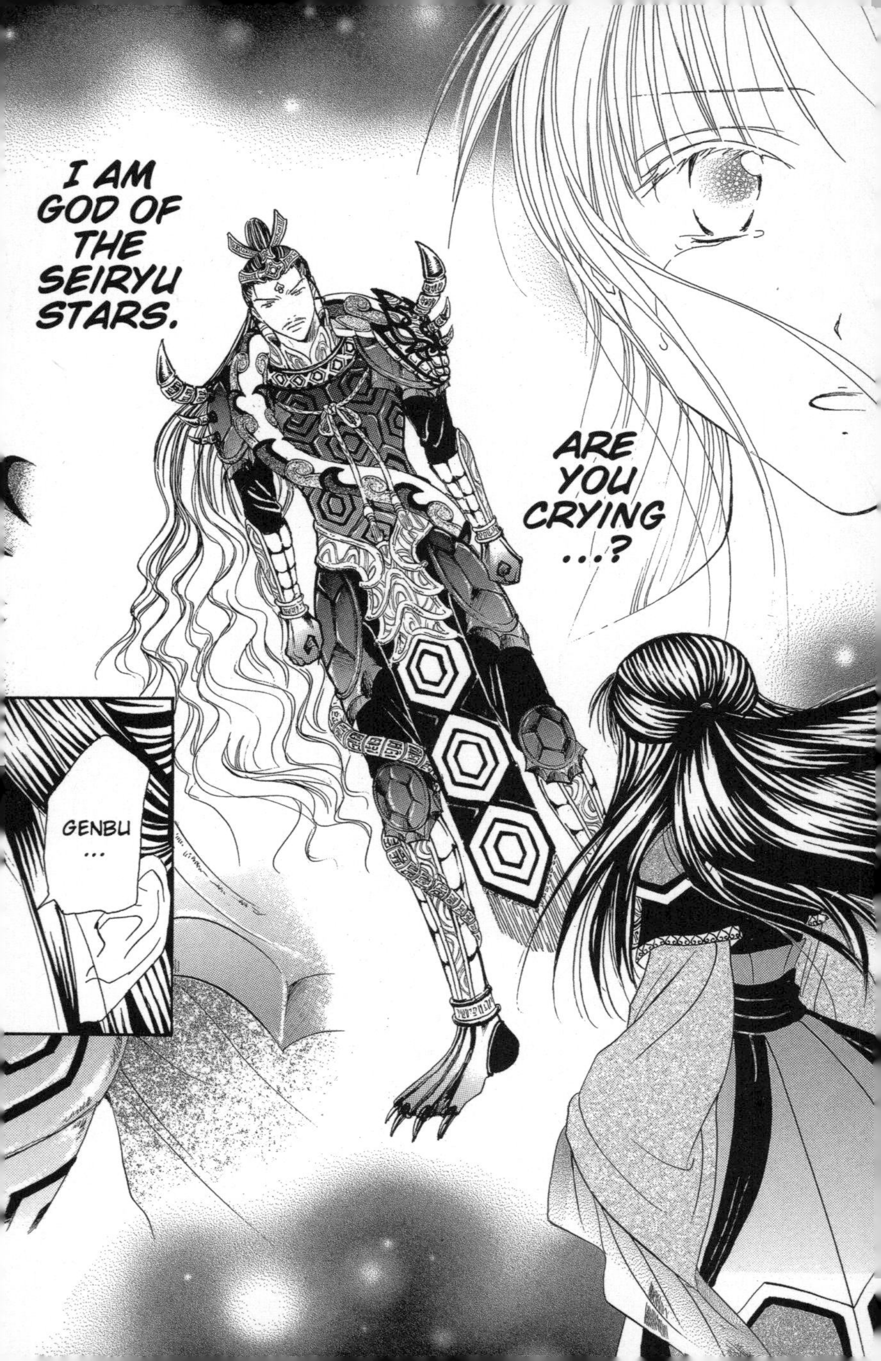
ARE YOU CRYING ...?
I AM GOD OF THE SEIRYU STARS.
GENBU ...

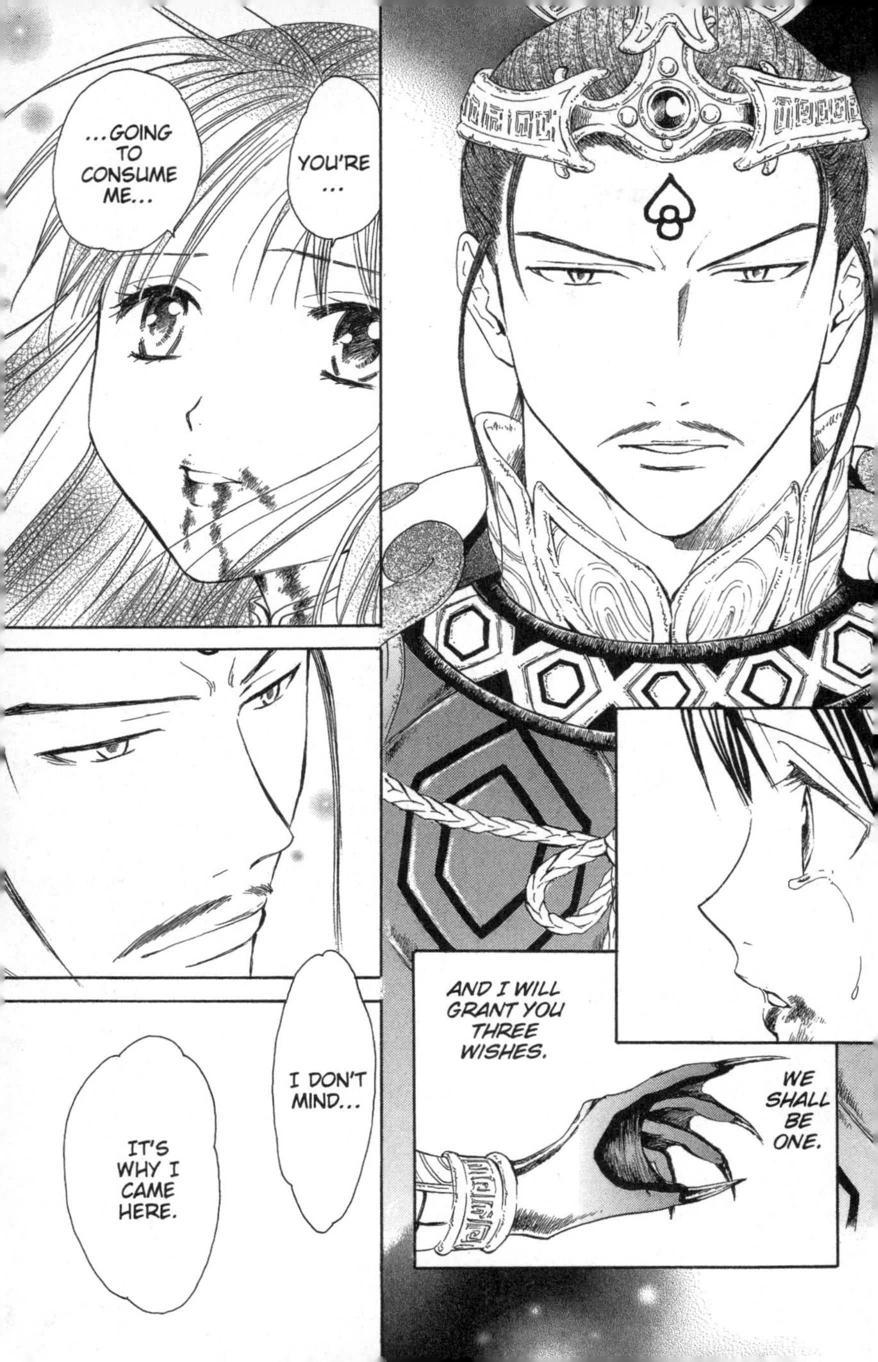
AND I WILL GRANT YOU THREE WISHES.
WE SHALL BE ONE.
YOU'RE ...
...GOING TO CONSUME ME...
I DON'T MIND...
IT'S WHY I CAME HERE.

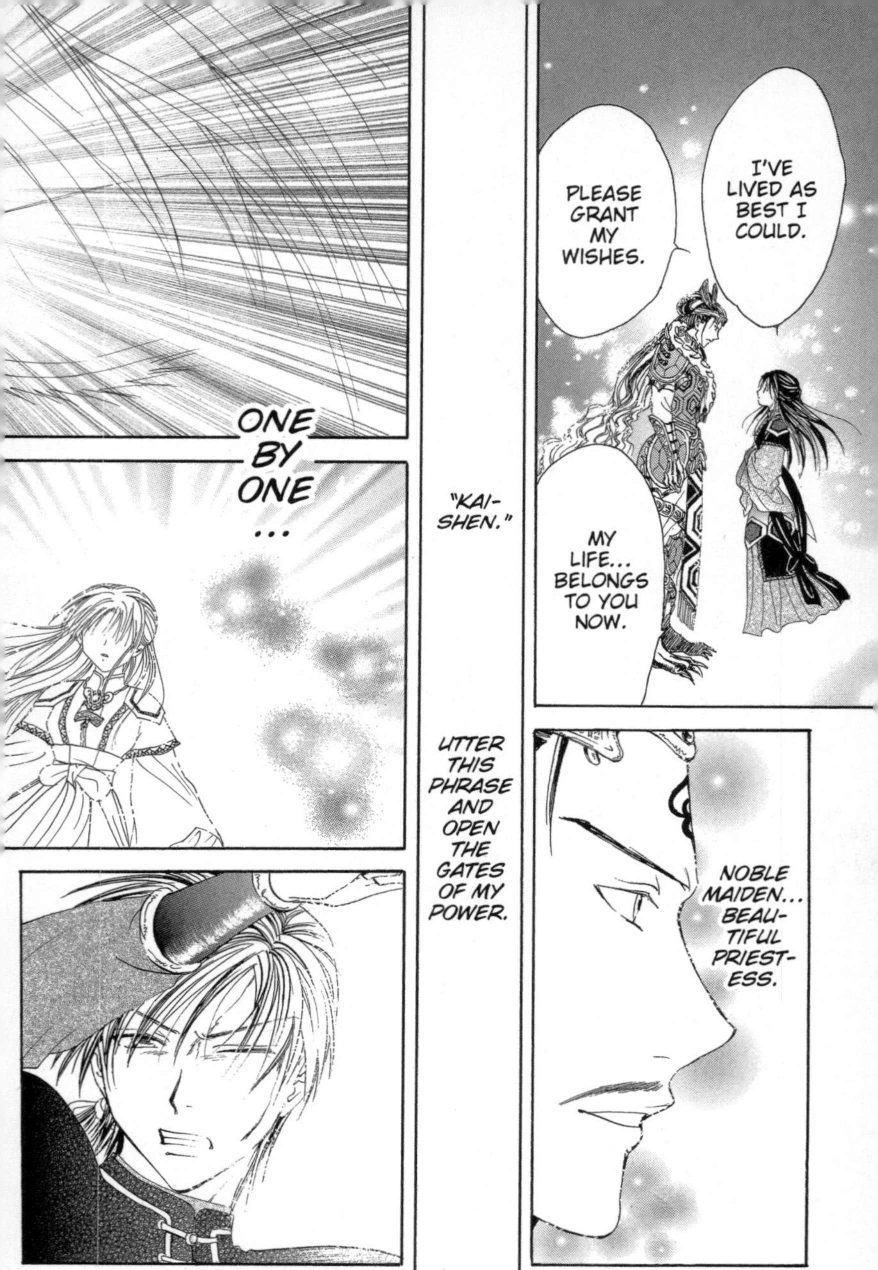
I'VE LIVED AS BEST I COULD.
PLEASE GRANT MY WISHES.
MY LIFE... BELONGS TO YOU NOW.
NOBLE MAIDEN... BEAUTIFUL PRIESTESS.
"KAI-SHEN."
UTTER THIS PHRASE AND OPEN THE GATES OF MY POWER.
ONE BY ONE...

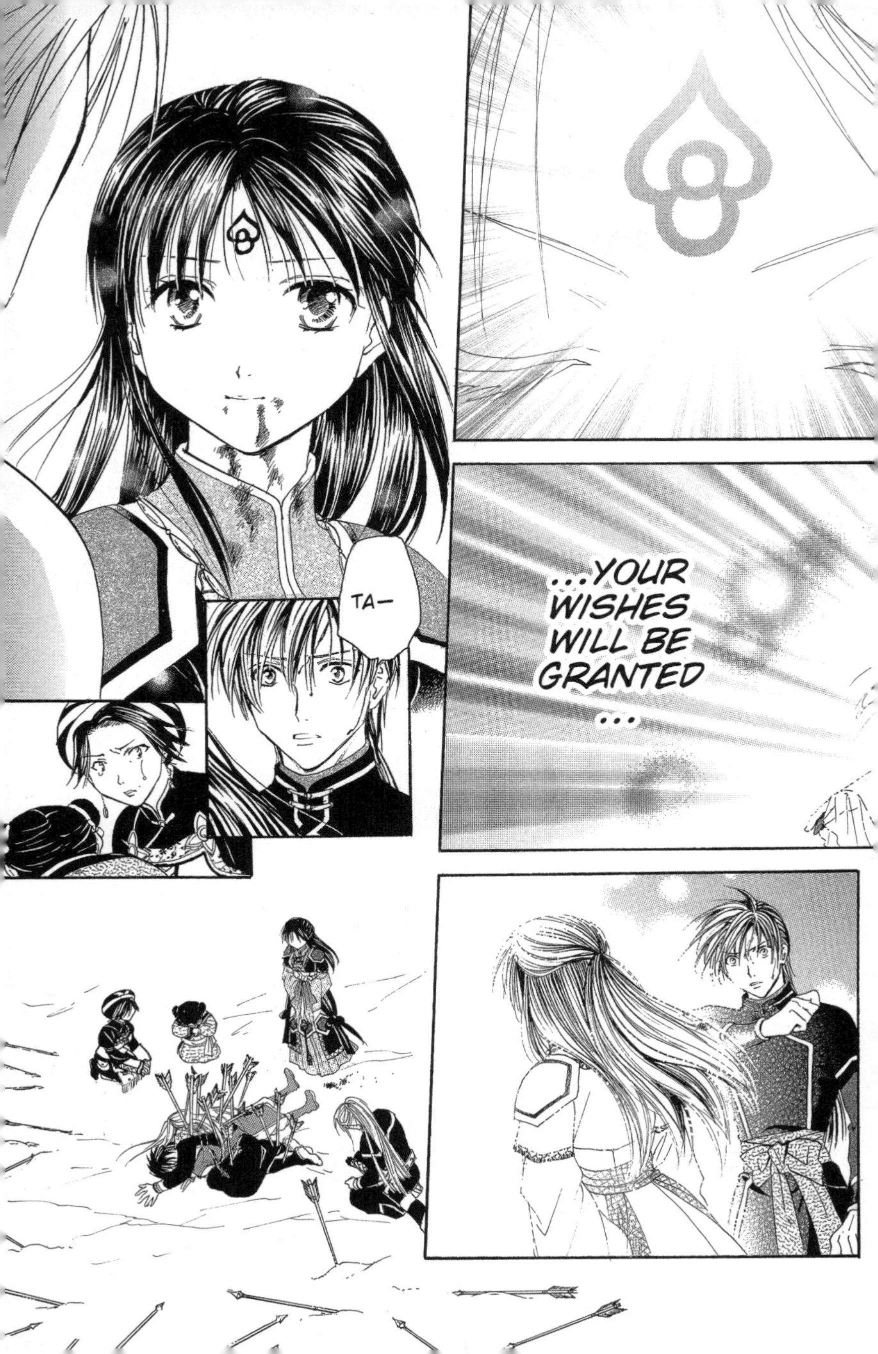
TA—
...YOUR WISHES WILL BE GRANTED...

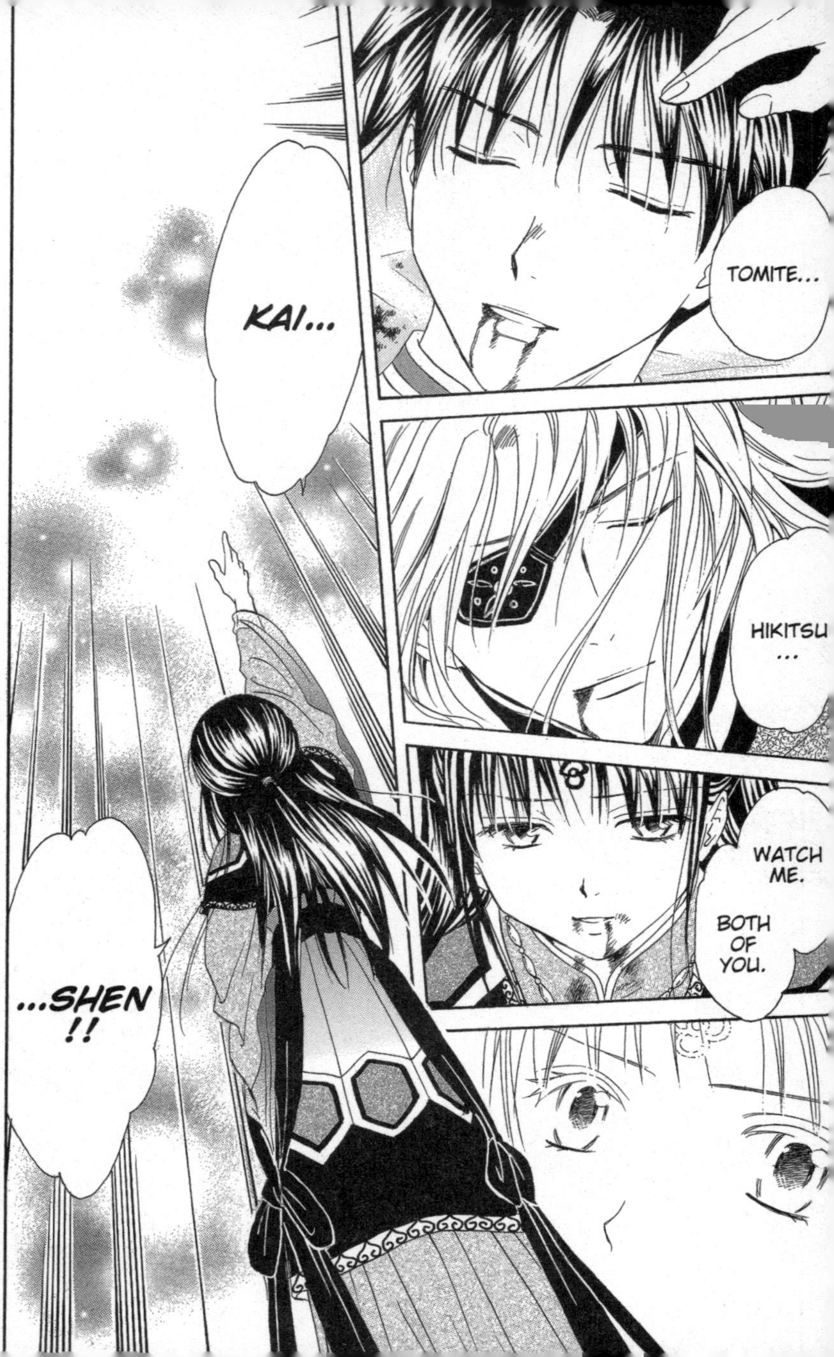
TOMITE...
HIKITSU ...
WATCH ME.
BOTH OF YOU.
KAI...
...SHEN !!

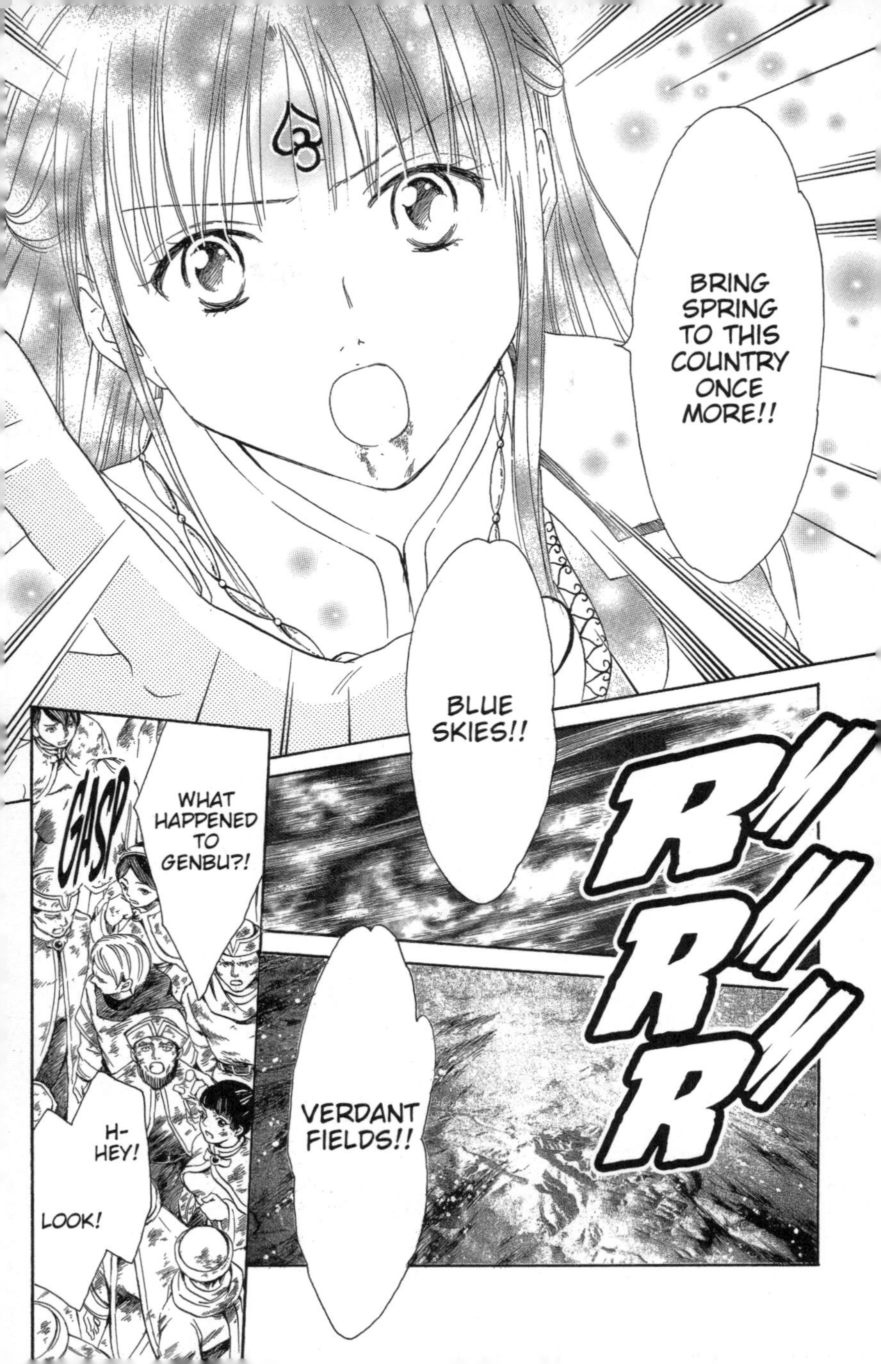
BRING SPRING TO THIS COUNTRY ONCE MORE!!
BLUE SKIES!!
VERDANT FIELDS!!
RRRR
WHAT HAPPENED TO GENBU?!
GASP
H-HEY!
LOOK!

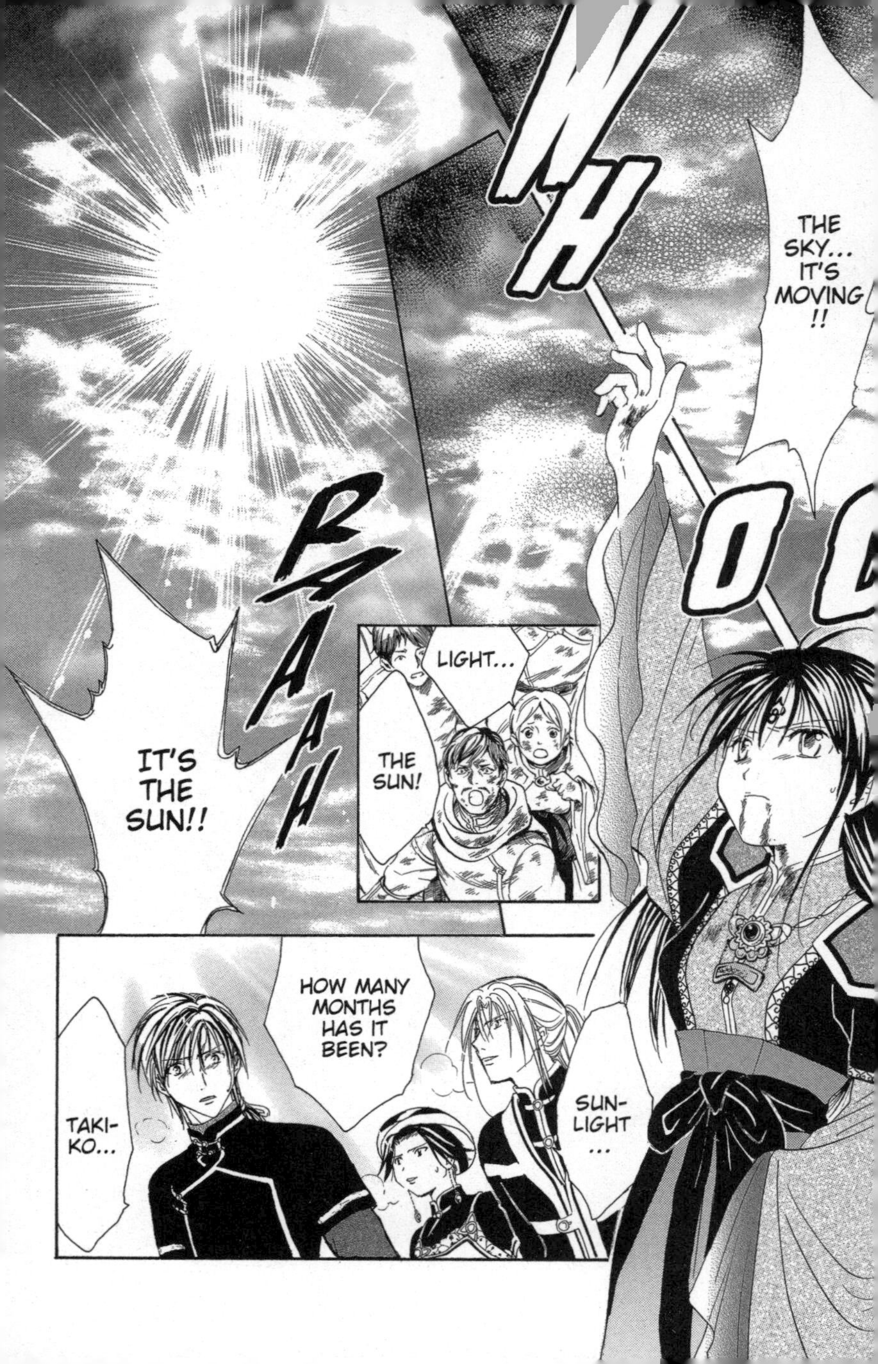
WHH
OOO
THE SKY... IT'S MOVING!!
RAAAH
IT'S THE SUN!!
LIGHT...
THE SUN!
SUN-LIGHT...
HOW MANY MONTHS HAS IT BEEN?
TAKI-KO...

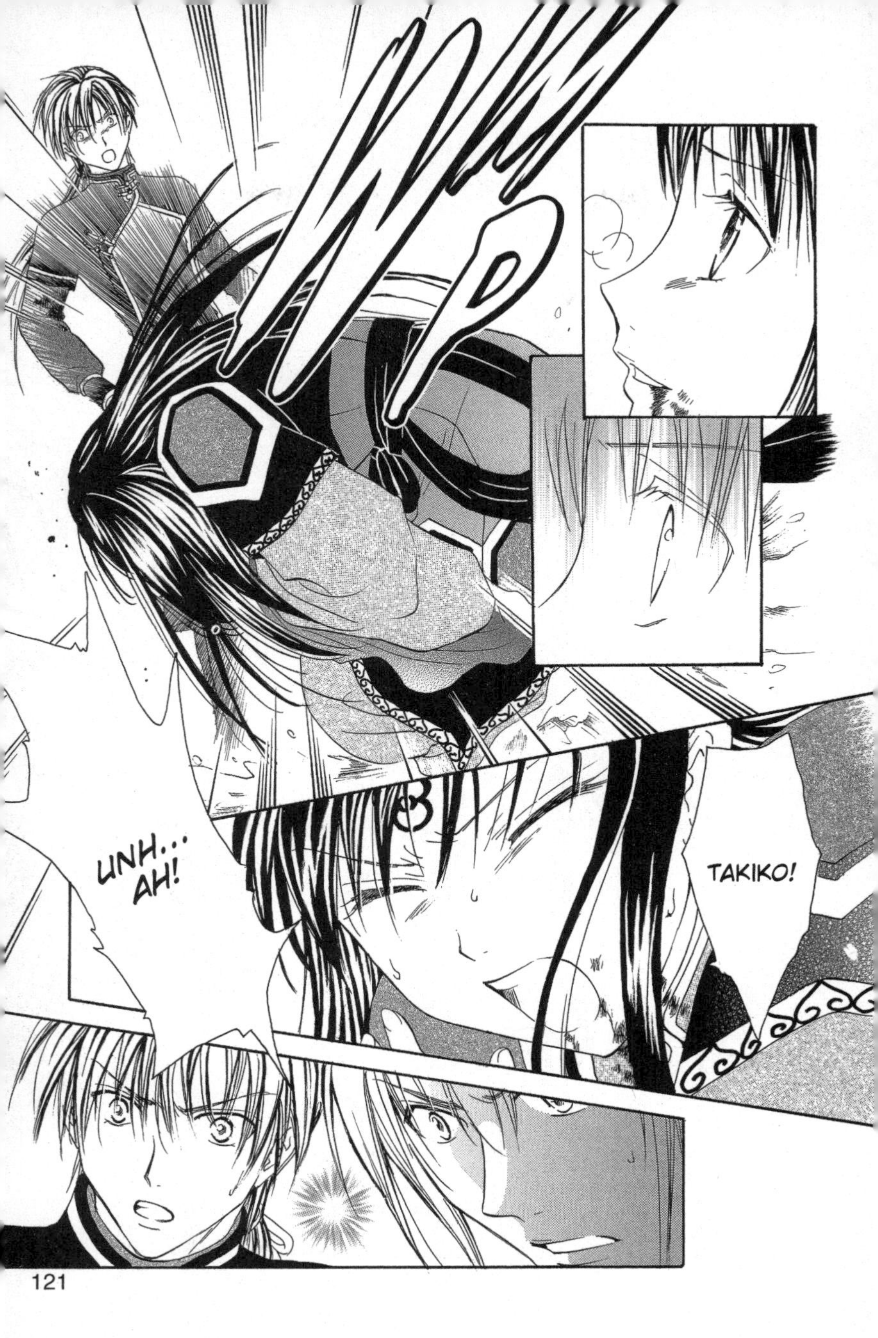
WHIP
TAKIKO!
UNH... AH!

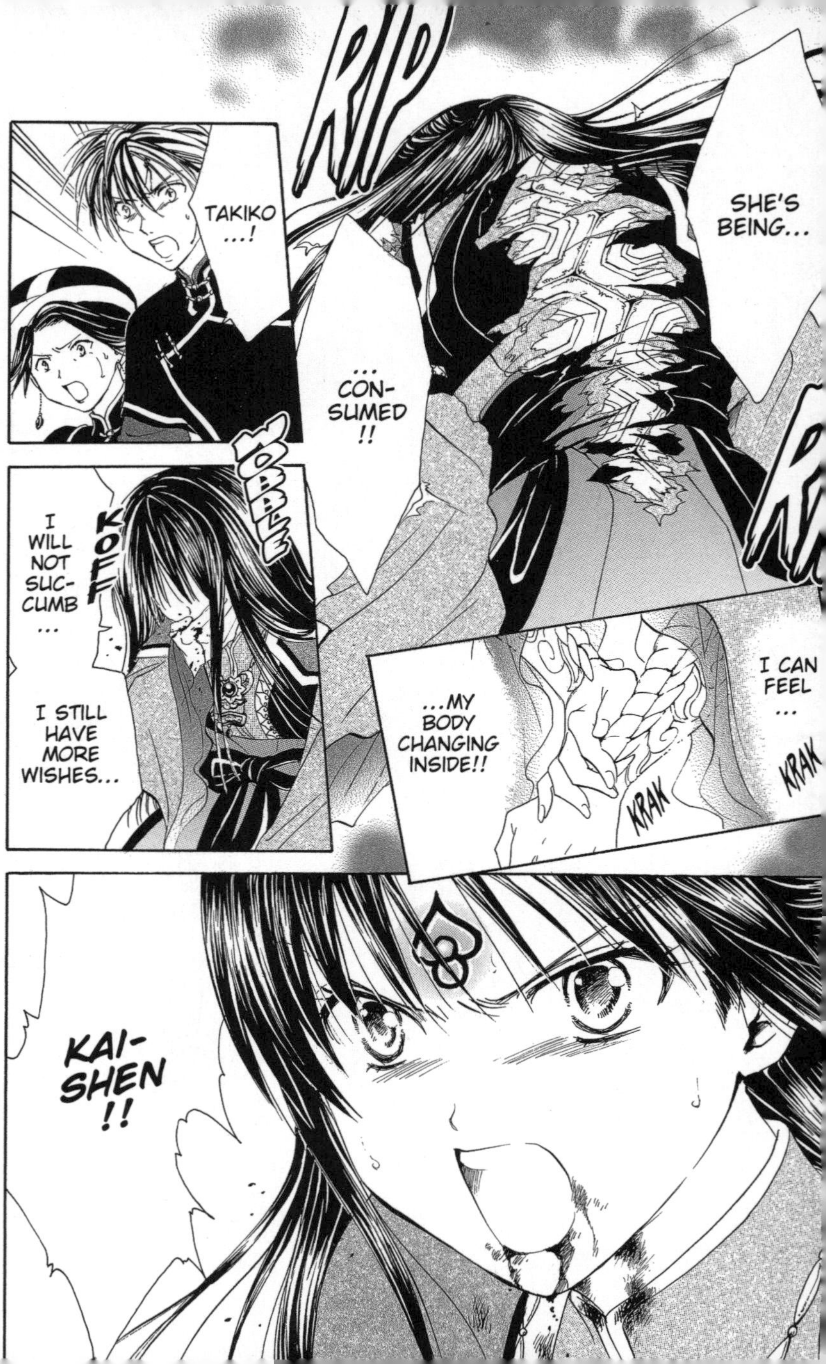
RIP
SHE'S BEING...
...CON-SUMED!!
TAKIKO...!
WOBBLE
KOFF
I WILL NOT SUC-CUMB...
I STILL HAVE MORE WISHES...
I CAN FEEL...
...MY BODY CHANGING INSIDE!!
KRAK
KRAK
KAI-SHEN!!

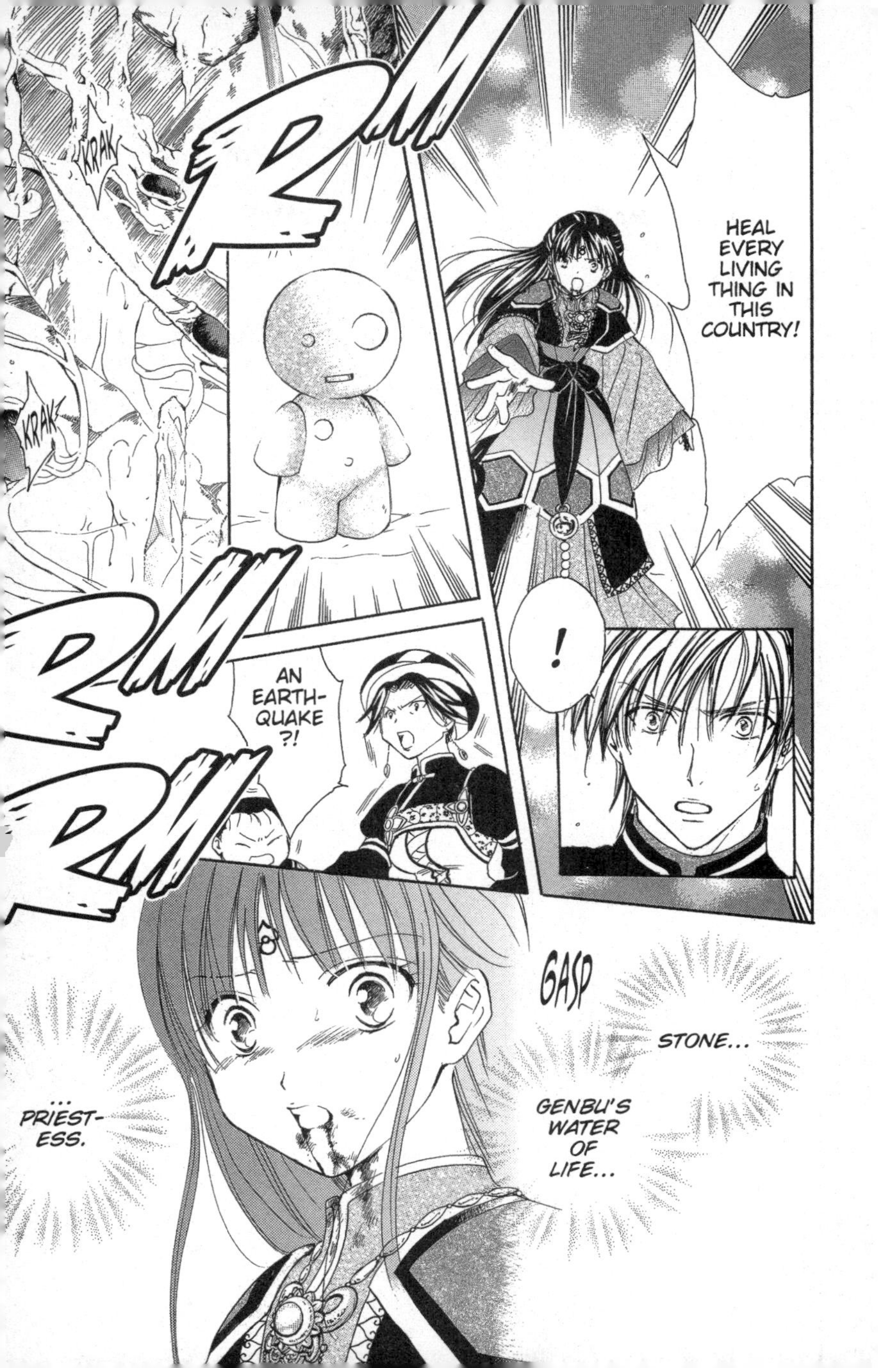
HEAL EVERY LIVING THING IN THIS COUNTRY!
KRAK
KRAK
!
AN EARTH-QUAKE?!
GASP
STONE...
GENBU'S WATER OF LIFE...
... PRIEST-ESS.

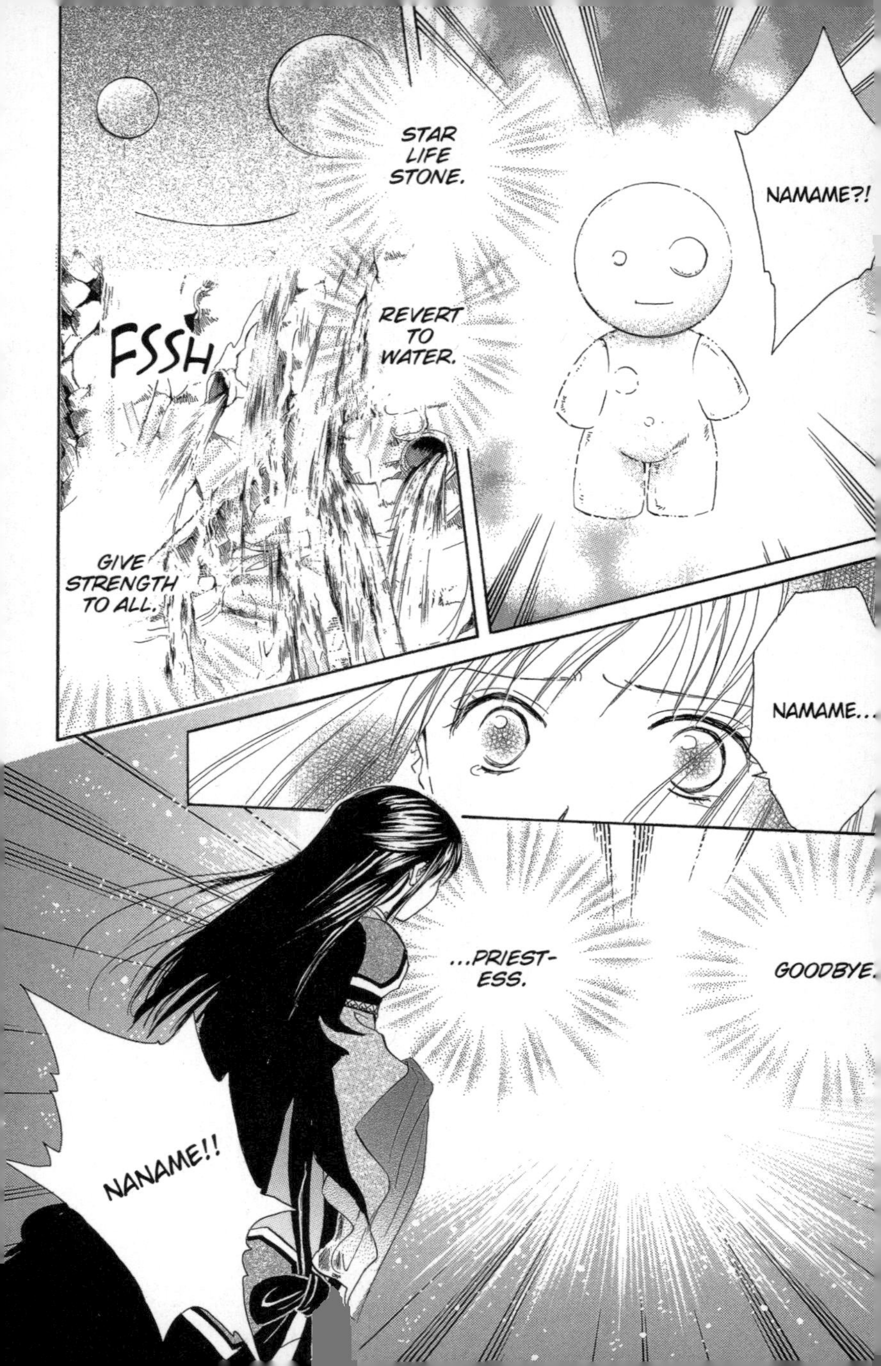
NAMAME?!
STAR LIFE STONE.
REVERT TO WATER.
FSSH
GIVE STRENGTH TO ALL.
NAMAME...
GOODBYE.
...PRIEST-ESS.
NANAME!!

FINAL CHAPTER:
LOVE THAT LASTS A HUNDRED YEARS
HER SECOND WISH WAS TO HEAL EVERY LIVING THING IN THE COUNTRY.
STAR LIFE STONE, REVERT TO WATER OF LIFE.
HELP OTHERS, AS THE PRIESTESS DOES.
THANK YOU, PRIESTESS.
NAMAME ...!
RM
AN EARTH-QUAKE ?!
KOFF KOFF
RM

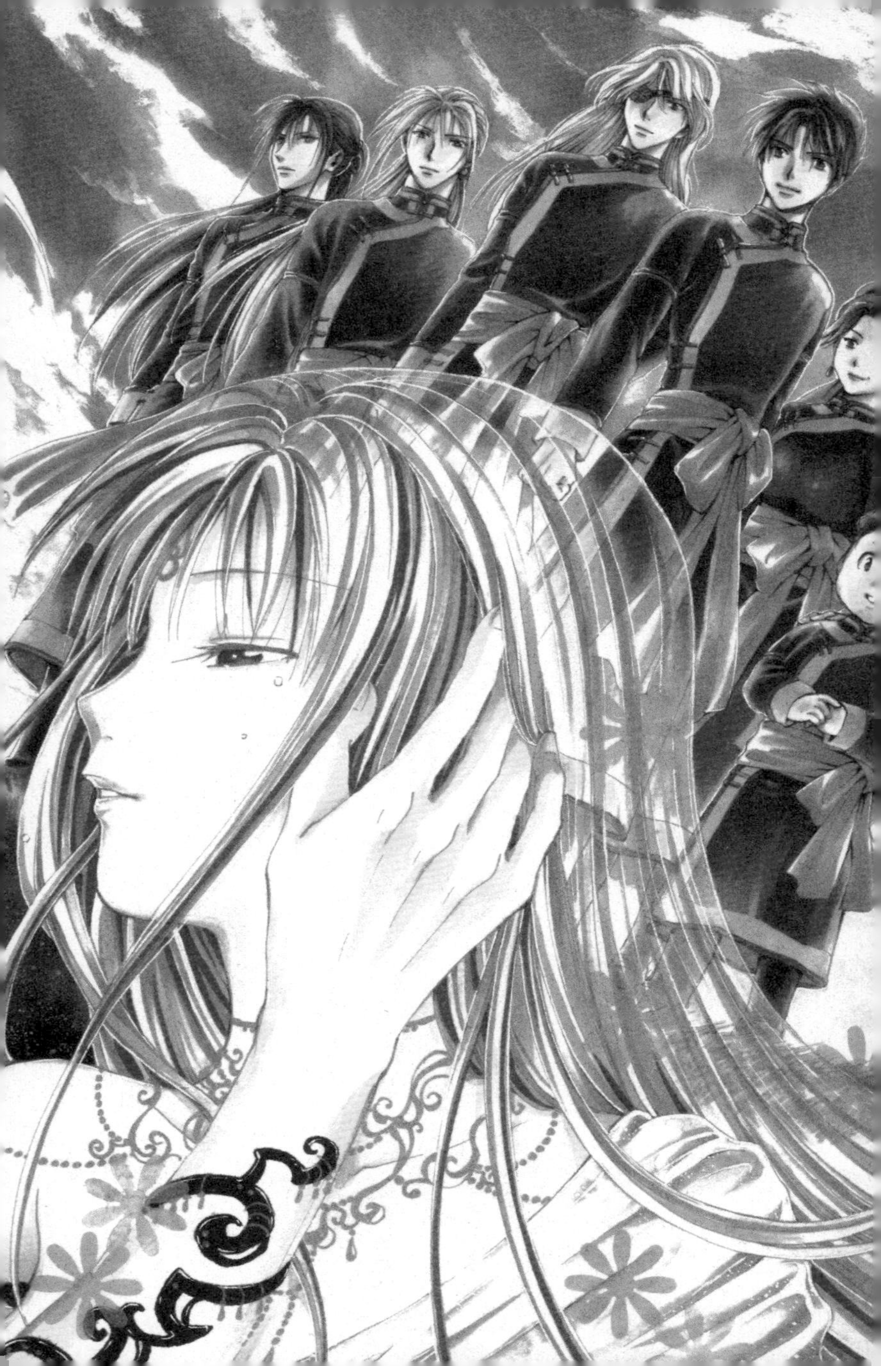

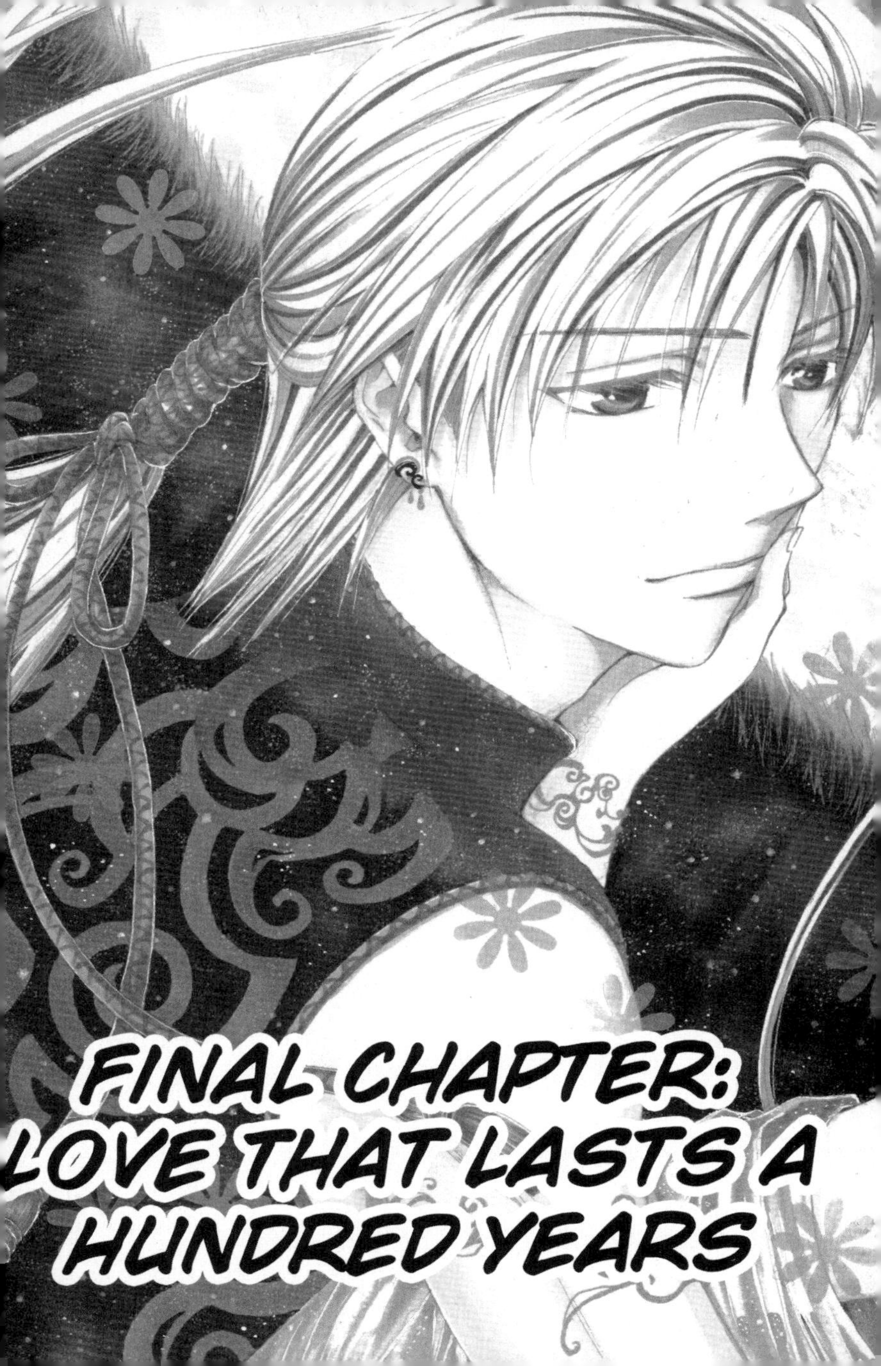
FINAL CHAPTER:
LOVE THAT LASTS A
HUNDRED YEARS

FUSHIGI YÛGI:
GENBU KAIDEN

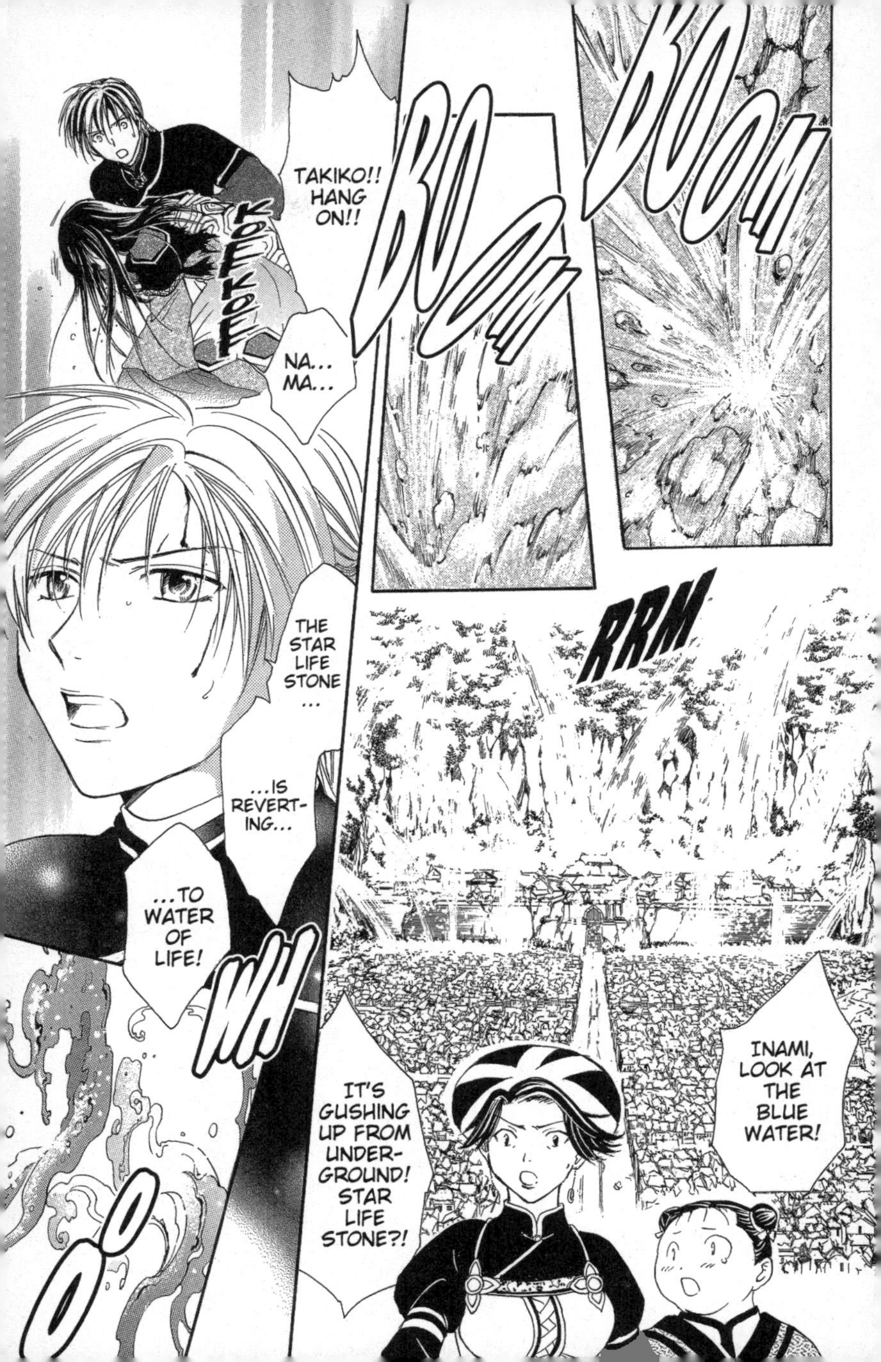
BOOM
BOOM
RRM
INAMI, LOOK AT THE BLUE WATER!
IT'S GUSHING UP FROM UNDERGROUND! STAR LIFE STONE?!
TAKIKO!! HANG ON!!
KOFF KOFF
NA... MA...
THE STAR LIFE STONE...
...IS REVERT-ING...
...TO WATER OF LIFE!
WH
OOO

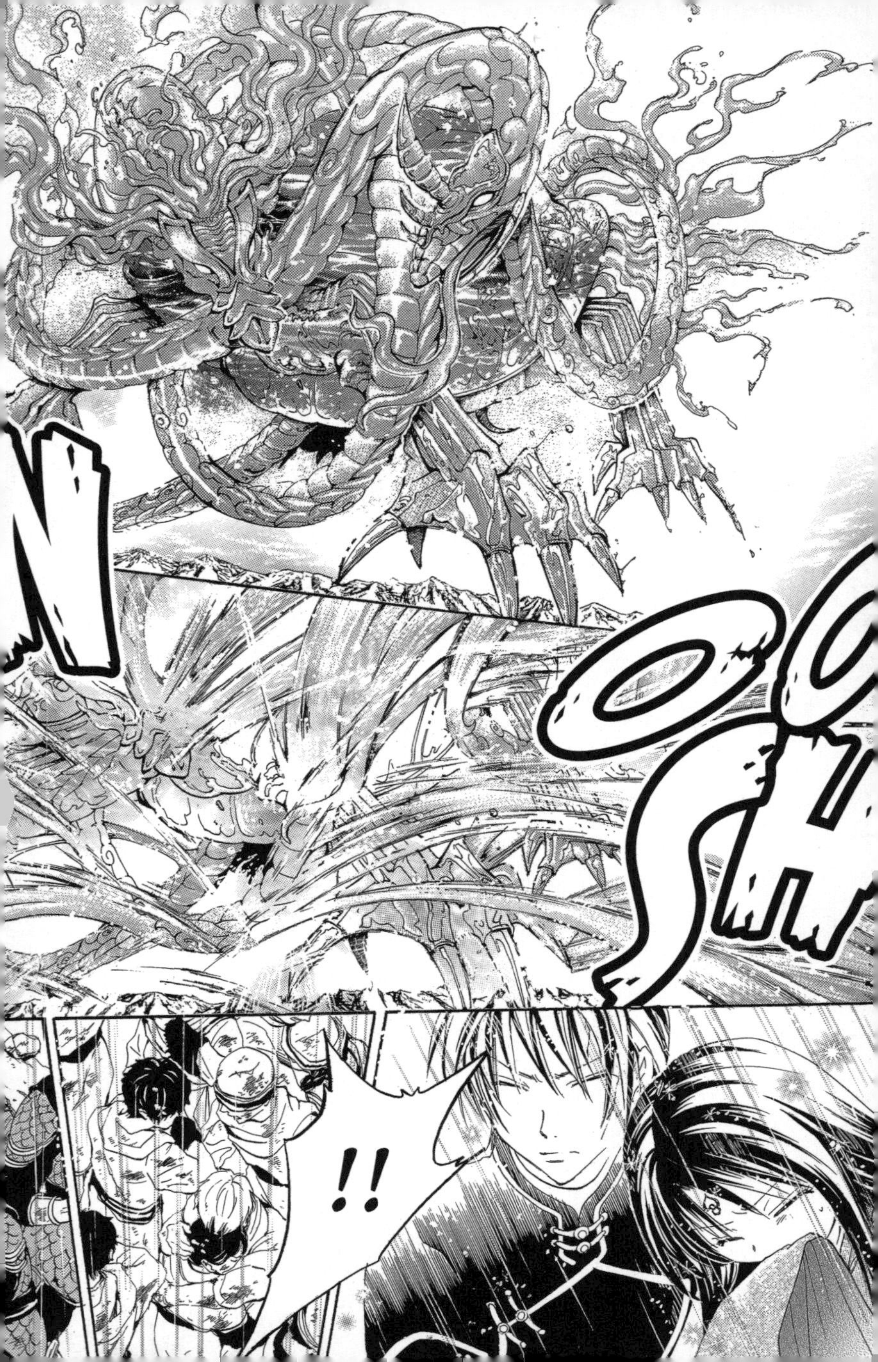
!!

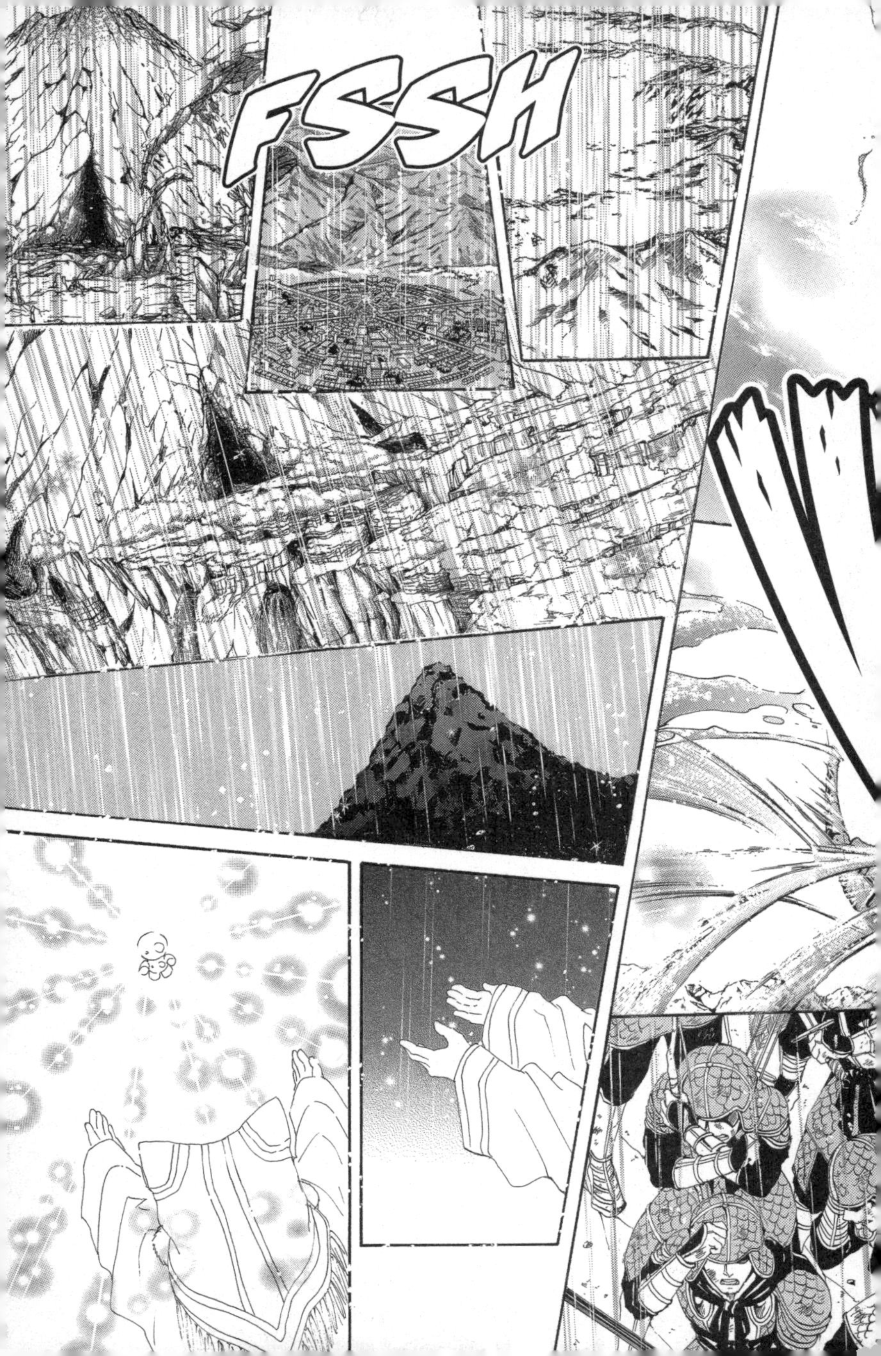
FSSH

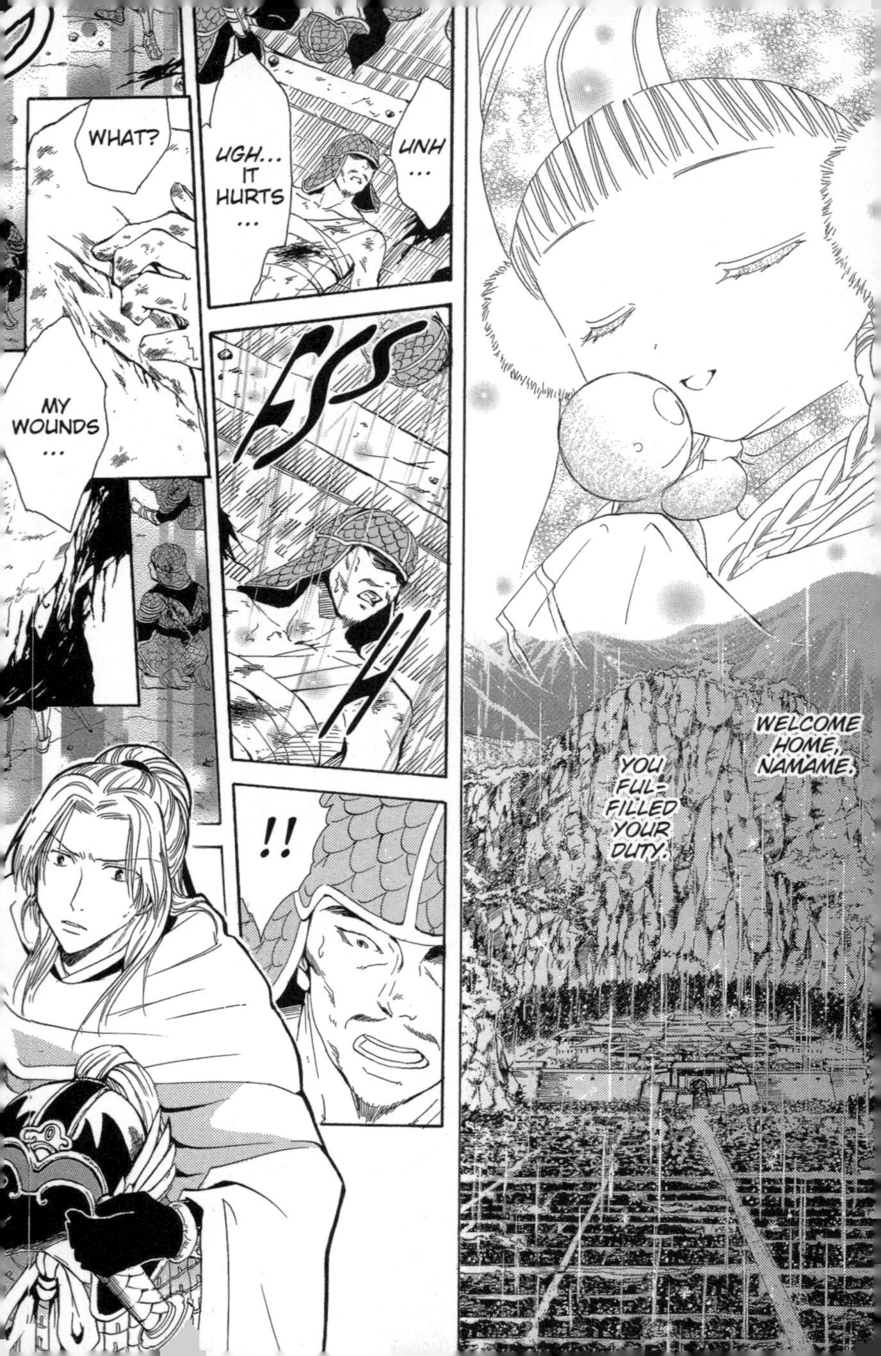
WELCOME HOME, NAMAME.
YOU FUL-FILLED YOUR DUTY.
UNH ...
UGH... IT HURTS ...
WHAT?
MY WOUNDS ...
FSS
!!

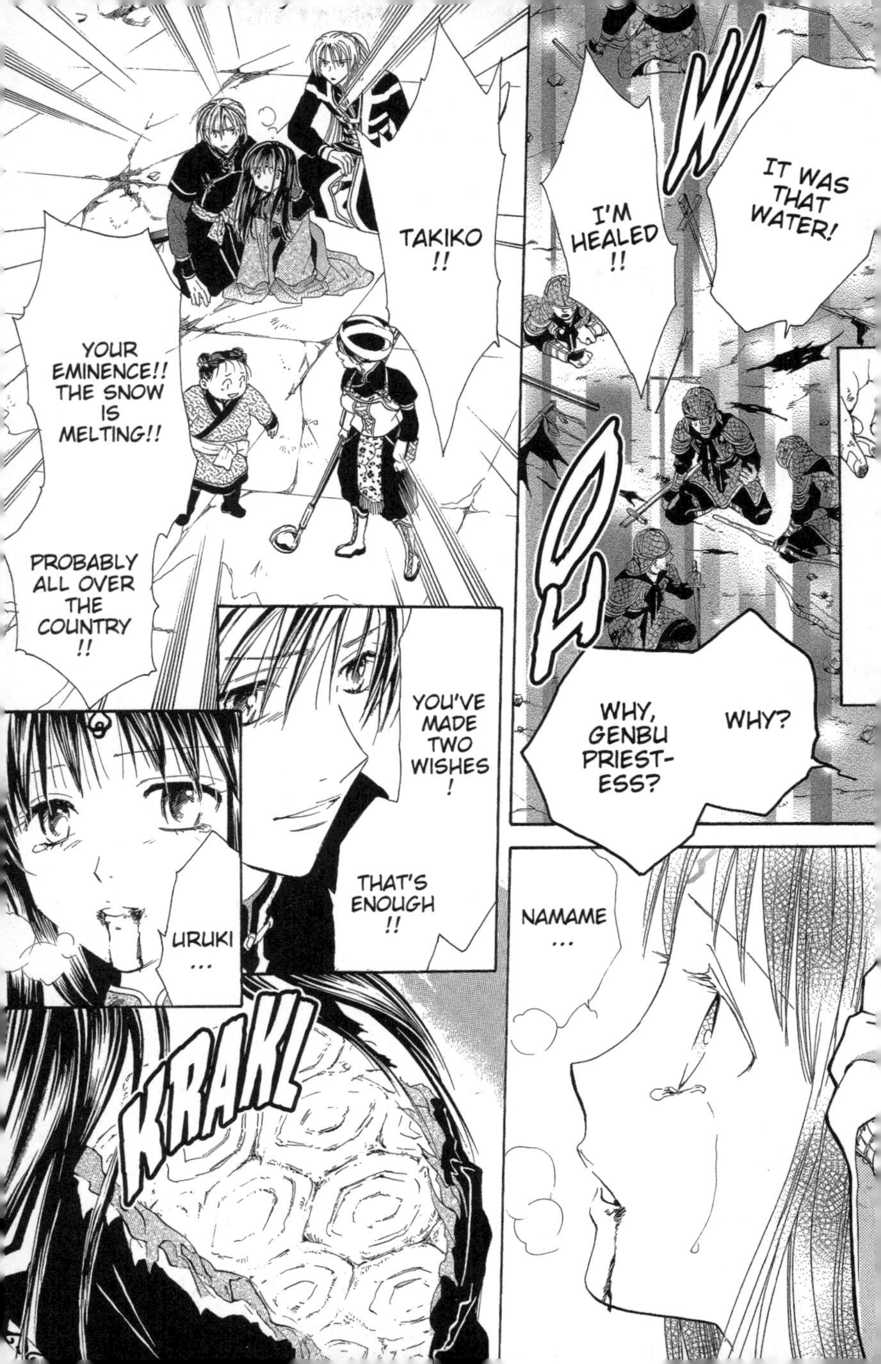
W
IT WAS THAT WATER!
I'M HEALED !!
O
WHY?
WHY, GENBU PRIEST-ESS?
NAMAME ...
TAKIKO !!
YOUR EMINENCE!! THE SNOW IS MELTING!!
PROBABLY ALL OVER THE COUNTRY !!
YOU'VE MADE TWO WISHES !
THAT'S ENOUGH !!
URUKI ...
KRAKL

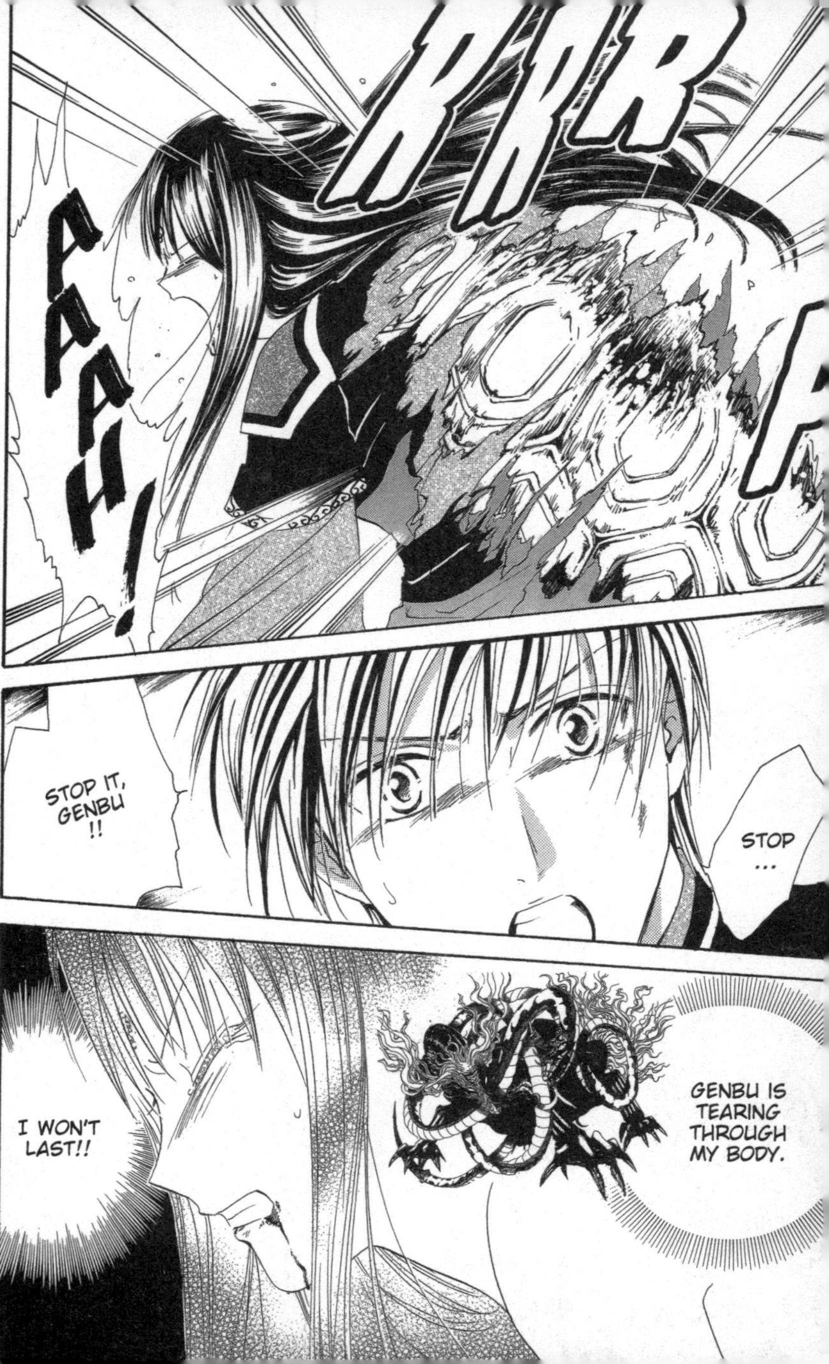
AAAH!!
STOP ...
STOP IT, GENBU!!
GENBU IS TEARING THROUGH MY BODY.
I WON'T LAST!!

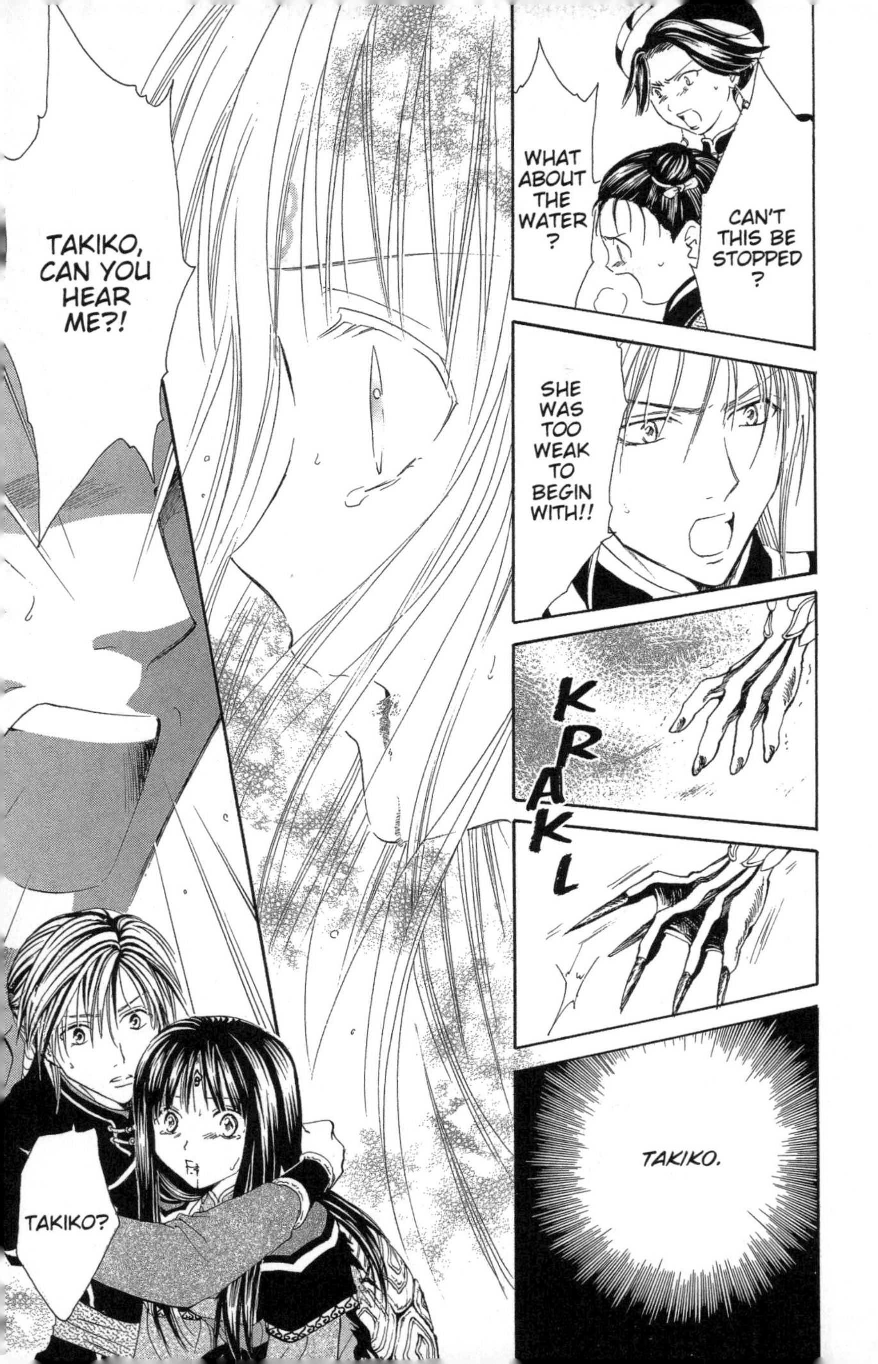
CAN'T THIS BE STOPPED?
WHAT ABOUT THE WATER?
SHE WAS TOO WEAK TO BEGIN WITH!!
KRAKL
TAKIKO.
TAKIKO, CAN YOU HEAR ME?!
TAKIKO?

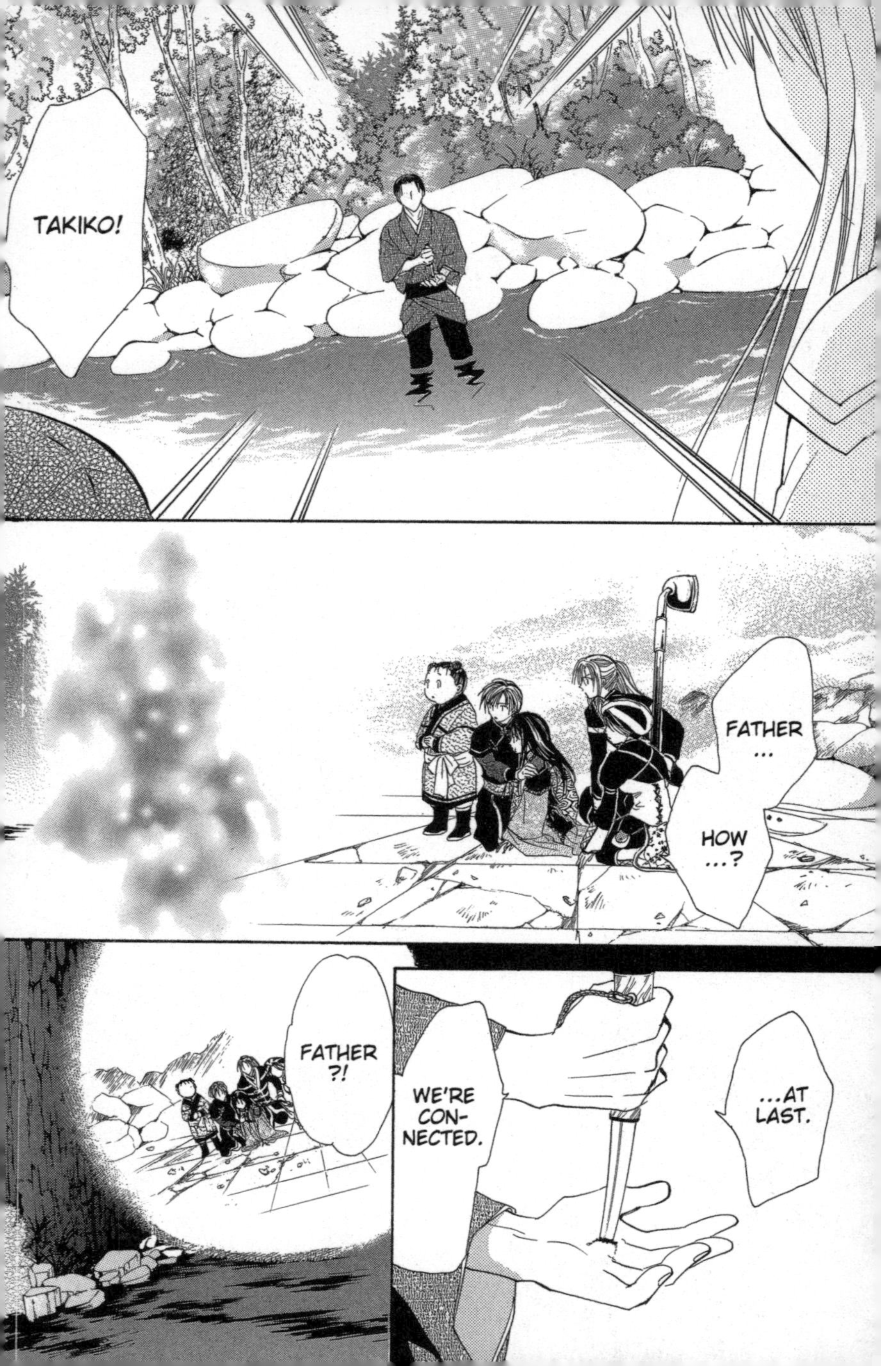
TAKIKO!
FATHER ...
HOW ...?
WE'RE CON-NECTED.
...AT LAST.
FATHER ?!

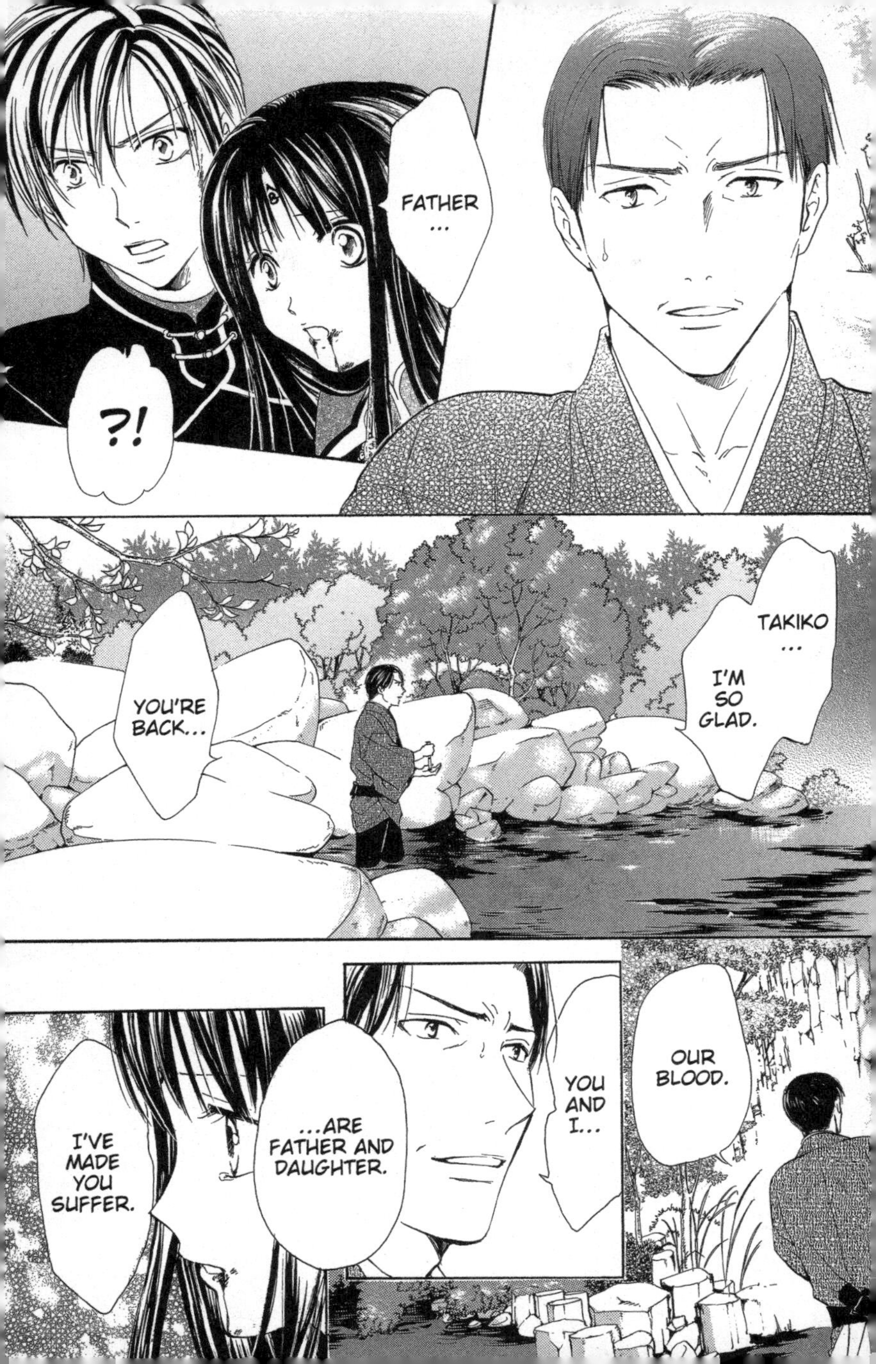
FATHER ...
?!
TAKIKO ...
I'M SO GLAD.
YOU'RE BACK...
OUR BLOOD.
YOU AND I...
...ARE FATHER AND DAUGHTER.
I'VE MADE YOU SUFFER.

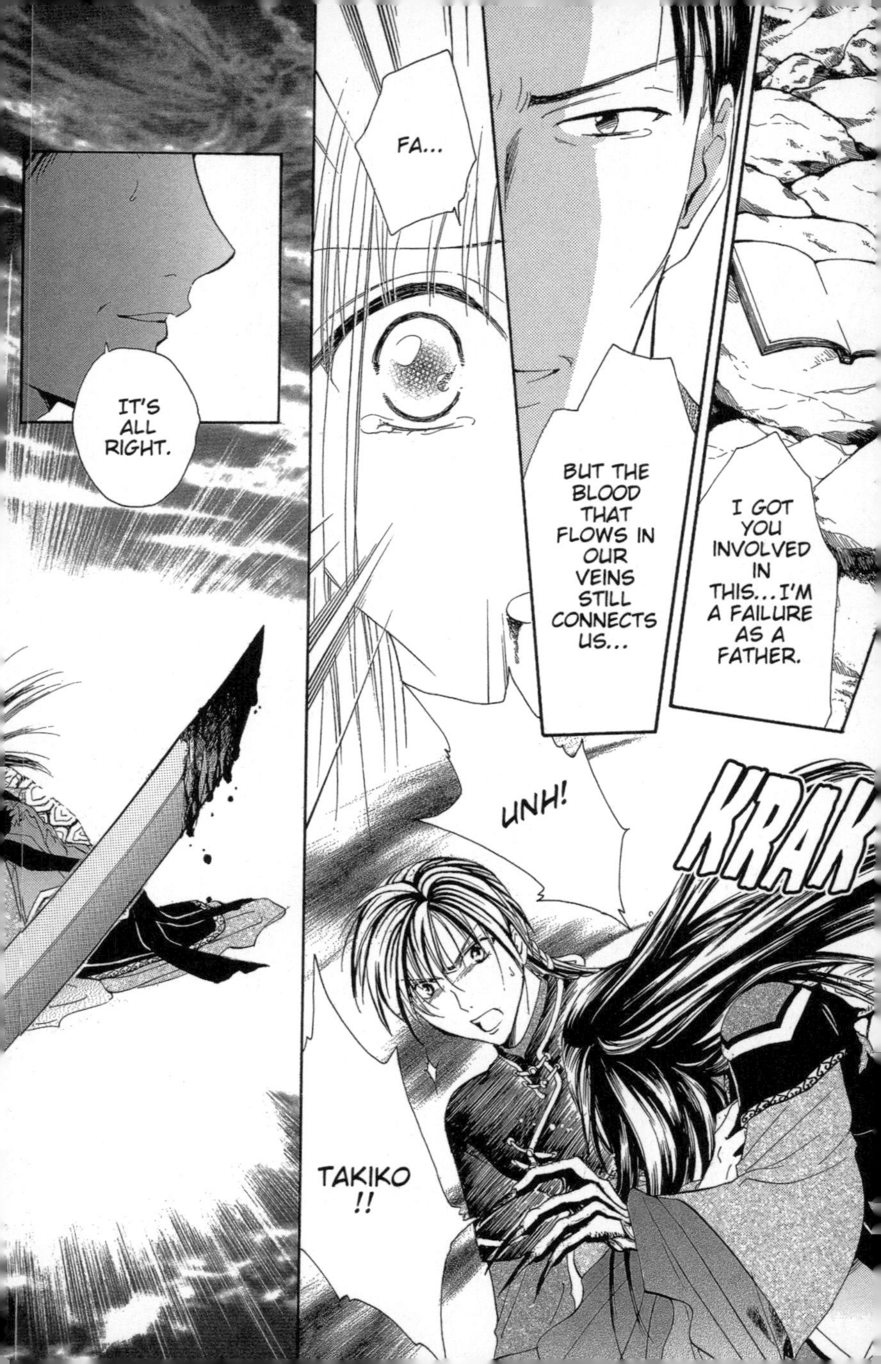
I GOT YOU INVOLVED IN THIS...I'M A FAILURE AS A FATHER.
BUT THE BLOOD THAT FLOWS IN OUR VEINS STILL CONNECTS US...
FA...
IT'S ALL RIGHT.
KRAK
UNH!
TAKIKO !!

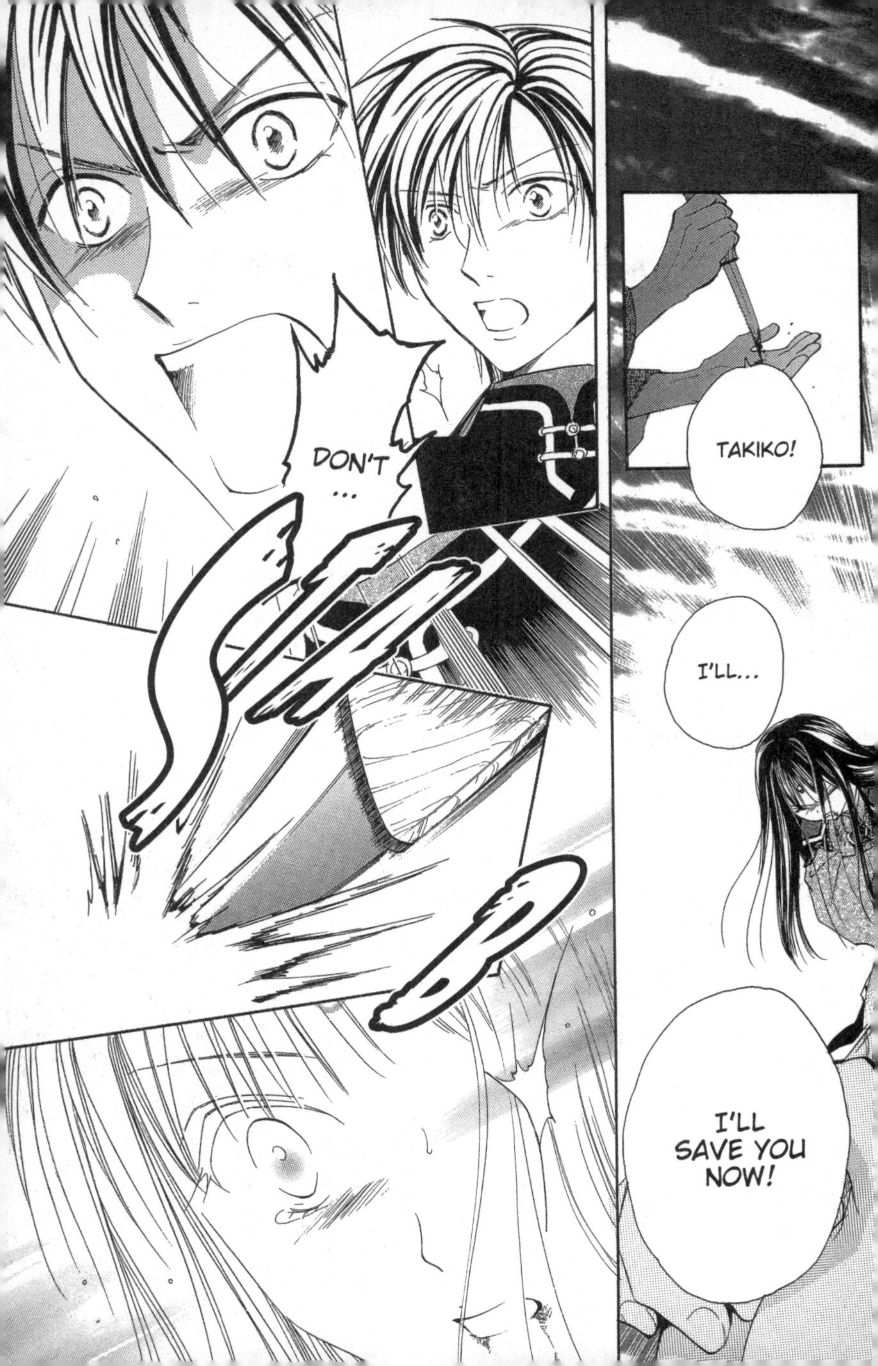
TAKIKO!
I'LL...
I'LL SAVE YOU NOW!
DON'T ...

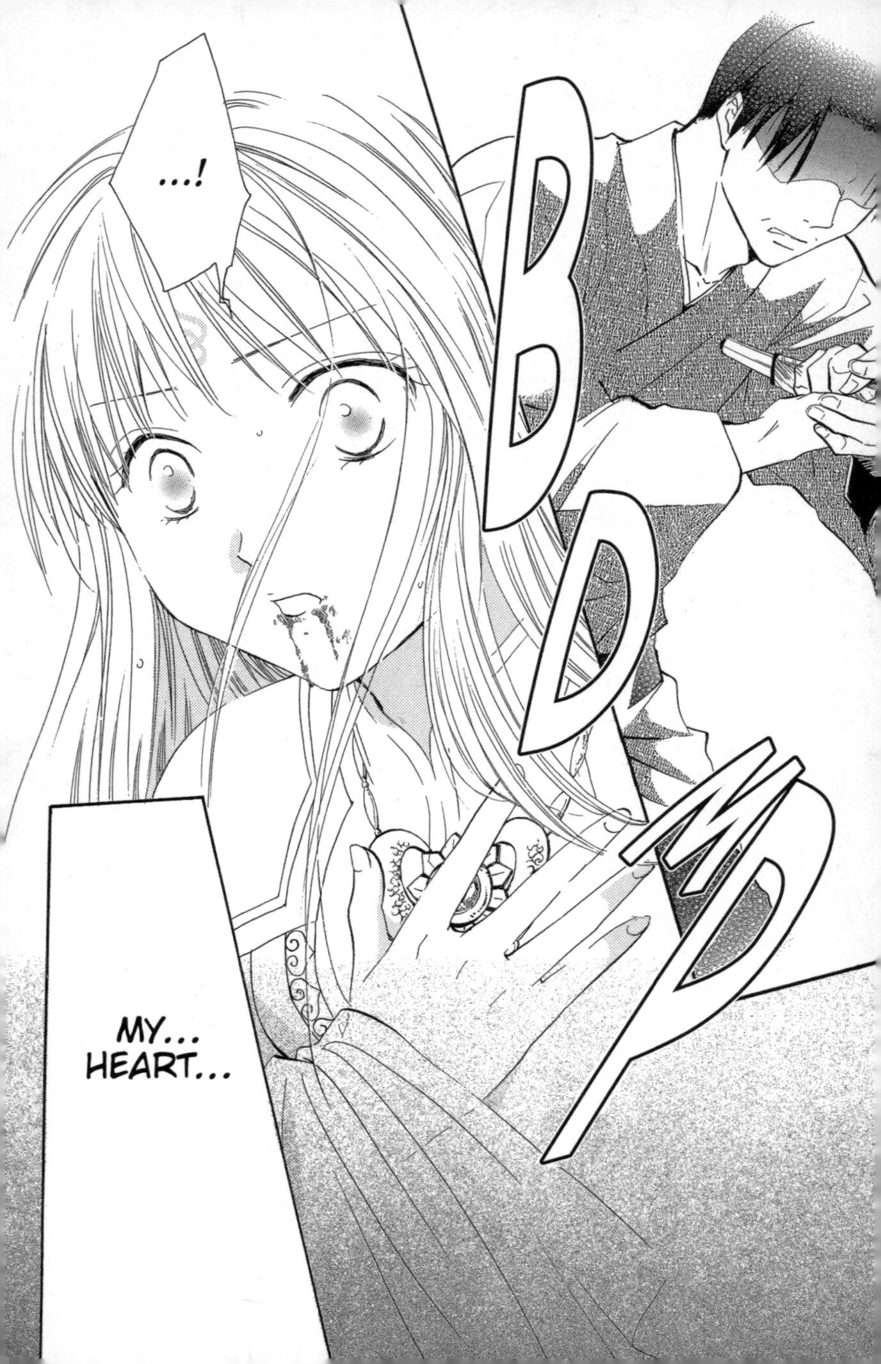
...!
BDDMP
MY... HEART...

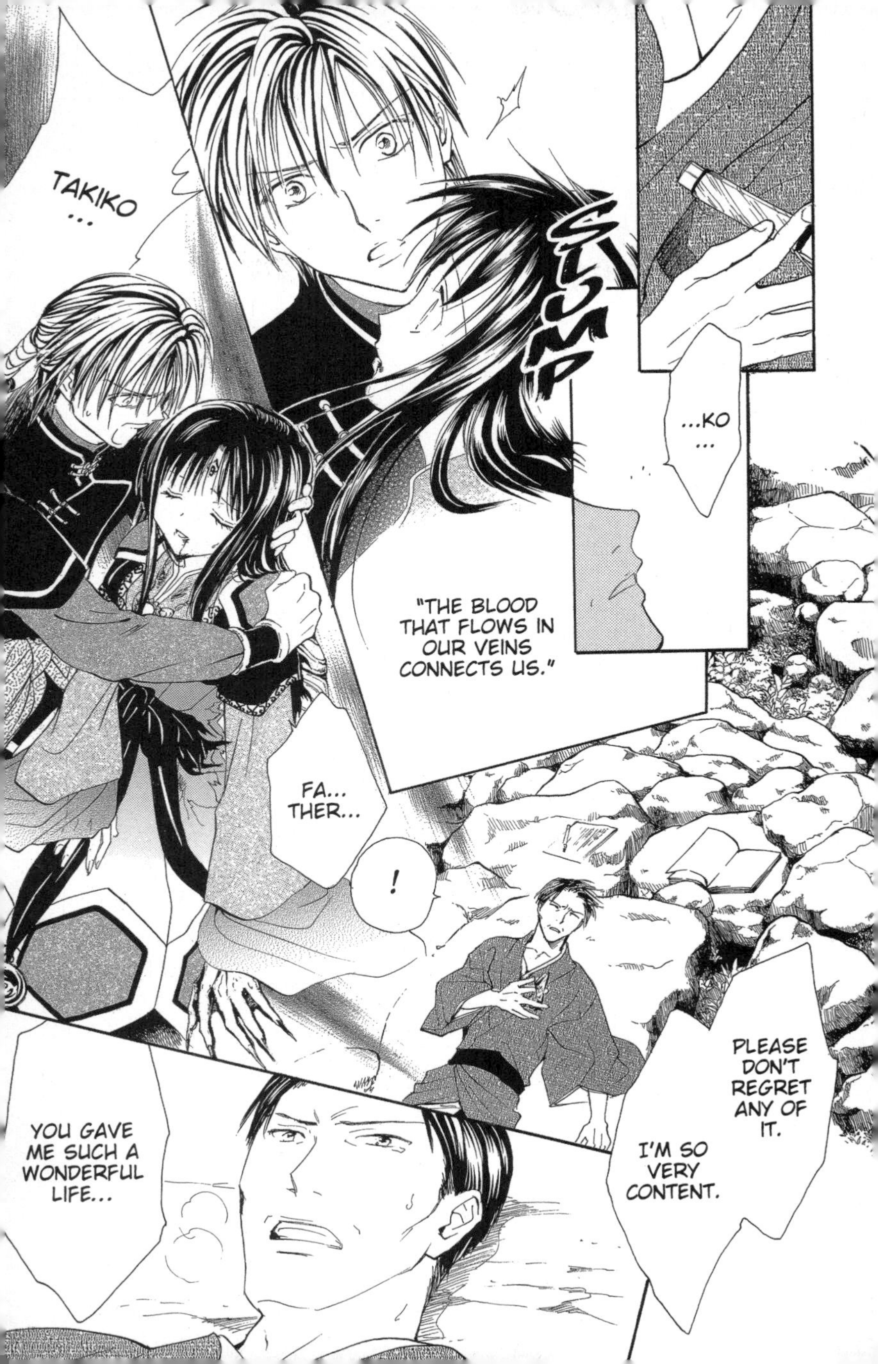
SLUMP
TAKIKO ...
...KO ...
"THE BLOOD THAT FLOWS IN OUR VEINS CONNECTS US."
FA... THER...
!
PLEASE DON'T REGRET ANY OF IT.
I'M SO VERY CONTENT.
YOU GAVE ME SUCH A WONDERFUL LIFE...

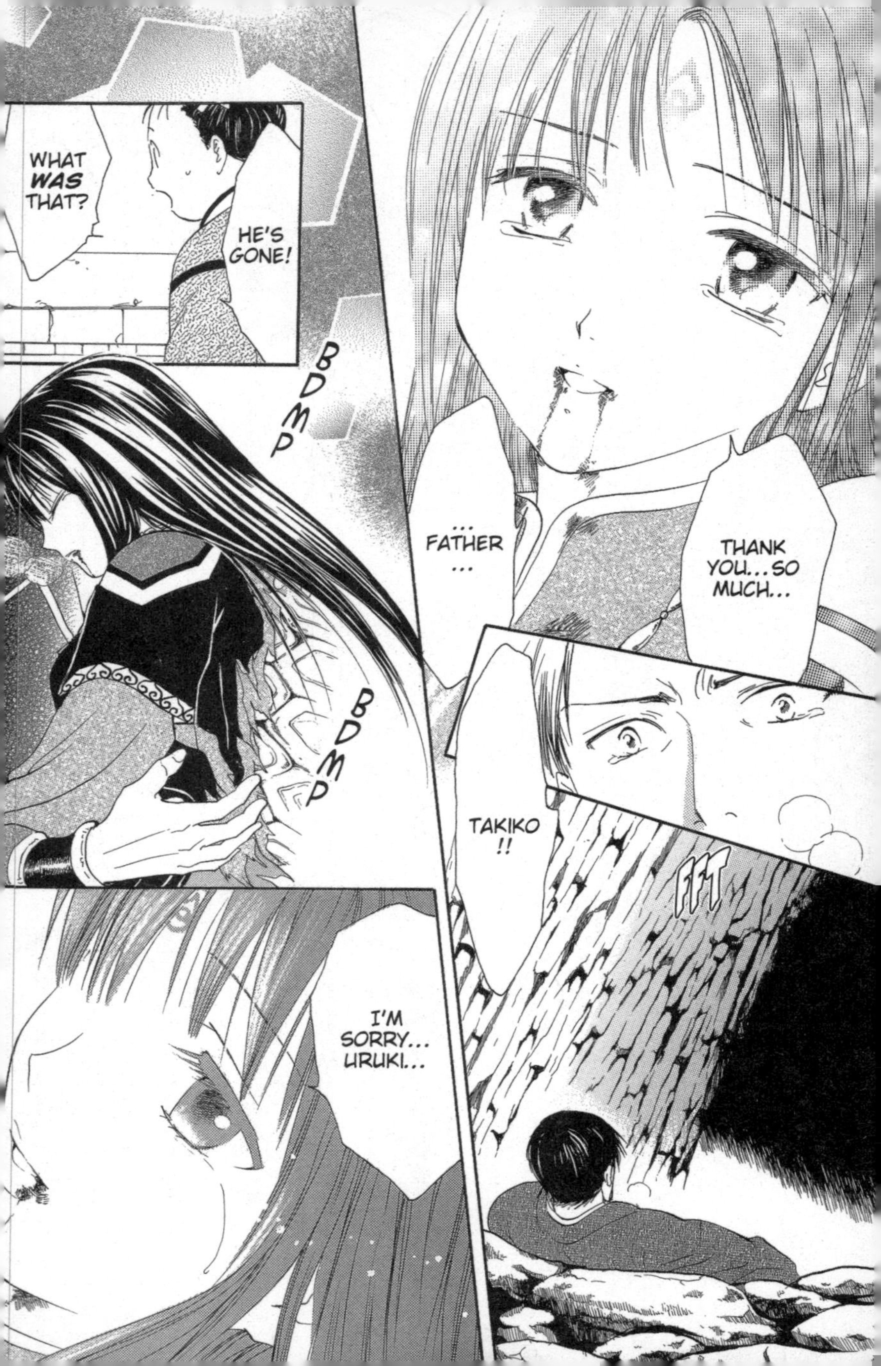
...FATHER...
THANK YOU...SO MUCH...
TAKIKO!!
FFT
WHAT WAS THAT?
HE'S GONE!
BDMP
BDMP
I'M SORRY... URUKI...

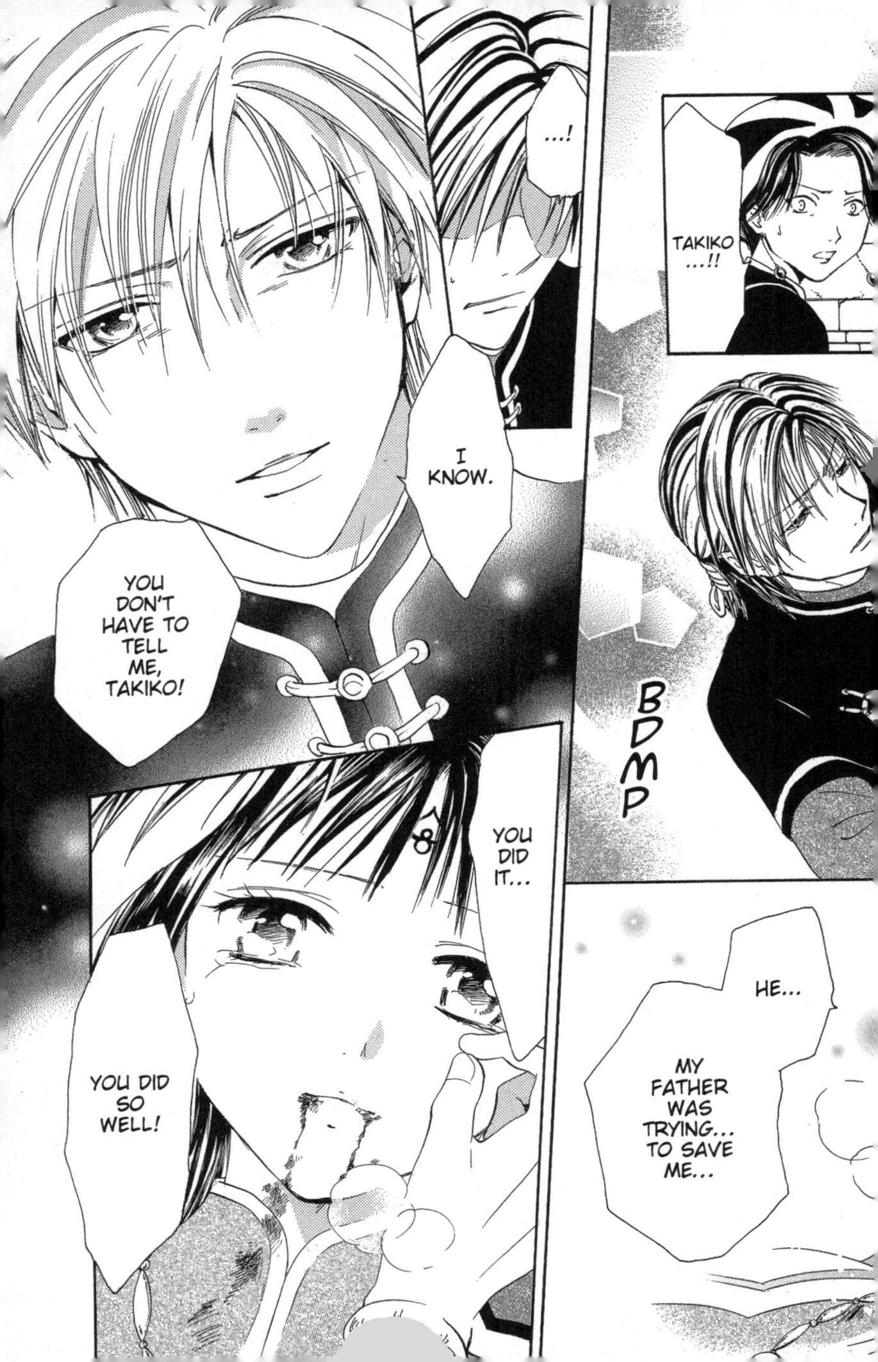
TAKIKO ...!!
BDMP
HE...
MY FATHER WAS TRYING... TO SAVE ME...
...!
I KNOW.
YOU DON'T HAVE TO TELL ME, TAKIKO!
YOU DID IT...
YOU DID SO WELL!

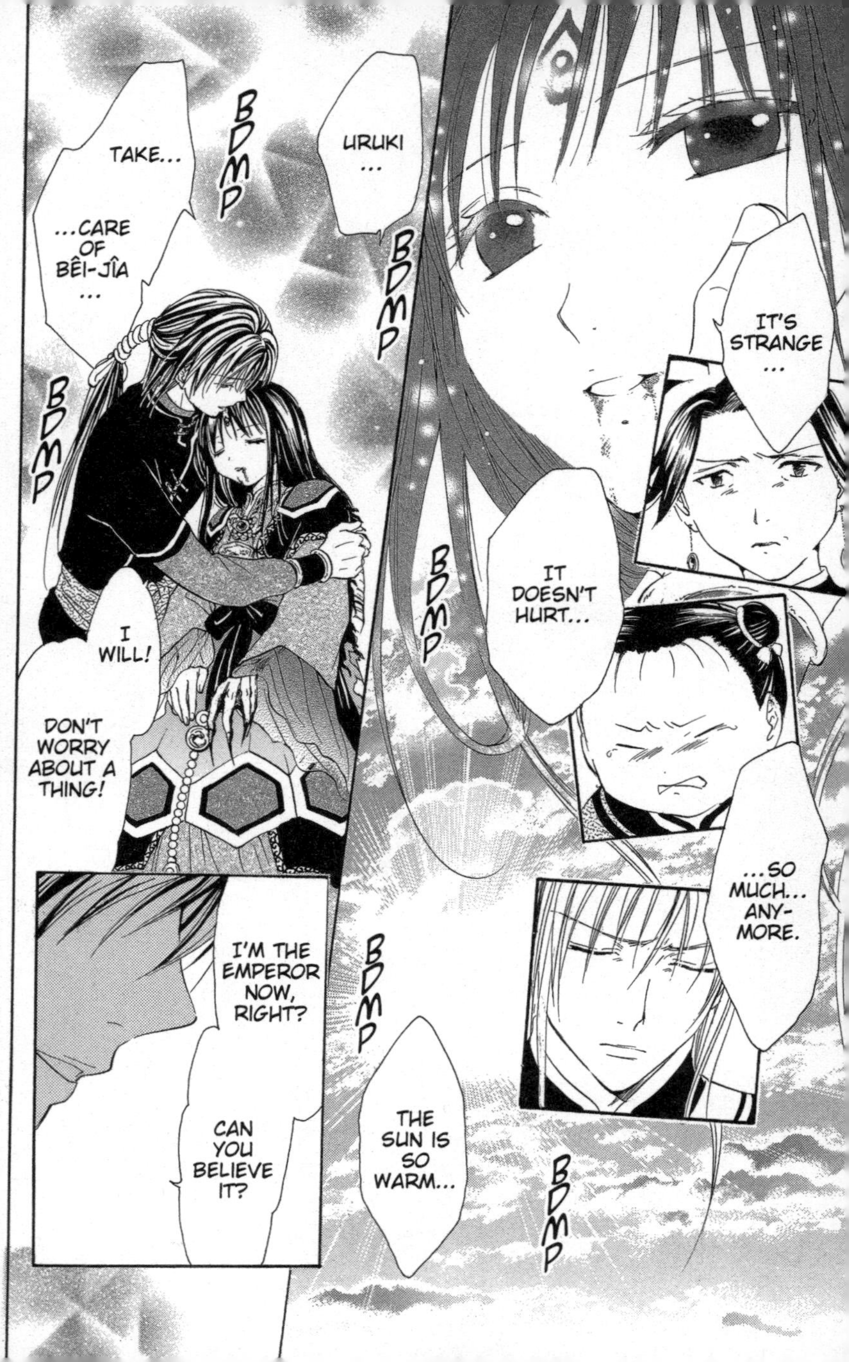
IT'S STRANGE...
IT DOESN'T HURT...
...SO MUCH... ANYMORE.
BDMP
THE SUN IS SO WARM...
BDMP
BDMP
URUKI...
BDMP
TAKE...
...CARE OF BÊI-JÎA...
BDMP
I WILL!
DON'T WORRY ABOUT A THING!
BDMP
I'M THE EMPEROR NOW, RIGHT?
CAN YOU BELIEVE IT?

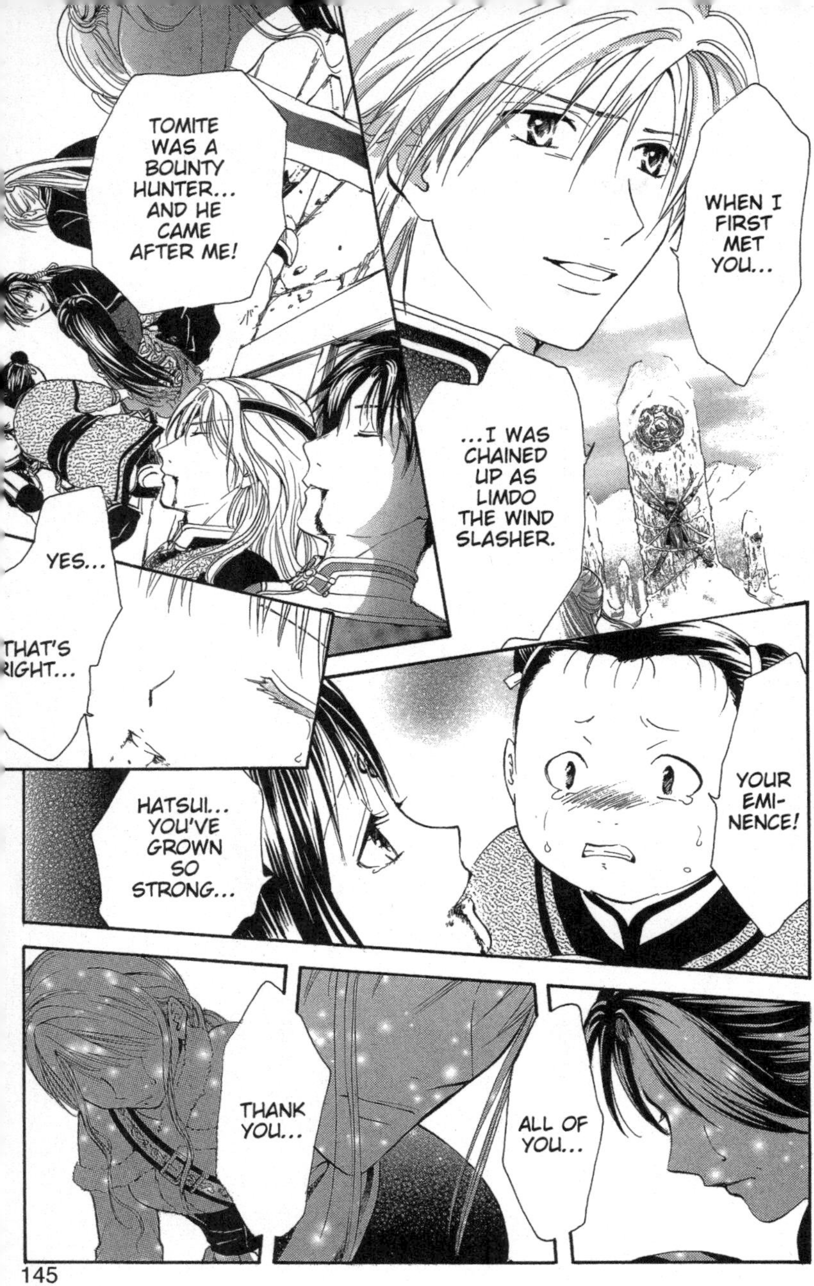
WHEN I FIRST MET YOU...
...I WAS CHAINED UP AS LIMDO THE WIND SLASHER.
TOMITE WAS A BOUNTY HUNTER... AND HE CAME AFTER ME!
YES...
THAT'S RIGHT...
YOUR EMINENCE!
HATSUI... YOU'VE GROWN SO STRONG...
ALL OF YOU...
THANK YOU...

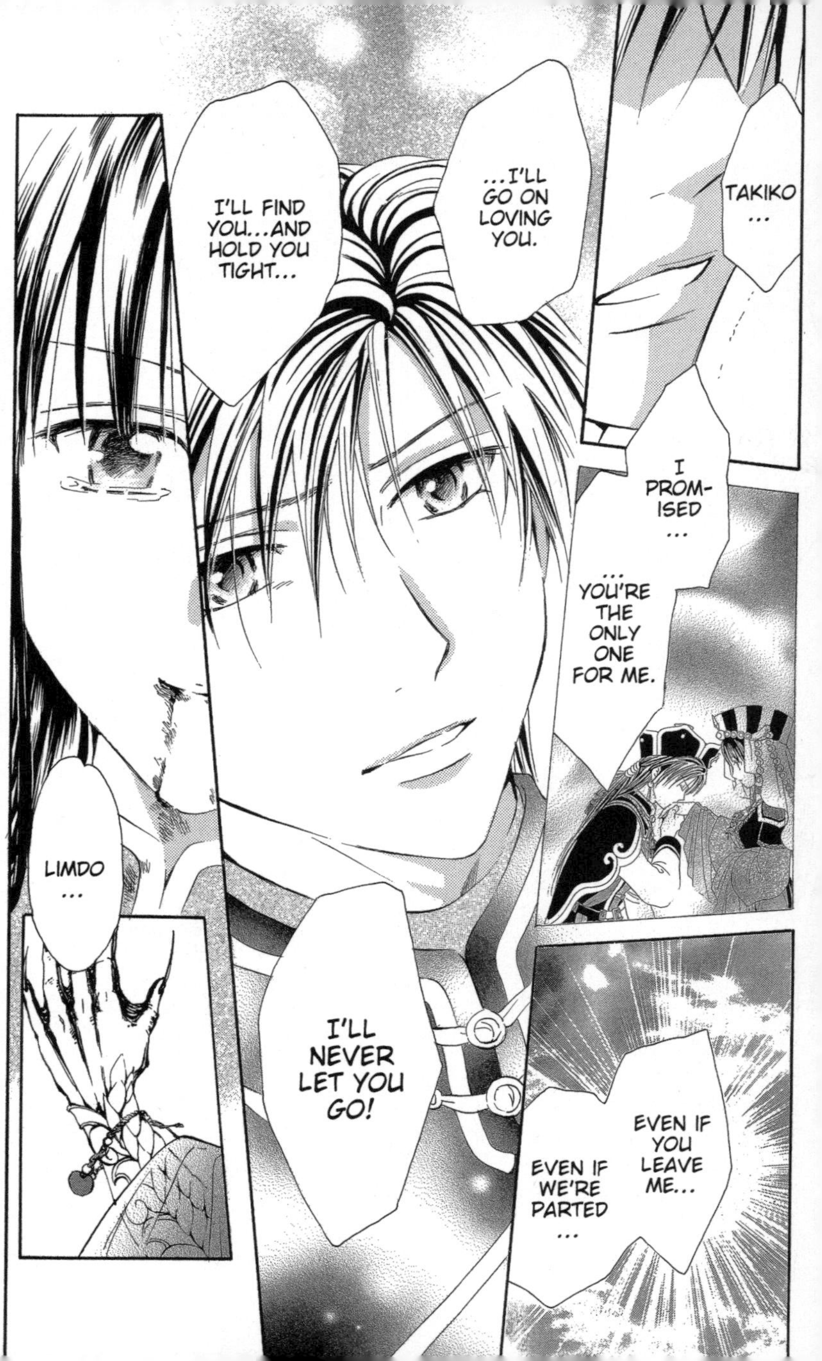
TAKIKO ...
I PROMISED ...
... YOU'RE THE ONLY ONE FOR ME.
EVEN IF YOU LEAVE ME...
EVEN IF WE'RE PARTED ...
...I'LL GO ON LOVING YOU.
I'LL FIND YOU...AND HOLD YOU TIGHT...
I'LL NEVER LET YOU GO!
LIMDO ...

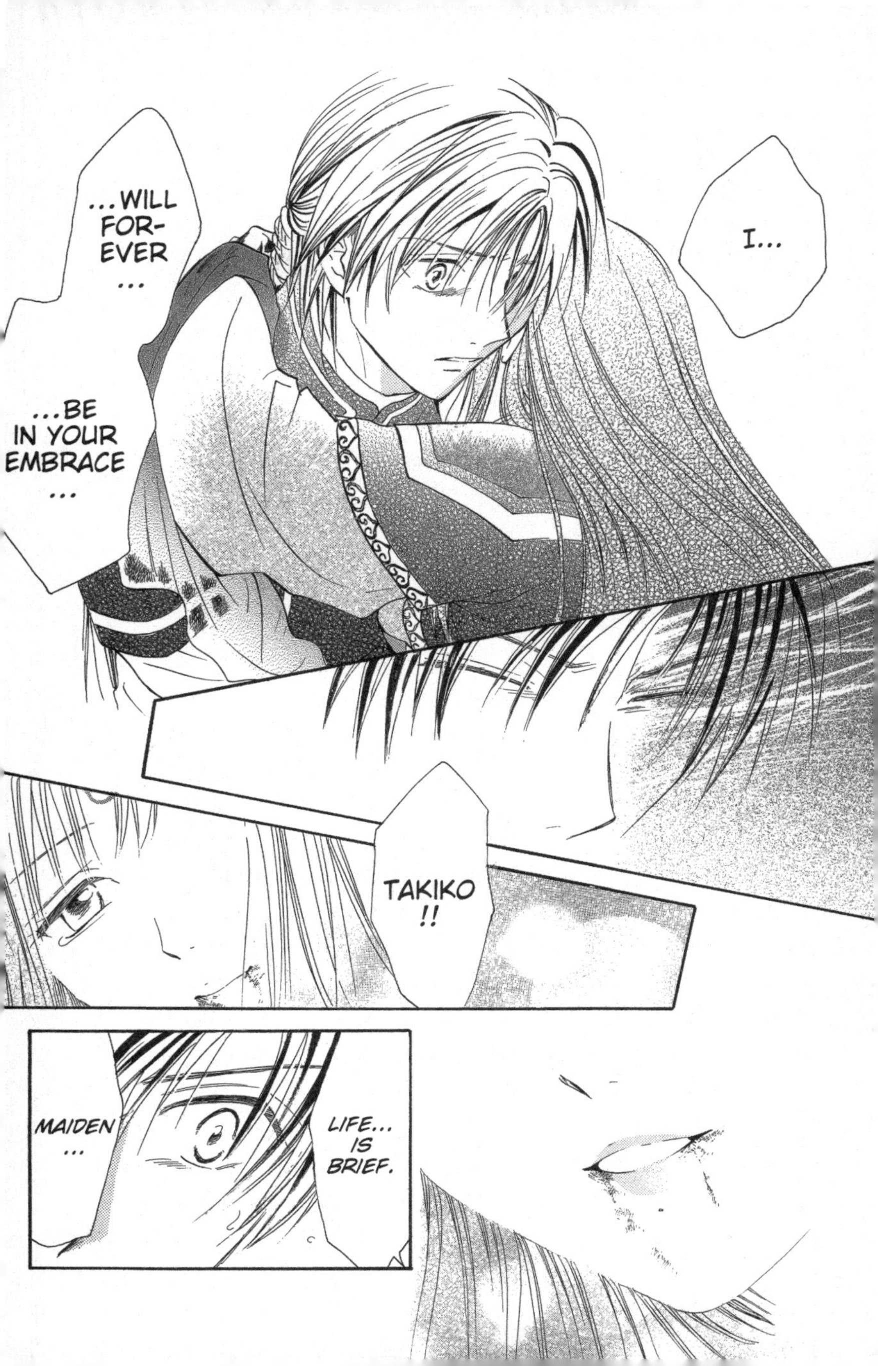
I...
...WILL FOREVER...
...BE IN YOUR EMBRACE...
TAKIKO!!
LIFE... IS BRIEF.
MAIDEN...

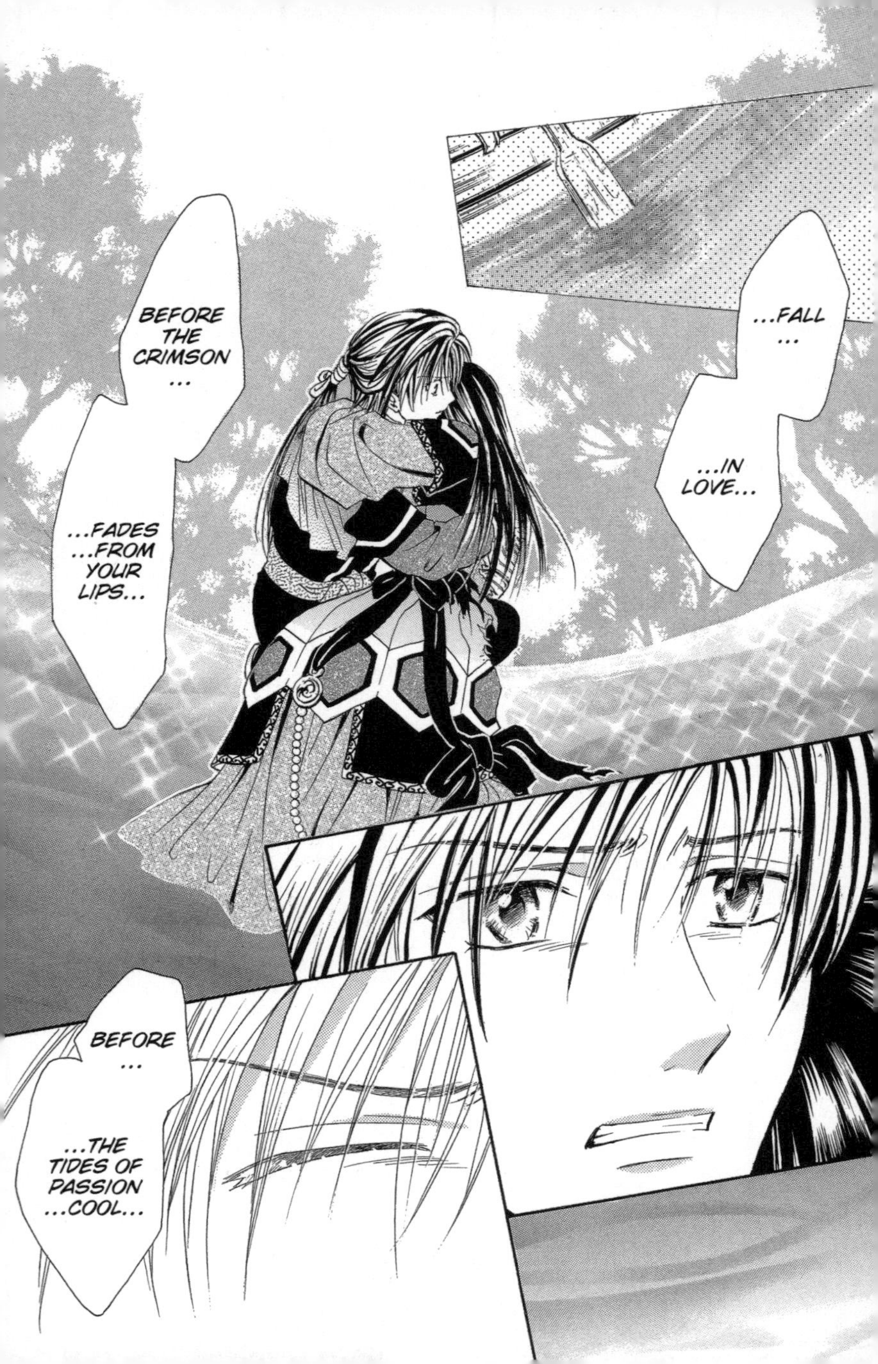
...FALL ...
...IN LOVE...
BEFORE THE CRIMSON ...
...FADES ...FROM YOUR LIPS...
BEFORE ...
...THE TIDES OF PASSION ...COOL...

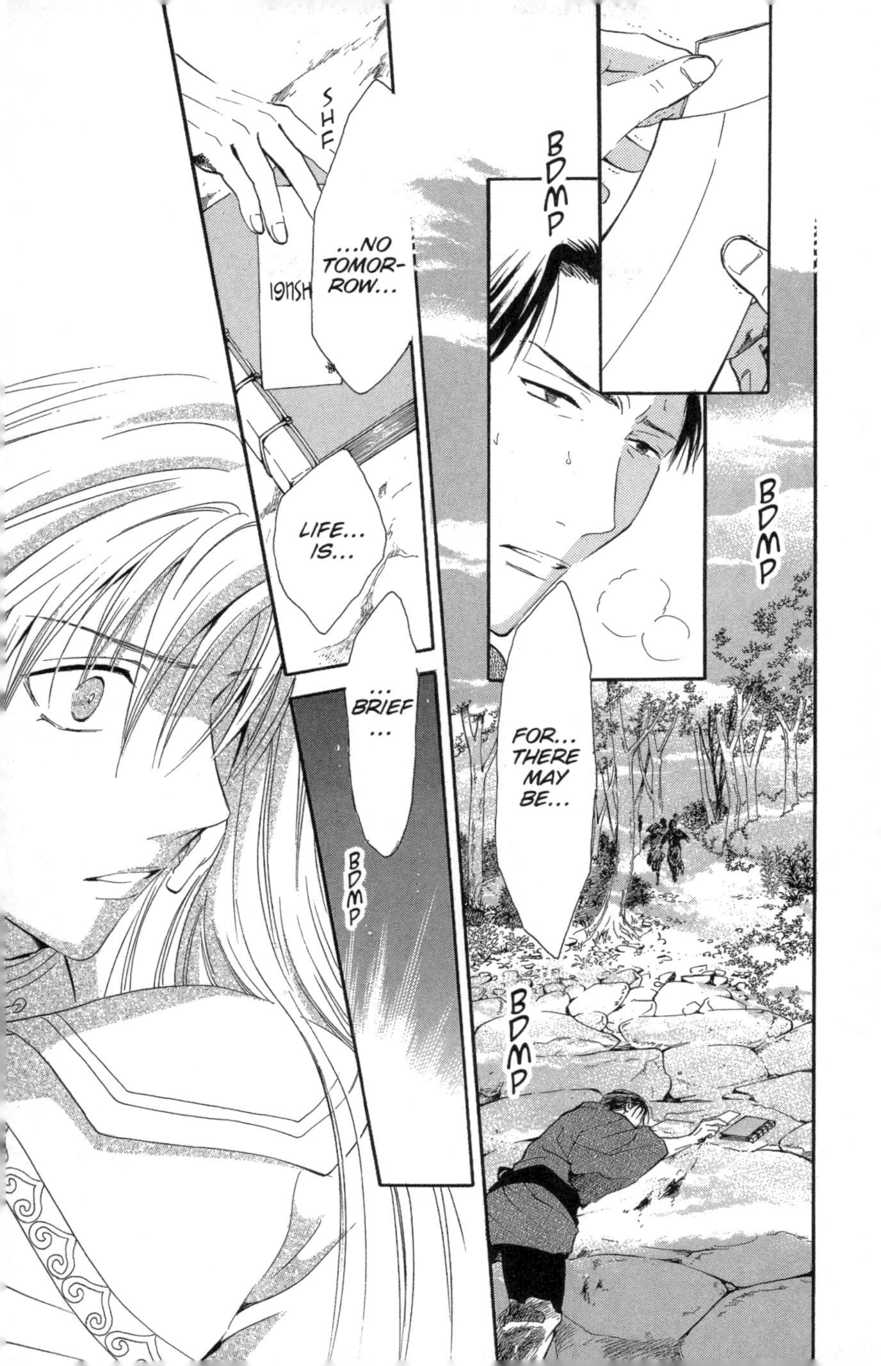
BDMP
BDMP
FOR... THERE MAY BE...
SHF
...NO TOMORROW...
LIFE... IS...
...BRIEF...
BDMP
BDMP

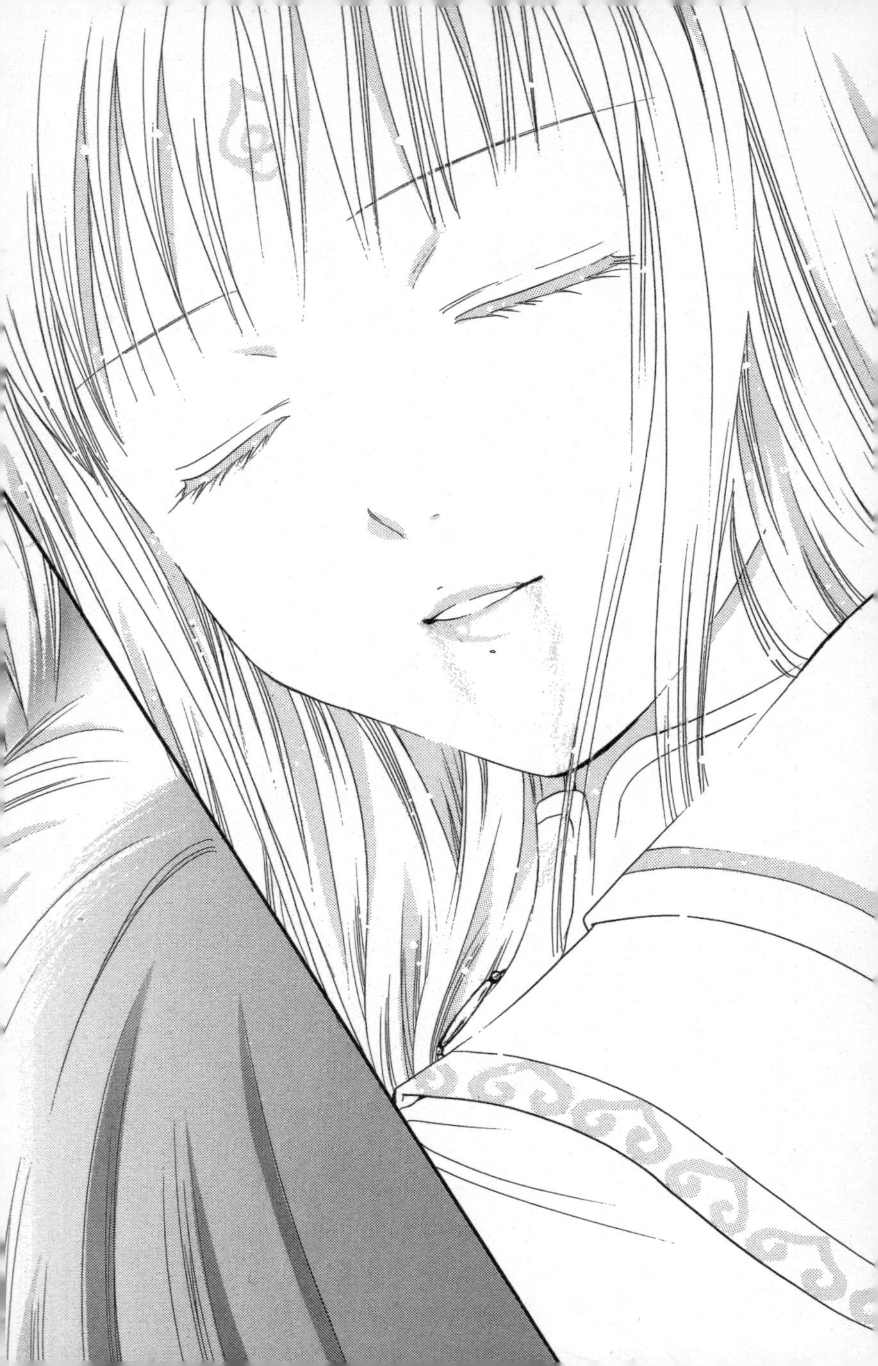

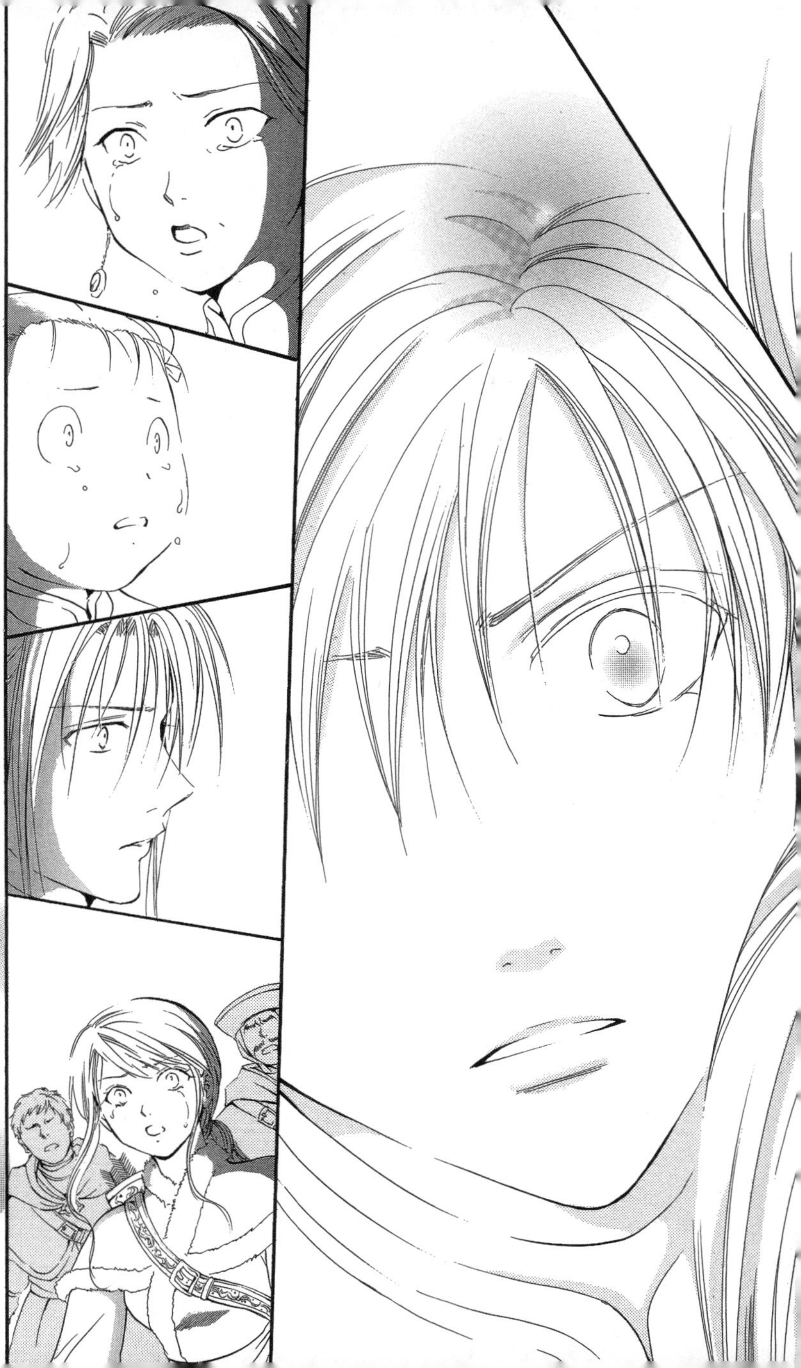

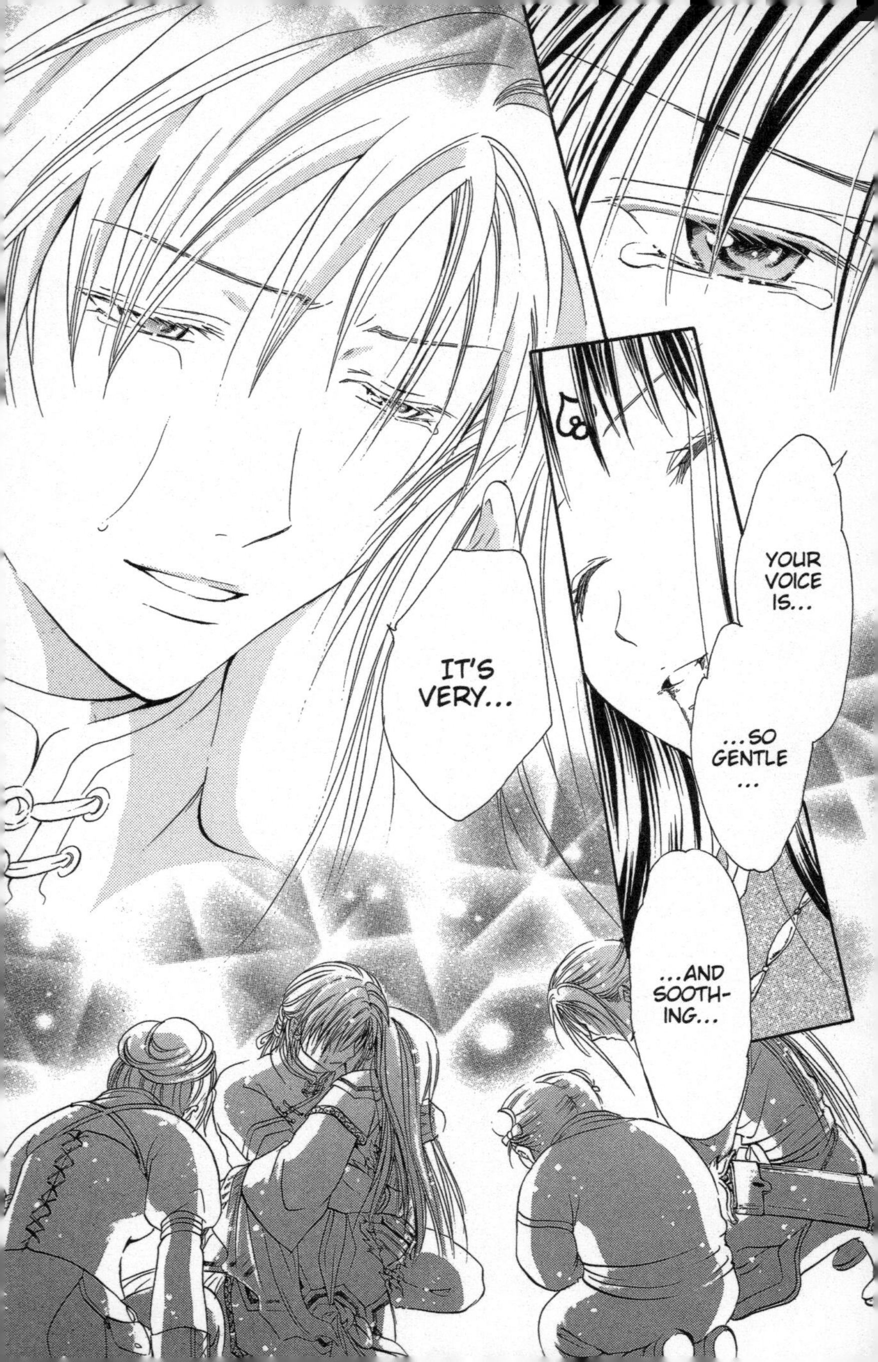
YOUR VOICE IS...
...SO GENTLE ...
...AND SOOTH-ING...
IT'S VERY...

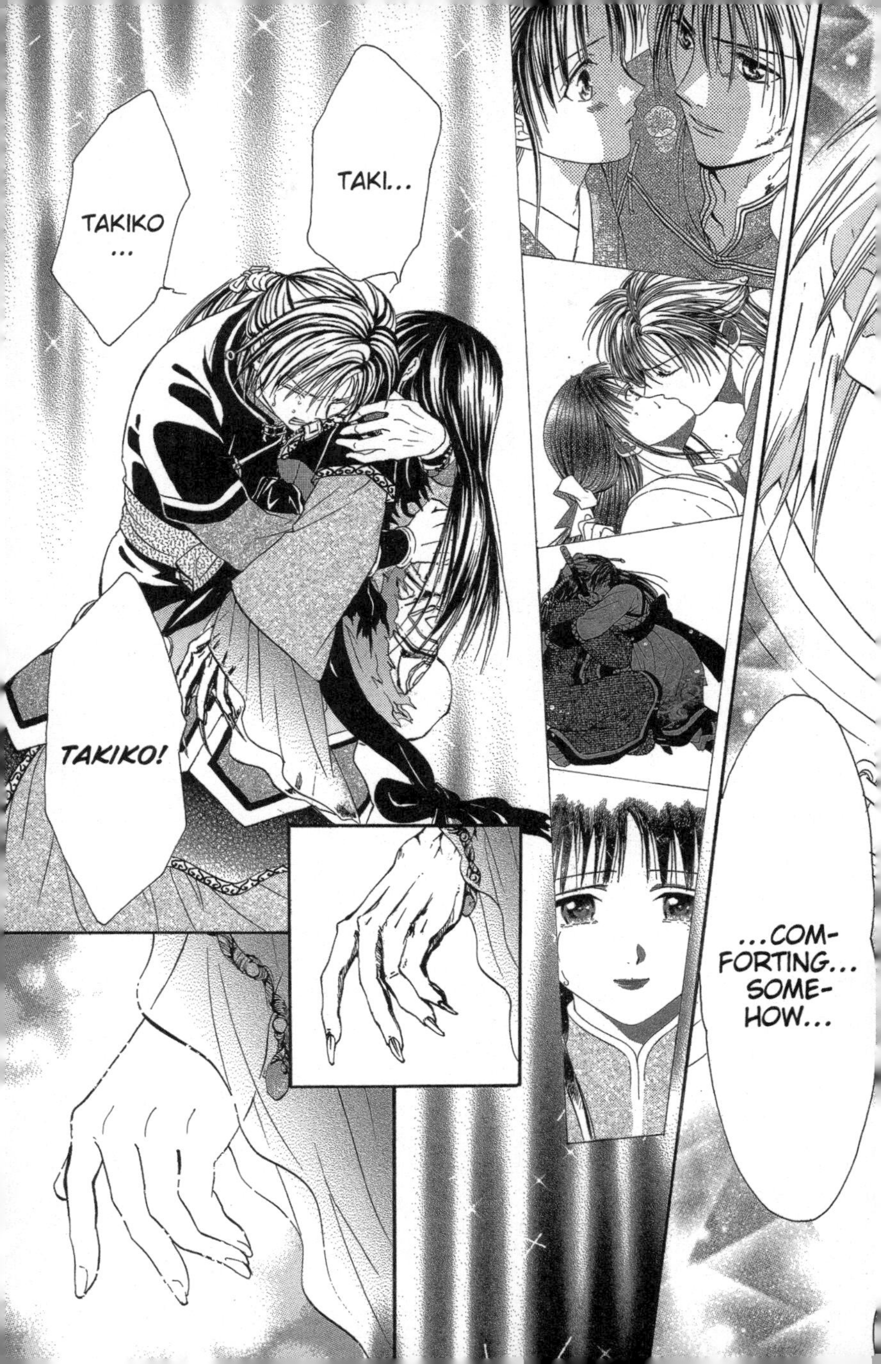
...COM-
FORTING...
SOME-
HOW...
TAKI...
TAKIKO
...
TAKIKO!

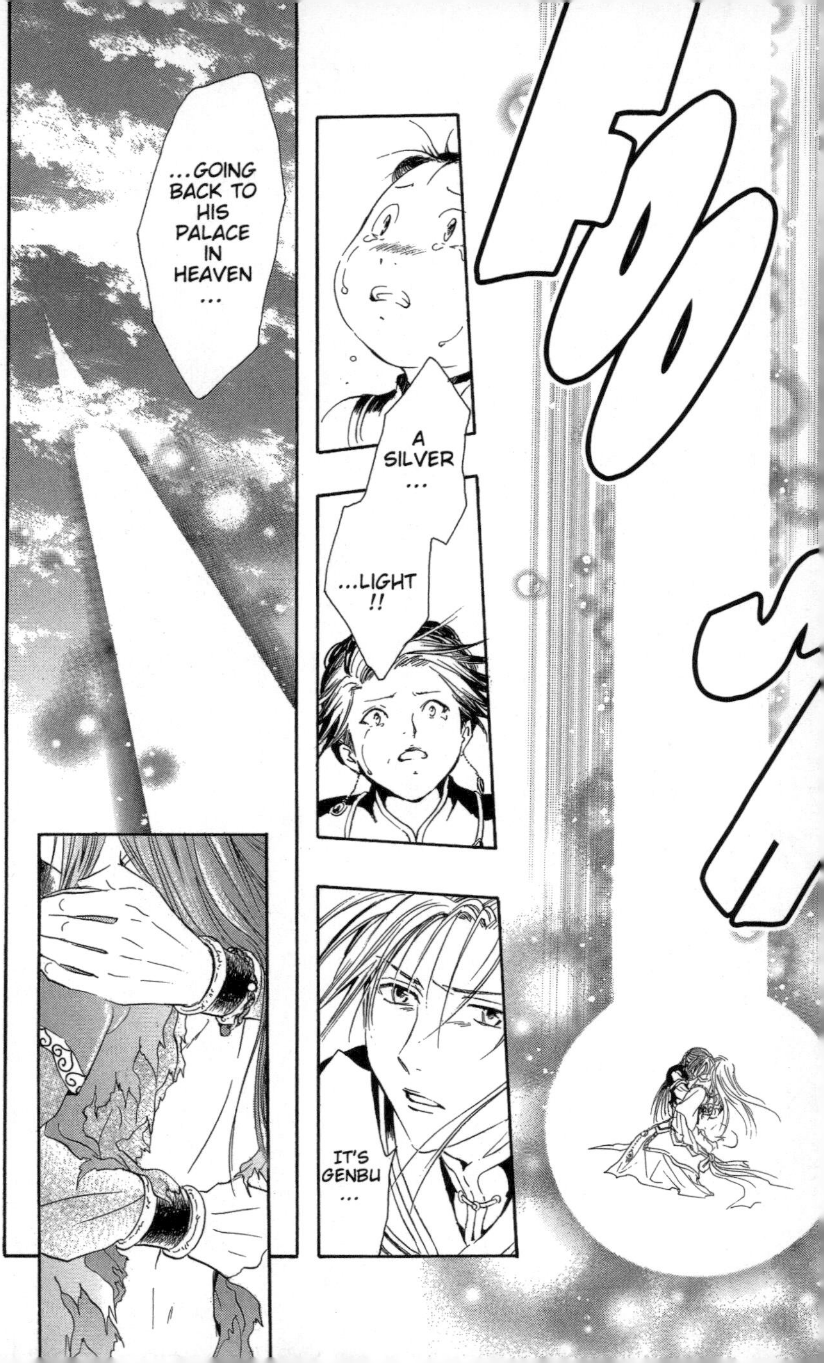
A SILVER ...
...LIGHT !!
IT'S GENBU ...
...GOING BACK TO HIS PALACE IN HEAVEN ...

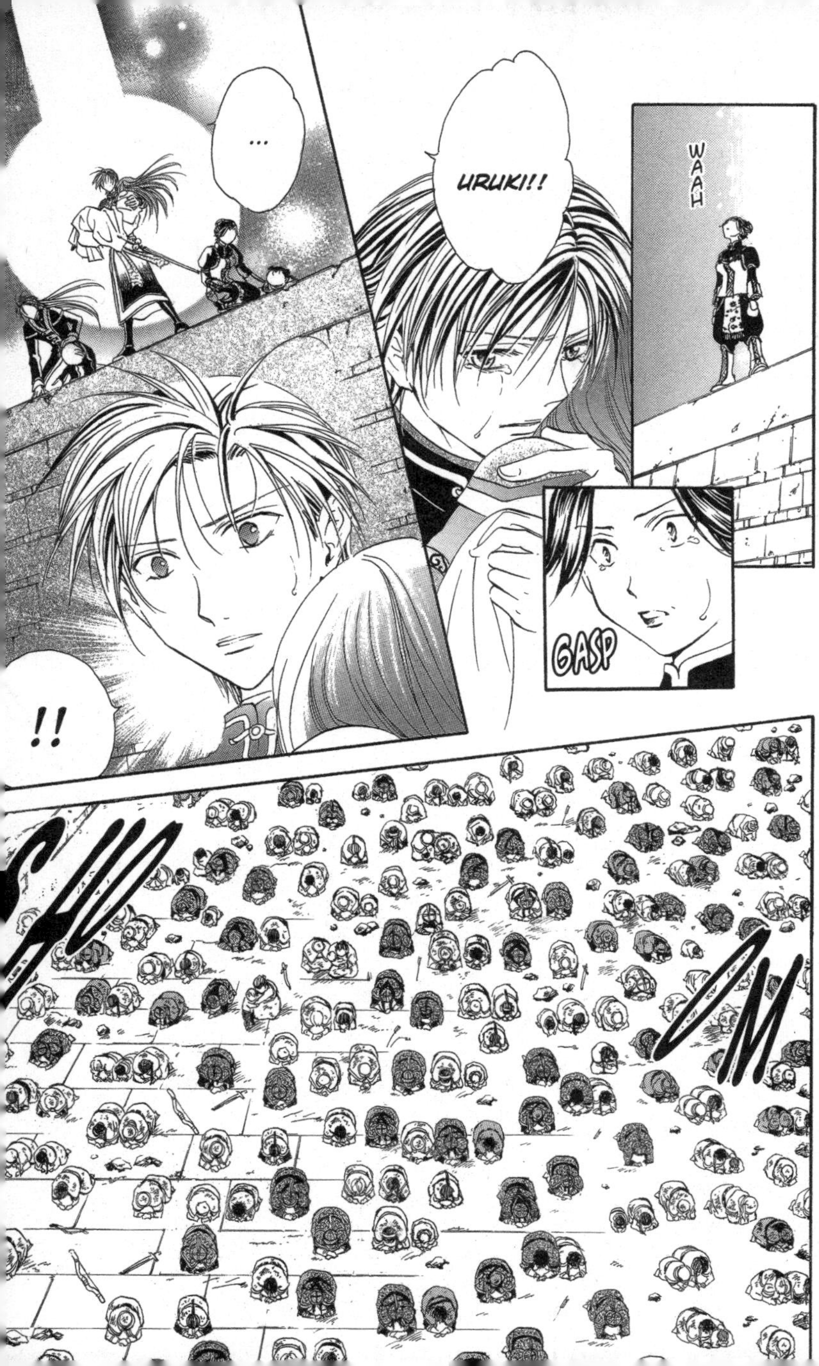

WAAH
URUKI!!
...
GASP
!!
SHU
OM

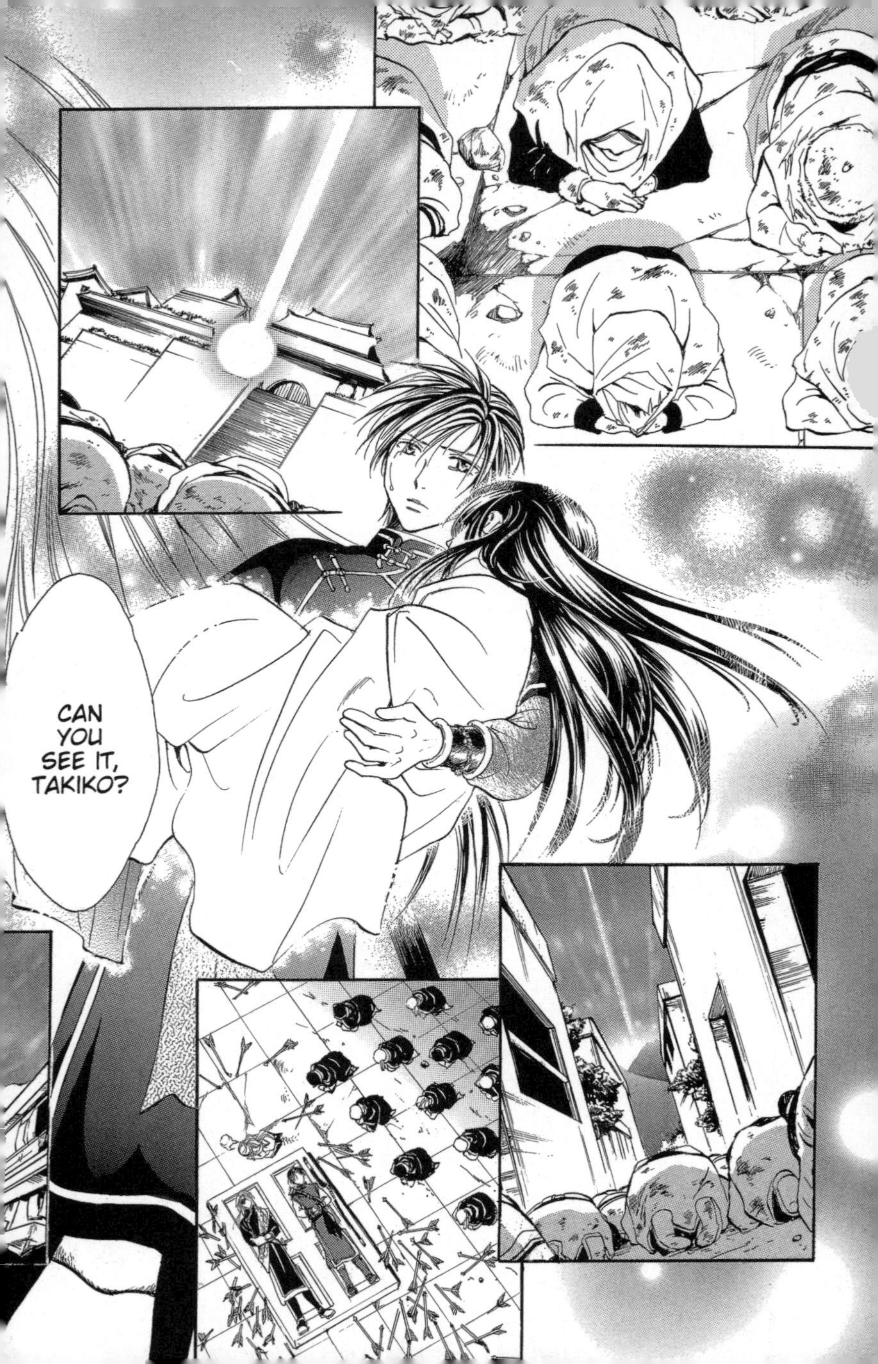
CAN YOU SEE IT, TAKIKO?

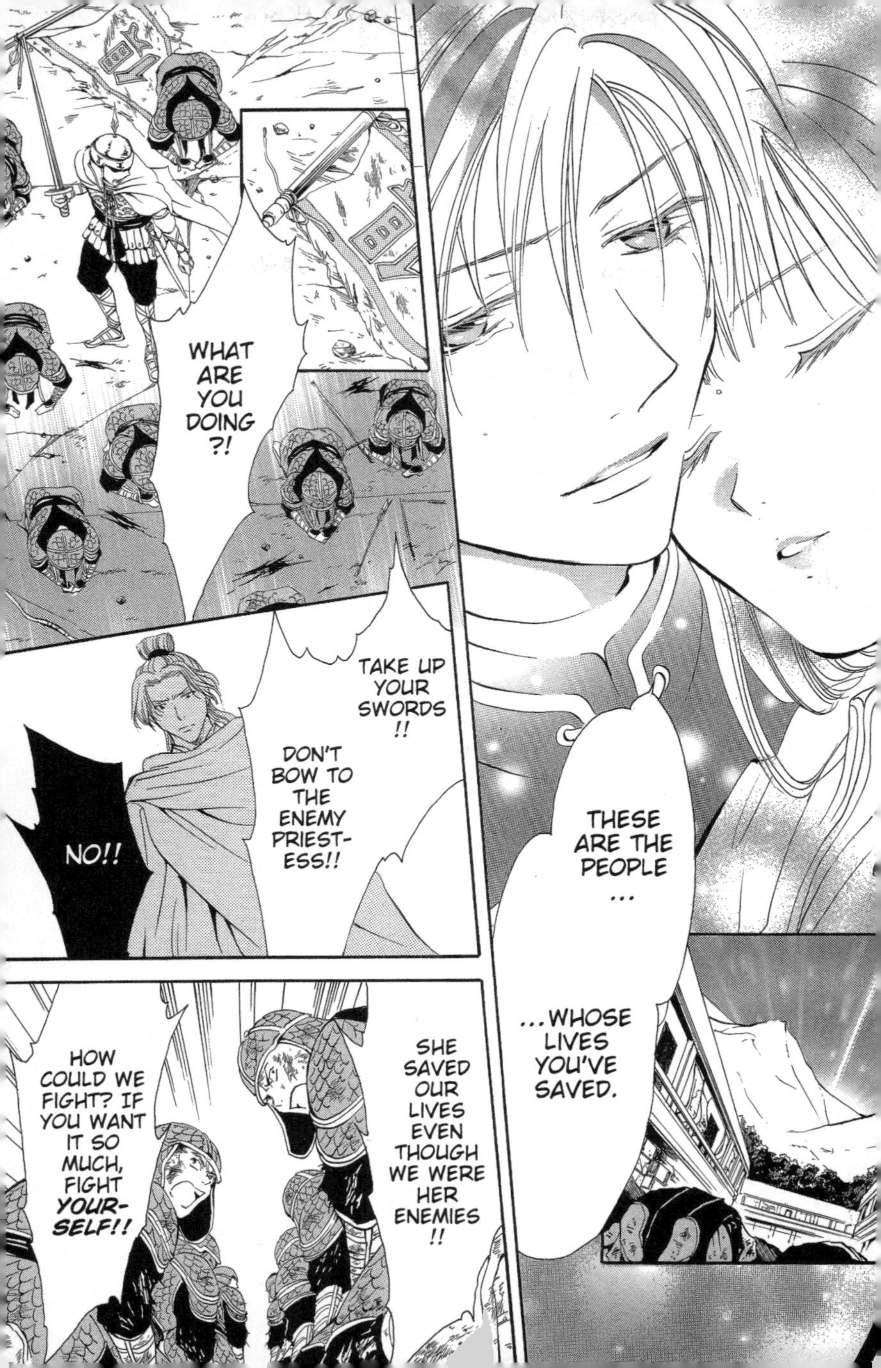
THESE ARE THE PEOPLE ...
...WHOSE LIVES YOU'VE SAVED.
WHAT ARE YOU DOING?!
TAKE UP YOUR SWORDS!!
DON'T BOW TO THE ENEMY PRIEST-ESS!!
NO!!
SHE SAVED OUR LIVES EVEN THOUGH WE WERE HER ENEMIES!!
HOW COULD WE FIGHT? IF YOU WANT IT SO MUCH, FIGHT *YOUR-SELF!!*

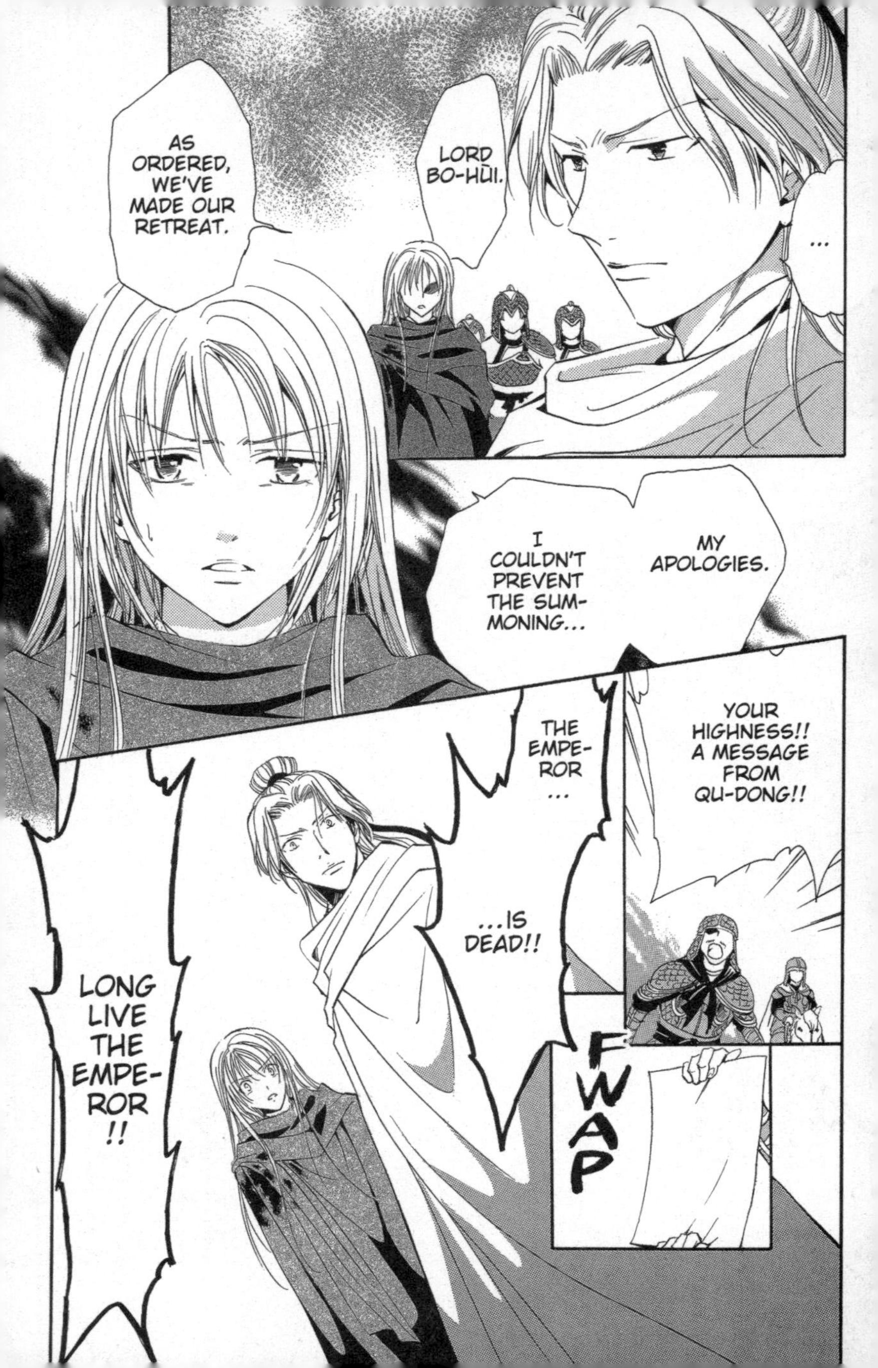
LORD BO-HŪI.
AS ORDERED, WE'VE MADE OUR RETREAT.
...
MY APOLOGIES.
I COULDN'T PREVENT THE SUM-MONING...
YOUR HIGHNESS!! A MESSAGE FROM QU-DONG!!
FWAP
THE EMPE-ROR ...
...IS DEAD!!
LONG LIVE THE EMPE-ROR !!

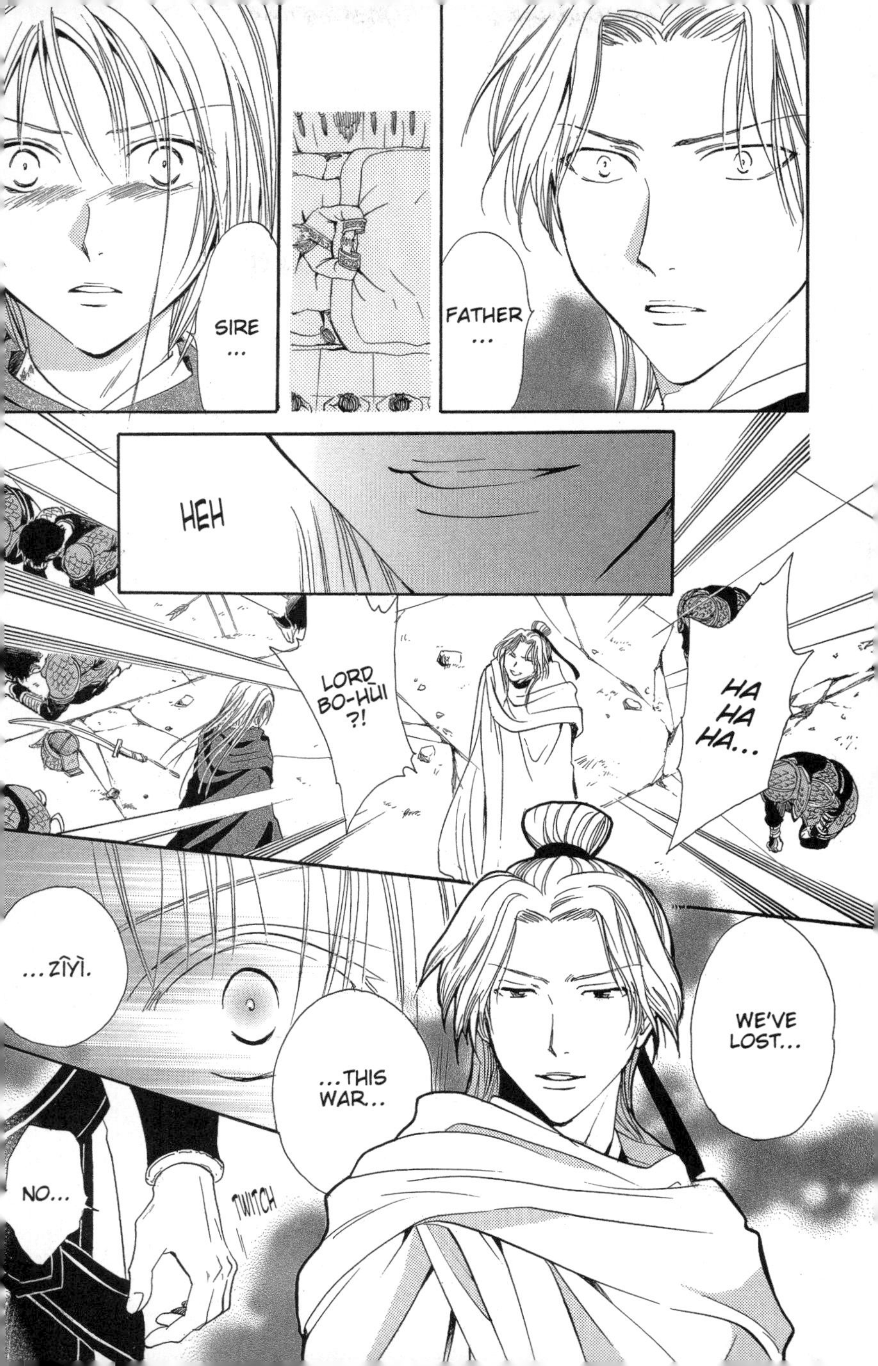
FATHER ...
SIRE ...
HEH
HA HA HA...
LORD BO-HÙI ?!
WE'VE LOST...
...THIS WAR...
...ZÎYÌ.
TWITCH
NO...

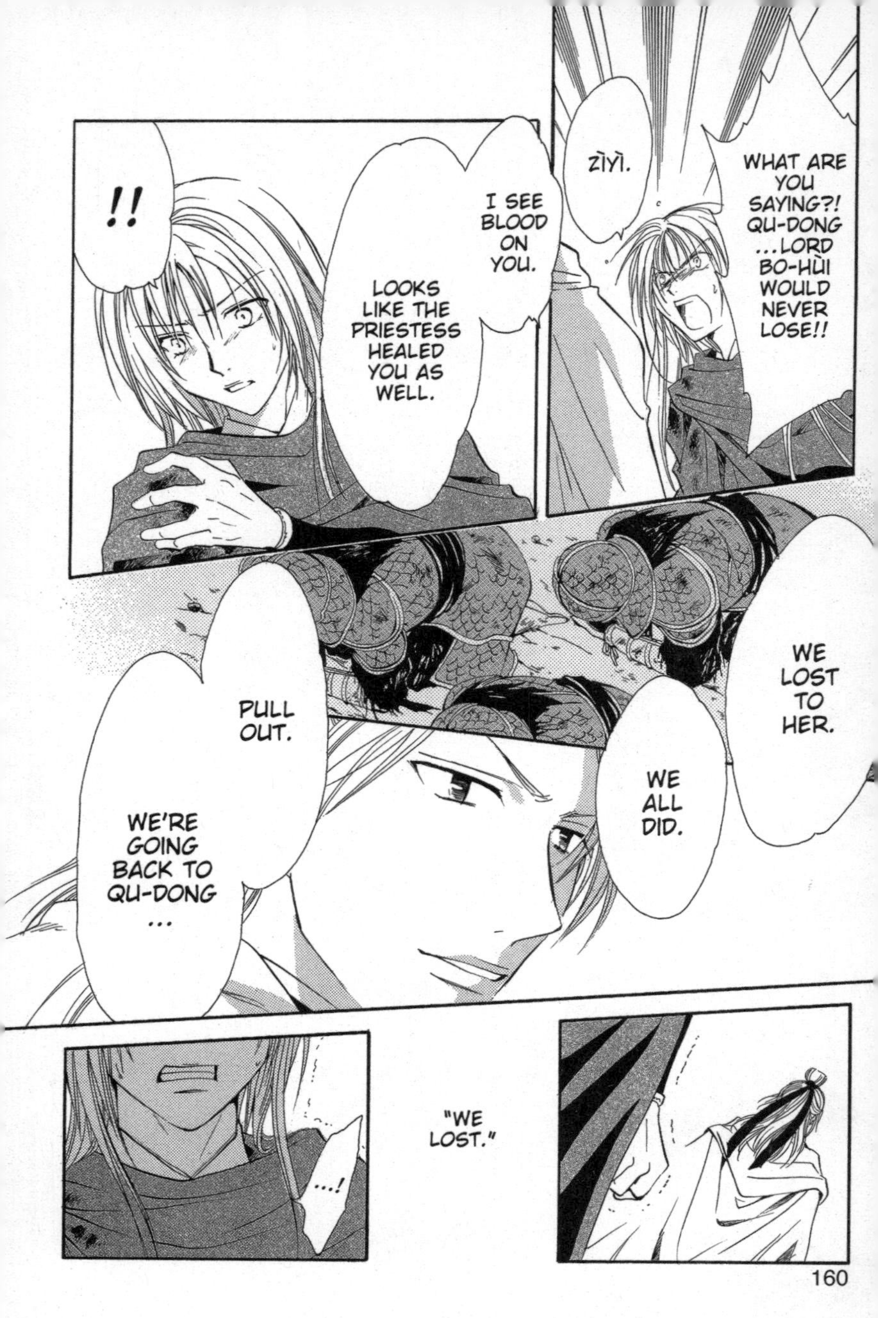
WHAT ARE YOU SAYING?! QU-DONG ...LORD BO-HÙI WOULD NEVER LOSE!!
ZÌYÌ.
I SEE BLOOD ON YOU.
LOOKS LIKE THE PRIESTESS HEALED YOU AS WELL.
!!
WE LOST TO HER.
WE ALL DID.
PULL OUT.
WE'RE GOING BACK TO QU-DONG ...
"WE LOST."
...!

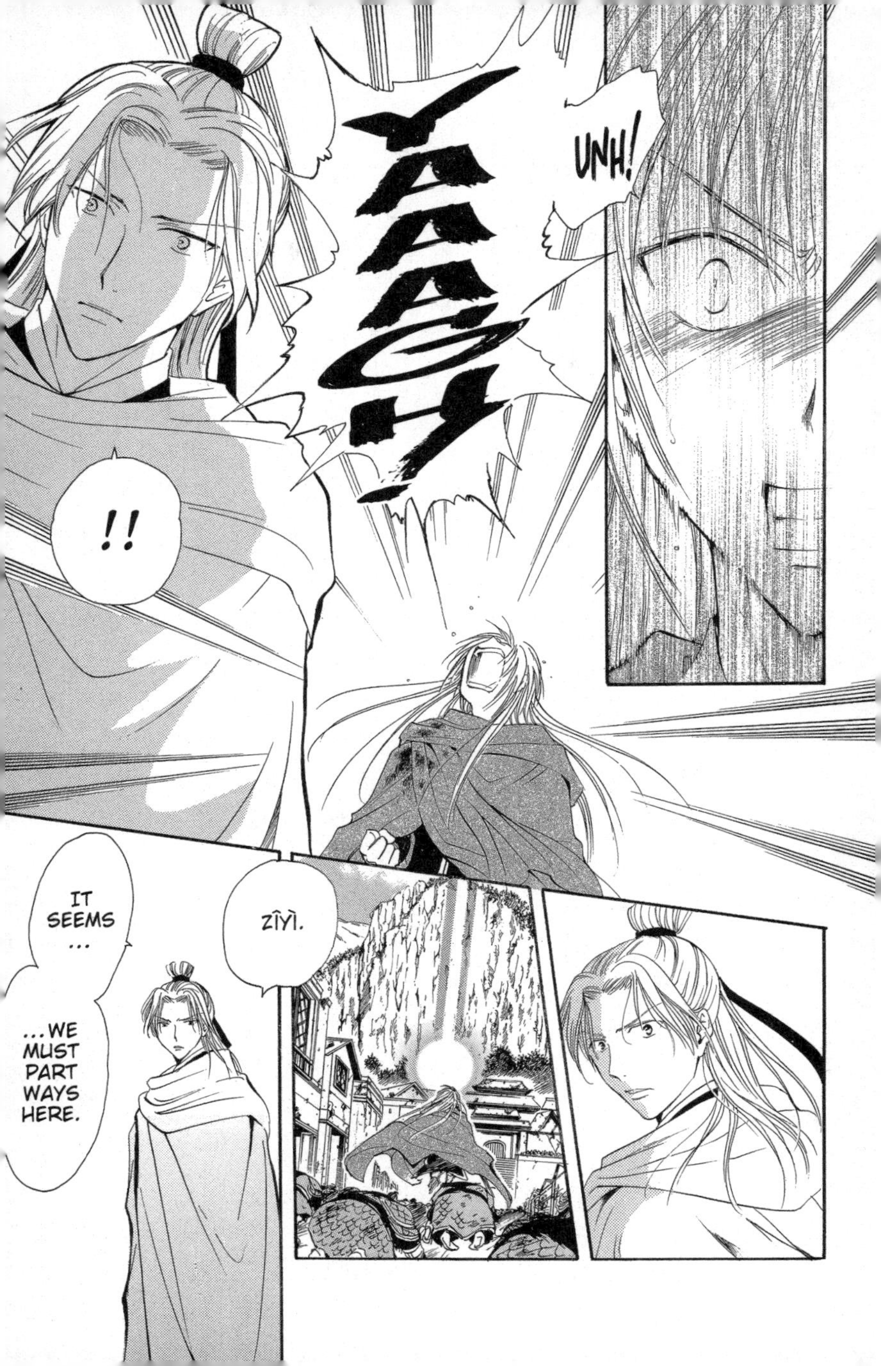
UNH!
YAAAGH!
!!
ZÎYÌ.
IT SEEMS...
...WE MUST PART WAYS HERE.

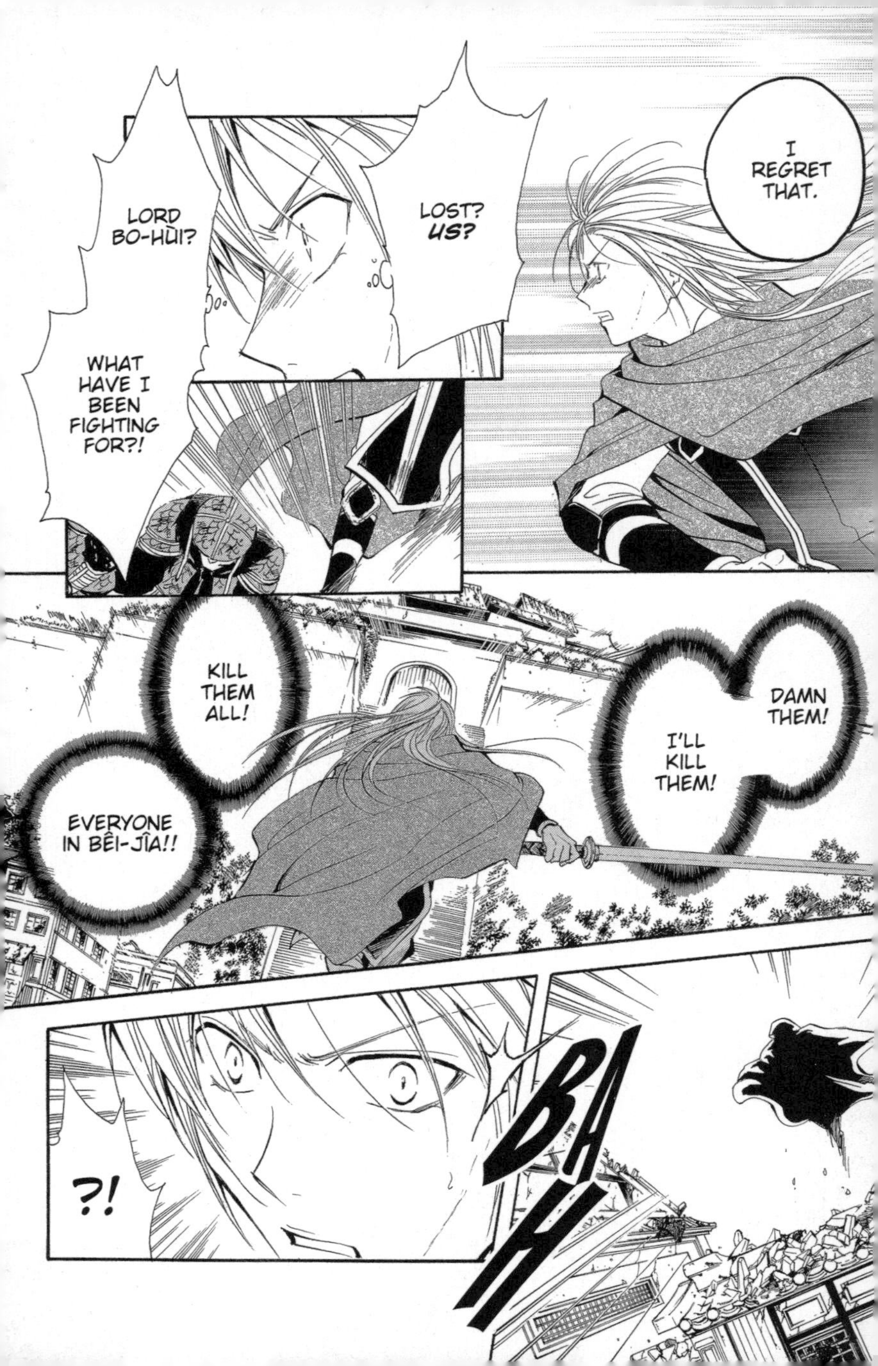
I REGRET THAT.
LOST? US?
LORD BO-HÙI?
WHAT HAVE I BEEN FIGHTING FOR?!
DAMN THEM!
I'LL KILL THEM!
KILL THEM ALL!
EVERYONE IN BÊI-JÎA!!
BAH
?!

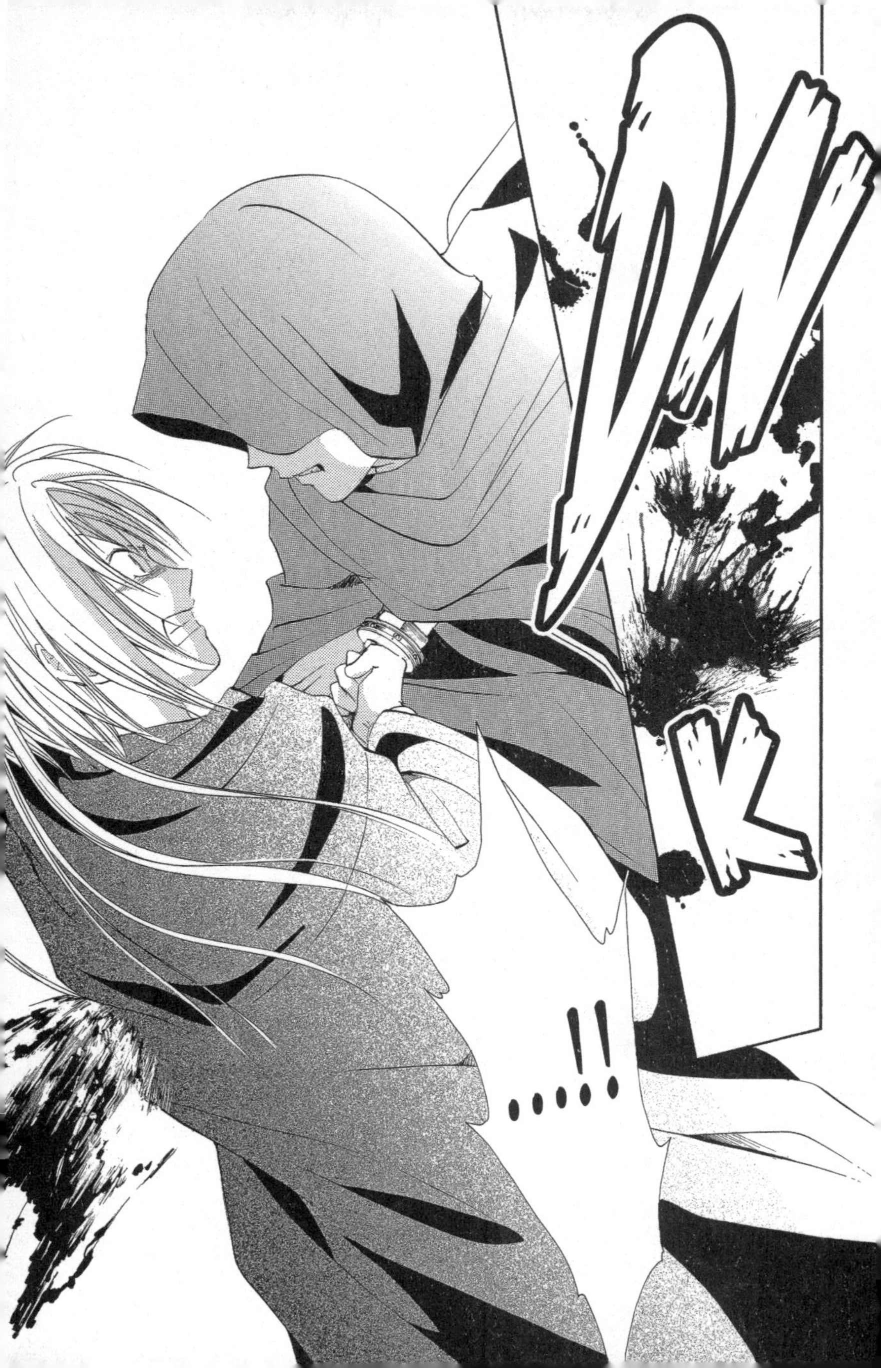
...!!

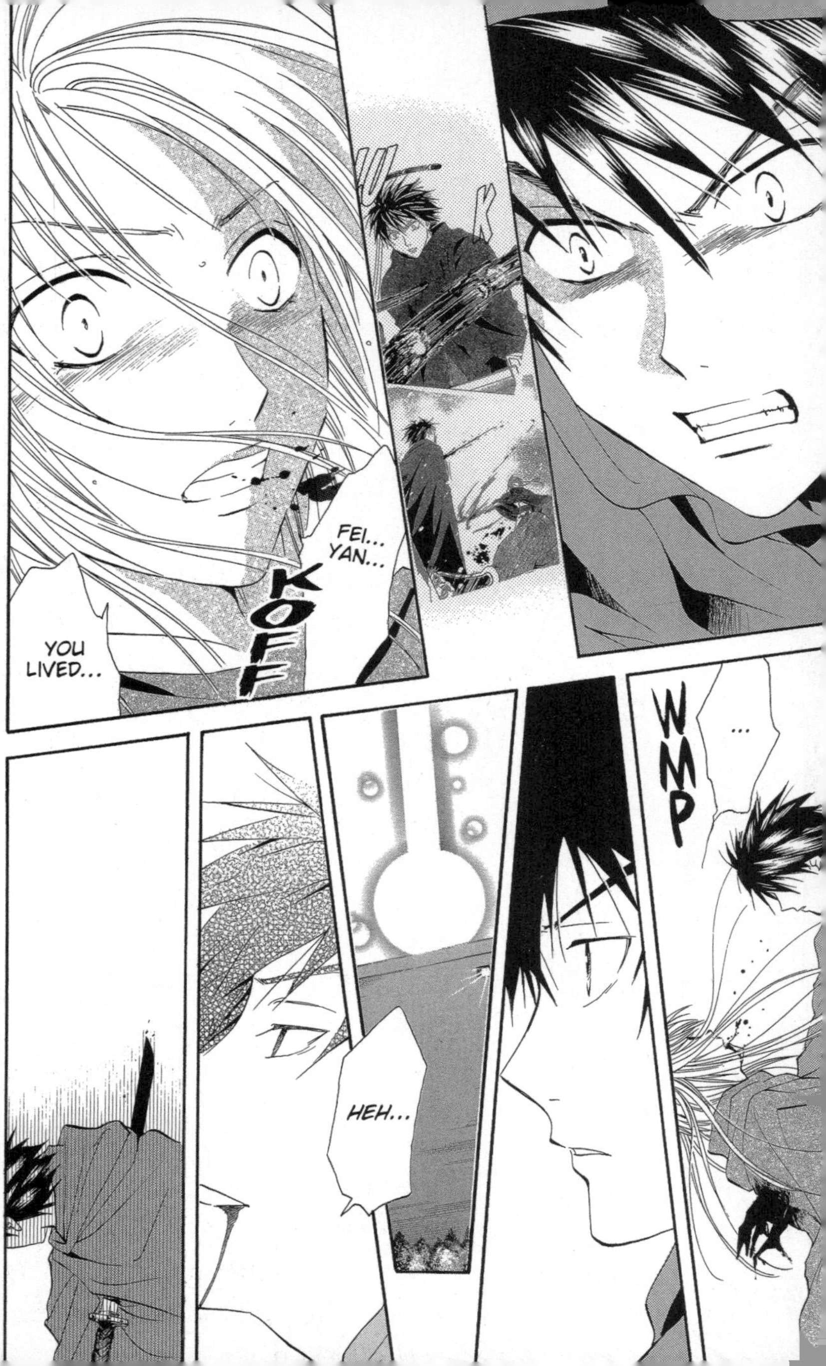
FEI... YAN...
KOFF
YOU LIVED...
WMP
...
HEH...

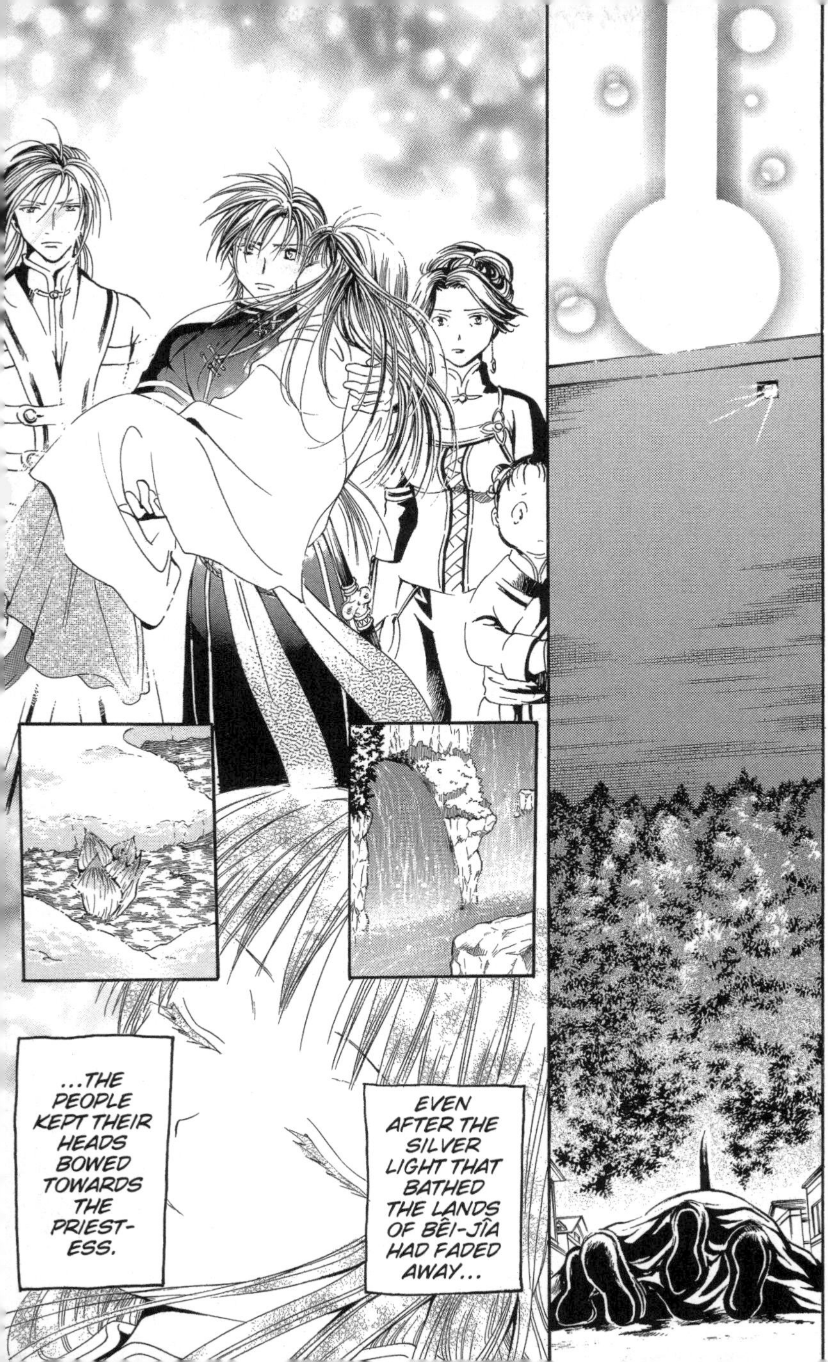
EVEN AFTER THE SILVER LIGHT THAT BATHED THE LANDS OF BÊI-JÎA HAD FADED AWAY...
...THE PEOPLE KEPT THEIR HEADS BOWED TOWARDS THE PRIEST-ESS.

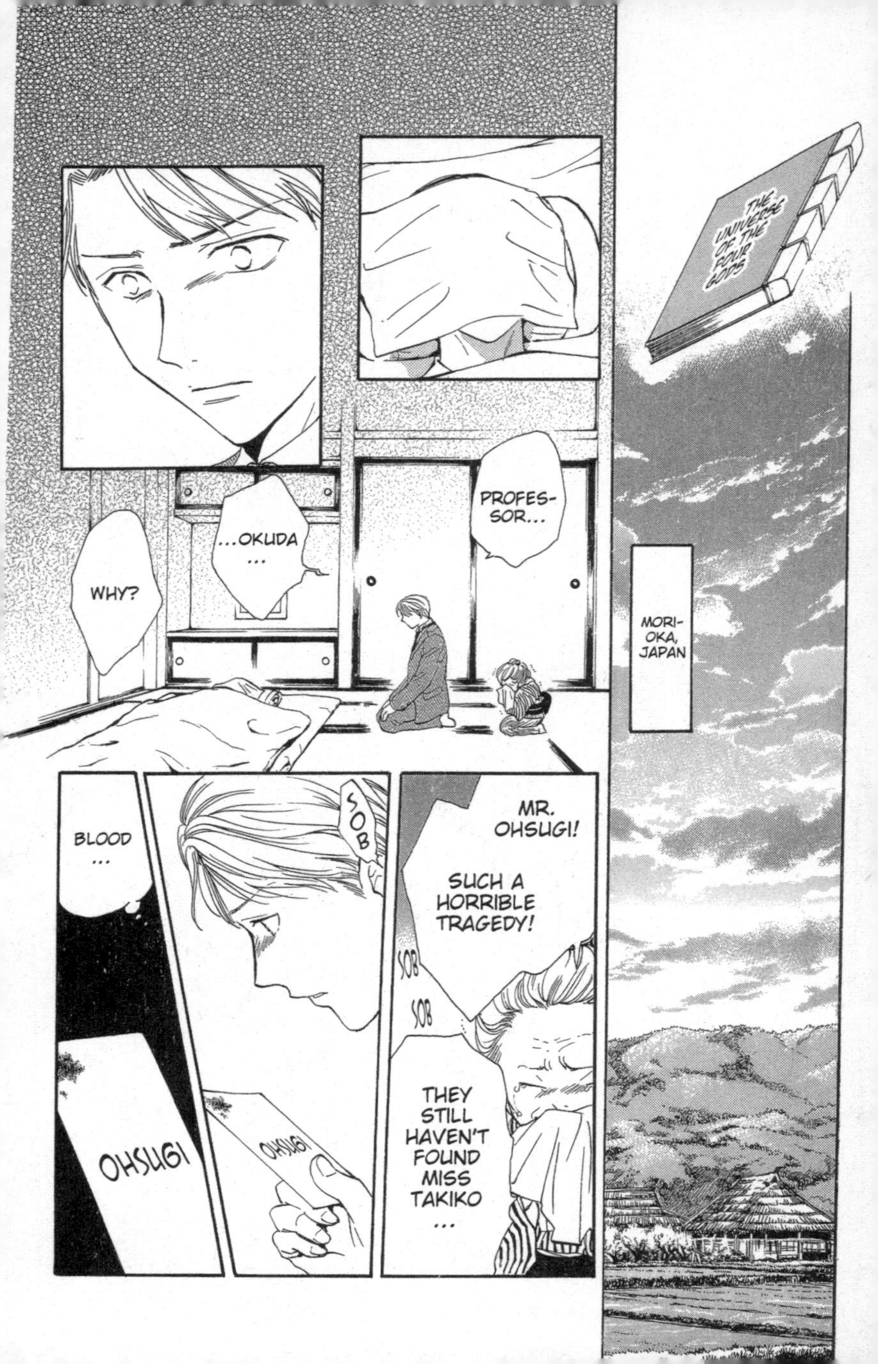
THE UNIVERSE OF THE FOUR GODS
MORI-OKA, JAPAN
PROFES-SOR...
...OKUDA ...
WHY?
MR. OHSUGI!
SUCH A HORRIBLE TRAGEDY!
SOB
SOB
THEY STILL HAVEN'T FOUND MISS TAKIKO ...
SOB
OHSUGI
BLOOD ...
OHSUGI

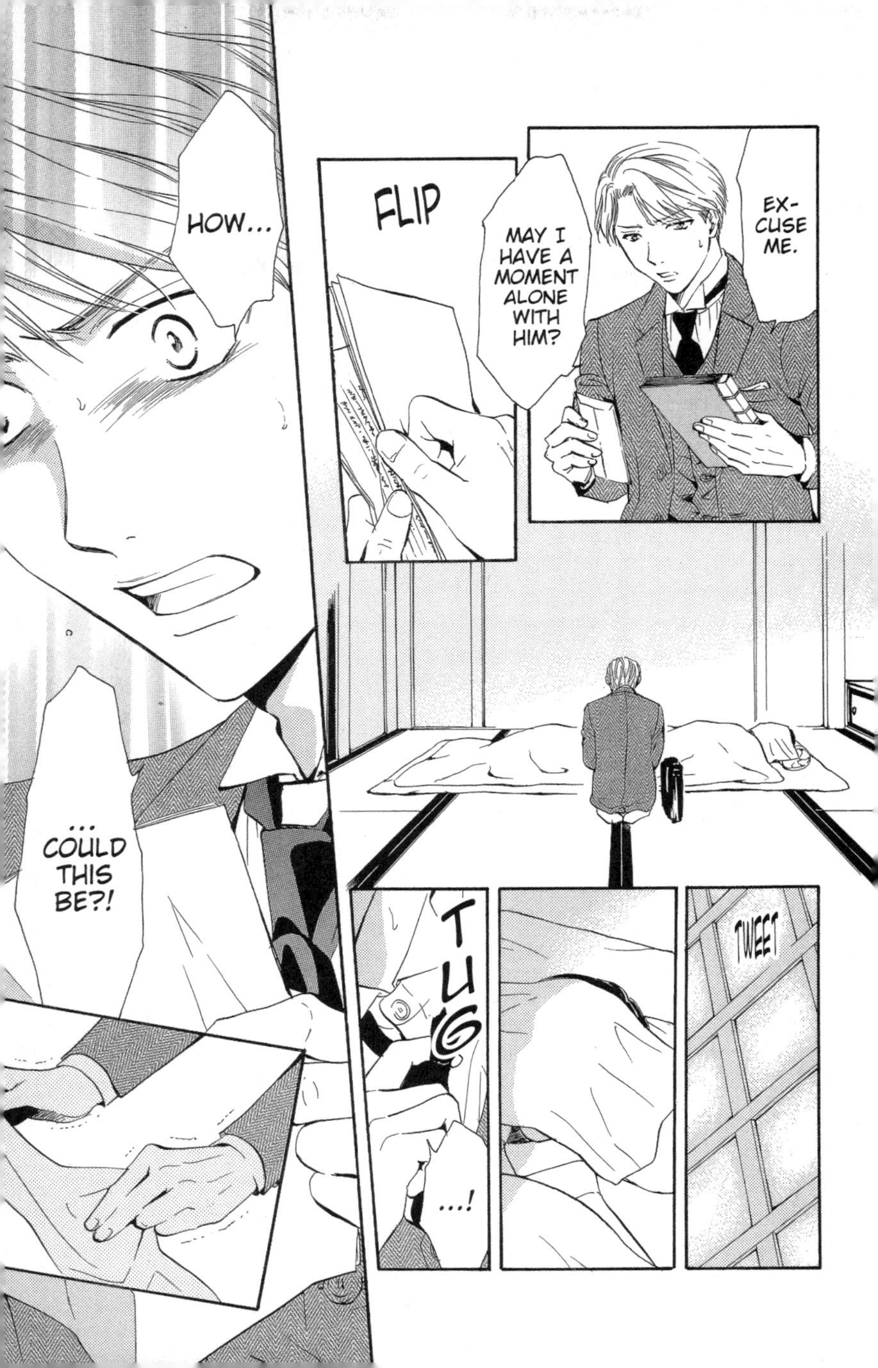
EX-CUSE ME.
MAY I HAVE A MOMENT ALONE WITH HIM?
FLIP
TWEET
TUG
...!
HOW...
...COULD THIS BE?!

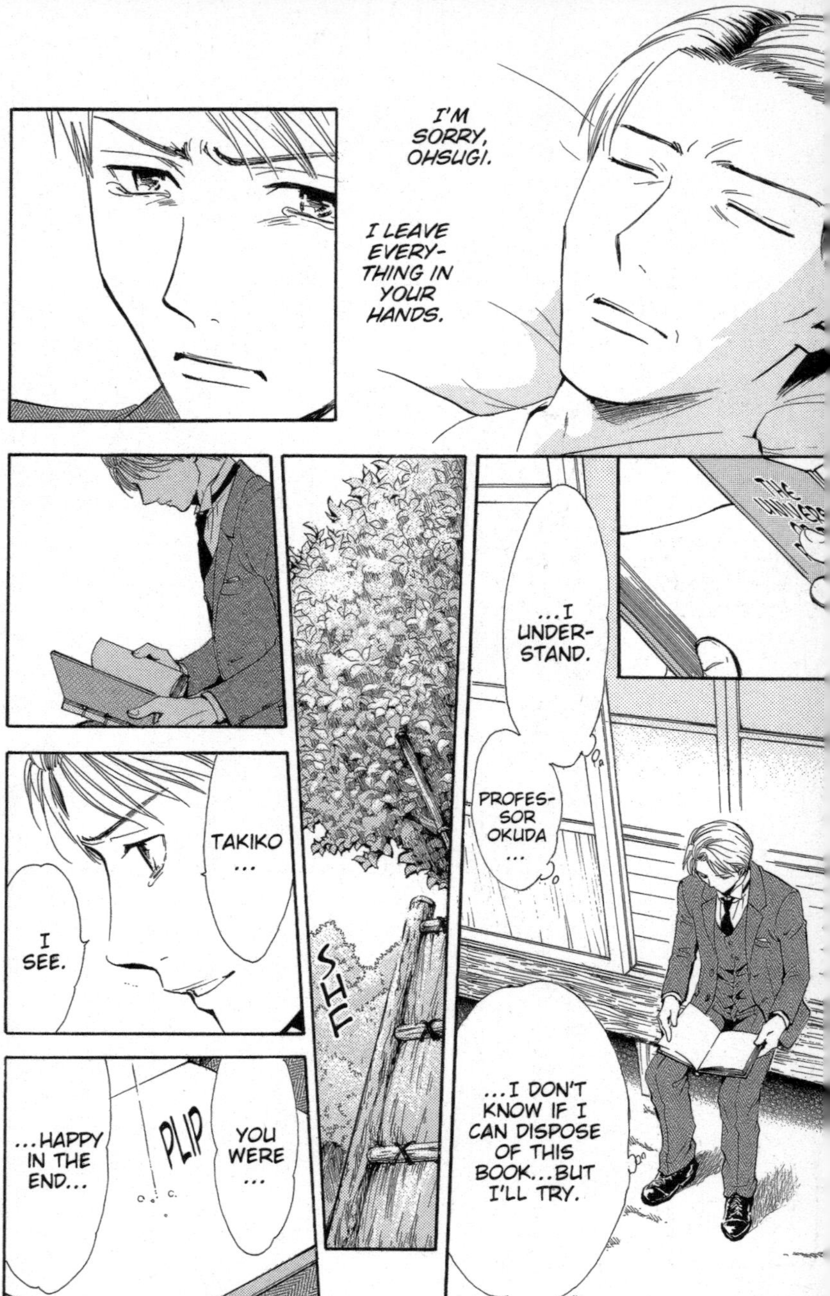
I'M SORRY, OHSUGI.
I LEAVE EVERYTHING IN YOUR HANDS.
...I UNDERSTAND.
PROFESSOR OKUDA...
...I DON'T KNOW IF I CAN DISPOSE OF THIS BOOK...BUT I'LL TRY.
SHFF
TAKIKO...
I SEE.
YOU WERE...
PLIP
...HAPPY IN THE END...

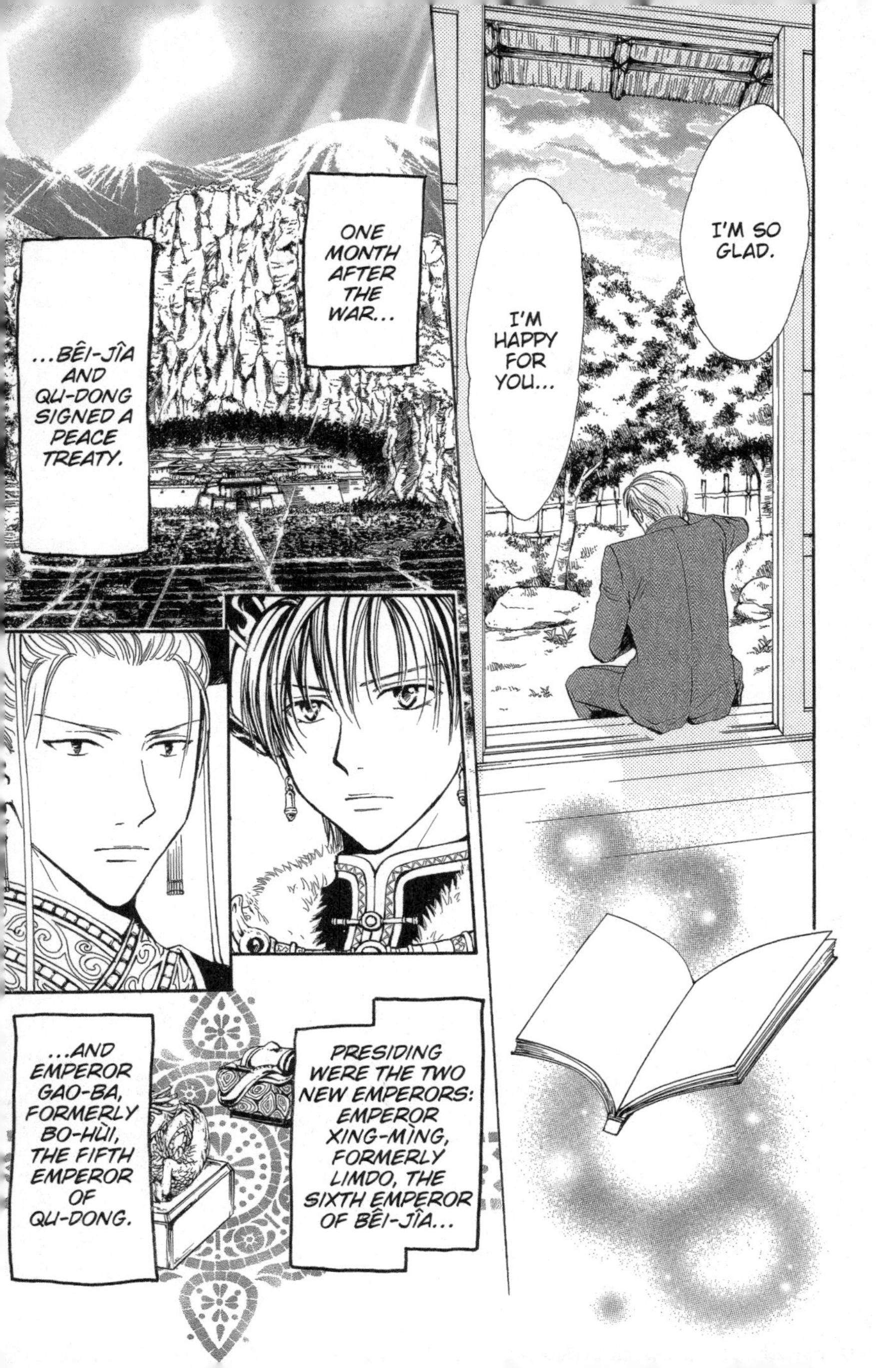
I'M SO GLAD.
I'M HAPPY FOR YOU...
ONE MONTH AFTER THE WAR...
...BÊI-JÎA AND QU-DONG SIGNED A PEACE TREATY.
PRESIDING WERE THE TWO NEW EMPERORS: EMPEROR XING-MÌNG, FORMERLY LIMDO, THE SIXTH EMPEROR OF BÊI-JÎA...
...AND EMPEROR GAO-BA, FORMERLY BO-HÙI, THE FIFTH EMPEROR OF QU-DONG.

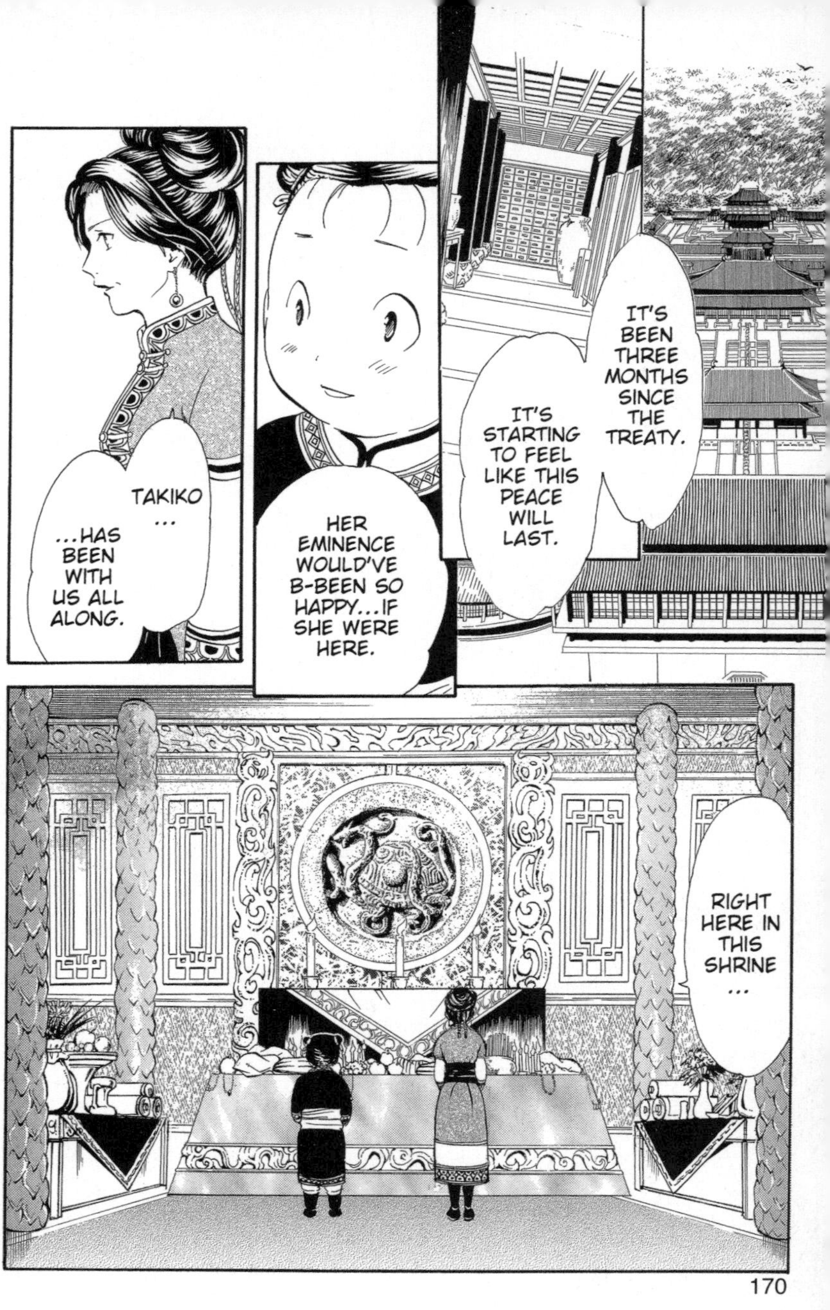
IT'S BEEN THREE MONTHS SINCE THE TREATY.
IT'S STARTING TO FEEL LIKE THIS PEACE WILL LAST.
HER EMINENCE WOULD'VE B-BEEN SO HAPPY...IF SHE WERE HERE.
TAKIKO ...
...HAS BEEN WITH US ALL ALONG.
RIGHT HERE IN THIS SHRINE ...

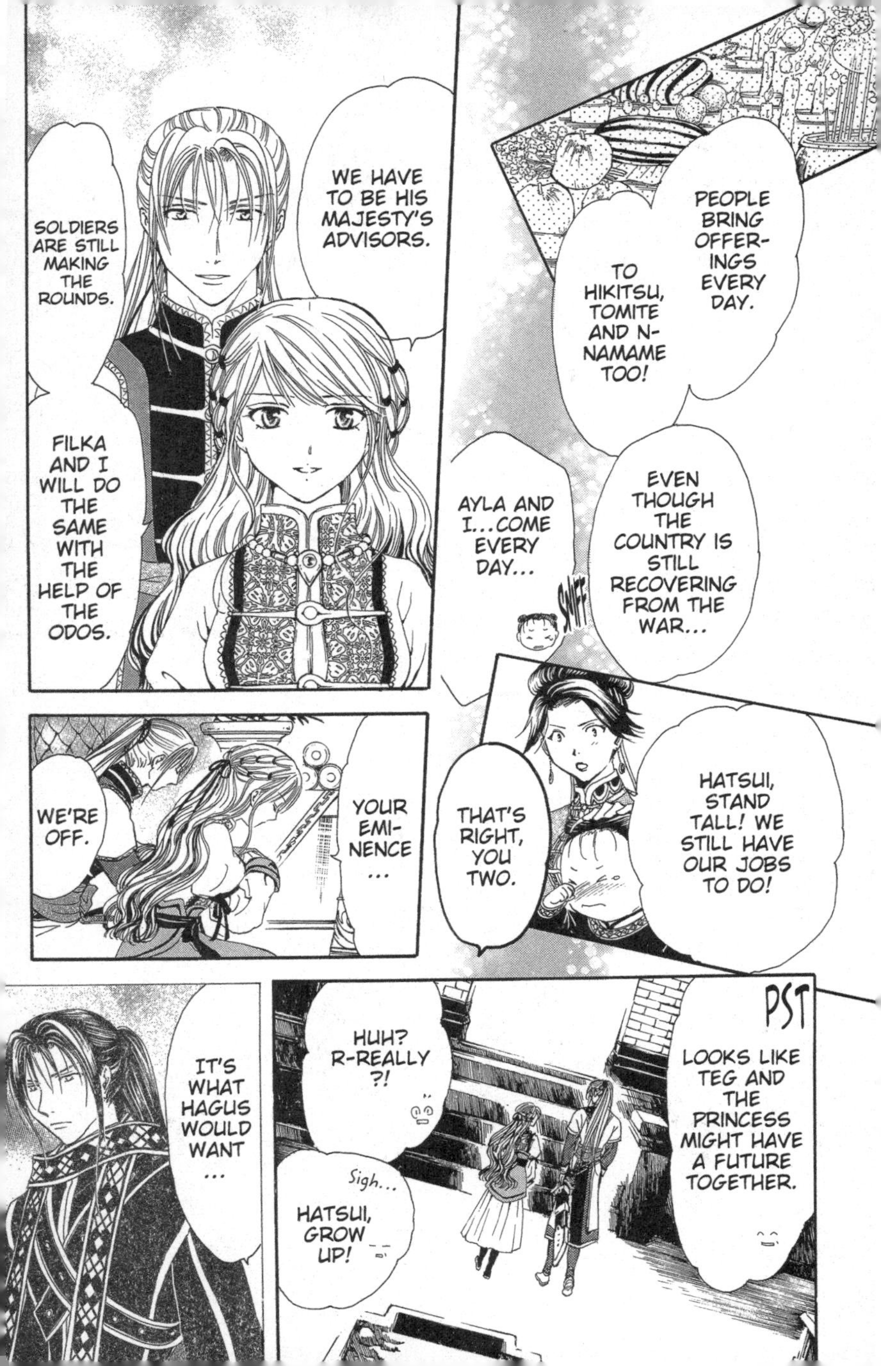
PEOPLE BRING OFFERINGS EVERY DAY.
TO HIKITSU, TOMITE AND N-NAMAME TOO!
EVEN THOUGH THE COUNTRY IS STILL RECOVERING FROM THE WAR...
AYLA AND I...COME EVERY DAY...
SNIFF
HATSUI, STAND TALL! WE STILL HAVE OUR JOBS TO DO!
THAT'S RIGHT, YOU TWO.
WE HAVE TO BE HIS MAJESTY'S ADVISORS.
SOLDIERS ARE STILL MAKING THE ROUNDS.
FILKA AND I WILL DO THE SAME WITH THE HELP OF THE ODOS.
YOUR EMINENCE...
WE'RE OFF.
PST
LOOKS LIKE TEG AND THE PRINCESS MIGHT HAVE A FUTURE TOGETHER.
HUH? R-REALLY?!
Sigh...
HATSUI, GROW UP!
IT'S WHAT HAGUS WOULD WANT...

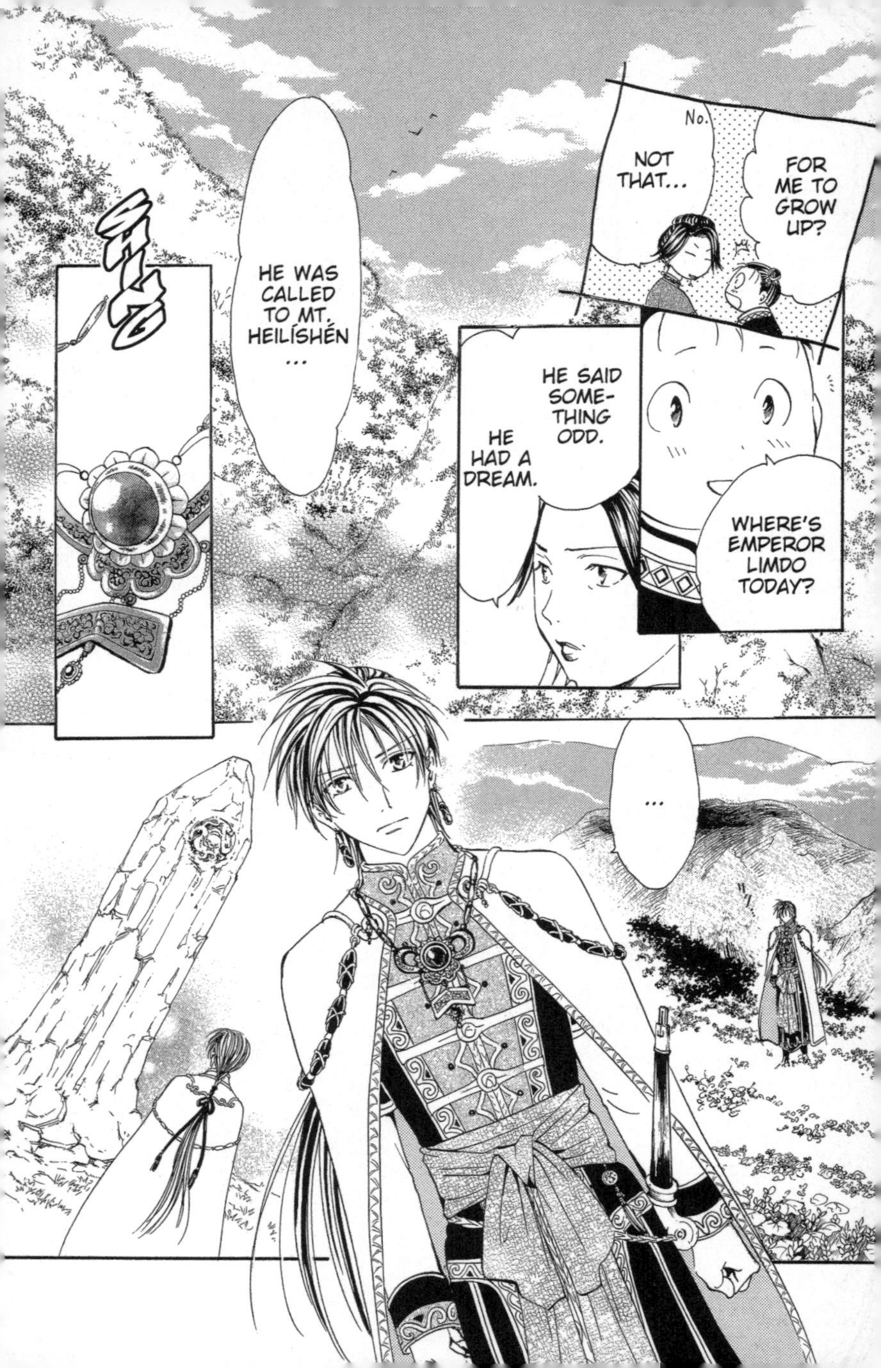
FOR ME TO GROW UP?
No.
NOT THAT...
WHERE'S EMPEROR LIMDO TODAY?
HE SAID SOME-THING ODD.
HE HAD A DREAM.
HE WAS CALLED TO MT. HEILÍSHÉN ...
SHING
...

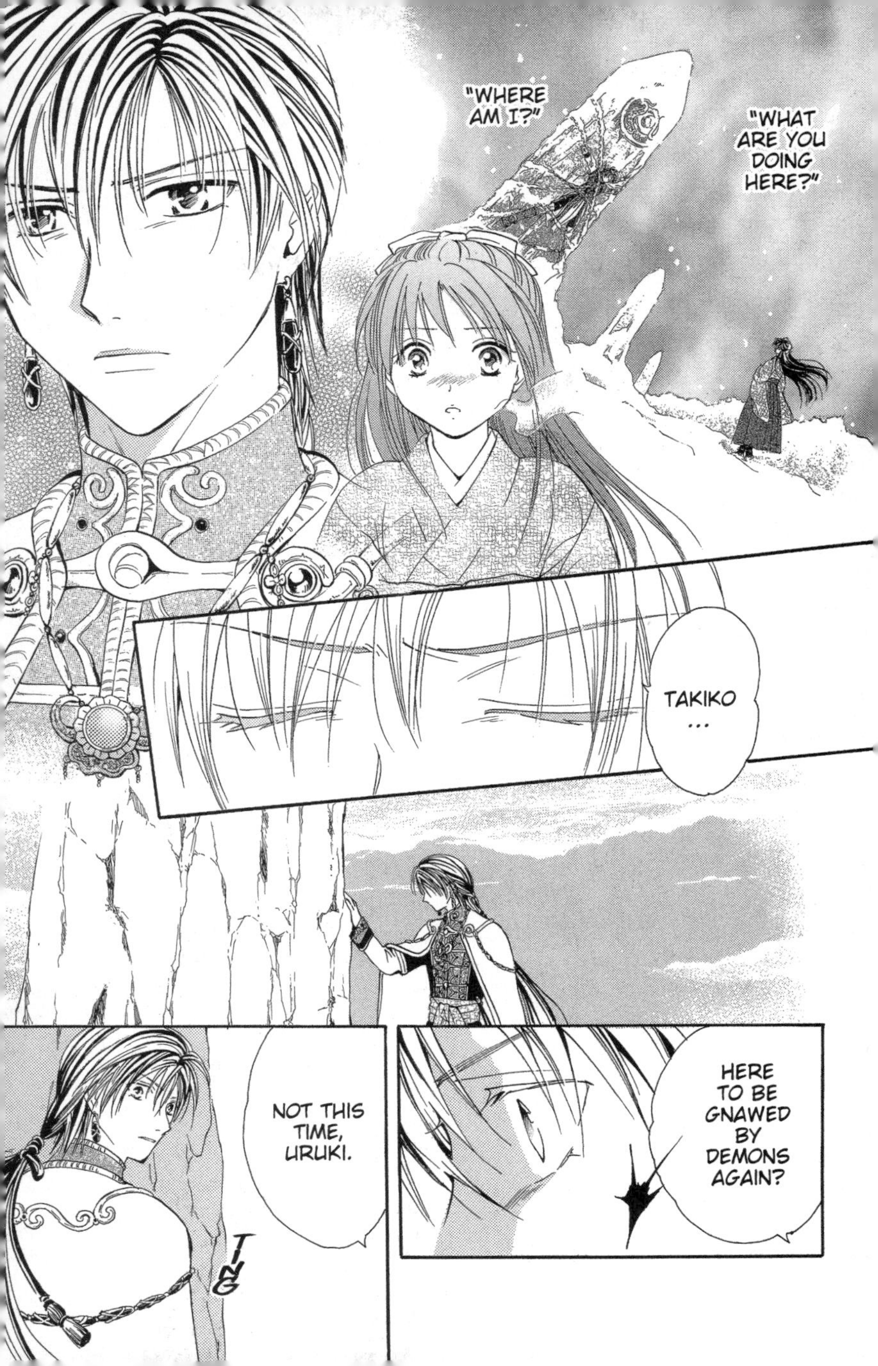
"WHAT ARE YOU DOING HERE?"
"WHERE AM I?"
TAKIKO ...
HERE TO BE GNAWED BY DEMONS AGAIN?
NOT THIS TIME, URUKI.
TING

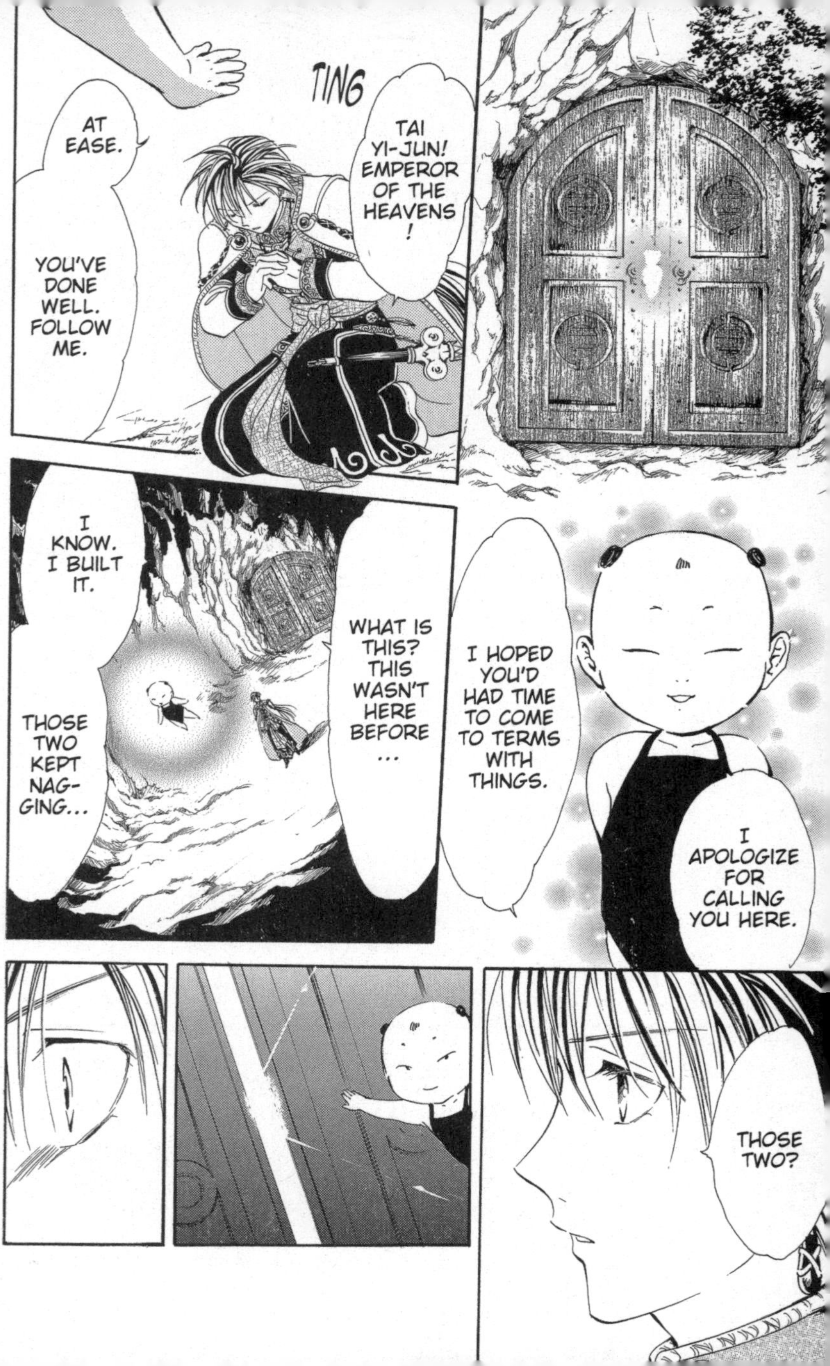
TING
TAI YI-JUN! EMPEROR OF THE HEAVENS!
AT EASE.
YOU'VE DONE WELL. FOLLOW ME.
I APOLOGIZE FOR CALLING YOU HERE.
I HOPED YOU'D HAD TIME TO COME TO TERMS WITH THINGS.
WHAT IS THIS? THIS WASN'T HERE BEFORE...
I KNOW. I BUILT IT.
THOSE TWO KEPT NAG-GING...
THOSE TWO?

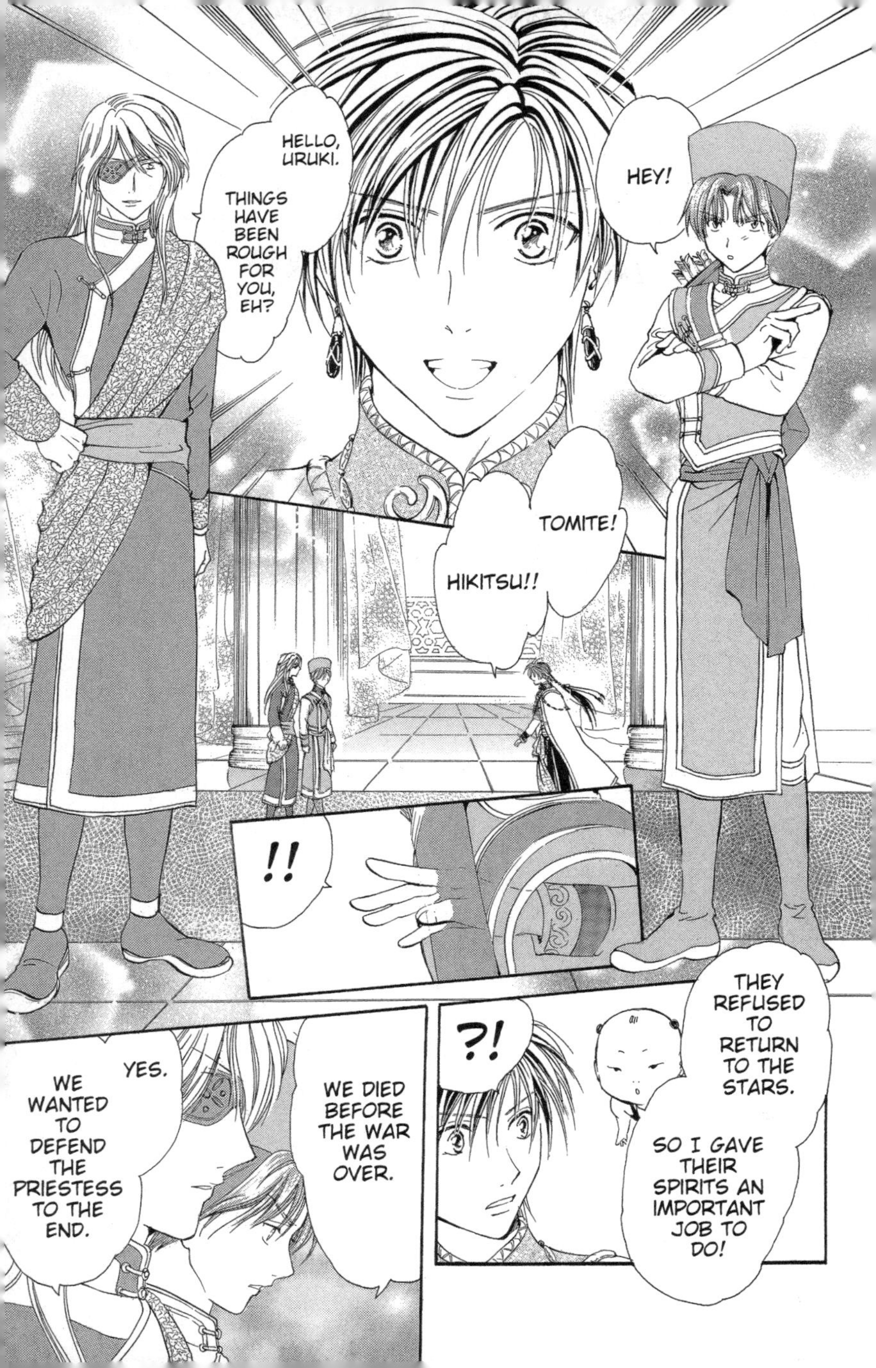
HEY!
HELLO, URUKI.
THINGS HAVE BEEN ROUGH FOR YOU, EH?
TOMITE!
HIKITSU!!
!!
?!
THEY REFUSED TO RETURN TO THE STARS.
SO I GAVE THEIR SPIRITS AN IMPORTANT JOB TO DO!
YES.
WE DIED BEFORE THE WAR WAS OVER.
WE WANTED TO DEFEND THE PRIESTESS TO THE END.

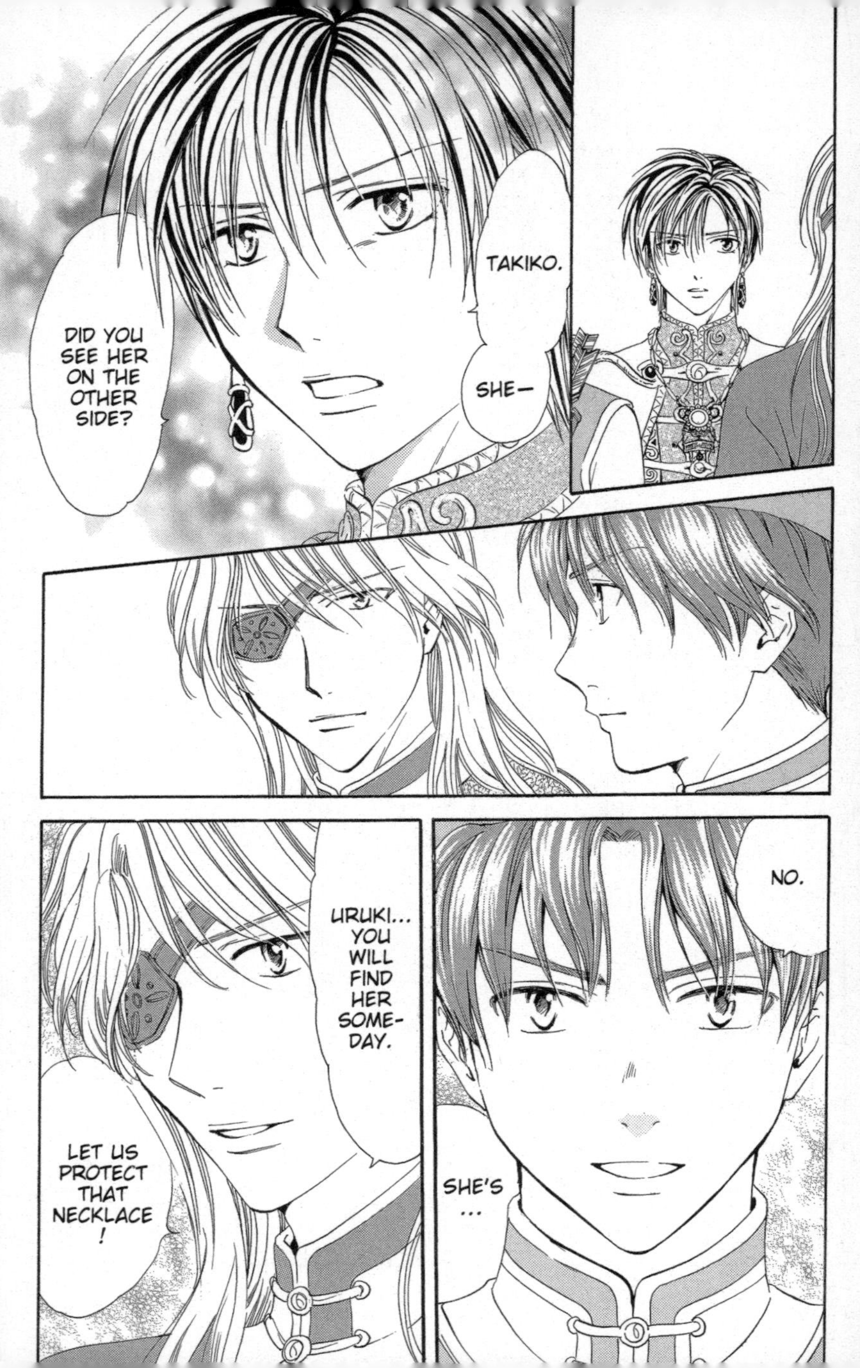
TAKIKO.
SHE—
DID YOU SEE HER ON THE OTHER SIDE?
NO.
SHE'S ...
URUKI... YOU WILL FIND HER SOME-DAY.
LET US PROTECT THAT NECKLACE!

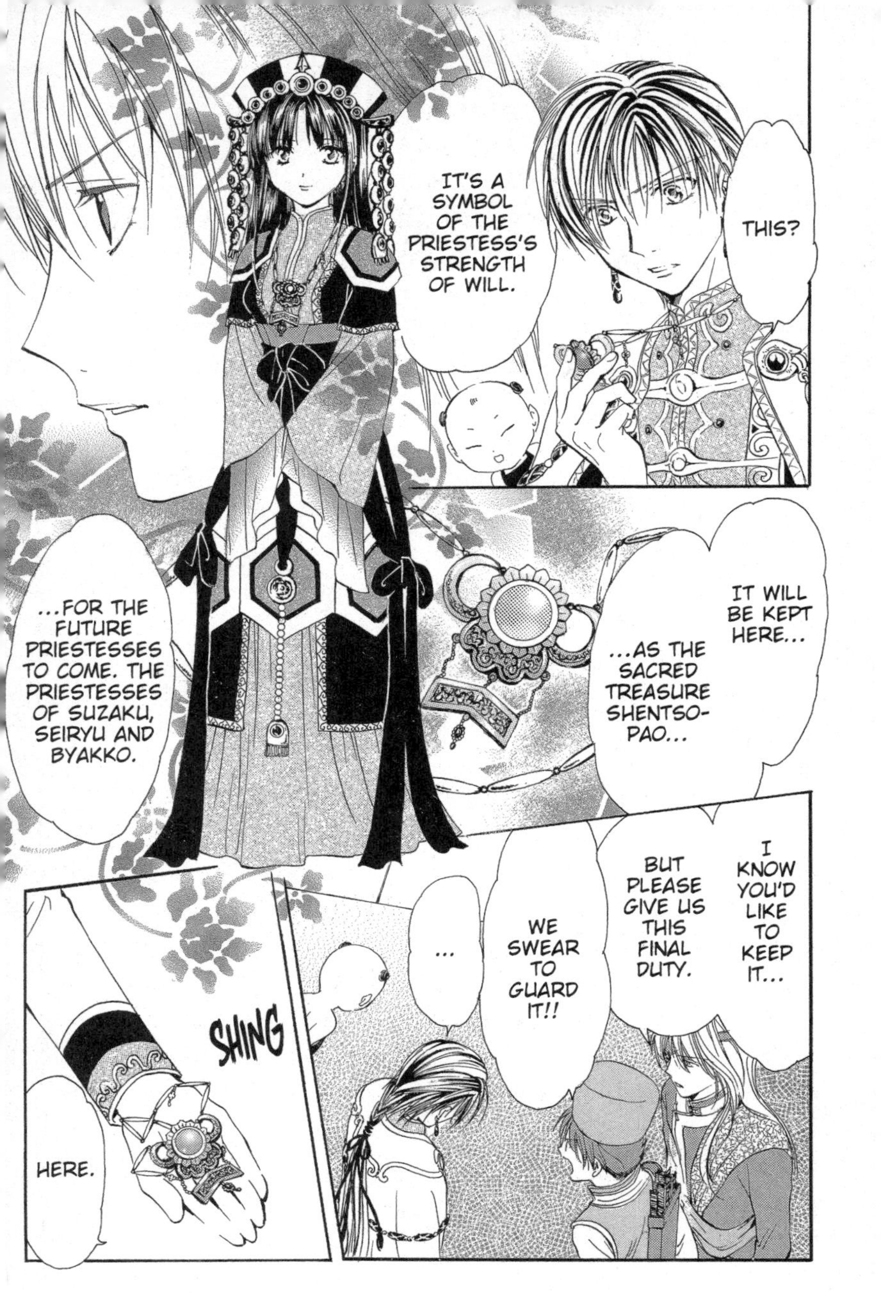
THIS?
IT'S A SYMBOL OF THE PRIESTESS'S STRENGTH OF WILL.
IT WILL BE KEPT HERE...
...AS THE SACRED TREASURE SHENTSO-PAO...
...FOR THE FUTURE PRIESTESSES TO COME. THE PRIESTESSES OF SUZAKU, SEIRYU AND BYAKKO.
I KNOW YOU'D LIKE TO KEEP IT...
BUT PLEASE GIVE US THIS FINAL DUTY.
WE SWEAR TO GUARD IT!!
...
SHING
HERE.

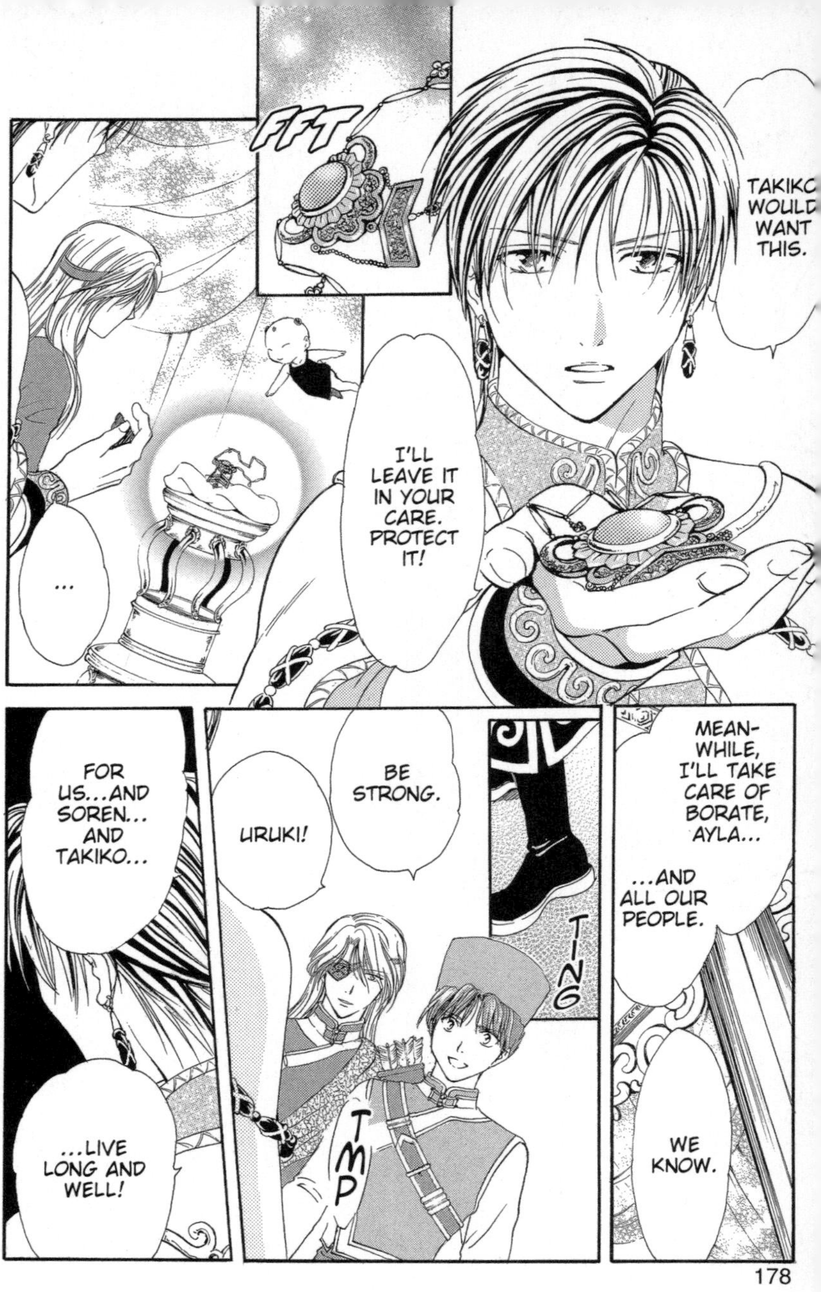
TAKIKO WOULD WANT THIS.
I'LL LEAVE IT IN YOUR CARE. PROTECT IT!
FFT
...
MEAN-WHILE, I'LL TAKE CARE OF BORATE, AYLA...
...AND ALL OUR PEOPLE.
WE KNOW.
TING
BE STRONG.
URUKI!
TMP
FOR US...AND SOREN...AND TAKIKO...
...LIVE LONG AND WELL!

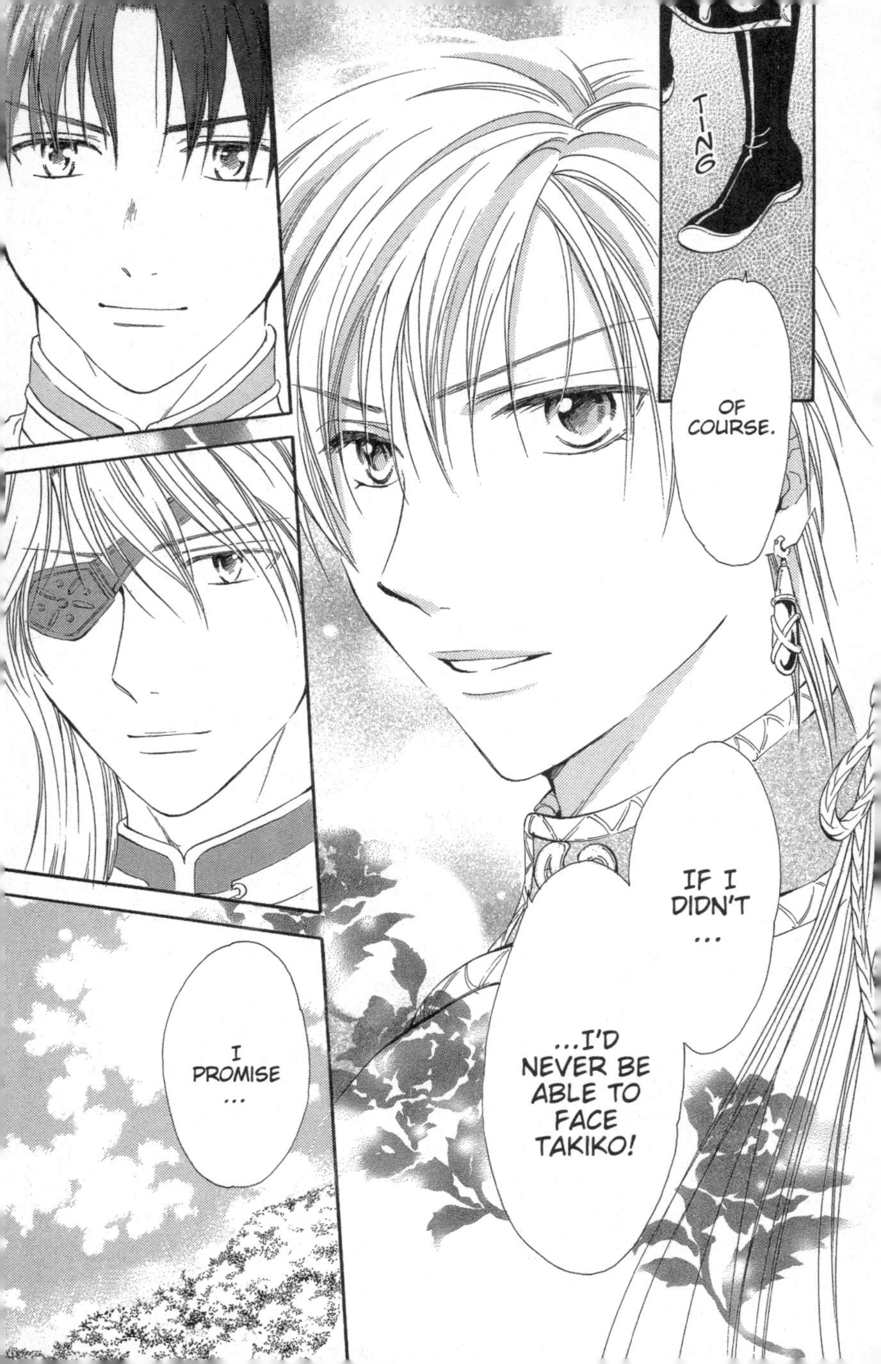
TING
OF COURSE.
IF I DIDN'T ...
...I'D NEVER BE ABLE TO FACE TAKIKO!
I PROMISE ...

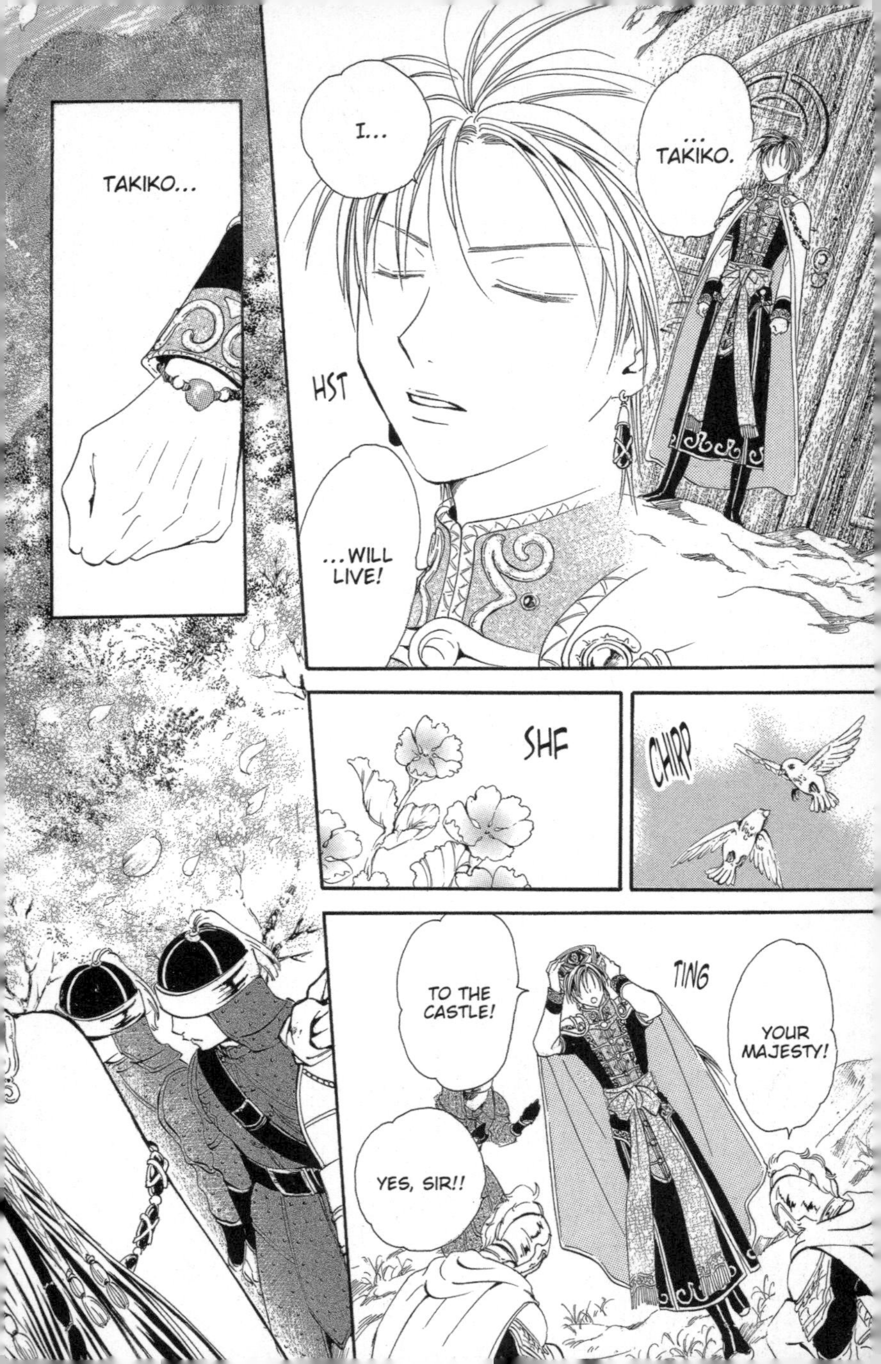
...TAKIKO.
I...
HST
...WILL LIVE!
CHIRP
SHF
TING
YOUR MAJESTY!
TO THE CASTLE!
YES, SIR!!
TAKIKO...

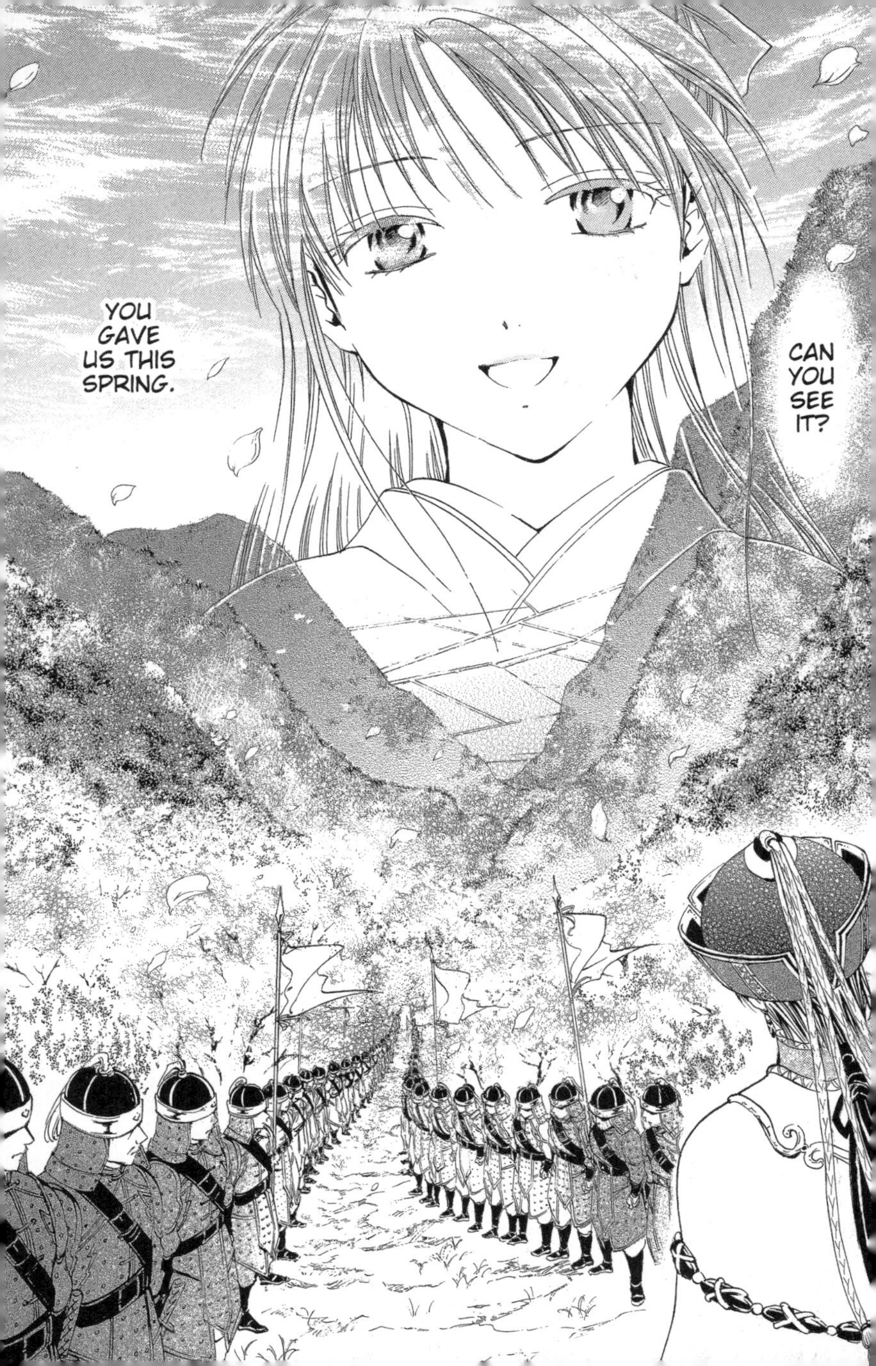
CAN YOU SEE IT?
YOU GAVE US THIS SPRING.

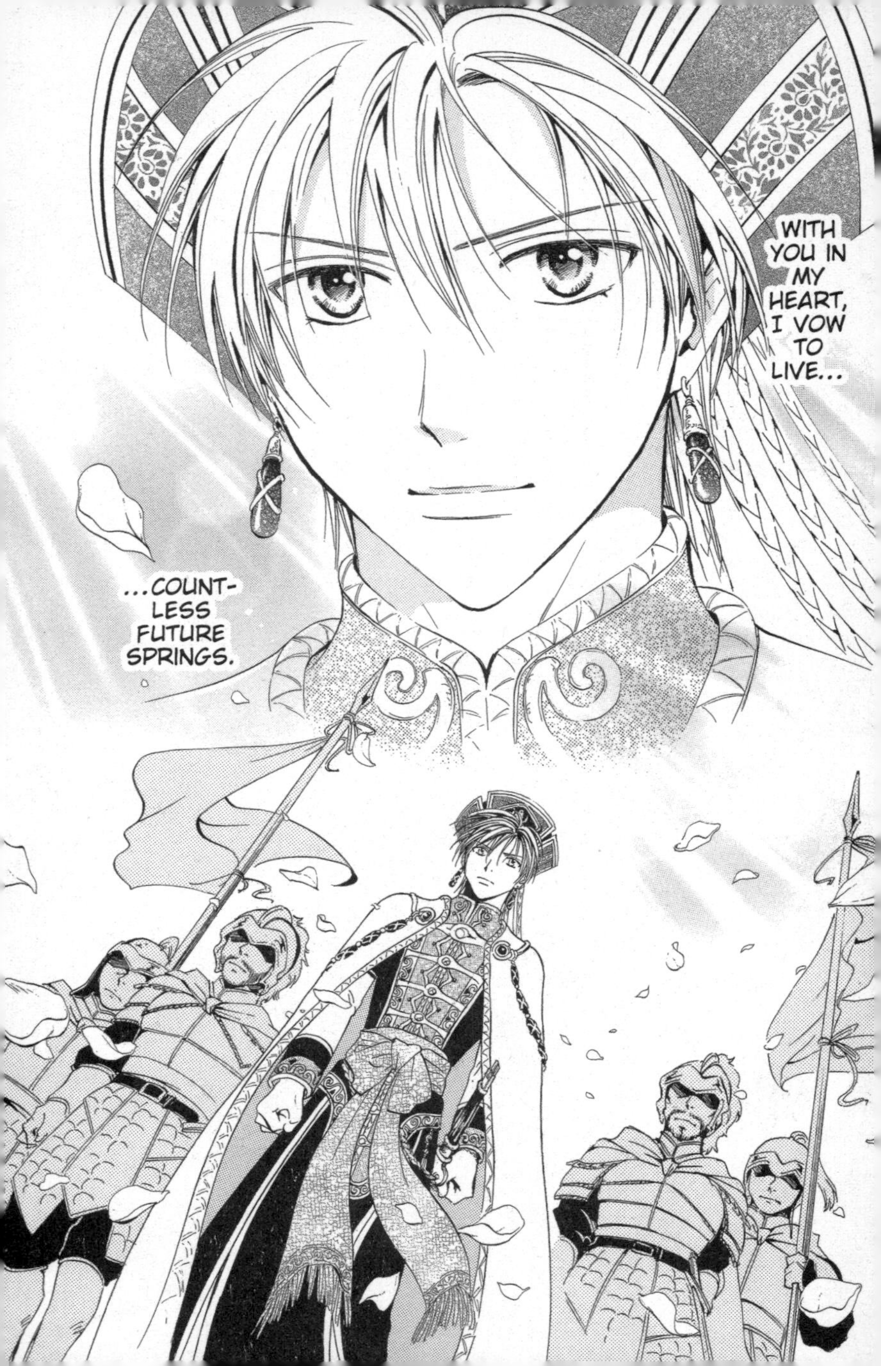
WITH YOU IN MY HEART, I VOW TO LIVE...
...COUNT-LESS FUTURE SPRINGS.

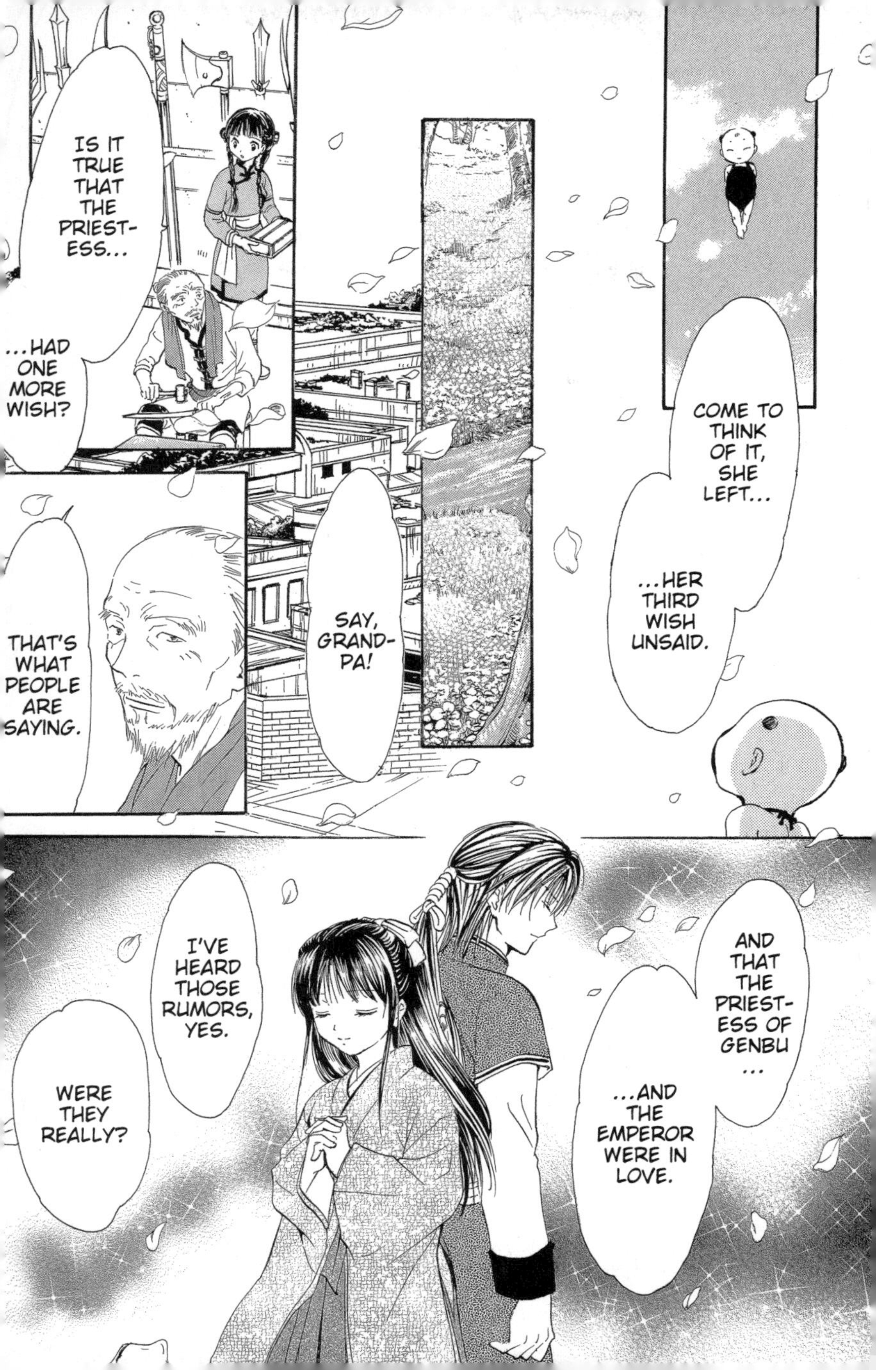
COME TO THINK OF IT, SHE LEFT...
...HER THIRD WISH UNSAID.
SAY, GRANDPA!
IS IT TRUE THAT THE PRIEST-ESS...
...HAD ONE MORE WISH?
THAT'S WHAT PEOPLE ARE SAYING.
AND THAT THE PRIEST-ESS OF GENBU...
...AND THE EMPEROR WERE IN LOVE.
I'VE HEARD THOSE RUMORS, YES.
WERE THEY REALLY?

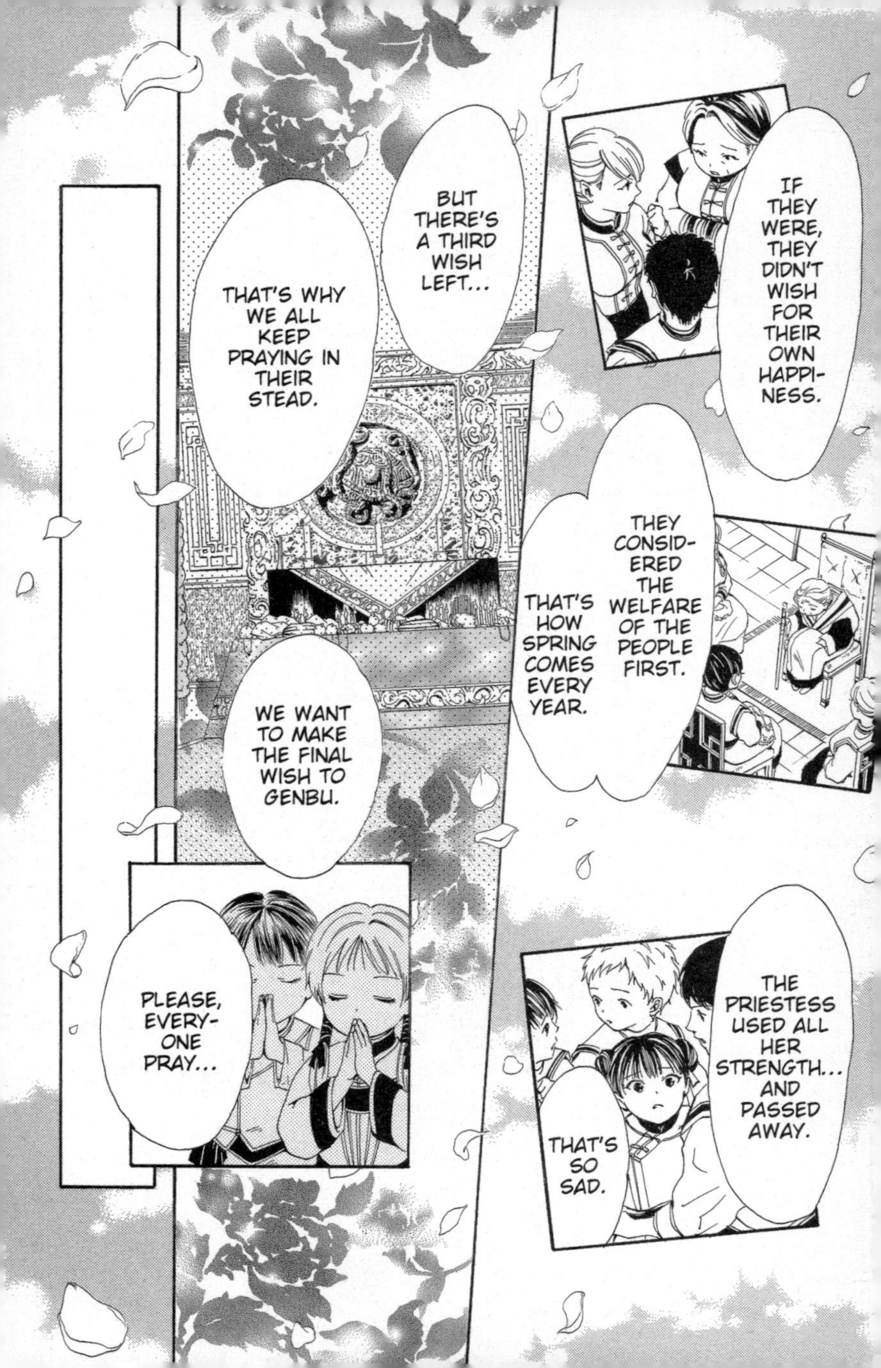
IF THEY WERE, THEY DIDN'T WISH FOR THEIR OWN HAPPI-NESS.
THEY CONSID-ERED THE WELFARE OF THE PEOPLE FIRST.
THAT'S HOW SPRING COMES EVERY YEAR.
THE PRIESTESS USED ALL HER STRENGTH... AND PASSED AWAY.
THAT'S SO SAD.
BUT THERE'S A THIRD WISH LEFT...
THAT'S WHY WE ALL KEEP PRAYING IN THEIR STEAD.
WE WANT TO MAKE THE FINAL WISH TO GENBU.
PLEASE, EVERY-ONE PRAY...

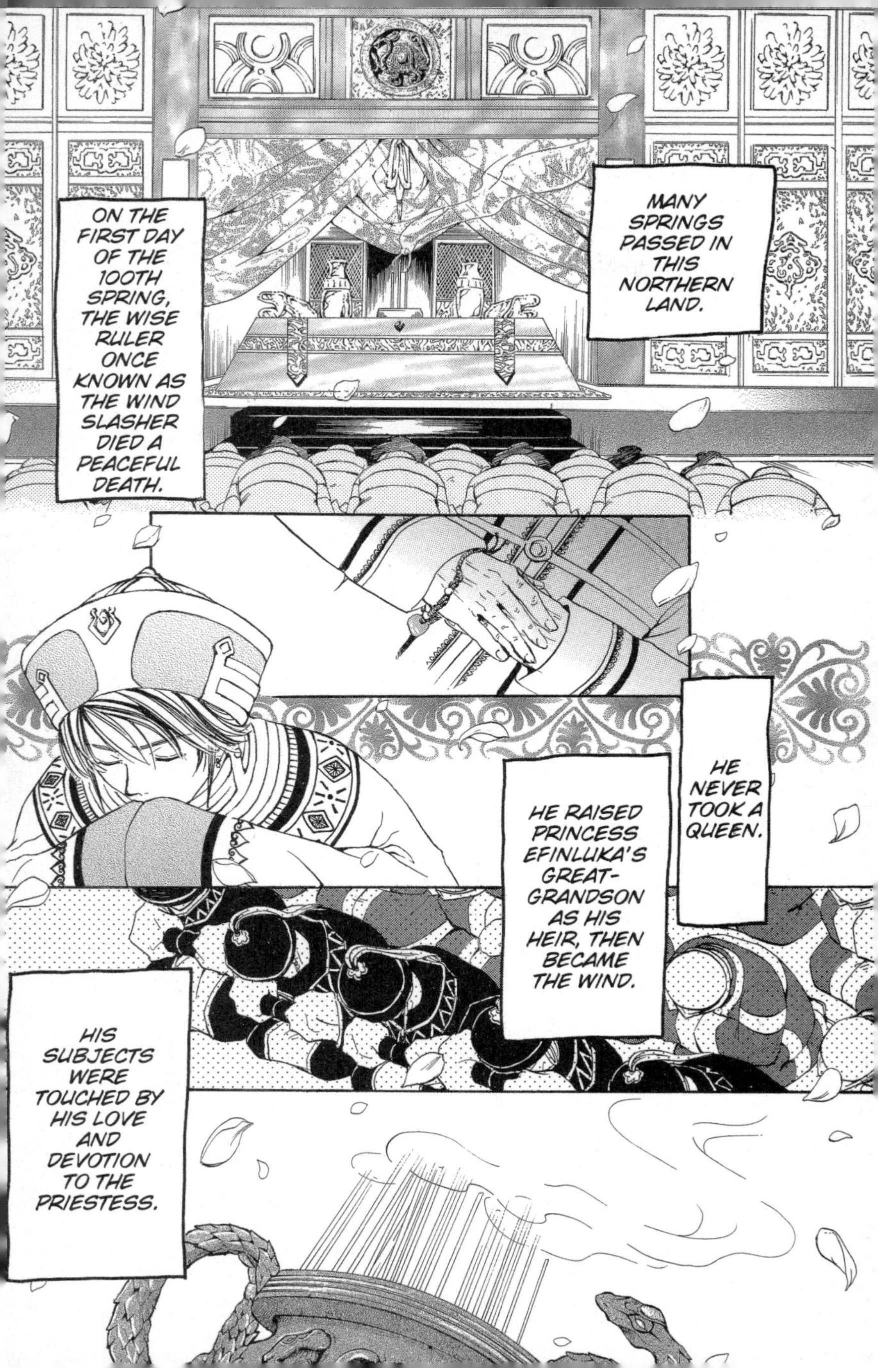
MANY SPRINGS PASSED IN THIS NORTHERN LAND.
ON THE FIRST DAY OF THE 100TH SPRING, THE WISE RULER ONCE KNOWN AS THE WIND SLASHER DIED A PEACEFUL DEATH.
HE NEVER TOOK A QUEEN.
HE RAISED PRINCESS EFINLUKA'S GREAT-GRANDSON AS HIS HEIR, THEN BECAME THE WIND.
HIS SUBJECTS WERE TOUCHED BY HIS LOVE AND DEVOTION TO THE PRIESTESS.

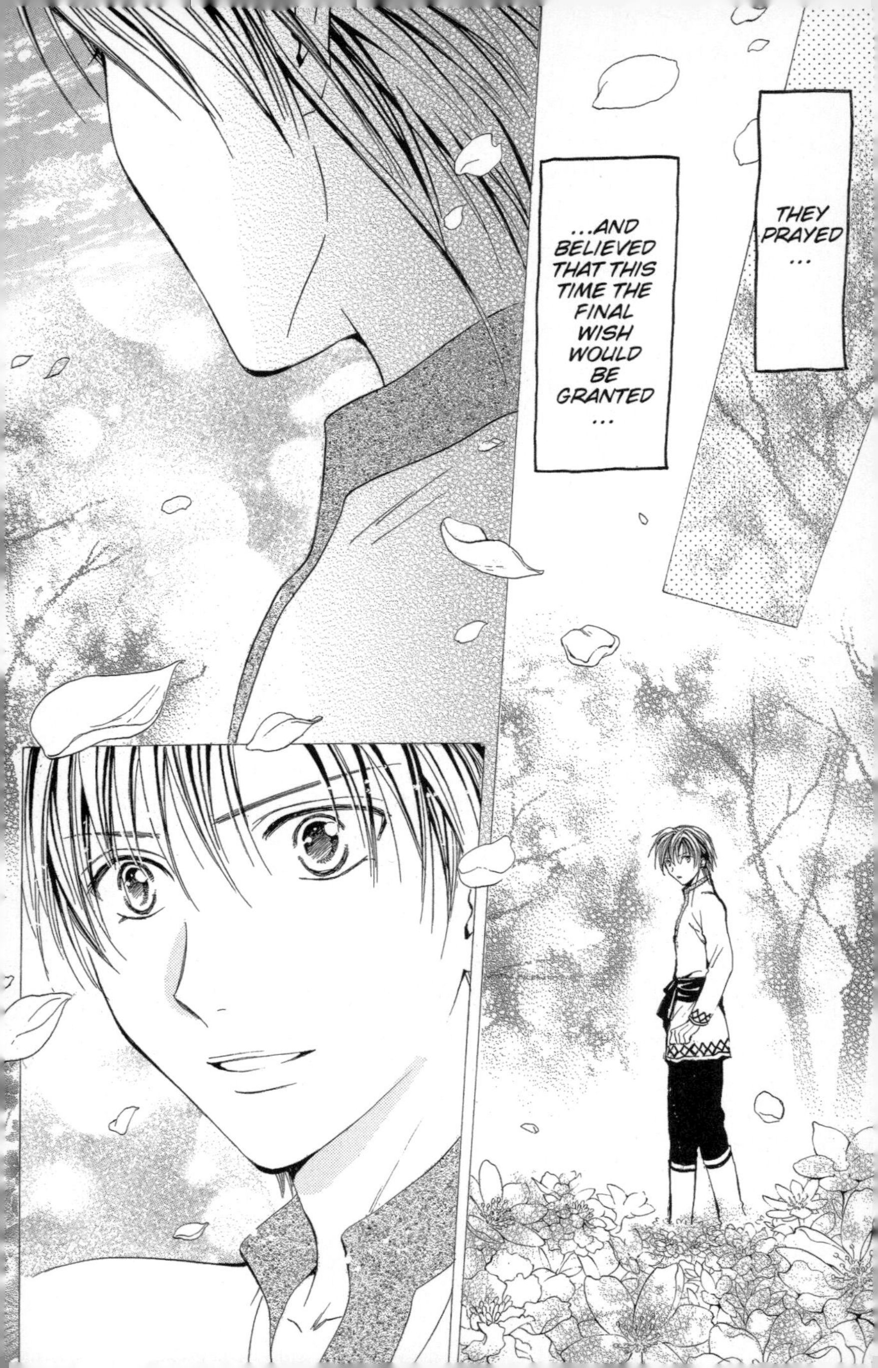
THEY PRAYED ...
...AND BELIEVED THAT THIS TIME THE FINAL WISH WOULD BE GRANTED ...

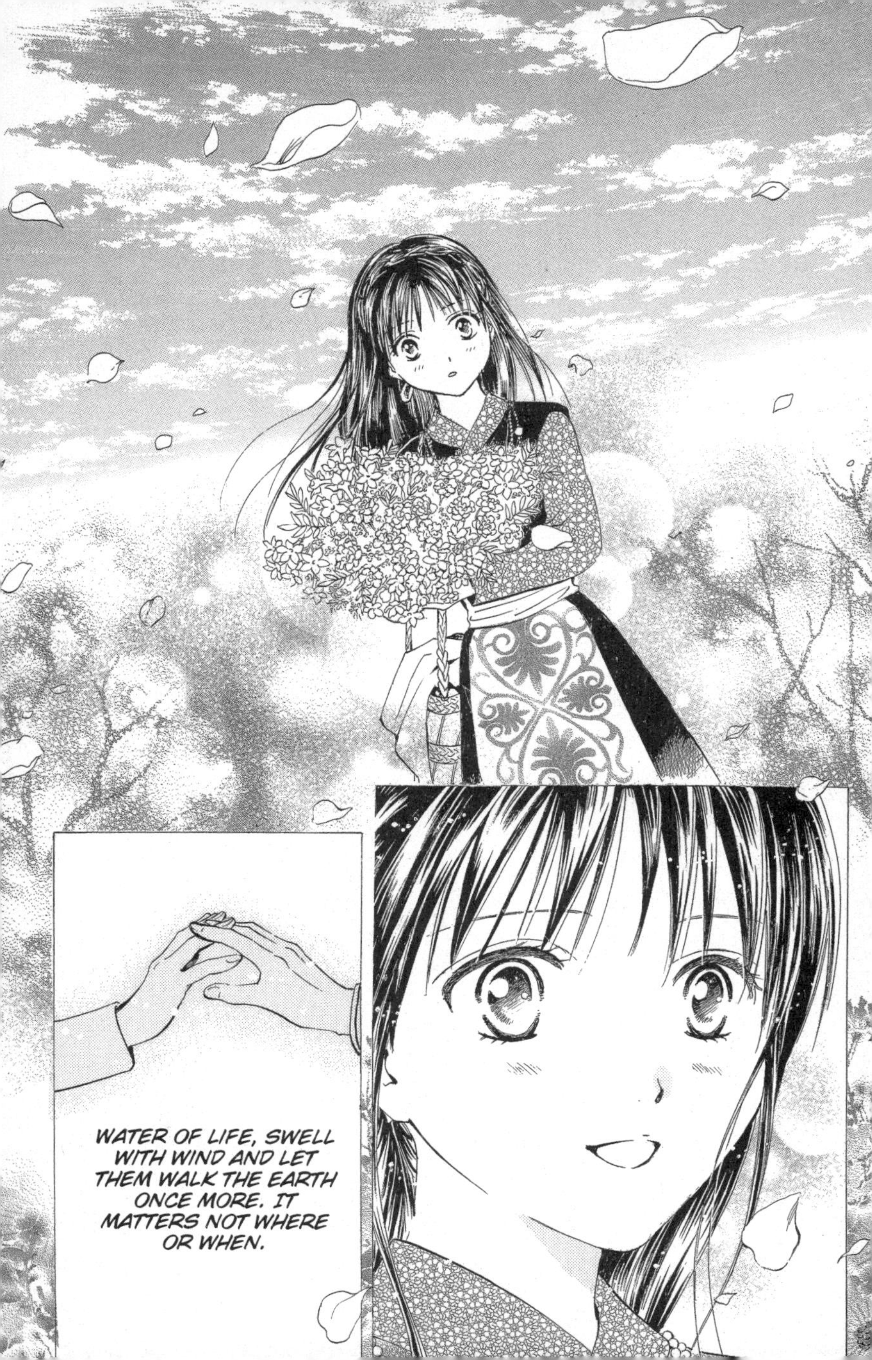
WATER OF LIFE, SWELL WITH WIND AND LET THEM WALK THE EARTH ONCE MORE. IT MATTERS NOT WHERE OR WHEN.

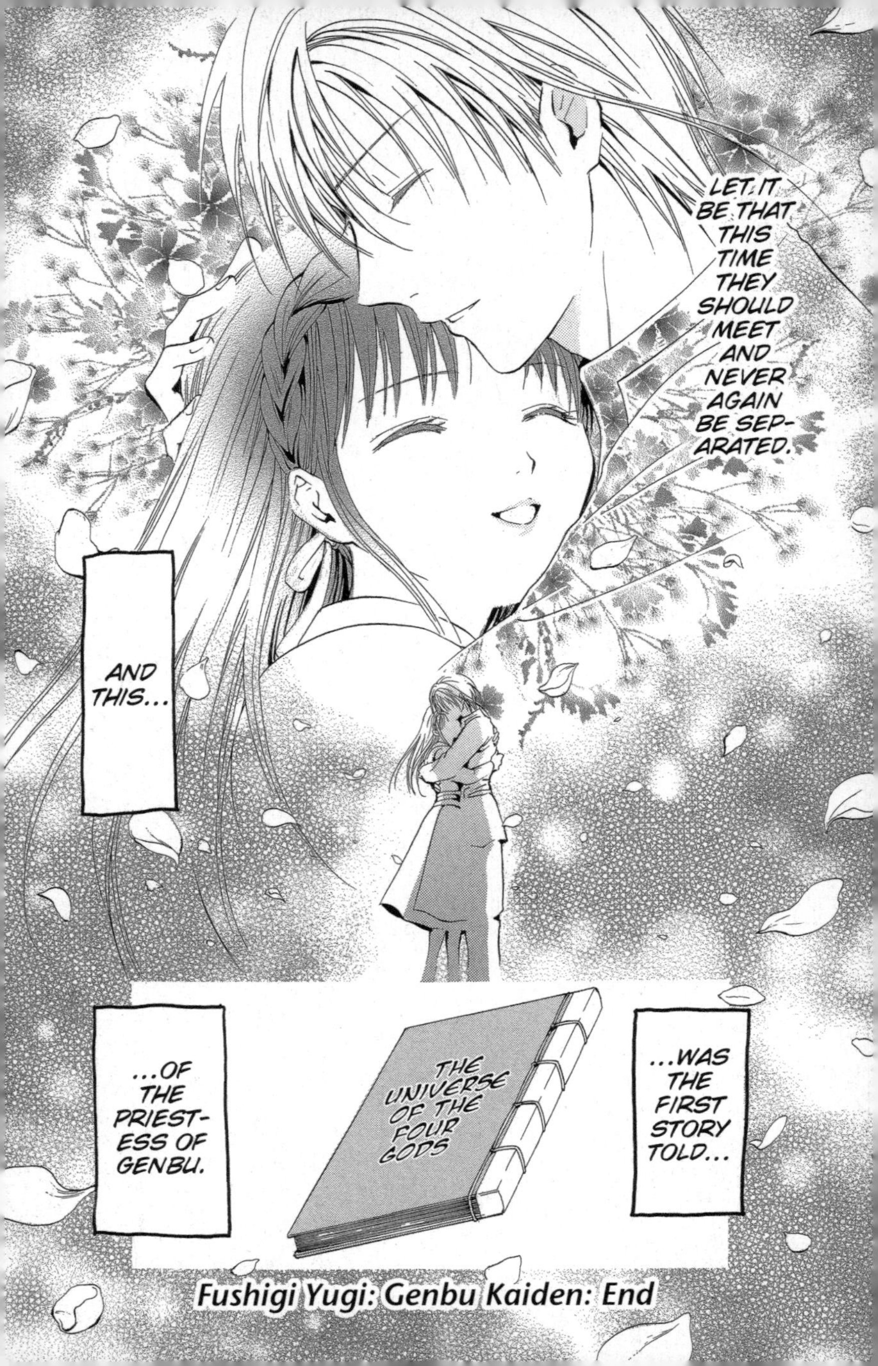
LET IT BE THAT THIS TIME THEY SHOULD MEET AND NEVER AGAIN BE SEP-ARATED.
AND THIS...
...WAS THE FIRST STORY TOLD...
THE UNIVERSE OF THE FOUR GODS
...OF THE PRIEST-ESS OF GENBU.
Fushigi Yugi: Genbu Kaiden: End

FUSHIGI YÛGI:
GENBU KAIDEN

It's been a whole year!! ✄✄

Seriously! It's me, Watase. One final hurried scribble!! ⁚ Finally, finally, we're at the conclusion of FY: Genbu Kaiden!! ♡

It's been ten years since this series began, extended by hiatuses, moving to a different magazine and so forth... ◊ It should've ended a couple of years ago, and I apologize to the readers who waited patiently for so long!! ✄ₘ(_ _)ₘ The plot of the last few volumes had been clear in my mind for a long time. From the very beginning, I received many letters from people who read the original *Fushigi Yugi*, saying, "Please don't let Takiko die!" I was so thankful that you hoped for her happiness!! (⊤⊤) How you feel after reading the ending will depend on how well I was able to convey my message... ⁚ A number of you might be aware that I myself lost a precious friend during my work on this serial. This event made me reflect a lot about issues of living and dying. The old FY also depicts a war, so death was inevitable...

Over the course of the series, a lot of ill-fated characters passed away. I too cried and felt the sadness. But when I came to a point in my life when I started to actually lose people close to me (my grandfather, my beloved dog, friends...) I began to focus not so much on the sadness but on how they lived. Obviously, it hurts terribly to say goodbye. I cried so much. But I felt that death wasn't despair, but only a temporary separation in the flow of life that continues into the future. The way you die reflects the way you lived. I tried to show that in my characters. Please take a good look at how they lived!

I'll keep drawing for the magazine *Flowers*, but I hope you'll be patient in waiting for the Byakko arc!! Sure, I want to work on it! Now that I've come this far, I can't die before I finish every arc. :) As long as the readers keep up their support, I'm sure that FY will resume again somewhere, someday.

Right now, I'm still working on *Arata: the Legend* in *Weekly Shonen Sunday* (the anime started in April 2013!), so please check it out!! ✄✄ Thank you so much for staying with me for such a long time!

STAFF♥

Kumiko Kuruma, Chika Ichikawa, Itsumi Ogura, Kayo Ohkuma, Hisako Kato, Satomi Tanaka, Chisa Nakatake, Yu Nishikawa, Chisato Hayatsu, Yumiko Higo, Ayako Mayuzumi, Sayaka Miura, Mayumi Miwa, Miki Yamazaki, Kaoru Yoshida, Yumiko Wakaba and others...

Lululu Books

Oeda, Ms. Megumi Nishizaki, Ms. Madoka Takao

Caramel Mama

Satoru Ohya, Tanaka and others...

Editors!

Kondo, Hayashi, Hikosaka, Taketaka, Yamauchi, Yamagata, Shinkawa, R. Komaba

Some of these are their maiden names... ʿ∪ Thank you, thank you so much! ₘ(_ _)ₘ So many of them... It was ten years, after all... ʿ∪